CONCEPTUAL & HISTORICAL ISSUES IN PSYCHOLOGY

Brad Piekkola

SAGE was founded in 1965 by Sara Miller McCune to support the dissemination of usable knowledge by publishing innovative and high-quality research and teaching content. Today, we publish over 900 journals, including those of more than 400 learned societies, more than 800 new books per year, and a growing range of library products including archives, data, case studies, reports, and video. SAGE remains majority-owned by our founder, and after Sara's lifetime will become owned by a charitable trust that secures our continued independence.

Los Angeles | London | New Delhi | Singapore | Washington DC | Melbourne

CONCEPTUAL & HISTORICAL ISSUES IN PSYCHOLOGY

Brad Piekkola

Los Angeles | London | New Delhi
Singapore | Washington DC | Melbourne

Los Angeles | London | New Delhi
Singapore | Washington DC | Melbourne

SAGE Publications Ltd
1 Oliver's Yard
55 City Road
London EC1Y 1SP

SAGE Publications Inc.
2455 Teller Road
Thousand Oaks, California 91320

SAGE Publications India Pvt Ltd
B 1/I 1 Mohan Cooperative Industrial Area
Mathura Road
New Delhi 110 044

SAGE Publications Asia-Pacific Pte Ltd
3 Church Street
#10-04 Samsung Hub
Singapore 049483

Editor: Luke Block
Editorial assistant: Lucy Dang
Production editor: Imogen Roome
Copyeditor: Bryan Campbell
Proofreader: Leigh C. Timmins
Indexer: Martin Hargreaves
Marketing manager: Lucia Sweet
Cover design: Wendy Scott
Typeset by: C&M Digitals (P) Ltd, Chennai, India
Printed and bound by CPI Group (UK) Ltd,
Croydon, CR0 4YY

© Brad Piekkola 2017

First published 2017

Library of Congress Control Number: 2016942802

British Library Cataloguing in Publication data

A catalogue record for this book is available from the British
Library

ISBN 978-1-4739-1615-9
ISBN 978-1-4739-1616-6 (pbk)

At SAGE we take sustainability seriously. Most of our products are printed in the UK using FSC papers and boards.
When we print overseas we ensure sustainable papers are used as measured by the PREPS grading system.
We undertake an annual audit to monitor our sustainability.

To my family and the Bozos—my foundation.
To my colleagues Chuck, Jennifer, Rachel, and Rob.
Most importantly, to my mentor and inspiration—Charles W. Tolman.

CONTENTS

FIGURES

ABOUT THE AUTHOR

Brad Piekkola received his PhD from the University of Victoria, Victoria, BC, Canada in 1989. His doctorate was in Personality/Theory. He taught Introductory Psychology, History of Psychology, Cognitive Psychology, Psychology of Personality, and Theoretical Psychology at Vancouver Island University from 1989 until his retirement in 2015.

COMPANION WEBSITE

Visit the SAGE companion website at **https://www.study.sagepub.com/piekkola** to find a range of free tools and resources that will enhance your learning experience.

For students:

- **Interactive Quizzes** featuring **Practice Questions** that help you engage with the phrasing of a question to identify clues to the answer and **Multiple Choice Quizzes** that test your understanding of key concepts covered in each chapter.

- Further reading on '**Key Thinkers**' in psychology. Look out for the **lightbulb icons** in the book which direct you to the website.

- **Helpful Weblinks** to additional resources relevant to each chapter, enabling you to expand your knowledge and explore your interests.

PREFACE

> It is peculiarly true of psychology that the value to the student depends upon his effort to relate the study to his own life-purpose. No subject is more deadening and trivial when treated as though it were contained between the covers of a book, the text, or of many books. (Hughes, 1928, p. 5)

In the spirit of Hughes, it is my hope that you will critically engage with what is presented in this text. Examine the issues and arrive at an informed opinion. Take it personally, agree or disagree, but engage with the material. Think it over.

To some people history is dead and irrelevant to the present. Yet the history of psychology is often implicit in its current practices. Knowing this history may help you in understanding the present state of the discipline and prepare you for your future engagement with psychology (Rieber and Salzinger, 1980).

The mainstream current of psychology emerged as dominant after much debate, and, in that, displaced or marginalized alternative perspectives (that may yet have value). Achieving dominance, the standard approach became the norm and was no longer questioned. It was codified in texts and treated as given, and incontestable. Its assumptions and conventions sank to the level of the implicit and are no longer scrutinized. In this there is always the danger of dogma, of assertions of incontrovertible fact. As the philosopher Bertrand Russell put it, "much education consists in the instilling of unfounded dogmas in place of the spirit of inquiry" (1932, p. 106). Inquire! Question!

It is not enough to know how to do psychology; you should be equipped to think, and to be able to justify why you do what you do. The spirit of inquiry is ill-equipped if one does not have a grasp of the underlying issues, unless one is informed. One must know why and judge for oneself whether it is wanting or not. Rather than education in psychology being a matter of formulaic, cookbook procedures, you need to be enabled to think critically about such practices and the presumptions that are their justification. I hope this book will help with that.

1

PSYCHOLOGICAL INQUIRY AS AN EVOLVING HUMAN PRACTICE

LEARNING OBJECTIVE

In this chapter we will consider what we know of the evolution of the universe and how, in the course of that process, life and mind came to be. This necessitates a consideration of hominin (formerly hominid) evolution, comparative psychology, and cultural evolution as aspects in the **emergence** and evolution of the mental or psychological. In acknowledging the biological as foundational to the emergence of mind, biology and neuroscience will be given their due, but not to the point of advocating **biological determinism**. The dependence of the psychological upon the biological will be established; however, it will be presented as relative given cultural evolution and its impact on **higher mental processes**. We begin with the beginning.

FRAMING QUESTIONS

- What is life?
- Where did it come from?
- What is mind?
- Where did it come from and what influences its characteristics?

INTRODUCTION

These are good questions. Among the ancient Greeks the theory of **spontaneous generation** was offered as an explanation of the appearance of at least some living creatures. Life and certain life-forms, it seemed, was generated all of a sudden, from inanimate matter, matter lacking life (Strick, 2000). It was a rather magical kind of appearance. Among the evidence supporting such a conception was the finding that maggots arose from decaying, lifeless meat. Similar origin explanations were offered for various insects, worms, frogs, and mice. Earthworms were thought to have been generated by the soil with the advent of heavy rain (Keeton and Gould, 1986). In the 17th century, van Helmont observed that if a shirt full of sweat were sprinkled with wheat and placed in a dark corner, mice would appear to be generated. The belief in spontaneous generation lingered as an influence among non-scientists until **Louis Pasteur** (1822–1895) demonstrated experimentally the correctness of the theory of biogenesis—that all living cells are the product of pre-existing living cells. Life begets life, not inanimate matter. That of course left unanswered where life came from originally.

Pasteur

In the 16th century two alternative, opposing viewpoints were put forward to address the vexing problem of the origin of life—**vitalism** and **mechanism**. To Driesch (1914) the main issue with which vitalism was concerned was whether the life processes could be accounted for in terms of organic (inanimate) factors or whether there was something autonomous and inorganic that was specific to those processes. The argument arose in response to René Descartes' (1596–1650) mechanistic explanation of physiological process. Descartes explained the operation of respiration, circulation, digestion, sensation, and bodily movement (Fancher, 1990). The body was an automaton and bodily processes were as mechanical as the springs and wheels of a clock. No soul or vital life force was required in its operation. The speculations of Descartes would in time be displaced by actual physiological research to which vitalism would eventually succumb. Biological phenomena increasingly were explained physically without needing to draw upon an undiscovered organizing and vitalizing force (Lanham, 1968).

The same sort of contentiousness has clung to the issue of mind. As with the question of life, there are physicalist and mechanist explanations. There are those for whom mind is qualitatively different from the physical and non-reducible to it, or fully explained by it. Others still, as I do, consider mind an expression of **emergent properties**, as a characteristic of organized matter when it achieves a sufficient level of complexity—a complex nervous system.

We humans did not always have the psychological wherewithal that we display today; nor are we guaranteed to possess it in the future. Our current level of functioning is the result of a long evolutionary process. This, if you accept the premise of historical development, is particularly true as it pertains to cultural forces that currently shape individual functioning and the quality of mind developed.

Imagine, if you would, the quality of mind needed to function in a post-nuclear, annihilated world. All social organization would have crumbled, including technologies, the electrical network, socially organized transportation of goods, hospitals, libraries, schools, and so on. The quality of mind needed to function under such preindustrial, socially backward conditions, would be of the primitive sort—uneducated and lacking the vast intellectual wealth which we collectively draw upon currently. The persons produced under such conditions would quickly revert to what was once referred to as the mind of the 'savage.' Among many early psychologists it was assumed that this intellectual lack of non-industrialized, uncivilized peoples was due to biological inferiority as opposed to cultural inferiority (see S. Gould, 1981, and Dewey, 1902, for a discussion).

The premise I will be putting forward, as you may have already inferred, is that mind and consciousness are qualities of action that are not innate. The character of the mind formed in any individual or group is a product of innate biological potential that is conditioned by cultural and historical forces. Consciousness, attention, reason, memory, and so on, are descriptive terms for qualities of action that develop in particular sociohistorical conditions. That means that mind is some non-natural, non-material existent, some 'entity' that is in any way separate from the body. To posit mind need not imply that it is something that has **ontological** status as a matter-independent entity or **substance** (as with the **mind–body problem**). By taking an evolutionary perspective on both **matter** and **mind** I intend to establish mind or mental phenomena as 'emergent properties' of evolved matter and to render the problem unproblematic.

1.1 FROM THE BIG BANG TO BIOLOGY

The development of the cosmos

To search for the origins of the universe (and later, life and the mental) is to be concerned with **cosmology**. This ancient concern received a massive boost and impetus from a discovery by Edwin Hubble in 1929. Hubble found that the universe was apparently expanding. That suggested the notion that at some point in the exceptionally distant past, all of the galaxies were contained within a single, inconceivably dense, original point (Hawking, 1988). This was the origin of the Big Bang, or the cosmic explosion from which the cosmos has been evolving. While incomplete, Tyson and Goldsmith (2004) have provided a synthesis of what is believed to have transpired since the initiating event.

When time began (the Big Bang), the energies of the universe were under immense pressure and heat and all of nature was a unitary force; relativity theory and quantum mechanics, the theories of the massive and the minute, could not be distinguished. With the cooling that occurred after the explosion the strong and weak nuclear forces separated, photons became pairs of matter/anti-matter particles and electrons and anti-electrons were produced. As cosmic evolution continued, weak nuclear and electromagnetic forces split and photons were further divided into matter/anti-matter particles but with slightly more particles of matter. All of this took the first three minutes. The matter became neutrons and protons and they formed nuclei to which electrons were eventually added. Very quickly, the three lightest elements were created: hydrogen (one electron and one proton), helium (two of each), and lithium (three of each). Despite the minor differences in numbers of electrons and protons these are qualitatively different elements and reflect the **quantity/quality dialectic** (see Box 1.1).

Hegel

BOX 1.1
THE QUANTITY/QUALITY DIALECTIC

Georg W.F. Hegel (1770–1831) introduced the quantity/quality dialectic as a logical principle by which the concepts of quantity and quality were related rather than abso-lutely opposed. In measurement one may discuss quantity as apparently free of quality, but Hegel proposed that with quantitative change there may be related changes in quality (Stace, 1924/1955). Consider the qualitative changes in water with quantitative changes in temperature: above 0°C it changes from a solid to a liquid and above 100°C it becomes a gas. Alternatively, consider the case of the elements in the periodic table. The addition (quantitative) of one proton and electron to helium results in the lithium atom. Helium is one of the *noble gases* but by adding a single electron and proton to the helium atom we get Lithium, an alkali metal (Turk, Meislich, Brescia, and Arents, 1968). Metals and gases are qualitatively different despite the close similarity in quantitative atomic structure.

The first billion years after the Big Bang was a period of cooling and expansion. Gravitational force drew matter together and, as the collecting size increased, the growing mass had greater gravitational draw. Gas clouds formed and eventually collapsed to form suns. Using helium and hydrogen these suns acted as forges which produced the remaining elements of the periodic table. Initially, the sun was able to release energy because it could combat the force of gravitational pull. Heavier elements were forged until the production of iron. This led to an increase in the star's mass to the point that it collapsed upon itself, exploded and sent the elements into the universe. In time comets, planets, and asteroids formed. Physics and chemistry were clearly in play at this point but the phenomena of biology and psychology had not yet appeared.

The emergence of life and biology

Living beings are dependent on the existence of the planet and the heavy metals found within it. It follows, from the scientific standpoint, that their presence must have been antecedent to those things that depend on them (Chaisson, 1981). Their existence was one of the necessary conditions for the maintenance of life, but how exactly did life come about? There is some debate as to what the pre-biotic conditions for life were, in other words, what material phenomena were necessary for life to arise. Darwin believed that the essential difference between the inorganic and the organic was that in the organic form molecular combinations have achieved a chemical complexity that supports the emergence of a self-replicating system (reproduction). Among modern biologists, some advocate the notion of a 'happy accident' or the idea that life was most improbable and miraculous—the chance random shuffling of molecular combinations; but to some it was the creation of a great deity (Fry, 1995). Ahrenius (1909, in Crick and Orgel, 1973) suggested the possibility of what he called 'panspermia.' By this he meant the transportation to earth of spores from other planets by radiation pressure or a ride on a meteor to explain the origin of life on earth. Crick and Orgel (1973) offered the possibility of 'directed panspermia'—that microorganisms were sent to earth by some distant technological society. Neither panspermia, however, speaks to the origins of life, only the transfer of life.

In the next section we will consider two influential theories of life or animate being that were taken up by philosophers and physiologists of the scientific era. It is an issue that has vexed humanity for centuries.

Whence life and is it special?

Prior to evolutionary theory there were two main explanations offered in accounting for life—the **mechanistic** and the **vitalistic**. Beginning with mechanism, Descartes (1641/1993) regarded the human body as a sort of machine, like a clock, composed of blood, bone, nerves, and skin that would operate as it did whether possessed of mind or not. The only difference would be that a body with a mind displays motions that are engaged due to a command of mind. To Thomas Hobbes (1588–1679) "life is but a motion of limbs" (1651/2012, p. 8) and is akin to automata (machines that are self-moved by springs and wheels) which can be considered artificial life. The heart is just a spring and the nerves are strings and, together with the joints which are akin to wheels, they give the body motion. Hobbes came under the influence of William Harvey (1578–1657), who showed that the movements of the heart and blood were akin to the operation of a pump (Watkins, 1955). Hobbes extended this mechanical mode of explanation to the operation of the body as a whole. Bodies are organic mechanisms. Even effects of the mind were due to some sort of mechanical agitation. What we call the thoughts of humans originate in sensation and that is caused by external objects pressing upon the sensory organs (Hobbes, 1651/2012). These then act upon internal mechanisms; external motions produce internal motions and that explains the mental. The mind cannot initiate anything since it is dependent on being set in motion by pressure exerted in the sense organs (Watkins, 1955). This, in brief, can be categorized as **mechanistic materialism**.

Unlike mechanistic explanations, the vitalists considered life distinct from natural mechanics and believed that it could not be sufficiently explained by physical or chemical laws or processes. There was something in animate beings that imparted a power called 'life,' something that the inanimate did not possess (Beckner, 1967). Such notions imbue everyday conversation. We find them in references to corpses as being 'lifeless' or to a 'loss of life.' This implied the invocation of **supernatural** explanatory principles that were anathema to the scientifically-minded. Francis Crick (1966), the co-discoverer of the double helix structure of the DNA molecule, arguing against vitalism, proposed abandoning the word 'alive' in favor of 'biological.' He further set the aim of biologists as the explanation of the biological in physical and chemical terms. Crick thus reclaimed the mechanistic principles that the vitalists took exception to.

A third alternative was offered by Oparin who, during the 1920s, rejected the mechanistic and vitalistic approaches in favor of explanation based on an evolutionary framework (Fry, 1995). Life, Oparin proclaimed, was an integral aspect of the development of matter but, he emphasized, the organization of biological phenomena possessed unique features. While debate has been vigorous and controversial (see Lahav, Nir, and Elitzur, 2001, for a more detailed discussion), the **continuity thesis** appears to be common to most *researchers* on the topic. According to this origins conception, life is continuous with antecedent inorganic matter since it continues to be composed of material forms, but these have become sufficiently complex as to support the 'emergence' of life. While the exact nature of the processes and constituents involved are up for debate, the continuity thesis establishes a **naturalistic** conception of the nodal conditions for the emergence of life. Whereas mechanism adopts an explanatory framework based on physics, and vitalism turns to explanation based on non-material forces, the continuity thesis posits the existence of a new scientific framework and subject matter—the biological. Biology represents a new branch of material phenomena that are qualitatively novel, possessing unique properties and processes.

Biology is qualitatively different from physics and chemistry. As a science it is concerned with life and living forms which are unique to it. Certain characteristics are to be found in the biological that do not exist in the antecedent inanimate conditions. While complete agreement regarding those characteristics that demark life is lacking, five are commonly accepted as distinguishing features (Lewis, 1995). These are (A) organization, (B) the use of energy and processes of metabolism, (C) homeostasis or the maintenance of inner constancy, (D) processes of irritability and adaptation (or reactivity to environmental change), and (E) reproduction and growth. The characteristics are so conceived (as distinguishing features) only as they are found in combination with each other. This is because they can be found operating in isolation in the non-living.

Being organized, living matter has a formal structure. A eukaryotic cell has a complex molecular framework including a cytoskeleton which contains microtubules and microfilaments and internal biochemical processes (Ingber, 2003). A railway is also highly organized but it cannot be considered alive. While not possessing metabolism as a cell does, a railway clearly uses energy to power its engines; and the engine does possess governors and other regulators to keep it operating within acceptable limits. Over history, railways have grown and developed (expanded and adopted new technologies) but they do not reproduce in any biological sense.

In contrast to mechanism and vitalism in biology, an alternative perspective toward the biological came from its conceptualization in **organicist** terms (Mayr, 1996). **Organicism** conceives of organisms as ordered **systems** (systems that are fundamentally different from systems that are non-living, such as a thermostat operates systemically but is lacking in life qualities). Unlike the order at the level of chemistry and physics, systems may possess properties that cannot be explained in terms of their components in isolation. Organisms, from the organicist perspective, have properties that are autonomous with respect to the physico-chemical, such as a historically acquired genetic program. Biological phenomena, by virtue of being alive, while built upon a physical and chemical basis, have unique properties which render the science of biology autonomous. Among these properties are hierarchical **levels of organization** or integration (see Box 1.2) and non-constant, shifting categories or groupings. Whereas the taxonomic classification is fixed in physics and chemistry (for example atoms, particles, and molecules), evolution leads to variation. Species in biology do not fit the traditional definition of classes since species lack an **essence** (a constant, unchanging nature): they have the potential of evolving and becoming what they currently are not (Mayr, 1987). They are temporally bound in their properties. A single species may split and take up different lines of development (a process known as divergent evolution). Biology adds a new source of causation in that the information that is accumulated historically, the adaptations that are made, are coded in the genetic program. The regularities to be found in biological processes lack the character of the universal physico-chemical laws.

Mayr does allow, however, that one may continue to speak of universality within a domain of interest. All of biology, for instance, is subject to natural selection as a universal.

Novikoff

BOX 1.2
LEVELS OF ORGANIZATION

Alex Novikoff (1913–1987), a distinguished biologist, developed the concept of 'levels of organization' or 'levels of integration' as a description of the evolution of matter through successively higher degrees of order and integration (Novikoff, 1945). As matter has evolved it has transformed from the inanimate level to the animate and, later on, to the social. The progression is both 'continuous' since it continues to be part of the ongoing process of matter recombining in greater degrees of complexity, and yet it is 'discontinuous' given the emergence of qualitative distinct phenomena. Higher-level phenomena are neither reducible to, nor explained or predicted by, lower-level laws or principles (although they remain active at their respective level). Natural selection, for instance, is a biological principle not evident in chemical level phenomena. The higher level includes the lower within it, but what were wholes at one level become parts at a higher level. The qualitative uniqueness of the higher-level phenomena also necessitates the establishment of methods that are appropriate to those phenomena (there is no point giving a questionnaire to a rock for instance). While it is a 'holistic' theory it allows, for purposes of analysis, the isolation of parts, while bearing in mind their integration into the whole structure in the concrete. At the human, societal level, historical, sociocultural factors like language and politico-economic forces are operative and infuse the process with qualitatively new, non-biological influences.

The concept of levels of organization is a popular conceptual scheme among biologists as an intra-biological principle (Solomon, Berg, and Martin, 2008). Under this understanding, biological phenomena are conceived of as existing at different levels of complexity and at each level there are emergent properties. The lowest level in biology is that of atoms and molecules. When these are sufficiently organized they form cells and they have the emergent properties associated with life. Over evolutionary time, cells combine to form tissues and tissues organize into organs with specialized functions. Organ systems (coordinated tissue and organ groups) are subsequently integrated within organisms at a higher level of complexity. Beyond the individual, organisms interact in more complex relations such as populations, communities, and their ecosystem.

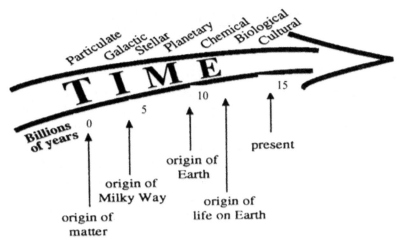

Some highlights of cosmic history are noted along this arrow of time, from the beginning of the universe to the present, including seven major epochs diagonally across the top. Cosmic evolution is the study of the myriad changes in the assembly and composition of energy, matter, and life, as well as the reasons for those changes. (Lola Chaisson)

Figure 1.1 The evolution of matter (including biology and culture)

Copyright © 2001 by the President and Fellows of Harvard College.

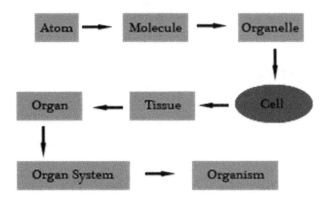

Figure 1.2 Levels of organization in biology

On Biological Autonomy: Reductionism versus Holism

Crick (1966) recognized levels of organization in biology and the notion that wholes at one level are parts at another. In cellular biology, he noted, cells are the wholes but comprise parts in tissue biology. Eventually, however, he came to believe the higher levels would be explained in terms of the lower and that this continued on to the atomic level. This is **reductionism** (the question of reductionism will be dealt with in greater detail in Chapter 2). Crick, in this, was rejecting emergence and proposing instead that something could be fully explained in principle by deconstruction to the smallest subcomponents whose nature would explain the larger complex. From his perspective, as a molecular biologist, it is not surprising that he believed that the more complex phenomena of biology are ultimately explained in chemical terms (and in the end in atomic terms). Among biologists who are holists (see **holism**) and **organicists** this fails to satisfy. According to Mayr (1996), the rejection of biological autonomy by **physicalists** (such as in its reduction to, and explanation in terms of, chemistry) involves delimiting conditions being imposed upon biological phenomena. By delimitation Mayr means that disclaimers of autonomy are justified by focusing on those aspects of biological science that exist in any science. By exclusion only those phenomena that are equivalent to the scientific characteristics of physics are acknowledged. Phenomena that are unique to biology like organicism, genetics and evolutionary causes are summarily dismissed.

In considering whether biology is an autonomous science, one is asking whether it differs from the sciences of physics and chemistry. According to Mayr (2004), the answer is yes and no; it is both continuous with the physical sciences and it is discontinuous in its emergent phenomena. This ambiguity is resolved when it is recognized that biology is actually two relatively different fields—mechanistic and historical biology. The mechanistic or functional branch is concerned with the biochemistry of organic processes, especially cellular, and explicable in terms of chemistry and physics. It is when one deals with issues pertaining to evolution that the importance of historical biology becomes apparent. Knowledge of historical development is not necessary to biochemical processes, but it is when the dimension of temporal change enters in.

It was when Charles Darwin (1809–1882) introduced his concept of evolution by natural selection in his *Origin of the Species* in 1859 that biology became autonomous as a science. The basic principles of the physical sciences were no longer applicable and had to be replaced by those which were relevant to the new phenomena. Darwin's scientific approach, furthermore, was not reliant upon the experimental method. To answer its questions this branch developed its own methodology—the historical narrative (Mayr, 1997). One would examine all known facts regarding a phenomenon (like dinosaur extinction) and then try to develop a scenario that accounted for it. This would then be tested by its fit or explanatory power and consistency with established evidence.

Darwin presented biologists with a different way of thinking. Since the ancient Greeks the multifarious phenomena of the living world had been conceived of in terms of **typology** or **essentialism** (Mayr, 2004) and an assumption of the fixedness of species. The great diversity was simplified by grouping individuals within which class members were considered identical; variability was overlooked or dismissed. Essentialism and the notion of permanent species were replaced by the novel concept of populations, which recognizes individual uniqueness, variability, and change, and replaces strict determinism with chance or random influences. Universal laws in biology were now of lesser importance because of variability and an emphasis on concepts like competition, **natural selection**, and changing ecosystems. It was in this discovery of principles or concepts specific to biology that its independence or autonomy became apparent. The most important difference was 'natural selection' as the driving force behind organic evolution.

Natural selection

Biological phenomena differ in nature from the physical and chemical in numerous other ways besides those already mentioned. To begin with, the animate, unlike the inanimate, had the emergent properties of growth, replication, reproduction, adaptability, and metabolism. The inanimate, furthermore, is not subject to 'dual causation' (natural law and genetic programs). The most important differentiating concept is that of natural selection, the driving force in organic evolution. Evolutionary biology, as contrasted with molecular biology, has a different conceptual framework and methodology (historical narrative). It deals with unique phenomena like extinction, hominin origins, and organic diversity, and these are not explained by natural laws. Natural laws in physical science tend to effect deterministic outcomes, but such **determinism** is not guaranteed with natural selection or 'sexual selection' (mating preferences). Evolutionary outcomes are usually the result of a number of interacting factors that are unpredictable; chance factors prevail.

The physicalist adopts a philosophy of reductionism whereby everything is reduced to the most basic parts and it is assumed that the whole has thereby been explained. In biological systems, in contradistinction, the knowledge of such properties is only a partial explanation since interactions between the parts occur at every level, and it is this which provides the whole (be it individual, social group, or ecosystem) with its outstanding characteristics. How the smaller units organize into larger units is crucial to the properties of those larger units. The **reductionist** ignores such organization and the consequent emergent properties.

One final difference that was emphasized by Ayala (1968) concerned **teleology**. Purpose in nature was not a concept found in the physical sciences. Teleological phenomena were consequently reformulated in the non-teleological terms of the physical sciences but in that, as Ayala determined, there was a loss of explanatory power. The concept was discredited because it had been equated with a belief in gods or as an event in the future that was an active agent in the present. Darwin, however, in the fact of adaptation, provided teleological processes in organic life a natural explanation, replacing theological teleology with scientific teleology. Teleological explanations can be found to be operative in at least three biological categories. The first is one commonly recognized in humans in which an end or goal state is anticipated in consciousness. Such purposeful activity has also been recognized in some animals although to a diminished degree, as when an animal is stalking game. Second, it is evident in teleonomic (motivated) systems of self-regulation like homeostatic maintenance of a steady body state despite fluctuations in the environment. Lastly, it is evident in anatomical structures that have evolved to serve certain functions like hands designed for grasping and teeth for tearing away flesh. Such biological adaptations have arisen because they support species' continued viability and reproductive capacities. So, while explanations that are teleological are inappropriate in the physical sciences, they have proven to be indispensable to biology and the investigation of organisms.

My intent here, in discussing arguments in favor of the autonomy of biology, was not so much to serve the field of biology as it was to lay the groundwork for the non-reducibility of psychological processes and to lay a foundation for what follows. We next contemplate biological evolution in terms of how this has contributed to the appearance of psychological attributes. Specifically, we will consider the evolution of the nervous systems as this is correlated with emerging psychological functions like sensation and perception.

1.2 BIOLOGICAL AND CULTURAL EVOLUTION

Levels of integration in mental evolution

Having established biology as an autonomous scientific domain, we next consider the continuity and discontinuity of biology and psychology. The discussion will briefly consider comparative psychology, the psychological functions of non-human animals as conceptualized by **Aleksei Leontyev** (1903–1979) which can be considered an extension of the theory of 'levels of organization' to psychological phenomena (Leontyev, 1947/1981b). This scheme serves a heuristic function for the categorization of cross-species psychological functions. In comparing species, it should be stressed that a successful comparative psychology, according to Tolman (1987), has to satisfy a minimum of two criteria. First, it would clarify, in a way consistent with the facts and without reduction to the biological, the unambiguously psychological nature of the comparison. Second, it must provide some account of its evolution. In this regard the approach of Leontyev established the concept of **activity**, the active connectedness of the organism with its environment, as a basis for his comparison. It is in the nature of this connectedness, in the adaptation both **phylogenetically** and **ontogenetically**, that differences in psychological levels, as stages in psychological evolution, were established. Leontyev identified the pre-psychological

Leontyev

category of Irritability, followed by the psychological planes of Sensitivity, Perception, Animal Intellect, and Consciousness.

It should be emphasized that these levels are intellectual differentiations or concepts in the sense mentioned previously with respect to biology. In the jargon of cognitive psychology, they can be considered **fuzzy categories** in that they lack hard and fast, segregating boundaries (see Box 1.3). There are what Novikoff (1945), in discussing integrative levels, referred to as **mesoforms** or intermediate forms that may exist at the transition points. Protein paracrystals, for instance, exist between inanimate crystals and primitive, unicellular organisms. Such intermediate forms should be expected to exist in the psychological levels of organization identified by Leontyev. As a comparative psychology it demonstrates the developmental continuity of the human psyche with primitive biological processes (Tolman, 1987). It further specifies how the more advanced psychological processes in humans are qualitatively discontinuous with the earlier forms and are not 'reducible' (see **reductionism**) to them. Furthermore, it incorporates later cultural evolution as a factor in qualifying the constitution of 'higher mental processes' and consciousness.

BOX 1.3
FUZZY CONCEPTS *AND* CLASSICAL LOGIC

Categories and concepts are closely related. A category is a group of objects or phenomena that have properties or qualities in common and a concept is a mental representation of a category. According to the 'classical view' of natural object concepts, concepts possess features that serve to define inclusion or exclusion from membership in a category (Medin, Ross, and Markman, 2001). A square, for example, is a figure having the necessary and sufficient defining characteristics of four right angles and sides of equal length. These are rigidly bounded defining properties. To Galotti (2014) the classical view can be traced to Aristotle in ancient Greece but it more likely begins with Socrates' **inductive definition**. In establishing an inductive definition of a concept Socrates investigated examples of the concept to identify what they had in common. In this he was seeking the something's 'essence,' or basic nature, and permanent characteristics (Hergenhahn and Henley, 2014). This, then, sets the stage for Aristotle's laws of logic (Runes, 1977) which apply to thinking in concepts.

(Continued)

(Continued)

According to the 'law of identity,' a thing or concept is identical with only that which is exactly the same as it. The 'law of non-contradiction' requires that a thing or concept cannot be identical with that which is not it; north and south for instance. The 'law of the excluded middle' asserts that there is nothing in between identity and non-identity; an absolute separation. Thus, no two concepts can be in any way related but, as Hegel demonstrated, opposite concepts are in relation and are partially defined by their relation (Stace, 1924/1955). Consider the terms up and down or north and south which are opposites but yet are related—try to separate the north and south poles of a magnet from each other. Research into conceptual thinking rather quickly ran into difficulties when adopting the classical view since not only did people fail to identify determining features, but their concepts were only loosely determined (Medin et al., 2001). While people may readily identify a robin as a member of the category bird, a penguin may not be, and yet a bat may (McCloskey and Glucksberg, 1978). Most natural concepts simply fail to conform to the classical view and are hence 'fuzzy' since the lines of demarcation lack clear differentiation.

Irritability

In developing his theory of the development of the mind, Leontyev (1947/1981b) began with the pre-psychic stage which involved the transition from the inanimate to organic, living matter. Matter enters the stage of biological evolution at this point. For life to occur in its simplest form the organism needs to be responsive to those substances that activate it positively and negatively (as supportive, or destructive, of life). This is **irritability** which, biologically, is a capacity to receive and respond to external stimuli (Lawrence, 2011). At its simplest, the single cell exchanges energy and materials with its environment. Such materials usually have to be converted into some form of energy, usually chemical, to support the functions of their biomechanical processes (Solomon et al., 2008). In cell metabolism various chemical processes transform this energy and thereby maintain homeostasis (an internal balance) and subsequent reproduction. As one moves from the single cell to multicellular organisms, irritability is essential to survival.

More complex forms of irritability can be found in the various multicellular organisms that are without a nervous system (the biological basis of psychological functions). The tropism is an example of this sort of irritability. In it there is an automatic movement evoked by physico-chemical processes in the parts of an organism. A common example is phototropism, a bending response that orients plants toward the source of light. It is triggered by blue light wavelengths and promotes the acquisition of light for photosynthesis (Solomon et al., 2008). In the case of phototropism, the plant was positively stimulated but a tropism may be negative as well. With gravitropism, plant roots display a positive tropism by growing toward the center of gravity but the stem tips display negative tropism by growth away from the center. To reiterate, such processes are of the pre-psychic type due to the lack of nerve cells.

Sensitivity

While continuous with the antecedent developments in biological evolution, this next stage is discontinuous in that a new biological mechanism—the nerve cell—has emerged. It marks the qualitative transformation from the biological, pre-psychic to the psychological level. While at first rudimentary, the nervous system itself evolves and becomes a sophisticated organ of connection and coordination. In terms of adaptation, the appearance of a nerve cell and, in time, a nervous system increases the speed of response to environmental conditions. Whereas a tropism is a fairly slow biochemical response, the electrochemical response rate of nerve cells is faster and more conducive to survival.

Irritability is a universal quality of the living contents of a cell and usually is made up of three main components: stimulation or environmental change and its detection, a reaction or signal conduction, and a response of some kind (Keeton, 1967). In unicellular organisms this all occurs within the cell but in multicellular organisms, like the sponge; slow conduction occurs in individual cells which then act upon adjacent cells. In such a system the rapid spread of an impulse over relatively large distances is not possible. With the further evolution of multicellular organisms, cells became specialized in the part they play in the survival of the organism. All animals above the level of the sponge have a specialized tissue for conduction, some sort of nervous system, although it can be quite primitive. At its simplest the nervous system is composed of two cells, as with jellyfish, specialized for reception and conduction. In such organisms there is no flexibility in reaction since there are no alternative pathways, but the reaction is quicker than a tropism. In most cases there are a minimum of three separate cells (sometimes specialized as receptor, conductor, and effector). Further increases in complexity result in more conductor cells interceding between receptor and effector cells. Eventually these become sensory neurons, motor neurons, and association neurons (interneurons). This expansion of conductor cells leads to increases in flexibility of response. Over a vast stretch of time these nerve cells formed into interconnected networks.

Nervous system development. Once the nervous pathway included several conductor cells there was greater response flexibility which is, of course, an adaptive development. There are more response options in support of survival—nature selects improved nervous systems. While we cannot speak to the ancient forms that evolved, given the lack of fossils,

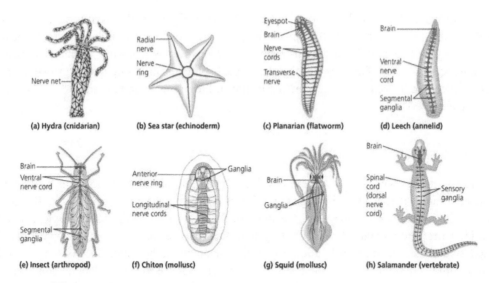

Figure 1.3 Different nervous systems

© Pearson Education, Inc., publishing as Benjamin Cummings

we can surmise how things may have been by way of comparison with current primitive organisms and their nervous systems.

Among the most primitive nervous systems are the 'nerve nets' of hydras (microscopic, water-dwelling organisms with a sac-like body). These have attained a level of organization in which there are separate nerve cells specialized for reception, conduction, and reaction. Rather than forming separate pathways, the conductor cells are interconnected and spread out through the body as a net. There is as yet no central control and excitation radiates to adjoining regions, decreasing in intensity as it spreads. This results in an exceptionally limited, localized responding. The jellyfish, in contrast, is a little more complex in that there is a slight degree of centralization. Two separate rings of nerves circumscribe the bell-shaped portion of the body and other nerve cells channel into these. This promotes swimming motions through the rhythmic contraction of the bell structure.

Over time there will be an overall trend in the evolving nervous systems. Centralization will arise in the formation of an elongated nerve cord that receptor and effector pathways pass through—a central nervous system. The pathways within the central nervous system become increasingly more complex and this is accompanied by increases in response flexibility. Nerve cells become more segregated and specialized in the functions they perform. The leading ends of the longitudinal central cord increase in their dominance over the remainder and gradually form into brains. Among vertebrates the most primitive form of brain develops three swellings at the end of the central nerve cord which, proceeding to more complex forms, can be recognized as the hindbrain, midbrain, and forebrain. As the bodies of animals increase in size and complexity, many cells cease to have direct contact with the environment. Natural selection led to the development of receptor cells specialized in the processing of biologically significant environmental information. Specialization of these conduction pathways leads to input and output channels to the central nervous system (the afferent and efferent nervous fibers). The afferent nerves subsequently become more particular in terms of the type and range of stimulation that they are responsive to. They become the specialized senses like vision, olfaction, echolocation, or the magnetic sense. It was the development of these sensory pathways, that are differentiated by the specific forms of energy they are responsive to, that Leontyev emphasized in distinguishing this first stage of psychic evolution.

In discussing the evolved adaptations that are the sensory systems, it is important to emphasize that these, and all other adaptations, reflect a coordination of an organism with its environment. The nervous system is commonly considered to be separate from the environment and reactive to it. It is conceived of as a discrete unit that uses input from the environment to determine and initiate appropriate responses (Chiel and Beer, 1997). Adaptive behavior can be understood, it is assumed, by focusing on the nervous system. This is misleading. The nervous system is embedded in the body and the body is embedded or integrated with the environment. Adaptive behavior is better understood, therefore, as a continuous and bi-directional interconnectivity and influence. There is unbroken and uninterrupted receipt-and-response-to-feedback from movement-in-the-environment. An octopus reaching for an object or a frog snatching a fly relies on ongoing input to coordinate its movements with its goal. The production of adaptive behavior depends on the properties of the environmental **niche** and ongoing feedback. In lamprey swimming, for instance, the generation of normal waves of bodily contractions depends on water hydrodynamics. If a lamprey is removed from water and swimming movement is induced, it produces inappropriate bodily movements. The water hydrodynamics are essential to the generation of coordinated behavior. There is a **mutuality** of organism and environment.

The **mutualism** of organism and environment, with respect to the senses, was emphasized by Gibson (1966, 1979/1986) in his '**ecological theory of perception**.' Emphasis in this theory was placed upon the adaptive significance of perceptual systems which are conceived of as inseparable and interpenetrating with the environment. Psychology, to Gibson, had long paid homage to evolutionary theory but failed to appreciate the mutualism implied in the proposition. Sensory/mental capacities evolved because they supported survival in a particular niche into which they fit. Organisms so conceived are products of nature and bound to nature—an organism that loses that connection suffers extinction.

Ecological theory of perception

A niche that is changing presents obstacles to survival, and that disentanglement has to be overcome to continue to thrive. Organisms are adapted to, and coordinated with, particular niches, and the adjustments they make may be species-/niche-specific. That is the point of evolution by natural selection—overcoming obstacles to survival through adaptation.

As a result, some organisms evolve heat detectors, some rely on echolocation, some are attuned to magnetic fields; they are niche-dependent and niche-adjusted. Sensation and perception can be considered evolved adaptations, currently serviceable, to lawful relations with relevant energy arrays (electromagnetic, chemical, acoustic) that encompass an individual. They act upon its sensory receptors which are attuned to those energies. In sensation, as in the subsequent levels of psychic evolution, this interpenetration and interconnectedness needs to be the contextual frame from which one understands Leontyev's formulation.

A concept central to appreciating Leontyev's classificatory schema and his approach to the psychological is that of 'activity.' This contrasts with the notion of **behavior**. Behavior, as conceptualized by behaviorists (learning theorists), represents an animal's engagement with the world as purely reactive to stimulus conditions—mechanical. Organisms are considered isolated from the environment, but it is the environment that determines behavior. Behavior, as Skinner (1953/1965) put it, was under 'stimulus control.' The concept of activity, in contrast, is one in which organisms are connected with their environment and by means of which they become oriented to the conditions of their existence (within their capacity). It is a unit of life that reflects the continuous, active engagement with the environment and is mediated by processes of **mental reflection** which orient the organism/subject to the realm of objects (Leont'ev, 1974–1975). Activity unites the organism with its environment and, depending on the level of development in the nervous system, **internalizes** that relation in a subjective form (from unconscious associations to conscious mental images and ideas). In what follows, the nature of the connection to the environment through activity will vary depending on the level of development of the nervous system being discussed.

Sensitivity and the psychological. When the level of *sensitivity* (the 'elementary sensory psyche') is attained there are two kinds of irritability now apparent, each with different functions. Firstly, there are those that are directly involved in the maintenance of life (the original form). Second, there is irritability with respect to properties that are not directly involved in the maintenance of life (Leontyev, 1940/1981a). The function of sensitivity is the capacity to sense; it mediates between environmental conditions and those activities of the organism that are involved in the maintenance of life. Whereas in irritability responses were to direct stimulation, in sensitivity the response is to a biologically relevant stimulus that is not experienced in its immediateness. Sensitivity thus introduces the function of orientation to distant conditions through the signaling functioning of intermediate energies (like light and sound waves which satisfy no biological need) that connect the organism to biologically significant conditions.

Leontyev speculated that sensitivity was originally undifferentiated, that is was not related to specific types of energies—the type of responding that occurred with the previous mentioned diffusion through nerve net. Over time this became more differentiated and specialized and reflected qualitatively different environmental conditions (light, sound, odors, et cetera). Coming under the influence of varying substances and energy forms meant differentiated responsiveness would better support successful assimilation of life-supporting sustenance. The conditions of existence necessitated that sensitivity be developed in the struggle to survive. The organism is better able to maximize its orientation toward sources of sustenance through sensory mediation. The processes of sensitivity are without direct life-supporting function, but support that by linking an organism with those conditions that do.

Organisms operating at the level of sensitivity represent a low level of processing in terms of the range of phenomena to which an organism adjusts and relates to. In contrast, humans have the power to relate to the world at a high degree of complexity. Looking about my office I see a computer, books, a lamp, fan, pencil, et cetera, and as I look out my window I can identify trees and birds, cars and roads. None of these things has any biological significance but they are the things of the world we inhabit. These are things composed of multiple qualities that act on a number of senses in concert—an apple can act upon vision, taste, touch, smell, and all of these go into our idea of an apple. Organisms operating at the level of sensitivity respond to properties of things but not to the thing in its totality, such as the apple above. Even though an object may simultaneously act upon different senses, that information is not integrated as a single 'mental reflection.' Wagner (1928, in Leontyev, 1947/1981b) pointed out that a worm, for instance, in search of food, relies upon a singular sense organ, like touch, even though it may possess other sensory capacities.

In his study of instinct, **Nikolaas Tinbergen** (1907–1988) offered numerous examples of creatures that respond to singular sensory qualities of a thing rather than the complex of sensations that may be available to it. As Tinbergen expressed it, "an animal responds 'blindly' to only part of the total environmental situation and neglects other parts, although its sense organs are perfectly able to receive (and probably do receive them)" (Tinbergen, 1951/1989, p. 27). There is a difference between the 'actual' and the 'potential' stimulus. For instance, during mating the male, three-spined stickleback will aggress against other males, but what it responds to is a singular quality of redness rather than the whole fish. Males have an intensely red underbelly so Tinbergen reasoned that it was that which elicited the fighting. Stickleback models varying in the degree to which they resemble the fish morphology (shape and size) but which possessed the red coloring, and a taxidermied stickleback lacking the red belly, were put into a holding tank. Attack was based solely on the color red, not fish-ness, even though the other properties of shape and size could be seen.

Tinbergen

Rabaud (1924, in Leontyev, 1947/1981b) found that spiders are attracted to the beating of an insect's wing as that is transmitted through the vibrations of its web. Upon reaching the source of the agitation it is wrapped in webbing. If the source of vibration was a tuning fork that too would be wrapped. Beyond the singular property of vibration there is nothing common to an insect and a tuning fork. Similarly, mosquitoes are drawn to copulate with females by the sound of their wings in flight and, as with the spiders, to a tuning fork producing the same frequency sound (Roth, 1948). This occurs despite the fact that the mosquito could tell by both sight and smell that tuning fork and female are different (Keeton, 1967). In each of

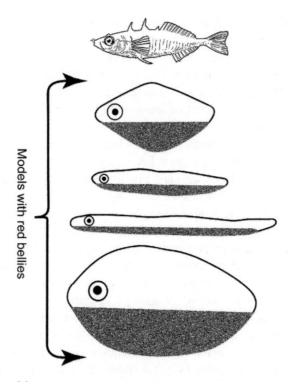

Figure 1.4 Stickleback models

With permission from intropsych.com/ch08_animals/releasers.html

these cases the creature was not responding to the thing—the fish versus model or the insect versus tuning fork—but to a single property of color or vibration. The information from two or more senses is not integrated in their effect on the organism. A mother hen, in response to one of its chicks vocalizing in distress at being tied to a stake, may engage in protective behavior, even when the chick is initially out of sight. Alternately, let the chick be in distress but its cries be blocked by an encasing glass dome, and now the hen, despite seeing the chick, ceases to respond to the situation (Bruckner, 1933, in Tinbergen, 1951/1989). It is the sound alone that promotes protective mothering.

While the characteristics of organisms at this level of psychological functioning are quite primitive, they can still, to varying degrees, adjust their behavior or, to put it another way, learn. **Classical conditioning**, or associative learning, and the transfer of a reflexive response to a neutral stimulus, demonstrates this. Simple earthworms were placed in a T-shaped maze and, if turning right at the choice point enter a dark, moist, inviting chamber. If the worm turns right it crosses over sandpaper and is shocked. Eventually, after around 100 repetitions, the sandpaper becomes a signal for the shock and the worm turns away from

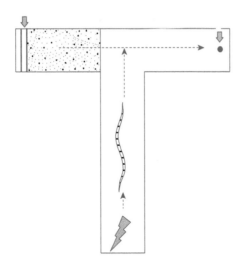

Figure 1.5   Flatworm t-maze learning

it, avoiding the shock (Schneirla, 1964, in Tavolga, 1969). Leontyev offered the example of a toad's **generalization**. A hungry toad was fed linearly-shaped worms repeatedly and then was presented simultaneously with a matchstick and a rounded piece of skin. It lunged for the matchstick (a generalization based on the shared property of shape). When the situation was reversed and a spider was the foodstuff, the round skin was later pounced upon. This was not a case of **abstract thought** but a purely mechanical response since the abstraction and generalization were in no way suggestive of consciousness. As Leontyev made clear, the processes we are dealing with are primarily reflexive or innate behavioral mechanisms, the type of learning identified by **Ivan Pavlov** (1849–1936) as classical conditioning. In general, as we move from the less complex, lower vertebrates to mammals, learning or forming associations is done more rapidly (less time and repetition) and with less errors (Munn, 1971). When it comes to mammals we enter the level of the perceptive psyche.

Pavlov

Perceptive psyche

The stage of the 'perceptive psyche' encompasses a new phase in the evolution of psychic reflection. Whereas the previous stage was characterized by responding to single properties of things, the activity of animals now involves an engagement with the world that is governed by many influences simultaneously. External reality is reflected in the form of things, or by combinations of those properties, rather than simple sensations evoked by separate properties. Most mammals and the majority of vertebrates are at this stage of psychic functioning (to different degrees). To Leontyev increased physiological complexity underpins this new form of **reflection**. The nervous system had undergone restructuring with the formation of a forebrain and afterwards a cerebral cortex.

In terms of mental content it is apparent that animals at this level possess representations (a mental reproduction of external objects and events). While we cannot see into the inner realm of mental reflections and representations, we can infer their existence from their effect on manifest activity. Leontyev drew upon Tinklepaugh (1928) to demonstrate this. Tinklepaugh extended the work of Hunter (1913) on delayed reaction, or the response to an absent stimulus. Hunter stated his interest as the determination of how long, after the cessation of a 'determining stimulus,' an image or idea is retained that can guide successful activity. Rats, raccoons, dogs, and children were trained to use a light as a discriminative stimulus for a reward location (a light came on at one of three possible locations indicating where food was available). After training, performance was delayed by being restrained for an amount of time. The maximum delay before forgetting the connection between light stimulus and location was ten seconds for rats, 25 seconds for raccoons, five minutes for dogs, and 25 minutes for children. The length of time for retention of a mental representation varied depending on the species.

Tinklepaugh sought to identify the representative factors that Macaque monkeys used in a version of Hunter's delayed reaction study. In pre-trial training a monkey was retained in a chair and two overturned cups, about six feet apart, were placed eight feet in front of it. Either a piece of lettuce or banana was shown to the monkey and then slowly placed beneath one of the cups. It was then commanded to retrieve the food. Once there was an established performance, the next step was to introduce the substitution session. After placing the banana under a cup, a wooden screen was used to block visual access to the cups; the unseen banana piece was replaced by lettuce. Given the retrieval command, the monkey raised the cup and started to reach for the food but stopped. A search ensued for the missing banana but not because lettuce was inconsumable. Later trials with the lettuce alone indicated that it was a desirable food source, but les preferable. Comparable sessions with children yielded similar results except the children vocalized their displeasure at the switch to a different, less desirable candy. The children displayed 'surprise' and 'disappointment' due to a retained, representative cue or idea of the substituted thing (and its collective properties and values). Tinklepaugh suggested a similar capacity should be extended to the monkeys. Comparable research by Bräuer and Call (2011) supports the existence of this capacity to 'individuate objects,' with respect to their properties, in great apes (chimpanzees, orangutans, gorillas) and dogs.

At the earlier stage of sensitivity the retentive capacity was with respect to links between separate sensory effects and motor responses. Rather than uniting around a single, dominant sensory stimulus, the surrounding reality is now reflected as separate images of separate things and not just elementary sensations. Now there is the new function of 'image memory.' This is further associated with changes in the capacity to differentiate objects (things not properties of things) and generalize on that basis. The scope of learning, the ability to adapt and make generalizations, has become much broader in the range of objects and situations that this extends to. In perception the animal's activity in the world incorporates more complex forms of differentiation, generalization, analysis, and synthesis. All of this is supported by further expansion and complication of the associative, integrative fields of the cerebral cortex and is thoroughly naturalistic. No substance called mind has to be introduced to account for mental processes.

In their symbolic processes, with their ability to recall past experiences, mammals have demonstrated a capacity to go beyond making adjustments to current situations. Beyond the immediately present, there is evidence of the influence of what is objectively absent but represented internally (Munn, 1971). Consider 'object permanence.' Piaget (1954, in Baillargeon, 1986) found that a child prior to about nine months of age displayed what might be called 'out-of-sight, out-of-mind.' When a desired toy is hidden from view by placing a cloth over it children cease their efforts to obtain it. They lacked a conception of an object continuing to exist when not within immediate perception. When object permanence is established, an object that is not part of immediate perception continues to exist mentally, and is known to have an independent existence. Search activity continues. This is what Tinklepaugh's monkeys revealed in their continuing search for the missing banana. The retention of a symbolic representation is of great importance in mental evolution because it sets the conditions for thinking and understanding (Munn, 1971). The shift to Leontyev's stage of animal intellect supports that judgment.

Animal intellect

The stage of 'animal intellect' or 'manual thinking' is found among highly organized animals, specifically the great apes—gibbons, orangutans, gorillas, and chimpanzees. While greatly expanding upon the mental capacities of lower animals the psyche of these creatures is still acting in the service of biological necessity. This contrasts with humans who, while still subject to biological demands, have forms of behavior that are governed culturally as well (Leontyev did not know at the time, but animal cultures have since been discovered). The animals operating at this level now clearly display thinking, but it is a form of thought that is qualitatively different from human reason. Things and their relations are now reflected upon, in the sense of ponder. Behavioral operations that they are able to perform, with respect to those things, as they mentally engage in problem solving. Action possibilities are ruminated upon.

Animals at the level of the perceptive psyche tend to engage in **trial-and-error** problem-solving by randomly acting, quixotically trying this then that, until luck brings them to the end sought. Operating at the level of 'intellect,' random activity may still be performed but the animal has the added capacity to work on the solution mentally. Different schemes of operation may be contemplated and then acted upon. Rather than responding to immediate conditions, the path to the goal is assessed and possibilities considered. Complex problems that require preparatory acts that set the conditions for the final resolution can be solved at this stage. The experiments on ape problem-solving by Köhler (1925/1957) influenced Leontyev greatly in this regard.

Working with chimpanzees, **Wolfgang Köhler** (1887–1967) developed problem-solving experiments in which a goal object (some food) could only be accessed by engaging in some preparatory activity. Direct access was negated. The conditions had to be rearranged. A tool or implement had to be used to achieve what the body alone could not. For instance, a female chimpanzee was confronted with food outside of her cage, beyond reach. Inside the cage and off to the side were a number of sticks. After a half hour of making various bodily attempts to reach the food she desisted. She had apparently taken no notice of the sticks even though they could not have been missed by her. A little later some younger animals took notice of the food. The caged animal immediately arose, took hold of a stick, and pulled the food within reach. An act of preparation (the extension of reach by a stick) led to accomplishment. During the interceding time the solution had dawned on the animal and the stick assumed 'instrumental value.'

In other two-phase problems food is raised to a height beyond reach by outstretching or jumping. Access required moving boxes beneath the goal and that they be piled up for climbing upon. Sometimes a combination of instruments was needed, such as climbing upon a box and using a stick for batting at the food to release it from its catch. Chimpanzees in arriving at solutions to these problems also displayed imitation, or what would now be termed 'observational learning.' They would repeat the performance observed of another if they were familiar with the action and understood it.

Figure 1.6   An ape's two-phase problem solving

One particular experiment was of especial significance to Leontyev because its solution required an intervening step that was contrary to the intended goal. Inside a large cage was placed a piece of food. The cage had three solid walls and one made of bars which the arm could pass through but through which the food could not be grasped. The opposing wall had a gap through which the food could be seen but beyond grasp. Attached to a tree, near the gap, was a stick that could reach the fruit (but not pull it up). The required preparatory act was to push the food away, toward the opposing bars, then to reposition to where it could then be grasped by reaching. What is remarkable about this is that the solution to the problem required doing the opposite of what was aimed at—the food must be pushed away rather than brought closer.

In the different problems that the apes were confronted with, they first engaged in random, *trial-and-error* operations which, by experimental intent, led to failure. This would be followed by a period of apparent rest and then what Köhler referred to as **insight** (the sudden appearance of a solution after survey of the situation as a whole). Such solutions would appear "*quite abruptly, and without visible external cause*" (Köhler, 1925/1957, p. 52, original emphasis). Apparently, the situation was pondered or thought about and the steps to solution brought together internally. The significance of this is apparent by comparison with animals at a lower level of ability.

In an experiment comparing chickens, rats, monkeys, and chimpanzees, the animals were placed behind a three-sided glass or wire mesh barrier which blocked direct access to food. The solution required turning back and around (Munn, 1971). Chickens and rats tried to get at the food by first trying to pass through the barrier directly, followed by random running around until accidentally obtaining the food (trial-and-error learning). Returned behind the barrier, the randomness continued until eventually the solution was firmly set. Monkeys and chimpanzees, in contrast, tended to go around the barrier from the start because they were not bound by the physically present. They apparently reconstructed the situation mentally and thought it over. According to Munn, many animals have been recognized for insightful behavior to some degree, under simple circumstances, but they fail to approach the primate level of resourcefulness and discernment.

In his analysis of Köhler's research, Leontyev emphasized the importance of two-phase (1. preparation, and 2. accomplishment) problem solving. The first, preparatory phase did not appear to be stimulated by the object the action was directed at, the stick or box for instance. Sticks do not in their natural relation to these animals elicit stick grasping; they are most often ignored unless they serve some ulterior purpose. The stick's significance is not biological although it serves a biological end. It is in the preparation of conditions for realization that 'intellect' makes its appearance.

There are four characteristics that distinguish the active engagement with the world at the level of intellect. First, there is a period of complete failure followed by sudden, successful solutions. Second, the successful solution is retained after one trial and repeated as needed. Endless repetitions are not needed to set the solution in memory and it is not subject to extinction when the objective associations break down. Furthermore, and third, the solution to one problem is easily transferred to other situations or potentially useful implements. If a stick had been used to extend reach but is unavailable, any elongated object suitable to the task is incorporated. Lastly, there is the emergence of the capacity to solve two-phase tasks involving 'preparation' and 'accomplishment.'

The performance of preparatory acts did not suggest to Leontyev that animals had the next step in mind, imagining it consciously. The first phase represents a reflection of the objective relations that exist between things in the situation—this is an expansion on the mere reflection of things at the level of perception. It is this increased reflective capacity that is the evolutionary advance and the greater objectivity that comes with it (Tolman, 1987). There has been a shift from the reflection of properties (sensitivity) to that of things (perceptivity) plus the relations between things (intellect). Generalizations at this stage also involve generalization of relations between things in objective circumstances in the form of interchangeable actions; trials are of previously developed operations, not random movements. Different approaches toward solution are attempted rather than random, happenstance trials and errors. Actions that were developed in other activities are detached from those activities and are made serviceable to novel circumstances. Objective reality is being dealt with more and more in the abstract and this lays a foundation for the thought capacity of humans.

Consciousness

The intellect displayed by the higher apes, to Leontyev, indicated that human thinking has its roots in biological evolution. As with each previous stage, consciousness involves further developments in the brain, such as greater size, weight, and complexity. Material reality, at the level of consciousness, is reflected, abstractly and conceptually, in terms of its separateness; in terms of its stable, objective properties. Consciousness and immediate experience may no longer be merged. There is direct, physical connection and a relatively independent, intellectual one. The realm of the intellect can be related to in its separateness from the objective realm, becoming an object of investigation in the capacity for self-observation. Humans began to gain control over nature and themselves rather than being biologically driven and reactive. There is a conscious reflection of the object world, of its attributes and relations, not accessible to direct perception.

In modern humans there are massive areas of the motor cortex devoted to the hands and to the organs of speech. These developments reflect the evolutionary pressures put on hominin evolution by labor (the intentional transformation of nature to satisfy human needs) practices. The need for fine motor movements in the hand was imposed by the production and use of tools and the need for communication, and its adoption effected developments in the mouth, tongue, and larynx. Washburn (1959) expressed the same idea when he wrote that the human hand and the expansion of the brain areas that regulate it were due to the selection pressure of tool use (a cultural development). Tools changed human morphology, and the patterns of life (effecting hunting, cooperation, and the need for communication). In their production and use, originality, memory, and foresight were favored and naturally selected for. There was 'mutualism' between brain development and human activity, each affecting the other. As Washburn concluded, "From the immediate point of view, this human brain makes culture possible. But from the long-term evolutionary point of view, it is culture which creates the human brain" (p. 29). To explain human behavior solely in terms of the brain is to engage in **biological reductionism**, thereby ignoring the significant role that culture plays in human history, both phylogenetically and ontogenetically.

According to Leontyev, the main difference between animal and human is that whereas animal psychic evolution is governed by general biological laws, humans entered the new evolutionary path of sociohistorical development and the emergence of labor. While many animals may work together to perform a task, like worker bees and ants, their activity is that of a collection of individuals. There is no division of labor. The labor process is characterized by the making of tools and by cooperative activity.

The tools' design reflects the properties of the object it was designed to be applied to, and incorporates the conscious, rational abstraction and generalization that went into its invention and production. An effective axe, for instance, corresponds to the properties of the object to be chopped or the knife for the cutting. While animals may make tools, the properties assigned to them are not fixed in the tool. As soon as the end has been achieved, the tool (such as the chimpanzee fishing stick) is dropped and becomes a stick again rather than remaining a tool. Humans, in comparison, retain their tools and improve on them. Leontyev contended animal tool use lacked the nature of a social process, a communal activity, and fell outside the level of human constructive activity. The labor of humans, he emphasized, was social from the beginning and involved, however rudimentary, a division of labor. Labor connects the individuals and mediates their conduct with the world and each other.

Leontyev's preferred example was that of the beater during collective hunting activity. The beater, working in concert with others, chases game away with pounding and banging. This is contrary to the personal end of obtaining food. In the collective activity, however, the game is being driven into ambush and another's arrow and spear. Each individual's personal need coincides with the needs of the others, and in concord they satisfy their common end by performing one of the operations required of the hunting activity as a whole. Contrary to Leontyev, it is now apparent that humans are not alone in this kind of division of roles. Collaborative hunting and a coordinated division of roles, for instance, has been found in the hunting behavior of lions (Stander, 1992). When a group is out hunting and comes upon game the animals slip into stealth. A couple of the animals spread out, circling behind the prey, while others engage in a slow, crouching advance. When set, the encircling lions chase the victim to the others waiting in ambush. Similar behavior has been found in wolves (Boesch and Boesch, 1989). The hunting behavior of some chimpanzees displays a more complicated division of labor that is more dynamic and flexible.

In Taï National Park (Côte d'Ivoire) chimpanzees relate their hunting actions to their fellows and engage in complementary, coordinated movements (Boesch and Boesch, 1989). In apparent premeditation, prior to the chase the situation is evaluated and conditions are set, shifting and adjusting with respect to each other and the prey, for the forthcoming pursuit (Teleki, 1975). The tactics suggest shared intentions and goals in the four complementary roles (Boesch, 2005). The driver begins the process by pushing the prey in a particular direction. The blocker closes routes of escape. The chaser pursues and the ambusher awaits the prey. There is an apparent sophistication in the cognitive processes comparable to human hunter-gatherers (Teleki, 1975). There is a deliberate, controlled quality to the stalking and chasing, often requiring involved, intricate maneuvers and complex strategies to isolate the target and corner it. Positioning and repositioning maximize spatial placement in a deliberate and complementary manner.

Animal consciousness

Whereas Leontyev regarded consciousness as a specifically human intellectual achievement, subsequent research suggests that the mental powers of some non-humans have surpassed the level of animal intellect or at least are transitioning to primitive consciousness, 'mesoforms' as it were. Wynn and McGraw (1989) believe that chimpanzee tool use is at the proto-human, Oldowan stone-flaking level of technological competence of two million years ago. A lack of actual stone flaking on the part of chimpanzees, they believe, is not representative of cognitive deficit since rocks are used to smash bone into fragments for use as puncturing instruments—a comparable performance. Furthermore, chimpanzees forage for stones to use as hammers and transport them to processing locations a half-kilometer away, a practice that is in evidence at Oldowan sites and is suggestive of conscious intent. The tool use of crows also suggests complex cognitive processes that rival those of chimpanzees (Emery and Clayton, 2004). Crows are skilled in making hooked tools by shaping and trimming twigs in order to extract insect larvae from trees. In the laboratory, a crow took a piece of straight wire and bent it into a hook tool (Weir, Chappell, and Kacelnik, 2002). That was then used to extract a food-containing bucket from inside a tube where it was previously inaccessible by beak or claw.

While animals may display evidence of being conscious or aware, it should not be assumed that they are fully conscious. Edelman (2001, 2003), in that regard, made a relevant distinction between 'primary consciousness' and 'higher order consciousness.' Primary consciousness is a state of mental awareness of objective phenomena and the possessing of images of the immediate present (with no accompanying sense of the past or future). While there is no awareness of the past, there is long-term memory that is acted upon. Prior experience supports current adaptations without awareness of the memory. Neither are those memories used to plan for the future. Something of the difference between this and higher order consciousness is indicated by analogy to certain types of brain damage in which a person, without being aware, responds appropriately to objective conditions. In the condition known as '**blind sight**,' for instance, a person is unaware of seeing but can visually locate objects that are in the person's blind region. If asked how they succeeded the person could not explain how. Let me offer possible animal examples.

Blind sight

Discrimination training (learning to distinguish between different stimulus categories) has been used to examine the capacity of animals to abstract and generalize, to act on a conceptual basis due to similarities and differences between things (Munn, 1971). An experimental test of pigeons demonstrated the formation of various **perceptual concepts** based on complex visual input such as 'person,' 'tree,' 'lake,' 'fish present,' the 'letter A,' or 'clothing type' (Domjan, 1993). Edwards and Honzig (1987, in Domjan, 1993) used pictures that either contained pictures of humans present or the same scene with humans absent as discriminative stimuli for reinforcement. If a pigeon pecked at a food-release disc, when pictures included humans food was obtained, but not if pecking when humans were absent from the photo. Pigeons learned to peck only to human-present discriminative stimuli. This was shown to not be memory for previously encountered pictures by introducing novel photographs to which conceptual generalization occurred. An animal like these pigeons may respond to a stimulus condition in ways that indicate responding to categories of things but that does not mean that they are conscious of those abstractions and generalizations. One might speak in that regard of implicit and explicit concepts where explicit implies higher order consciousness and a state of being "conscious of being conscious" (Edelman, 2001, p. 113). There is awareness of the situation and of oneself in the situation, and there is a sense of past, present, and future.

Evidence of burgeoning consciousness in animals is apparent in research into more complex cognitive functions. Investigations into abstract concept formation had formerly been restricted to mammals and humans, but avian species are beginning to demonstrate such capacities despite dissimilarities to mammalian brains (Pepperberg, 1998). The African Grey parrot, in particular, has been shown to possess greater categorization and concept formation skills than other birds. One parrot, named Alex, learned to distinguish between, and designate with English words, more than 80 different kinds of objects, shapes (triangle, square, pentagon), colors, and material makeup (wood, paper, cork), and can make quantitative designations up to six units (Pepperberg, 1998). This was established through verbal questioning. More surprising was his ability to answer questions correctly with respect to the abstract categories of similarity and dissimilarity. Shown two wooden triangles in blue and yellow, for instance, upon which no previous tests had been performed, he could correctly answer to "What's same?" and "What's different?" Several bird and animal species have demonstrated the same intellectual capacity (Maier, 1998).

Another intellectual capacity formerly thought to be distinctively human was that of reasoning, but research with chimpanzees has demonstrated a capacity for reasoning by inference and by analogy (Domjan, 1993). A transitive inference is one based on relational similarity between three or more things. For instance, if you know that a jet airliner is larger than a bus and an aircraft carrier is larger than an airliner you can infer that the carrier is larger than the bus too—a transitive inference. Gillan (1981) tested this capacity in three chimpanzees. They were presented with canisters of the same size and differently colored lids (red, blue, black, white, orange) which had greater or lesser amounts of food, say red > blue > black > white > orange. In pairs they were taught that red had more food than black, then that black had more than white and white had more than orange. When subsequently offered the novel pairing of black and orange they chose black, which was a correct transitive inference. Similar findings have been obtained with pigeons (Fersen, Wynne, Delius, and Staddon, 1991) and rats (Davis, 1992).

Gilllan, Premack, and Woodruff (1981) studied analogical reasoning in animals. This involves reasoning based on likeness or equivalence due to prior relations. A previously learned relation is generalized to a novel situation because of similarity or equivalence. Chimpanzees, for instance, were tested for analogical reasoning with respect to objects familiar to the animal such as locks, torn cloth, knives, padlocks, or a paint brush. In one test the animal was shown a key and a lock on one side and a closed paint can on another for which a choice had to be made between a can opener and a paint brush. The functional relation was that of opening and the correct choice was opener. Or a piece of paper and a pencil were shown with the closed paint can and the choice between opener and brush (correct choice). The chimpanzee Sarah reasoned correctly on 15 out of 18 attempts.

Space does not permit reviewing the extensive literature on cognitive functions in animals, but the evidence has broadened extensively on what was available to Leontyev (see Byrne, 1995; Greenberg and Harraway, 2002; Roberts, 1998; Wynne, 2001). Animals have specialized sensory systems for processing relevant information in the niche they occupy and the challenges they must accommodate. Different animals display varying capacity in concept formation from 'perceptual concepts' and **abstract concepts** to a 'sense of time,' and from quantity to numerical processing. Differences in short-term/working memory and long-term memory capacities including specialized memory functions (like extensive spatial memory for food caches in nutcrackers) have been found. There is also evidence of reasoning and communication. This does not invalidate Leontyev's categorical scheme of mental development, but it does mean that reconsideration of the capacities of different species may challenge some of his interpretations and possibly require new categories. What is established is that those processes that constitute the mental and are designated by the term 'mind' are of natural origin and require no **dualistic** explanation.

1.3 HOMO SAPIENS

The first possible **hominin** species was *Sahelanthropus tchadensis* of six to seven million years ago, but the best evidence is that of *Australopithecus*, an intermediate bipedal form between ape and human, of about four million years ago (Lewin and Foley, 2004). The earliest intelligent hominin, associated with the appearance of stone tool use, was the *Homo habilis* species around two-and-a-half million years ago. They had a body structure similar to australopithecines but a brain of about 650cm^3 compared to around 400cm^3 for australopithecines. *Homo erectus* appears around two million years ago with a brain up to 1,350 cm^3. During this period significant developments included systematic hunting, the use of fire and home bases, and large tool construction (cleavers, picks, and hand axes). Their technologies suggested greater cognitive complexity in their conceptualization and manufacture. Substantial developments arise with the transition from *Homo erectus* into *Homo sapiens* genus about 150,000 years ago. Tool technologies are more finely crafted and of increased diversity. Strategies for foraging are more efficient and social organization is of greater complexity and includes symbolic expression and developed language. Included in this superspecies are the subspecies of *Homo neanderthalensis* (70,000–30,000 years ago) or 'archaic' Homo sapiens and modern *Homo sapiens* (the past 50,000 years).

The Neanderthals, or 'archaic' *Homo sapiens*, evolved from *Homo erectus* and had a modern-sized brain (Haviland, 1997). The tools they produced were classified as Mousterian technology, which was lighter and smaller than the tools of their predecessors and of greater variety. There were axes and scrapers, but also tools for sawing wood and points for spear heads. Such weapons meant greater sources of food became available. Evidence suggests efficient hunting techniques of small and large game such as bison and elephant, cooking, and the use of leather for clothing manufacture (Scrupin and DeCorse, 2008). There are fossils of aged individuals and indications of recovery from serious bone injury that suggest care for the handicapped and elderly (Haviland, 1997). There is also evidence of the burial of the dead, especially given the intentional positioning of the body. To Schepartz (1993) that indicates symbolic (conceptual) thinking and awareness of one's species as distinct from the rest of nature, and of a sense of self. Besides symbolism and cognition, there is reason to believe Neanderthals had developed language abilities.

Somewhere between 45,000–35,000 years ago Neanderthal populations gave way to modern humans (Lewis-Williams, 2002). The most apparent indicator of the transition was in the Aurignacian tool technology's greater refinement and the expanding range of tools. Patterns in temporal migrations were recognized and used to predict movement and improve hunting tactics, hunting having become a highly organized social activity. Humans had developed modern language, could converse in sentences about abstract ideas, and had an apparent awareness of the past and future. Fully developed language capacity was a significant advancement in biological evolution (Scrupin and DeCorse, 2008). Through language use and production humans create and communicate standardized meanings which further support the transmission of culture (beliefs, customs, technologies, and skills). Since the perfection of language, human history has been dominated by cultural evolution rather than biological evolution. Luria (1966/1967) maintained that the development of language provided a new method of communication and a tool for the ordering and regulation of mental processes. It was in verbal communication that the higher mental functions (those that expand upon the innate, elementary, biologically-based psychological functions) originated. The methods developed for interpersonal verbal communication were adapted to intrapersonal needs and purposes. This resulted in conceptually mediated perception, abstract thought (and inner speech), and voluntary forms of attention, recall, and behavior. The basic laws of biological evolution recede to the background or are subsumed into new laws that govern social relations and the process of sociocultural evolution (Vygotsky, 1930/1994).

Vygotsky
Luria

As **Lev Vygotsky** (1896–1934) and **Alexander Luria** (1902–1977) wrote, over the course of human historical development there was a change in the relation of humans to nature as they transformed from biological beings to cultural beings (Vygotsky and Luria, 1930/1993). In the course of this, humans began to gain supremacy over nature and expansion in technologies. Whereas animals are almost wholly dependent on their inherited traits, humans learn to master cultural products, technologies, and intellectual tools, which liberate them from enslavement to the environment. Cultural behavior differs from natural behavior in that it is learned, socially not biologically transmitted, and involves abstractions and conceptual generalizations (Park, 2000).

The development of conceptual understanding, or the mental representation of categories, is particularly significant. Concepts free people from the necessity of storing massive amounts of **concrete** impressions and overwhelming, copious detail (Vygotsky and Luria, 1930/1993). A concept is a general meaning and object of awareness that can be thought about (English and English, 1958) and supports orientation to the object world. By means of concept formation humans can classify or arrange objects around common properties, meaningfully understand and explain experience, and reason effectively (Medin et al., 2001). Categories and concepts help in making sense of the world and to profit from experience. One can make predictions based on past categories of experience and plan effective action. Meaningful understanding can be communicated to others and passed across generations. In effect, humans construct for themselves a world of meanings that mediates between the individual and the immediate environmental conditions.

Our ancestors, as Clark and Piggott (1965/1990) observed, created a cultural cushion between them and the environment, enabling them to resist immediate pressures and formulate conscious choices of action. The process was relatively slow in its development, at the time of the emergence of modern *Homo sapiens*, but it has certainly accelerated immensely over the last two millennia. Even in those earlier more primitive times humans had developed a sociocultural world that transcended the capacity of the isolated individual and made people ever more interdependent in the cultural context. As Heinrich and McElreath (2003) put it, tools, kayaks, boomerangs, and bows, along with myriad other implements, are technologies that embody within them knowledge and skills that no individual could figure out in a lifetime.

The Neolithic revolution

In the initial phase of modern human existence (the Upper Paleolithic, around 40,000–10,000 BC) our ancestors followed the hunter-gatherer lifestyle. In this pre-agricultural period the human group (small bands) was very much at the mercy of natural conditions (Clark and Piggott, 1965/1990). Food supplies had not been brought under control. Fruit, grains, vegetables, and game were subject to chance environmental forces that were little understood. As a result, the hunter-gatherers had to remain wanderers in search of sustenance and pursuit of migratory animals. The transition from the hunter-gathering lifestyle to agriculture was both slow and rapid, taking 20,000–30,000 years before its large scale adoption (Leakey, 1981). Increasing sedentism (a shift from nomadism to settlement), perhaps where resources were plentiful, was followed by a gradual adoption of domesticated plants and animals (Lewin and Foley, 2004). All of this set the stage for the Neolithic Revolution associated with the emergence of agriculture. There were three major locations where the shift took hold: the eastern Mediterranean (8,000 BC), northeastern China (5,000 BC), and Mesoamerica (3,000 BC).

The agricultural revolution led to a massive reorganization in human modes of existence and marked the beginning of modern societies, and resulted in changes to human consciousness and mental powers. Modern humans, as Lewis-Williams (2002) pointed out, are anatomically the same in terms of their nervous system as the people of the Neolithic period and have a consciousness that is culturally determined. The human nervous system has not changed but the consciousness of humans has evolved with cultural growth (societal knowledge has expanded and been made available and, as it is incorporated, so grows the consciousness). That is consistent with Vygotsky, who hypothesized that as a function of the transition from one historical form to another, not only the 'contents' of consciousness changed, but also the 'structure' of higher mental processes, underlying the concrete forms of psychological activity (Luria, 1976). The process whereby the primitive human (the Neolithic type) is transformed into the cultural human does not coincide with biological evolution (Vygotsky and Luria, 1930/1993). Over the course of the historical development of humans there was a change in the relation with nature in which humans changed their own nature, developed it, and altered their way of life, becoming more active than reactive.

The commitment to the farming lifestyle, according to Leakey (1981), led to the necessity to defend the land. Whereas the key to survival for the hunter-gatherer was sharing, which increased the possibility of the whole group surviving in the long-run, the farmer-herder relies upon saving seeds and breeding pairs for future productivity. The hunter-gatherer would have shared his last goat, but the farmer could not for the sake of future yields. Competition was replacing cooperation in the struggle to secure the best resources. The agricultural revolution brought about an increase in productivity and that had an impact on the evolution of human practices.

With control over food production surpluses becoming the norm, each home could feed a larger family. The increasing population eventually led to a surplus in humans beyond the requirements of farming (Leakey, 1981). A social division of labor and labor specialization, as well as the rise of villages and towns, and finally cities and civilization (the city-state), came into existence. Communal life, based on kinship and egalitarianism, was being replaced as political organization transitioned from band to tribe and chiefdoms (kin-ordered societies), to the agricultural state system (Scrupin and DeCorse, 2008). The state is an institutionalized, bureaucratized institution that governs large territories and populations. The system was increasingly hierarchical in organization and usually involved great social inequality associated with the control of food surpluses and associated economic activities. Freed from fieldwork, people took up specialized occupations—carpenter, baker, potter, milliner, and so on. Associated with each specialized activity were particularized vocabularies that expressed the relevant concrete and abstract ideas that were relevant to the particular occupation (Derry and Williams, 1960/1970).

Higher in the power ranking, new occupations arose in response to increasing societal complexity related to commerce, religion, the military, and the various levels of government. The state sanctioned laws which were commonly maintained by the use of force (Scrupin and DeCorse, 2008). The protection of land resources and of the state also led to the necessity of an army (Leakey, 1981). Conflict was probably always with humans but not at the level of organized warfare. When one band of hunter-gatherers encroached on the territory of another, the lack of commitment to the land left the option to resist or move on. If resistance occurred, it was not all-out annihilation. The forming of armies and improvements in killing weaponry during this period is associated with the first evidence of mass aggression and warfare. The original indications of war as lethal violence between groups existed in Mesopotamia around 3,000 BC and China about 2,500 BC (Cioffi-Revilla, 1996). Barbarity and cruelty are synchronous with high levels of civilization and political systems with ruling elites. That the archaeology, the monuments and paintings, of warfare disappear beyond 10,000 years ago hints at the close connection of the sedentary lifestyle with mass aggression (Leakey and Lewin, 1992). This was also the period when human slavery was instituted (Scrupin and DeCorse, 2008). For good or ill, humans were shaping their world, altering it, and—in the process—themselves, in how they acted and how they thought.

Intellectual tools

The invention of tools clearly had an impact on the human capacity to impose their purposes on nature and to effect desired changes. The development of farming tools and irrigation systems, of carpentry and metallurgy, and so on, all bear witness to the transformative power in human activity. What is less apparent is the degree to which humans have turned their power to observe and understand to the mastery of themselves. Besides physical technologies, humans have also developed systems of psychological technologies by means of which they have come to exercise directive control over their natural psychological capacities.

While I would not want to suggest that humans invented speech as a means for interpersonal communication, its incorporation into mental processes has transformed speech from a means of interpersonal influence to an intrapersonal mediating mechanism in intellectual operations. Language to Vygotsky had a two-fold function as (A) a means to social coordination of collective activities, and (B) as a tool for thinking by speech internalizing and wedding with non-verbal thought as inner speech (Van der Veer and Valsiner, 1991). A tool for social interaction became a tool for internal activity. Not only is practical activity brought under verbal control, but abstract intelligence is increased in its power by the acquisition of meanings and knowledge that have been incorporated into language (Vygotsky, 1978).

Tool and **sign** use were of particular importance in the transformation of the biological human into the socialized human (Luria, 1979). Natural (elementary, biological) psychological processes become higher psychological processes by the active use of signs (words, numbers, maps, symbols, clocks, et cetera). The creation and use of signs meant that humans were transforming themselves from the outside (Leontiev and Luria, 1968). The history of the development of signs is therefore also the history of the gradual increase in self-control through the adoption of sign technologies. Tool and sign use thus contributed to the development of individual consciousness and the active orientation to the objective conditions of living.

The expansions on elementary memory are an example of the transition to higher mental processing through the appropriation of the mediating mechanism of signs (Vygotsky and Luria, 1930/1993). Signs were the first tools developed to support natural memory. West African storytellers, for instance, used golden figures to represent aspects of a narrative and to serve as aids in recall. The quipu of ancient Peru is a further example of such a device. Knotted strings hanging from a stick support recall by each knot representing a specific piece of information. When a particular technique became widespread in a cultural group it assumed a conventionalized meaning and became a means of communication. Memory, therefore, that is supplemented by abstract sign systems is qualitatively different from elementary memory. The organic basis is not altered, but the method of remembering is. The improvements to memory therefore rest upon the development of systems of signs and how they are developed. The development of writing, in particular, represents the evolution of the preservation and communication of meaning through an objective memory (Olson, 1993).

Of all the sign systems that have been created to support memory, writing is one of the most efficient, but it did not appear in its current form overnight. In fact, writing systems developed over thousands of years and did so in stages (Clodd, 1904). In the first 'mnemonic' stage the memory devices like quipus became a means of communication whereby a message was retained by encoding into knotted designs and was passed to others at a distance. In the 'pictorial' stage a picture of a thing represented the thing by obvious resemblance (the first evidence being in Sumeria in the fourth millennium BC—Schmandt-Besserat, 1986). While not an efficient system for complex communication, pictographs are used to transmit ideas in the modern world and can be understood without knowledge of the local language, such as pictures of a knife and fork indicating food (Gaur, 1992). In the 'ideographic' stage the figure is no longer a picture in that it has assumed a representative, symbolic function. The images now represent an idea rather than a thing and have a generalized meaning (Haviland, 1997). A crown placed above a house, for instance, could symbolize a royal palace. In a more abstract form a cross enclosed by a circle was used in Mesopotamia as the sign for sheep (Schmandt-Besserat, 1986).

Hieroglyphic writing developed out of ideographic, but differs in that the picture was converted into a symbol related to the sound of a word (Scrupin and DeCorse, 2008). This was Clodd's (1904) 'phonetic' stage which was marked by a picture becoming a phonogram (representative of a word sound or phoneme). In the verbal form a whole word was signified by the picture, in the syllabic form syllables were depicted, and in the alphabetic a letter

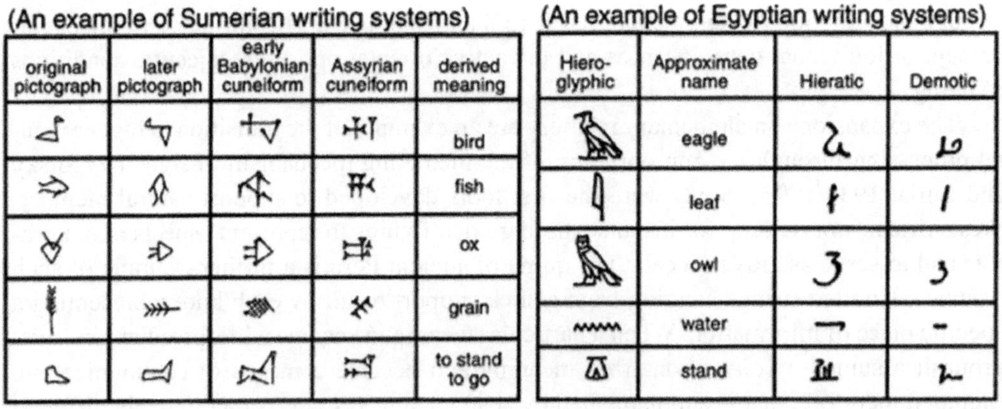

(An example of Sumerian writing systems)

original pictograph	later pictograph	early Babylonian cuneiform	Assyrian cuneiform	derived meaning
				bird
				fish
				ox
				grain
				to stand to go

(An example of Egyptian writing systems)

Hiero-glyphic	Approximate name	Hieratic	Demotic
	eagle		
	leaf		
	owl		
	water		
	stand		

Figure 1.7   Ancient writing systems

signified a sound. In syllabic writing characters represented sound sequences or consonants, such as in Arabic and Hebrew writing systems (Olson, 1993). There were 22 graphic signs and they could be used to represent a much broader range of meaning. Developing out of the syllabic system, the alphabetic system, perfected by the ancient Greeks around 750 BC, had a separate symbol for each vowel and consonant. Memory is involved in the learning and subsequent encoding and decoding of the alphabet, but individual memory is surpassed in that the written word, as a form of information storage, can be passed from one generation to another, supporting new developments and expanding accumulating knowledge (Gaur, 1992). How modern, enculturated humans remember and what they know, the whole of human experience, has accumulated in texts and other recorded symbol systems, an external societal memory, has expanded human memory and is the necessary condition for cultural-historical development (Vygotsky and Luria, 1930/1993). All of this is due to external memory based on the use of signs.

The development of mnemonics was a further factor in the development of internal memory. In ancient times the art of memory was a part of rhetoric and concern was with accurate recall in the delivery of long speeches (Yates, 1966/1992). Oral recitation made great demands on memory (Danziger, 2008). Poets and storytellers drew upon memory aids such as rhythmically strumming an instrument, or the use of meter and rhyme, to support their performance. Simonides of Ceos (5th century BC) is accredited as the discoverer of mnemonics when he realized that orderly arrangement supported recall (Yates, 1966/1992). At a banquet where he was delivering a poem the roof collapsed upon the guests just after he stepped outside. He was asked to help identify who was who from the mangled remains. He envisioned the room and where each person sat and was able thereby to make the identification. By doing this he created the mnemonic strategy of the 'method of loci.' In the 1st century BC a textbook was written to guide orators in memorizing their delivery. Two types of memory were identified in the text: natural, innate memory, and artificial memory which required training in order to improve on the natural type.

When written texts were developed the reliance on individual memory was not so important (Danziger, 2008). As you read this text you are likely unaware that the transmission of the written word itself has undergone substantial reform since its introduction. In classical antiquity, however, the physical characteristics of the written page worked against easy reading (Achtemeier, 1990). Manuscripts lacked separation of words by spaces between them, punctuation, and sentences. Since the words ran together, ancient readers lacked external signals to support the identification of linguistic structure. During the medieval period, and prior to the invention of the printing press with increased text availability, the link between memory and writing was being emphasized because of the rarity of books (Danziger, 2008). One way that text memorization was improved was in better organization of the text on the page. Mnemonic aids like spaces between words, then paragraphing, and later punctuation supported the retention of ideational content. Chapters and chapter titles followed, and in the

1300s indexes were created for the scriptures as well as tables of contents (Crosby, 1997). These location systems within the text made for easier referencing and were needed in the universities, the church, and courts of law (Danziger, 2008). Medieval libraries were also expanding and needed a system for locating manuscripts so catalogues, which were eventually alphabetized, promoted the easy access of voluminous written materials.

In our own times the transition to widespread literacy and the need for symbolic communication of the last century has broadened and transformed the general consciousness of the population. Much of the modern world demands a capacity to read to function effectively, and a person bereft of that capacity leads an ineffective existence. One's orientation to city life depends on reading signs and schedules. Jobs depend on reading to fill out employment application. Health depends on reading drug prescriptions. On and on it goes. One's chances of adapting to current life conditions are greatly diminished by impotence in literacy. Literacy, as Scribner (1984) pointed out, is a social (not a biological) achievement that is transmitted culturally.

Without going into the details, other sign systems were developed by humans that furthered the organization of their activities and aided them in regulating their own conduct. Numeric notation was developed in Mesopotamia and Egypt around 3,500 BC (Chrisomalis, 2010). In the late Middle Ages and the Renaissance, Europe was involved in developing a quantitative model of reality and the use of numbers became more widespread (Crosby, 1997). The emergence of mercantilism further spurred that development. The general public began to learn quantification as the cash economy began to pervade all forms of life. The use of money in everyday affairs affected the consciousness of the people using it (Kaye, 1988). During the mid-14th century, and traceable to the monetization of society, there was an intellectual movement called the 'science of calculation.' The calculators had the new habit of measuring, which became important to the practice of science. An arithmetic mentality was developing.

To this one could also add the impact of the measurement of time and the creation of calendars for the organization of social activity, or how maps helped people become oriented in physical space. The point is simply that in their creative activities and in their cultural developments, human conduct and thought, the consciousness of the day, was being brought under cultural influences more and more, while the brain had remained constant—we are still the species Homo sapiens. As Thurnwald (1936) put it, although objects and meanings have been created by humans, people have become ever more dependent on such devices and ideas. If we underwent a technological collapse in the delivery of electricity, communication, and shipping networks, we would be lost. Societal organization would collapse. The food supply would be localized and you would have to provide for your needs yourself. We would quickly revert to a hunter-gatherer state of affairs. Without the educational system and knowledge networks our consciousness would become primitive in content and organization over a few generations. We would become dependent on those psychological mechanisms that evolutionary psychologists like Buss (1995) emphasize. Psychological mechanisms would be those that are coded in the brain and which were adaptive and supported survival and reproduction in the pre-Neolithic period. Life would not be as we know it (or understand it).

In this chapter we have considered the evolution of the physical universe. In the process we considered how the emergence of biology set the conditions for the development of elementary psychological functions in animals and humans. We ended with a consideration of the effect that sociohistorical and cultural developments had on the establishment of higher mental functions. In the next chapter our concern will be with the appearance of philosophy in the West and of the issues that arose for them. In particular, we will survey the modes of explanation that were developed to account for what they observed and were trying to understand. In doing so it will be shown how these explanatory frameworks influence modern interpretations of psychological phenomena.

SUMMARY

The known universe evolved from the Big Bang and the issuance of subatomic particles and atoms, followed by biological and cultural evolution.

- Life was explained in terms of the theory of levels of integration and emergent properties.
- Mechanism and vitalism were rejected as viable accounts of life.
- Life was shown to have the new qualities of metabolism, homeostasis, growth, reproduction, and evolution by natural selection.
- The first mental processes were an expansion on the biological property of irritability. Sensitivity involved a nervous system and specialized nerves responsive to specific types of energy (the senses). This was followed by the perceptive psyche, animal intellect, and consciousness.
- Hominins themselves have undergone evolutionary stages: australopithecines, Homo habilis, Homo erectus, and Homo sapiens (including Neanderthals and modern humans).
- Hominins developed tools and language which achieved their greatest perfection in modern humans. A new form of evolution—cultural evolution—surpassed biological evolution. Sign systems were singled out in particular as a major force in shaping individual consciousness.

SUGGESTED READINGS

Leontyev, A. N. (1981). *Problems of the development of the mind*. Moscow: Progress Publishers.

Novikoff, A. (1945). The concept of integrative levels and biology. *Science*, *101*, 209–215.

Vygotsky, L. S. and Luria, A. R. (1993). *Studies on the history of behavior: Ape, primitive, and child* (V. I. Golod and J. E. Knox, Eds. and Trans.). Hillsdale, NJ: Lawrence Erlbaum Associates. (Originally published 1930.)

Want to learn more? For links to online resources, examples of multiple choice questions, conceptual exercises and much more, visit the companion website at
https://study.sagepub.com/piekkola

2
HISTORICAL CONCEPTUAL ISSUES

LEARNING OBJECTIVE

In this chapter we will look at the philosophical roots of psychology including some examples of how these basic concepts can be found in modern psychology. Two broad branches of metaphysics—ontology and epistemology—will be the focus. More specifically we will consider:

- The mind–body problem (including reductionism and holism)
- Appearance versus reality
- Rationalism versus empiricism
- Realism versus anti-realism (including relativism, constructionism, skepticism, and phenomenology).

By connecting these to modern psychology you should come to appreciate how these issues were merely repressed in the turn to scientism and have remained implicit throughout.

FRAMING QUESTIONS

- Why should Greek philosophy be of a concern? What does it have to do with modern psychology?
- What philosophical issues are embedded in modern psychology? Where do questions of ontology and epistemology appear?
- Why are subjectivity and free will problems in psychology?

INTRODUCTION

In this chapter we will be considering the philosophical roots of psychology. Some would argue that psychology has nothing to do with philosophy, but the emergence of psychology as a discipline involved the wedding of philosophical subject matter to physiological method (Koch, 1985a). Traditional philosophical problems like the mind–body problem, questions of knowledge and what could be known, continued to be issues. Initially, psychology continued to be categorized as a division of philosophy rather than a science. Ebbinghaus (1911), who initiated research into memory, considered psychology to be the handmaiden and servant of philosophy. This association was further indicated by the titles of the first two journals devoted to the new approach: Bain's *Mind*, founded in 1876, and Wundt's *Philosophische Studien* in 1881 (Boring, 1929). By the 1890s a 'new psychology' based on experimentation was being advocated as a replacement for the old philosophical psychology (Boring, 1929). There were many in psychology who wanted to distance themselves from philosophy altogether and to become an experimental discipline freed of uncorroborated fanciful speculation.

The tradition of disciplined reasoning about human affairs, the method of philosophers, was being derisively dismissed as 'armchair psychology' (Koch, 1985a). Psychologists, it was argued, would have to learn the scientific method and move from the armchair into the laboratory (Heidbreder, 1933). In this process psychology would leave behind a vast history pertaining to psychological knowledge that existed in the humanities and in natural language categories (Koch, 1985a). Respect for scholarship would dwindle as the emphasis on empirical practices arose. The creation of the psychological laboratory was significant in this transformation in that it signified the intention of psychologists to become recognized as members of the naturalistic, experimental sciences (Hilgard, 1987). It further signaled the separation of psychology from speculative philosophy.

The eradication of philosophy from psychology was not immediate, but the process was well under way by the early 1900s. By that time a number of psychologists were contending that the scientific-experimental practices of chemistry and physics were equivalent to a philosophy of science unfettered by worthless **metaphysical** haggling (Robinson, 2000a). The ascendance of experimentalism, and to some **scientism**, was prefigured in these discussions. The founder of the *American Journal of Psychology*, G. Stanley Hall, was proposing that the 'new psychology' should be focused on the physiology of mental states and adopt natural science methods, eschewing metaphysics. The journals were filling with laboratory reports that adopted technical terms drawn from biology, physiology, and physics, and had no resemblance to the 'old psychology.' In their efforts at being scientific the proponents were zealously disavowing any affiliation with philosophy.

Watson

The apex of the transition, at least in North America, was best reflected in **John Watson's** (1878–1958) 'Behaviorist Manifesto': "The time seems to have come" he wrote, "when psychology must discard all reference to consciousness; when it need no longer delude itself into thinking that it is making mental states the object of observation" (1913a, p. 163). Watson preferred his students to have nothing to do with the mind–body problem but admitted that consciousness was a tool psychologists worked with (presumably in objective observation). Nonetheless, the question of the proper use of consciousness was a matter for philosophers, not psychologists. Despite psychologists' assertions of their liberation from philosophy, that did not mean that they in fact had cast off their metaphysical shackles. Not all were convinced that philosophy could be left behind.

Boring (1929), in his history of experimentation in psychology, acknowledged that "psychologists have never succeeded in avoiding metaphysical discussion" (p. 249). One's facts, according to Vygotsky (1934/1986), such as experimental results, are examined from the perspective of some theory and, because of that, cannot be extricated from philosophy. Even observations would come to be judged as **theory laden** by philosophers of science, meaning that what is selected for observation is under the direction of some theory (Greenwood, 1990). Vygotsky (1934/1986) further asserted that the avoidance of philosophy is itself a philosophy and may lead one into inconsistencies. As Heidbreder (1933) judged, Watson's emphasis on objective phenomena was itself a metaphysical issue. Such an assertion involved **epistemological** knowledge claims about an external world that was accessible to all (a claim that remains contentious to this day). Furthermore, Watson's dismissal of consciousness as a topic of concern for psychology did not rid it of the matter. It slipped back in through the method of observation which implicitly involves awareness of what is being observed (Price, 1960).

As you may have inferred from the foregoing, in this chapter we will be examining the philosophical roots of psychology. The issues to be discussed were explicit in the 'old psychology' and implicit in the 'new.' No matter how much one may protest that psychology has liberated itself from philosophy, philosophical concerns still inhabit psychological practices and explanations and should be exposed. Koch (1985b) queried "Are we conceptually independent of philosophy?" and answered "Most of our ideas have come from the twenty-six centuries of philosophy preceding the birth of our partition myth" (p. 90). To Hume (in Report of the Secretary, 1909) "psychology without philosophy is blind" (p. 66). Or, as Dewey (1920/1948) expressed it, theory (think armchair speculation) is empty and valueless unless tested in practice; but practice without theory, conversely, is a mere agglomeration of meaningless facts. The question you should be asking yourself is whether psychology should do without metaphysics when, as William James (1890/1950) put it, "Metaphysics means nothing but an unusually obstinate effort to think clearly" (p. 145).

2.1 ON THE NOTION OF GREEK PSYCHOLOGY

There has been a tendency among historians of psychology to trace the roots of psychology to the ancient Greeks. Hunt (1993), for example, proposed that the formation of psychology as an academic discipline had been foreshadowed for a long time; the Greek philosophers had delineated its subject matter. This idea is no longer as acceptable as it once was. The problem to Smith (2005) rests with the fact that there was no social activity called psychology at the time. Just because perception and memory were being studied and discussed does not mean that this was 'psychology.' The term psychology was not in use at the time. Nonetheless there has been a false assumption that because people over the ages have been studying memory, perception, or thinking they were referring to an unchanging realm, the knowledge of which remains constant. Terms like 'mind,' 'perception,' 'memory,' and 'emotion,' from the perspective of constancy, would be in reference to **natural kinds** (rather than such psychological categories being **human kinds**). If such terms refer to biological processes, uninfluenced by cultural developments, the designation may hold but, as Smith contended, even though such terms were in use in the past does not mean that they held the same conceptual meaning as is current. To assume so is to fall into the danger of **presentism**, of reading the present into the past. That psychologists and ancient Greeks used the same terms does not mean the Greek usage was psychological. What Smith questioned was what a history of psychology could be before there was a social activity called 'psychology.'

Although there had been long discourse regarding human nature and mental processes, there was no actual discipline called psychology until the mid-1800s (Richards, 1996). What discussion there may have been was neither scientific nor experimental. Furthermore, the proposition that the questions being asked have remained the same, and that just the methods have changed, does not hold unless one believes that the early Greeks were asking the same questions that psychologists ask. Richards was not suggesting that there is no connection historically, but that these predecessors were not engaged in what psychologists have been pursuing. That their inquiries led to discussions of topics like perception or child development, and provided terms that modern psychologists adopted, certainly establishes a historical connection. The issues contemplated, however, were in reference to a different context and had a different purpose. As Danziger (1990a) explained, that terms remain contemporary should not suggest that their usage in past discourse referred to objects that remained the same and therefore reflected real, natural (hence constant) objects. It is quite possible that this neglects radical changes in the objects under discussion over time. Historians of psychology therefore need to examine and compare the different usages of the terms and attend to local contexts (sociohistorical) before doing a comparison (Smith, 2005).

I am not going to be so bold as to challenge the foregoing concerns, but still intend to take you back to the ancient Greeks—not as psychologists but as philosophers, particularly with respect to the modes of explanation that they developed. The problem of explanation is an important methodological issue that has been a key aspect of science historically, and psychology, of course, lays claim to being a science (Tolman, 2011). It is a matter of what assumptions one works from regarding what exists, what is fundamental, how true knowledge is to be acquired, and so on. Mainstream psychology, the dominant approach, is full of

ONTOLOGY

Monism

Idealism		Materialism	
Objective	Subjective	Mechanistic	
Dialectical			Phenomenalism
Reduction	Emergence		
	Solipsism	Elemental	Holistic

Dualism

Interactionism, Occasionalism, Double Aspect Theory,
Psychophysical Parallelism, Epiphenomenalism

Free Will versus Determinism

Free Will	Determinism	
	(Agency)	Fatalism
Incompatibilism		
Compatibilism		

EPISTEMOLOGY

Rationalism versus empiricism

Appearance versus reality

Realism			Anti-realism
Direct realism	Indirect realism	Solipsism	
Presentationalism	Representationalism	Skepticism	

Relativism

Nihilism

Figure 2.1 Categories of philosophical concepts for psychology

empirical generalizations devoid of anything that resembles an attempt to explain the facts obtained. At best, the causes of obtained experimental results are intended to serve that purpose. Rather than giving an explanation, descriptions of phenomena are drawn upon in the service of, or in lieu of, explanation (Brown, 1963). The methods of explanation are classifiable in a number of ways, for instance the type information that is drawn upon in explaining a phenomenon: genetic or developmental findings, intentions, functions, and empirical data. A further classification scheme unmentioned by Brown, but implicit in the foregoing, is in terms of the ontological and **epistemological** foundations that precede any inquiry. Psychologists, as Sanford and Capaldi (1964) determined, maintain (or should maintain) a particular interest in epistemology and in methods since both apply to matters of sensory processes, perception, and how the world is conceptualized (and thus explained). That is our current concern, the core themes of which are denoted in Figure 2.1 and are organized into categories.

2.2 THE TRANSITION TO THE PHILOSOPHICAL

When the Greek city states appeared around 800 BC they preserved aspects of mythology and religion from antecedent times (Bryant, 1986). These practices involved ritualism, sacrifices, and magic that were intended to avert the retribution of gods and disaster, such as drought, and to reap benefits through worship. The central themes were fertility cults, nature spirits, and various deities. The belief in nature spirits reflects a type of explanation known as **animism** and explanations of natural phenomena in terms of human qualities, like gods controlling lightning or rainfall, is called **anthropomorphism**. At the beginning of the 6th century BC a new kind of social being appeared—the philosopher intellectual—and their efforts after understanding led to the development of rational ways of thinking. All attempted to move beyond supernatural beliefs and adopt **naturalistic** explanations of physical phenomena. In medicine, explanation had been accounted for on the basis of the inculcation of illness by the gods; such supernatural influences gradually came under suspicion (Falagas, Zarkadoulia, Bliziotis, and Samonis, 2006). Under the influence of Hippocrates (approximately 460–370 BC), explanations were being sought in terms of natural phenomena to account for disease. Detailed histories of patients were developed including age, sex, behavior, and the environment, as well as a meticulous examination of the patient. In consequence, the treatment of illness became more a matter of observation and experimentation and the maintenance of careful records. Successes and failures would in the end lead to better understanding of a disorder and of corrective procedures, however primitive by our standards.

BOX 2.1
THE FIRST PERSONALITY THEORY

Despite the dismissal of the notion that the Greeks were doing psychology, there is one area of modern psychology that they did have an influence on and that is personality (or character as it was originally termed). Besides his medical work, Hippocrates observed that people tend to display stable characteristics that differentiate them from one another and that these fell into four distinct categories (which are now called 'types'). This, according to Allport (1961), was momentous in the history of psychology since it was the most ancient psychological theory known.

In an attempt to account for the observed similarities and differences, Hippocrates offered a biological explanation based upon excesses in hypothesized humors (bodily fluids roughly comparable in conception to hormones). These were blood, black and yellow bile, and phlegm. The sanguine type had an excess of blood and was characteristically hopeful. The melancholic (black bile) was overly sad. The choleric (yellow bile) was irascible and the phlegmatic (not mucous, a pituitary product) tended toward apathy. That humors did not exist is irrelevant. What matters is the introduction of typological explanations and explanations of personality sought at the biological level.

Hippocrates' theory clearly influenced modern psychology. For instance, in his research with dogs, Pavlov (1928, in Hothersall, 1995) identified four types of nervous system based on the speed and strength of classically conditioned, learned associations. Depending on how quickly they learned the association, and the degree to which the acquired response was subject to discrimination and generalization, the dogs were classified as sanguine, choleric, melancholic, or phlegmatic. There is a further affinity in the work of Thomas and Chess (1977) on the influence of temperament (innate constitution related to emotional stability) on personality, which led to the identification of three types—difficult, easy, and slow-to-warm-up. The best parallel, though, is found in Eysenck (1970, in Cervone and Pervin, 2010). Eysenck identified what he considered to be the two basic dimensions of human personality—neuroticism and extraversion introversion—and he showed how they related to the Hippocratic classification scheme (see Figure 2.2). Eysenck recognized that the humoral causes of the old theory had been repudiated but he showed how its typological insights could be incorporated into his own approach.

(Continued)

(Continued)

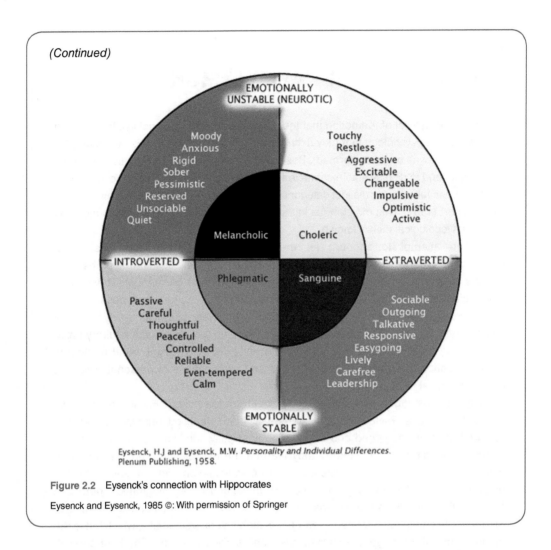

Eysenck, H.J and Eysenck, M.W. *Personality and Individual Differences*. Plenum Publishing, 1958.

Figure 2.2   Eysenck's connection with Hippocrates

Eysenck and Eysenck, 1985 ©: With permission of Springer

The first philosophers

The birth of philosophy in Greece is associated with Thales of Miletus (640–550 BC), who turned away from supernaturalism and sought within nature a means of accounting for natural processes (Lamprecht, 1955). Thales and other Milesian philosophers abandoned traditional mythology, although the existence of cults and the worship of gods persisted among the general public for many centuries (Lloyd-Jones, 2001). In their explanations the Milesians drew upon the materials available to them and, being technologically primitive, that was provided by their unaided senses (Fuller, 1945).

Two questions confronted the Milesians and they were dealt with in ways that never became outmoded: (1) 'What is the universe in reality?'; and (2) 'How is experience generated by it?' (questions of ontology and epistemology). Ontologically they were preoccupied with 'physis' or nature at its most basic level. They aimed to explain the phenomena of the world by seeking their origins in what was most essential (Waterfield, 2000). In doing so they introduced a concern with **substance** or the fundamental basis of all that is, that existed prior to everything. Epistemologically, they were interested in the role of perception in knowledge and what could be known—the relation between the knowing subject and the known object (Wright, 2009). The Milesians had no notion of the possibility that our sensory experiences could deceive us regarding objective reality and were thus **realists**, but doubt would soon arise (Fuller, 1945).

The Milesians introduced the idea of first principles (what would become known as **metaphysics**) and were seeking knowledge of a material nature (hence they were **materialists**). The first principle that concerned them was that from which all existing things are formed, a 'substance' which persists despite qualitative changes (Waterfield, 2000). There would be disputes regarding how many there were (introducing the issues of **monism, dualism**, and **pluralism**) and what their nature was. For Thales it was water (monism). It is unknown why he chose water but it is speculated that the necessity of water for life may have been a factor (Fuller, 1945). For Heraclitus (535–475 BC), on the other hand, the underlying unity of things was fire; not the fire of common experience, but an ethereal fire of the heavens (symbolic or metaphoric). Heraclitus was known for stressing change (**Becoming**) and fire may therefore symbolize the universal process of transformation. To Anaximander (610–546 BC) the ultimate substance was what he referred to as the 'Boundless'; it underlays all that is (Lamprecht, 1955). For Pythagoras (570–495 BC) number was behind everything in the world—an underlying mathematic ordering principle.

Undoubtedly, to the modern understanding, with our knowledge of the Big Bang and energy, the ancient Greeks sound primitive and simplistic in singling out water or fire. I must ask you to remember that they did not have the advantage of thousands of years of accumulated inquiry to draw upon. They were starting with basically nothing and had to rely on their sensory impressions, their observations, and their capacity to think. That Thales was wrong in his speculations about water, to the historians Garraty and Gay (1972), was trivial compared to the importance of his endeavor to establish nature as a comprehensible order.

When Heraclitus proposed that everything is in constant flux he introduced a problem for those attempting to develop a conception of what is true. According to Parmenides (approximately 515–450 BC), it was not possible to have knowledge of that which is changing continuously (Stace, 1920). He argued as follows:

- How can one know with any certainty that which may be something different tomorrow?
- In order to arrive at a true understanding one must seek what is eternal, constant and abiding (**Being**), amidst change.
- The material world revealed by the senses is of 'Becoming,' of appearance and illusion.
- Truth, which is in 'Being,' is revealed not by the senses but by reason.

Upon epistemological grounds this was challenged by Parmenides. Whereas others had relied upon their observations to develop their theories of knowledge (**empiricism**), Parmenides was the first to go beyond merely stating his position but to support it with logical reasoning (Fuller, 1945). The ultimate determiner of truth was reason, and when the senses conflicted with reason it was reason that prevailed (**rationalism**). For the first time a distinction was made between reason and sense, and the problem of epistemology and the **appearance versus reality** distinction was introduced. Whereas **materialism** maintains that reality is discovered through sensory experience, Parmenides represents **idealism** because the ultimate principle of 'Being' is a concept, an abstract thought discovered by reason rather than through the senses (Stace, 1920). Materialism and idealism, while different, are both **monistic** positions.

The first **pluralist** was Empedocles (495–430 BC). All things, he proposed, are composed of four ultimate particles or roots—fire, water, earth, and air (Lamprecht, 1955). This is a form of **elementalism**. Change occurs at a macroscopic level, the level of ordinary experience, but it is at the microscopic level that these roots exist. Roots are changeless but they come together and separate through the forces of love and hate (think attraction and repulsion), and that accounts for manifest change. Things change through the redistribution of the unchanging particles. Developing this, the early **atomists** Leucippus (ca. 5th century BC) and Democritus (460–370 BC) replaced the roots with a pluralism of atoms (indestructible and indivisible elements) which differed in size and shape. Atoms are inherently in motion, obviating the need to posit love or strife, and they existed within a void. The atoms were permanent and unalterable (satisfying Parmenides requirement) and their coming together accounted for the qualitative changes associated with growth, change, and decay. Leucippus was the first to introduce the idea of **mechanism** (and by implication **determinism**) with the notion that atoms undergo change of place and rearrangement in a wholly mechanical way (Fuller, 1945). Leucippus and Democritus were complete materialists in that everything for them was just a collection of atoms (Waterfield, 2000). The mind or soul was conceived of being composed of fiery atoms that possess the greatest mobility and provide movement to living beings. As the fiery atoms come together with mass they become alive and conscious and as they lose mass they pass into sleep and, with further losses, coma and death (Fuller, 1945). To Democritus qualitative differences are explained by **reduction** to quantitative differences and qualitative change was explained by reduction to spatial movements. A discussion of the distinction between elementalism and reductionism is provided in Box 2.2.

BOX 2.2
REDUCTIONISM, ELEMENTALISM, AND ATOMISM

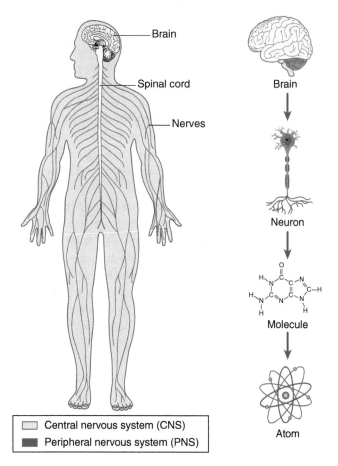

Figure 2.3 The peripheral and central nervous systems

To appreciate the difference between elementalism and reductionism I must remind you of the concept of 'levels of organization' since the distinction applies here. A level represents a position within an organized phenomenon whereat each member of a level

(Continued)

(Continued)

shares in the essential features, qualities, and properties that distinguish it from higher and lower levels. Furthermore, the incorporation of the lower level into the higher involves 'emergent' characteristics that accompany the increase in complexity.

Consider the human body. While the body functions as an organized whole, analysis has identified various subsystems (nervous, respiratory, gastro-intestinal, and cardiovascular) that, while interconnected, can be differentiated by the functions they enact. These systems have been analyzed into further component parts (cellular, intra-cellular, molecular, and atomic). Elementalism seeks to understand a complex phenomenon by breaking it up into component parts. Each system of the body (respiratory, reproductive) is an element of the organism (within each system the organs are elements and within them the cell elements). All these components are biological and remain at the same level. These elements are non-reductive. In Figure 2.3, the nervous system is a whole but it includes the brain, spinal cord, and peripheral nervous system as elements. So too is the neuron an element since it remains at the biological level.

Unlike elementalism, reductionism involves two different domains or levels of orga- nization and explains the higher level in terms of the lower-level phenomena. Explaining the functions of cells, tissues, organs, and so on in terms of molecular functions and properties would be reductionist (as in Figure 2.3, the molecules—chemical and atoms— physical are reductive). So too would be the explanation of higher mental functions in terms of the underlying biology while ignoring the influence of the sociocultural-historical level in their development. The impact of language, of ideas and meanings, would be lost in such an explanation. The significance of this was expressed by White (1942):

> With words man creates a new world, a world of ideas and philosophies. In this world man lives just as truly as in the physical world of his senses. Indeed, man feels that the essential quality of his existence consists in his occupancy of this world of sym- bols and ideas—or, as he sometimes calls it, the world of the mind or spirit. (p. 372)

Therein lies the problem of reductionism—a dismissal of the significance and inherent uniqueness of emergent phenomena. 'Atomism,' lastly, represents both reductionism and elementalism in that all phenomena, mental or otherwise, are explained by the arrange- ments of atoms which are elements of the physical level.

Levels of integration, by incorporating lower levels into a larger, organized whole, rep- resents 'holism.' Analysis into elements can occur within such a stance, but emphasizes that such elements are abstractions, products of analysis, and that they possess only intellectual independence.

When Parmenides distinguished between reason and sense, appearance and reality, he introduced what has remained an epistemological problem that still confronts modern psychology—to what degree, if any, do we have access to an objective reality? That became an issue that the next group of Greek philosophers would take up.

The problem of subjectivity

Whereas the previous discussion was focused on a search for first principles, a starting point or foundation for arriving at knowledge, the next group will begin to challenge that very possibility. Collectively they are known as **sophists** and **skeptics**. Through their clever arguments they questioned whether solutions to the problem of what 'is' could ever be achieved or known. Examining the claims of their predecessors, they noted how at variance they were with each other regarding

what was fundamental and concluded that their assertions were extravagant and unjustified. In this they introduced epistemology as their central interest. Compared to the naturalists the Sophist movement was essentially humanistic in shifting interest from physical nature to humans (Lamprecht, 1955).

Leading the change, Protagoras (5th century BC) observed that people differed in their determinations of what was true and concluded that speculations on metaphysics had no worth (Fuller, 1945). There is no appeal possible to some universal standard (such as objective reality) regarding what is or is not. The 'truth,' furthermore, changes as opinions alter over time. What 'appears' to be true or false to an individual is the only truth or falsehood that can be acknowledged, and that is variable. To Protagoras "Man is the measure of all things." What is real is what is experienced by the senses and, if what is real is only what is provided through the senses, reality means different things to different people (Lamprecht, 1955). What one person perceives as real may be so for that person but it may not be for another. This introduces the epistemological position of **relativism**. Once the individual becomes the measure of everything there can be no appeal to anything beyond personal experience, and personal experience varies over individuals. Rather than some independent truth, what is true is relative to the individual.

Plato (427–347 BC) responded to Protagoras with the 'self-refutation argument.' As a relativist, it was argued that Protagoras would have to admit the truth of those who contend he was in error and that his own position was therefore false (Burnyeat, 1976). To Burnyeat it may be a false doctrine to Protagoras' opponents, but that does not necessitate Protagoras conceding his own position as false and theirs as correct. He is asserting the truth for the person making the judgement, but that does not commit him to endorsing it as true for him.

Gorgias (483–375 BC) carried the reasoning of Protagoras a step further by discounting the possibility of communicating one's beliefs to another. Like Protagoras he contended that there was no real existence beyond appearance (Waterfield, 2000). The senses could be of no avail as the senses were known to deceive—the apparent bending of straight sticks in water for instance (Fuller, 1945). Reason was no help since the power of reason to know any reality, other than changing sensible experiences, was contested. (Given the impossibility of knowing objective reality this becomes an example of **solipsism**, an **anti-realist** perspective, since one is locked within a realm of subjectivity.) Even if it were possible to know objective reality, Gorgias believed that one could not communicate what one knew to another. That was because language is the means of sharing ideas, but language, in the conveyance of ideas, is just noise. With vision, for instance, a spoken word about what was seen and the audible sensation produced by speaking could convey nothing of the optical sensation associated with sight. Whatever one's idea of truth may be, the words by which it is communicated are not like the truth, and one cannot be certain that the words create a concept in the mind of another that resembled one's own. With that his solipsism becomes the position known as **nihilism**. Words were deceitful since they were not the things being referred to (Waterfield, 2000). So it was, too, with words regarding some real world. In the final analysis, the human condition is not of knowledge but of belief. There is, however, as Waterfield noted, a possible inherent contradiction in this. If what Gorgias is proposing linguistically can be comprehended, that would mean his belief could be communicated to another, as I am doing in writing this (and assuming you understand). He is relying on the possibility of communicating to communicate the impossibility of communicating.

Plato's forms

Plato would develop the aim of Parmenides to seek truth in permanency; and that was not to be found through sensory experience. The world of experience, of particular things that are changing and variable, for Plato was unreal (Lamprecht, 1955). He posited, instead, the existence of a realm of '**forms**' or pure ideas, fixed and permanent, the reality of which underlies the imperfect manifestations of sensory experience (mere appearance). This is in line with Parmenides' argument for truth in 'Being.' Plato reasoned that there must a permanent, non-changing realm that truth can rest upon, but sensory impressions are variable. Sometimes the very same object looks large and sometimes small (the effect of distance). He thus reasoned into existence a realm of idea from which, and to which, knowledge and truth are derivable and referred. Knowledge became a matter of recollection, of regaining access to forms (pure ideas), which one had before the soul entered the body. These ideas were innate or inborn and, because of that, represent an example of **nativism**.

Whereas Plato believed reason (rationalism) could reach beyond false sensory impressions and grasp what was real, the Skeptics like Pyrrho (360–270 BC) promoted disbelief in sensory experience and extended it to thinking (Fuller, 1945). Whatever was true was simply beyond the reach of the human mind. As above, every statement regarding true reality can be countered by an opposing proposition that is just as well founded, and thinking cannot decide between them. Those who made claims of certain truth against the falsehood of others were simply **dogmatic** (Palmer, 2000). Truth had not been discovered but that did not foreclose on further inquiry. The rational thing to do, they argued, was to suspend all judgment (Fuller, 1945). Assertions as to truth and falsehood were merely opinions. Avoiding arguments of self-refutation by asserting the truth of their position, they did not claim the certainty of uncertainty. Their position, they argued, was probable rather than established. Having left open the possibility of future surety, the Pyrrhonian skeptic did not stop seeking the truth.

Epicurus (341–270 BC) and his followers rejected the position of the Skeptics. They contended that the charge of self-refutation was still open in that if nothing could be known one couldnot know that nothing can be known (O'Keefe, 2010). The Skeptics were not, however, proposing truth but an attitude of suspended belief. Having no doctrine, their doctrine could not be self-refuting. A different challenge came in the form of the 'argument from concept formation.' To develop their position, the skeptic must have some knowledge—the knowledge of terms ('knowledge,' 'true,' 'false') and their meanings. Furthermore, concepts are acquired empirically. As a result of recurring experiences with classes of objects a concept develops for that phenomenon. The skeptic, by verbally stating a position, demonstrates knowledge of word meaning, as well as how the senses reliably connect to the world (to that I would add the reality of those to whom they communicate).

Additionally, the 'inaction argument' challenged that if one did not trust the senses there would be no reason to act one way or another (such as avoiding cliffs). Appearance can still be a criterion for acting. Epicurus argued that if the senses are doubted one has no criterion for distinguishing true from false. A distinction was therefore made between sensations and judgments based upon sensations regarding objects. Judgments, opinions or preconceptions, form from repeated sensory impressions and these are confirmed or disconfirmed by subsequent experience. That is the basis of our acting successfully or not in the world. There is reason, then, to rely on the senses.

The problem of free will

Leucippus and Democritus had, in their atomism, advocated determinism. At the human level this posed a difficulty since it implied that what people do is not within their determination and relieves them of **agency** or **free will**. While aspects of the problem had been under discussion already, it was Epicurus who clearly recognized a problem and, most likely, initiated the free will controversy (Huby, 1967). Before that, Plato and Aristotle (384–322 BC) had acknowledged the part played by heredity and experience in human conduct, but they failed to consider how that could lead to determinism. In the context of criminal responsibility, Aristotle had discussed voluntary and involuntary actions. He made the case that every action is voluntary that is initiated by the actor. Involuntary actions suggested the idea of a defense upon the basis of determinism (and, therefore, non-responsibility) but Aristotle passed over it. Free will seemed obvious to him since people clearly initiate actions but, where Aristotle left the issue at that, Epicurus recognized a problem.

Epicurus mostly accepted the atomistic theory of Democritus, but was reluctant to accept complete determinism (and the related idea of **fatalism**). He accepted that only atoms exist, and that all else comes to be through their interactions, but saw a problem in the account of Democritus (O'Keefe, 2010). To Democritus, atoms flew about the void in all directions, colliding and combining, but he failed to account for that motion. To achieve that, Epicurus added the properties of weight and swerve to atoms. Due to weight, atoms move downward at an equal rate (an intuition of gravity?) but, under those conditions, they could not collide (their movements would be perpendicular—Fuller, 1945). To allow for interaction, swerve, unpredictable shifts in direction, was added. That introduced an element of unpredictability to motion and was the means by which Epicurus avoided absolute determinism and fate. Epicurus thus established the problem of free will versus necessity (the modern perspective will be dealt with in Chapter 12).

The Stoics (see **stoicism**) rejected the notion of free will and put forward a position that mixed base materialism and religious idealism (Duncan, 1952). They rejected the idea of a transcendent god, outside of the world, arguing that God was within the world, directing its events. The capacity to act and be acted upon belongs to corporeal phenomena only, so God must be corporeal too, pervading the material realm (a position known as **pantheism**). This reflects their effort to avoid dualism of body and soul or corporeal and spiritual but still preserves what was of value in idealism, especially reason. They believed in a completely rational yet material universe. Every event is under the control and direction of reason and therein lies destiny. One cannot know one's ultimate destiny but, while the individual may try to resist it, it is preordained and happens for a reason. Acceptance and detachment were advised for peace of mind since resistance was futile. In this they were the first to propose complete determinism since Democritus had not addressed the problem of free will other than by implication (Gould, 1974). This of course renders the notion of choosing, to resist or accept, problematic since choice is illusory under complete determinism.

In the foregoing I have tried to introduce some central issues in the history of philosophy that still play a part in modern psychology. There are other issues that arise in modern philosophy that will also have a bearing on recent explanations and practices, but I will leave those to later chapters where their impact has greater immediacy. For now, we will consider how the topics we have considered can be found in the 'new psychology.'

2.3 PHILOSOPHY IN PSYCHOLOGY

In revealing ontological and epistemological issues in psychology the treatment will not be exhaustive, space precludes that. I will try to indicate the pervasiveness though by beginning with a consideration of the widespread practice of experimentation. In conducting an experiment there is an implicit assumption of realism. One measures the adequacy or inadequacy of the tested hypotheses against an objective reality that is presumed to exist and is accessible. Also, ontologically, the majority of experimental psychologists are 'materialists.' Whatever psychological phenomena may be, it is generally assumed that they do not involve some non-material, spiritual or ideational substance but a brain process, which does not mean that idealism does not exist; where it does, it is usually unintentional. This is indicated by theories of perception.

The British psychologist Michael Eysenck defined perception as "the processes involved in producing organized and meaningful interpretations of information from the environment" (2000, p. 259). This implies that we have access to the environment of which we are informed and which is therefore knowable—a realist proposition. Similarly, perception is "the conscious experience of objects and object relations" (Coren, Ward, and Enns, 1994, p. 17). Fine; no problem. According to Tavris and Wade, however, perception is "the process by which the brain organizes and interprets sensory information" (1997, p. G-8). This has anti-realist connotations and leads to idealism. Whereas materialists maintain that 'reality' is discovered through the senses, idealists consider the sensory world 'appearance' (Stace, 1920). What we have access to are not the things sensed, but sensations (even those not directly); we are without access to an objective reality, hence anti-realism. Confined to subjectivity, what are known are the organized and interpreted sensations, not objective phenomena. In such 'constructionist theories of perception', perception is the end result of an inferential process (Eysenck, 1990) and what we 'know' is the result of inferences, not things as they are in the world. I don't suggest that this was what was intended. I am sure that constructionists believe themselves materialists and realists, but their explanations push them into anti-realism and then idealism.

Ontology and psychology

Monism, dualism, and pluralism

Materialism is a common stance in psychology. It is evident in biopsychology and neuropsychology where cognitive functions and motivation are explained in terms of cerebral processes, the limbic system, neurochemicals, and hormones. Another example would be the computer modelling or computational strategy in cognitive psychology to account for human information processing as analogous to computer data analysis. Mental processes are computational processes of the organism, not of a mind. In personality psychology, McCrae and Costa (2003) offer a materialistic account of personality that is also elementalistic and reductionist. They claim the structure of personality is composed of five universal 'basic tendencies' (elements) that account for patterns of thought, action, and feeling which are biologically based (reduction). All attempts to account for psychological processes in terms of biological processes are materialist in nature.

Idealism is less pervasive but it does exist. An obvious example of idealism in psychology can be found with advocates of phenomenology. According to Kendler (2005), phenomenologists focus on the subjective nature of consciousness. It is basic to human existence and, because of that, phenomenology precedes psychology as a natural science. Experience of the world depends on consciousness. Without it there would be no experience and without experience there would be no science. On the other hand, it is further proposed that what we do occurs within the internal world from which we cannot escape. Primacy is thus given to mind and that is idealism. When one is locked within the realm of subjectivity, in the realm of mind one is pushed into solipsism and idealism. That is what happened to Gestalt psychology as well.

Despite doing research into perception, which suggests access to objective reality, Gestalt psychologists focused on immediate experience as their subject matter. Immediate experience, what is perceived, is not an aspect of the real world, of objective reality. Writing of the physical world, Köhler (1947) proposed that "it can never become directly accessible to me" (p. 19). Gestalt psychologists are thus trapped within a phenomenalist subjectivity.

Materialism and idealism are monist positions but, while not common, dualism has had its representatives in psychology. One recent example is Eccles (1989), a Nobel laureate for neurophysiology. Eccles modernized Descartes' interactionist theory of mind and body—that mind and body are two separate substances, completely independent, but which influence each other through the interface of the pineal gland. Eccles replaced the pineal gland with a hypothesized 'Liaison Brain.' The Liaison Brain, located in the cerebral cortex, was the basis for the mutual influence of what was called World 1 (the physical realm) with World 2 (subjective experience, consciousness). Eccles also went beyond dualism, in conjunction with Popper, in adding a third realm: World 3, or the world of culture. The addition of World 3 provides an example of pluralism (although I may be stretching things to consider culture a substance).

Elementalism, holism, and mechanism

There are many versions of elementalism in psychology. McDougall (1908/1950) emphasized instincts that were thought to be separate impulses toward different types of actions. More recently, motor neurons, sensory neurons, and interneurons can be considered elements of the nervous system and traits as elements of personality. Titchener (1898) wrote that he was seeking the 'structural elements of the mind' which he independently grouped as sensations (and subsequently, ideas) and affection (feelings). William James (1842–1910) and the gestalt psychologists argued against elementalism in psychology by taking a holistic position. Thought, to James (1890/1950), presents itself to us as a unity and it is in analysis and abstraction that the so-called elements enter. In the gestalt tradition, likewise, Cassirer (1911, in Ash, 1998) regarded elements to be conceptual discriminations rather than an underlying reality of conscious phenomena.

Mechanism is also well represented in psychology. Broadbent (1958), a pioneer in cognitive psychology, drew upon communications engineering (specifically telephonic systems) to discuss limitations on attention in terms of input, limited capacity processing, and output which he believed would be found to be based on physiological structures. The multitudinous sensory input was more than could be attended to and, so as not to be overwhelmed, a filtering mechanism was hypothesized, which selected some for attending to and excluded the rest. This led to the information processing approach to cognition which is based on computer analogies. You may recognize it in terms of memory flow diagrams involving input, short-term and long-term storage modules, and control processes of encoding and retrieval. The mind is an information processing mechanism that operates like a computer. Similarly, 'connectionism' is a 'brain metaphor' model of the mind intended to replace the 'computer metaphor' model (Rumelhart, Hinton, and McClelland, 1986) which, nonetheless, was itself based on a computer simulation of hypothesized brain mechanisms.

Pythagorean psychology

The Pythagoreans established the notion that mathematical regularities underlie all phenomena (Winthrop, 1960). The faith in the underlying mathematical order was strengthened by Galileo and Newton and has led to its adoption in the social sciences. That is not to suggest that there is some sort of numerical mysticism in psychology, but that there is a reliance on the search for mathematical order in psychological phenomena. Few would go so far as Murphy (1967) in proclaiming himself a Pythagorean (given its number mysticism), but would possibly agree with him that psychology has been captured by mathematical obsession. I am not about to suggest that the use of statistics is any way Pythagorean. In those instances where theory is driven by mathematics, however, rather than mathematical regularities being discovered in psychological phenomena, I would contend that the Pythagorean spirit is represented.

Consider the use of 'factor analysis' by Raymond B. Cattell (1905–1998) to create a theory of personality structure that was supposed common to all people. Mathematically, factor analysis takes very large data sets and bundles them on the basis of statistical relatedness into smaller, underlying, unifying dimensions called factors that are conceived of as independent (at least in Cattell's usage). For this he used the more than 3,000 trait terms (terms describing qualities of a person, like affiliative or pugnacious) identified by Allport and Odbert in 1936 (Cattell, 1966). I won't go into the details, but Cattell mathematically reduced the list of descriptive terms to 16 Personality Factors that were unitary (a single, uniform entity). Does this represent the true nature of personality, or is it a fabrication determined by statistical procedures being given primacy? To some personality psychologists like Allport (1937), personality is a unified whole with which factor independence is inconsistent. Given unity, "factors often seem remote from psychological fact, and as such they risk the accusation that they are primarily mathematical artifacts" (p. 245). Sometimes the factors don't even make psychological sense. For example, Endler, Hunt, and Rosenstein (1962) found three factors: interpersonal, inanimate, and the third they named 'ambiguous' because they could make no sense of it. To give credence to what makes no sense, and this is the point in terms of Pythagoreanism, is the assumption that an underlying mathematical order guides inquiry and explanation.

Appearance versus reality

The distinction between appearance and reality enters into psychological inquiry most clearly in sensation and perception. From the outset, a major area of concern for psychologists was the susceptibility of humans to illusory perception. Various illusory line drawings were being produced through the last half of the 19th century (see Figure 2.4) that demonstrated a discrepancy between the actual physical stimulus and its perception (Murch, 1973). Such disparities led Helmholtz in 1866 to introduce a distinction between the 'distal stimulus' and the 'proximal stimulus.' The distal stimulus referred to the objective object or event (think reality) and the proximal stimulus referred to the sensory representation of that stimulus in the nervous system (appearance).

The same general issue found its way into personality theory too. Endler (1984) proposed that, in doing research, one cannot conclude that an experimenter's perception of a situation will accord with that of an experimental participant. That meant that each individual's interpretation would have to be considered. A distinction had to be made between the 'actual situation' (reality) and the 'perceived situation' (appearance). As Block and Block (1981) noted, each person's experience is unique and due to solipsism we are not in a position to appreciate what the meaning of a situation is for any individual. While solipsism is certainly a danger, if one is proposing that the perceived situation allows no access to objective reality, what Block and Block are really addressing is the 'problem of other minds.' That is the proposition that no one can have personal access to another person's subjective experience, only their actions, and will therefore never appreciate what their subjectivity is actually like.

I should point out that there is the possibility that appearance and reality are not wholly opposed. Leontyev (1981b) proposed distinguishing between 'meaning' and 'sense.' Meaning is the socially developed and transmitted understanding that is passed from one generation to the next (based on access to a common reality). Sense is an individual's personal attitude or understanding based upon unique experience with the matter of concern (appearance). While pro-life and pro-choice advocates can agree that abortion is the cessation of pregnancy, their subjective sense is different. Pro-life supporters believe that aborting a human embryo is the murderous taking of life, whereas the pro-choice lobby believes it is the right of a woman to decide, before an embryo can be designated a person, whether a pregnancy is wanted and not be forced into motherhood.

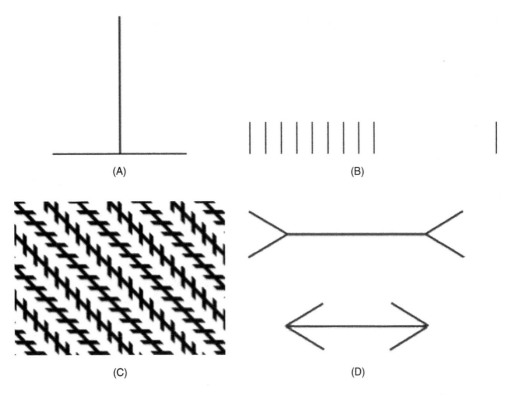

(A) Vertical-Horizontal Illusion (1852): Despite being the same length the vertical line appears longer.

(B) Oppel Illusion (1854): Despite being the same length the filled-in portion appears longer than the blank portion.

(C) Zöllner Illusion (1860): Despite being parallel the hatch-marked lines appear to converge.

(D) Müller-Lyer Illusion (1889): Despite being the same length the upper horizontal line appears longer than the lower.

Figure 2.4   Early illusions

You may have noticed that the reality/appearance distinction also involves the problem of knowledge or epistemology. This is because some suggest that all that can be known are appearances. There is more to psychological philosophy than ontology.

Epistemology and psychology

It is safe to say that most experimentalists, if not all, intend to be realists. In practice they are both rationalists and empiricists in their search for knowledge. Many adopt the 'hypothetico-deductive method', which is an approach to conducting research which advocates formulating predictions as a result of deduction from a theory (based on prior observations—empiricism), testing them experimentally and assessing them through comparison with obtained results. The formulation of deductions involves reason (rationalism) and the conclusions of acceptance or rejection is based on the experienced results (empiricism). The whole procedure is based on the realist assumption of an objective reality which is accessible and knowable. Their practice, what they do, is realist, but when it comes to their theories (explanations) they may slip into anti-realism. We already noted this with perception theory and saw how that can lead to skepticism and solipsism. Then again, there are others who take this stance intentionally.

One position which is intentionally anti-realist is that of phenomenological psychology because their starting point is consciousness (a reasonable but problematic commencement). Kendler (2005), mentioned previously, proposed that science begins with experience, but then restricted what was available in arguing that "We operate in an internal world from which we cannot escape" (p. 320). In his phenomenological approach MacLeod (1944) made the case that "all psychological data become 'subjective'" (p. 200). Objectivity and subjectivity are properties of the perceptual field within which subject (self) and object are points of reference. Subject and object share in the characteristic of being segregated aspects of a common perceptual field. If what is known is the perceptual field, we are trapped in subjectivism; and skepticism and solipsism follow from that. There is, however, a form of subjectivism that is not anti-realist or at least aspires to some form of realism.

Modern theories of perception tend to promote **indirect realism**. The adherents believe that there is an objective reality that acts upon the senses but which is inaccessible. As a result, what is known of reality are the mental representations (the ideas and images) formed through sensory experience. This is also known as **representationalism**. As Helmholtz originally put it, the ideas produced by vision are formed due to an impression being made upon the eye. As a result, *"such objects are always imagined as being present in the field of vision as would have to be there in order to produce the same impression on the nervous mechanism"* (Helmholtz, 1867/2000, p. 2, emphasis in original). What the object is exactly we do not know. The ideas we have of things are only symbols that we use to regulate activity in order to achieve desired results which are judged effective if the expected sensations arise.

This contrasts with **presentationism**, which is the proposition that the world presented to experience is the world as it is (**direct realism**). The mainstream theory of perception is representationalist, but it was challenged during the mid-twentieth century by Gibson. He had begun as a representationalist but then began to marvel at the degree of success people have operating in a world to which they have no access. How remarkable it is that there are so few car crashes when driving is based on best guesses about traffic flow. To correct this, Gibson (1979/1986) developed an 'ecological approach' to perception. According to Gibson perceptual systems evolved because they are designed to give us access to objective phenomena and are adaptively beneficial.

Psychology also has its relativist representatives. Scarr (1985) maintained that every person has their own version of reality of which we try to convince others. So-called scientific facts cannot be separate from the individual scientist; they are not discovered, they are invented. What makes one scientific theory better than another is its persuasive power (not in its agreement with reality). Gergen (1985), in his **social constructionism**, argued that the supposed objective criteria by which events and entities have been identified are either non-existent or highly constrained by social contexts, by history and culture, and are thus socially constructed. Social constructionism makes a number of assumptions that challenge the assumption that knowledge is objective and ahistorical.

To begin with, science does not reflect the nature of the world. What is taken to be an experience of the world does not determine the terms through which the world is understood. The words an individual uses to make sense of the world, rather than being a reflection of reality, are socially constructed artifacts transmitted through communication. An examination of changes in historical understanding (accepted meanings), or cultural variations in explanatory concepts, testifies to the primacy of the social in knowledge and explanation. In consequence, the degree to which any understanding is maintained over time is due to processes of social negotiation and persuasion. What any particular group considers to be reality is socially constructed. What is considered true is conditional upon the historical moment and the social group, not objective reality—and that is relativism.

Gergen (1997) developed his anti-realism further in proposing that the social constructionist rejects a realist metaphysic; the world as experienced is not the world as it is. Science which posits an accessible and knowable reality is dismissed. There is nothing objective that can disprove any belief system. All that any theory can be measured against are just the social conventions of shared meanings that vary between groups. Given no accessible reality to affirm or disaffirm beliefs, there is no ground for silencing any community of believers. That is not a demand for putting an end to science though, just so long as it is conceived of as yet another form of discourse and meaning construction. Theories (beliefs, understandings, explanations) do not correspond to anything 'real' against which claims to truth or adequacy can be assessed.

To Hibberd (2001), Gergen has adopted the form of skepticism called 'nihilism' because he rejects empiricism and realism (Hibberd's usage of nihilism here leaves out the aspect of incommunicability). Social constructionism, to Hibberd, is silent regarding what exists because description is a language game and completely constrained by language. Claims to knowledge are only relevant to discursive practices within a closed language system which does not represent reality or truth. We cannot talk about what occurs or exists, but only converse about the 'talk-about-things.'

Given the rejection of objectivity, the social constructionist makes no statement regarding actual affairs beyond oneself. That raises a difficulty for me since Gergen does allow for communities of believers and for persuasive arguments. Presumably the communicants exist in objective reality and are accessible to each other. If so the door opens to the rest of the objective field since that is where the communicants are to be found. Not only that, communication implies an objective medium. As Gibson (1966) pointed out, besides the stimuli provided by the natural world (which Gergen rejects), humans respond to symbols like language; but there are no symbols that do not have their basis in material processes. The verbal symbol is conveyed by sound waves and the written symbol is conveyed by light waves. There is thus an implicit realism in communicating that contradicts Gergen's main assertion.

In his analysis of constructivism, Tolman (1980) allowed that theories are constructed but that did not mean that theories could not reflect objective reality. Granted observations are theory laden—guided by assumptions regarding what constitutes knowledge, what acceptable methods are, and what inferences are permissible. In that sense it is fair to say that knowledge is relative, given different assumptions, but that does negate objective reality, its accessibility, or its reflection in theory. The issue is whether the skeptics are correct or whether we can make a rational connection to an objective reality. The problem and the answer, to Tolman, lie in the assumptions one starts with. All philosophies (and psychologies) begin with an initial premise that is ultimately unjustifiable. For those who opt for subjectivism it is the undeniability of consciousness that has to be asserted. For the materialist it is objective reality that cannot be denied and which has to serve as a basis for knowledge. One position is not more justifiable than the other. Neither position has a preferred status. It is just as difficult to prove the existence of material reality beyond subjective experience as it is an unobservable mind or consciousness. Nonetheless, depending on the choice made, there are consequences that follow and reasons for preference.

In choosing consciousness as a starting point one is confronted with the accompanying difficulty of making objective reality accessible, beyond its experience, and the attendant problems of anti-realism. Traditional materialism, on the other hand, has failed to adequately account for consciousness and mental phenomena, other than to dismiss them altogether as non-existent or reduce them to some material phenomenon like neural mechanisms. That is a dominant stance among neuropsychologists. While most psychologists are unaware of it, I would be remiss to not remind you that the theory of levels of integration (Chapter 1) was a materialist solution to this difficulty. The issue will be more fully covered in Chapter 6 when we deal with the mind–body problem.

The intent of this chapter has been to indicate the philosophical roots of psychology and the continued existence of philosophical issues in psychology. It seems fitting therefore to close with the following quote from Koch (1985c): "Our problems, concepts, terminology, questions have grown out of the history of philosophy; and any position, theory, model, procedural decision, research strategy, or lawlike statement that we assert presupposed philosophical commitments" (p. 944). I hope I have demonstrated that.

SUMMARY

- Psychology may not be traceable to ancient Greece but its philosophical roots can be.

- The 'new psychology' may have repressed philosophical issues but that did not mean liberation from them. There can be no question that psychology incorporates epistemological considerations.

- The scientific method is inherently epistemological and psychology has given special status to it as a means of establishing objective truths. There is in that an assumption of access to an objective realm which reflects philosophical realism.

- Not all share in this realist conviction. Anti-realism in the form of relativism, skepticism, and nihilism has representatives in modern psychology.

- Psychologists have not freed themselves from ontological considerations either. While the majority adopt a materialist stance, their explanations at times lead them into subjectivism and that, in the end, renders their stance idealist. Some, the phenomenologists, intentionally assert subjectivism as their starting point and are ultimately idealists.

- Despite protestations to the contrary, psychology has not liberated itself from inherent philosophical considerations. An awareness of these issues, in place of their dismissal, may better serve psychologists in their efforts to explain their subject matter and avoid the logical pitfalls to which they have been vulnerable.

SUGGESTED READINGS

Gregory, R. L. (1987). *The Oxford companion to mind*. Oxford: Oxford University Press.

Hergenhahn, B. R. and Henley, T. B. (2014). *An introduction to the history of psychology* (7th ed.). Belmont, CA: Wadsworth/Thomson Learning.

Robinson, D. N. (1981). *An intellectual history of psychology* (rev. ed.). Madison, WI: The University of Wisconsin Press.

Want to learn more? For links to online resources, examples of multiple choice questions, conceptual exercises and much more, visit the companion website at
https://study.sagepub.com/piekkola

3
SCIENCE AND PSYCHOLOGY

LEARNING OBJECTIVE

Before psychology became a science it had a difficulty to overcome: it had to demonstrate that it could even be a science. That has been the basis of its abiding neurosis—anxiety over not being considered scientific, which prompted the diagnosis of 'physics envy.' In the late 18th century Kant determined that psychology, defined as the analysis of mind through introspection, could not be an experimental science (Hergenhahn and Henley, 2014). Since it was not a physical thing, the mind could not be investigated objectively. **Introspection** was no aid since the mind would not hold still for analysis. Additionally, the introspective process itself would influence the mind, interfering with its independent observation. Furthermore, and perhaps most significant to psychology's struggle to prove itself, a scientific subject matter required precise mathematical applications and mind was immeasurable. What it means to be a science, and whether psychology can lay claim to such status, is the topic of this chapter. We will consider the following:

- What does it mean to be scientific and when did humans become scientific?
- Scientific thinking versus common sense.
- Physics envy and psychology as a science.
- Natural kinds versus human kinds.
- A question of ethics.

FRAMING QUESTIONS

- What is science and does psychology qualify as a science?
- Did humans only become scientific during the Renaissance?
- To be a science must psychology forgo subjective human experience?
- Is psychology both a science and a branch of the humanities (the study of human experience including philosophy, art, religion, literature, and so on)?

INTRODUCTION

'Science' is defined as "**1** Systematized knowledge derived from observation, study, etc. **2** a branch of knowledge, esp. one that systematizes facts, principles, and methods" (Webster, 2002, pp. 571–572). Science thus encompasses a broad range of human pursuits that resist being categorized by the application of the scientific method. Certainly, Aristotle's biological investigations qualify despite the lack of the methodological rigor that characterized 19th-century biology (Mayr, 1997). The distinction between Aristotle's approach and biology proper suggests that scientific thinking and practice has evolved as a cultural pursuit. Where one marks the beginning of science is going to be determined by what one constitutes science as. Some would contend that science begins with the ancient Greeks, in Thales' turn to nature in search of non-mythical explanations of phenomena for instance. Others would go further back to technological inventiveness, primitive medicine, and other knowledge-based practices.

To Dewey (1925/1958) science has its roots in the arts and crafts, in the technologies associated with medicine, war, navigation, metal and wood work. Such practices were marked by an intellectual attitude of inquiry generated from the attempts to control things of the object world, including other people, in order to establish more assured and stable outcomes. It involved a move away from being under the oppression of immediate events, things, and conditions, that began with the employment of appliances and tools in the pursuit of ends.

Prehistorically, proto-humans had to be realists. Without knowledge of the world and its regularities they, as biological beings, were subject to its contingencies. Nonetheless, through empirical observations, certain orders, certain regularities, were eventually noted. The plant realm became an exploited resource for food and medicine, as well as material for artifacts like clothing, shelter, and tools; and that involved a form of scientific reasoning (Crump, 2001). Tool-making *homo habilis*, some two million years ago, left the first artefactual evidence of the usefulness of observation and generalization (Leakey, 1981). With observation and generalization, implements can be rendered more useful by taking notice of their beneficial qualities, like hardness, and then incorporating them into future products. Certainly the age of tool production was exceptionally primitive, but it reflected, to a degree, a scientific attitude of discovery and perfection through subsequent practice.

Invention can be considered a precursor to the scientific approach that characterizes the 16th and 17th centuries. In prehistory, it was through invention that humans were gradually able to transcend their dependence upon the natural conditions of their existence and increasingly gain control and mastery over those conditions. One may distinguish between these practices and science, as we normally understand it, as the difference between accidental and fortuitous discovery and a program of systematic observation and standardized methods. Does that mean that primitive inventiveness can be called science? To Sarton (1952) it did. It commences with the first attempts to solve the problems of living. No matter how awkward those solutions were, such expedients were generalized, rationalized, perfected upon, and set the ground for more adequate, rational approaches. To Hurd and Kipling (1964) a first step in developing the scientific attitude toward knowledge acquisition was the observation of regularities in nature. That is not to suggest that this is science, as we understand it today, but it does suggest germinal forms.

3.1 THE PATH TO SCIENCE PROPER

Science is a form of inquiry and the intellectual means for inquiry were themselves a product of cultural evolution. A number of intellectual tools had to be developed, like rational thinking and mathematics, before scientific inquiry could become a standardized, methodological procedure. Each generation built upon the advances of its predecessors and drew on the accumulating understanding and explanatory principles. Many such explanations may originally have reflected magical, supernatural thinking, but over the centuries these would become ever more naturalistic and exacting.

According to Hung (1997) there were two stages to scientific growth—the 'phenomenal stage' and the 'theoretical stage.' During the phenomenal stage the inquirer takes note of what is detectable and observable, available to the unaided senses. As a knowledge-gathering procedure, observation is the primary tool of investigation followed by the use of **induction**. Facts are gathered and organized (regularities, similarities, and differences are noted) and phenomena are classified and categorized. Only gradually would active experimentation arise. What experimentation existed among ancient peoples was a haphazard undertaking involving unorganized trial and error (Sarton, 1952). Discoveries were more accidental than deliberate.

It would not be until the 17th century that the theoretical stage became evident (associated with Galileo and Newton). At that point abstract theories were developed to explain observed phenomena and to make predictions that could be tested. Whereas the senses were the primary tool during the phenomenal stage, rational thought is the primary tool for scientific advances. To this can be added three phases that occurred in the development of instruments (Jones, 1967).

- During the first phase the senses and memory were supplemented with specially contrived devices like rulers, balances, and clocks (measurement, the assignment of numbers to varying things based on common properties, was also significant—Crump, 2001). Memory was enhanced by writing and drawing.

- The second phase is associated with the period of Galileo. It was typified by the telescope and microscope, devices that extended the range of the human senses.

- The third phase started with the invention of the magnetic compass by the Chinese. Third phase devices responded to physical effects that were inaccessible to the human senses. They converted a stimulus (magnetism, radioactivity) that humans do not perceive into one that humans have sensitivity for (a needle pointing north or a Geiger counter clicking).

The history of scientific procedures and instrumentation is, of course, the history of the cultural development of the means by which humans have expanded their inquiry into natural phenomena, including their own capacities and limitations.

Early science

To Boring (1929), simply observing natural phenomena and recording observations does not make science. Scientific observations are selective, made in the interest of rendering rational generalizations. The first experiment proper in the ancient world was conducted about 100 years after Aristotle by Aristarchus (310–230 BC). While no conditions were manipulated, the conditions had to be planned and carefully selected for the measurements he required in his inquiry into nature. He awaited the moon to be exactly half full then recorded the angles between sun, moon, and observer, forming a triangle. From this he estimated the relative distance between sun, moon, and earth. Already mathematics and measurement had a significant role. Aristarchus concluded, wrongly, that the distance from earth to sun is twenty times the distance between earth and moon (when it is actually 400 times). Regardless, it was the planned nature of this selective observation that made it experimental.

BOX 3.1
THE FIRST PSYCHOLOGICAL EXPERIMENT

Avicenna (980–1037), or Ibn Sina, was a famed Arabic physician. He was the first person to apply experimental procedures to the study of affect or emotionality by attempting to correlate emotional states with physiological reactions (Alexander and Selesnick, 1966). A terribly ill person (deep depression) was brought to him and his analytic approach involved what can only be described as a precursor to the lie detector. Placing a finger on the fellow's pulse he mentioned the names of various provinces and attended to the quickening of the pulse. Increased rates directed subsequent questioning to districts of that province, then towns, streets, and people. Through this procedure he identified a young woman with whom the fellow was hopelessly in love. Avicenna recommended marriage and his patient was cured.

Long before the experimental method of controlling and manipulating variables had been established in the West, Avicenna conducted an experiment into the psychology of emotions that anticipated these advances (Yaroshevsky, 1990). In the experiment, two sheep were provided with fodder that was identical in terms of quality and quantity. Where their conditions differed involved one of the sheep having a wolf tethered nearby. That sheep could not eat, withered away, and died while the other thrived. Translating this into the language of modern scientific psychology, confounding variables, the quality and amount of food, were controlled. The factor manipulated, the independent variable, was the presence or absence of the wolf, and the result (death versus thriving) was the dependent variable. Avicenna revealed, experimentally, the deleterious impact of overwhelming affective states (undue stress) on wellbeing.

Roger Bacon and Leonardo da Vinci

After the fall of Rome, around 400 AD, Europe went into the Dark Ages. It was a period involving the domination of the Church over public life and belief. What constituted inquiry and knowledge became the logical examination of matters of faith based on deductive logic. Around 1,000 AD, universities appeared and centers of learning began to emerge and, in time, Aristotle would be rediscovered and incorporated into theology. Pedagogy involved debate and logical deductions from authority (Church doctrine and Aristotle) as the principle means of seeking and disseminating knowledge. During the 13th century Roger Bacon (1214–1292) would develop arguments that would represent a transition to a more scientific approach to seeking knowledge (Hurd and Kipling, 1964). Instead of giving priority to argumentation, debate, and logical formulation, Bacon would favor empirical demonstration.

According to Bacon, there were two modes of knowing—by argument and by experience (Power, 2013). While reason and argumentation may compel us to admit a conclusion, they lack the power to alleviate the doubt that experience does. A lot of spurious beliefs were, at the time, being accepted that observation would readily disprove, such as the notion that only goat's blood could break down diamonds. Only experience and experimentation, not debate, could support the demonstration of truths. Bacon further contended that in such endeavors the adoption of mathematics was important. While Bacon considered experimental science the best means of establishing truth, he offered no discussion of the procedures that would be involved. He wrote of others who were conducting experiments, but what was being done resembled magic more than scientific tests (Thorndike, 1914). For instance, gout had been found to be effectively treated by tying frog's legs to a sufferer's feet for three days; and the alchemists were engaged in their transmutational researches of turning gold into lead. Nonetheless, it was a beginning.

During the 15th century, Leonardo da Vinci (1452–1519) discussed the scientific method but not in any systematic way (Blake, Ducasse, and Madden, 1960). While his practice revealed an appreciation of it, he appears to have lacked a conscious awareness of the principles of method. Nevertheless, he emphasized the importance of experience, the necessity of experimentation, and the indispensable value of mathematics. In his appeal to experience and demonstration, for the confirmation of theories, he also asserted the importance of replication (repeating demonstrations) as a check on the consistency of results and to guard against accidental findings. Repetition also meant varying conditions in order to eliminate irrelevant factors and to highlight what was essential. He frequently formulated hypotheses (an important aspect of later scientific practice) as suggestions in need of corroboration or elimination through investigation.

3.2 EARLY SCIENCE: KEPLER, GALILEO, FRANCIS BACON, AND NEWTON

During the later Middle Ages and the Renaissance, a quantitative model was entering daily life (Crosby, 1997). Measurement was becoming fundamental to practices like counting and temporal organization (mechanical clocks displaced the position of the sun in the sky and church bell ringing in regulating daily life). Precise quantities replaced measures like 'medium-sized-piece' in glassmaking and other formulas. Calculation was becoming a widespread practice. An economy based on money was emerging. All this was made easier by the gradual displacement of Roman numerals by the Arabic decimal system. An 'arithmetic mentality' was beginning to take hold and a 'science of calculation' was transforming formerly qualitative distinctions into quantitative ones (Kaye, 1988). Every quality imaginable was thought to be subject to quantification.

Fundamental to the scientific approach of Johannes Kepler (1571–1630), consistent with the age, was his emphasis on mathematics and what was essentially a Pythagorean metaphysics (Burtt, 1952/1980). According to Kepler those qualities that are real exist in the mathematical harmony that undergirds the realm of the senses. The real world is constituted by quantitative characteristics alone and what differences exist are in number only. Mathematical relations can be found in all objects that impact the senses and certain knowledge has to be of quantitative characteristics—perfect knowledge is mathematical knowledge.

For his part, Galileo (1564–1642) emphasized a distinction between **primary qualities**—those properties inherent to matter, such as shape, quantity, and motion, and **secondary qualities**—sights, sounds, and other sensory experiences produced by primary qualities acting on the senses (Galileo, 1623/1957). In making that distinction, Galileo emphasized the common evidence of sensory illusions and discounted the trustworthiness of the senses (Burtt, 1952/1980). Faced with the realm of sensible experiences, it was necessary to isolate a particular phenomenon and examine it completely in order to intuit those simple elements (elementalism) by which the phenomenon may be expressed in mathematical form, to quantify what was sensed. If performed adequately, the sensible facts were no longer needed because the elements extracted were the real constituents.

By religious conviction, Galileo proposed that God created the world as an 'immutable mathematical system' that allowed for certainty of scientific knowledge through the mathematical method. Mathematics was a form of thought that operates in a sphere of total abstraction from specific instances (Whitehead, 1925). The general conditions transcend the particular entities (the sensible facts) and are the basis for entering into mathematics and mathematical logic. General conditions can be investigated without specifying particular entities. In Galileo's metaphysics time and space were fundamental categories, and the real world was one of bodies reducible to motions depicted mathematically (Burtt, 1952/1980). The 17th century produced an approach to scientific thinking that was framed by mathematicians for the use of mathematicians (Whitehead, 1925). The mathematical mind had great capacity to deal with abstractions and to engage in a train of reasoning that was reasonable so long as it was abstractions that one wanted to ponder.

There were three steps to Galileo's method: intuition, demonstration, and experiment (Burtt, 1952/1980). As just mentioned, this involved examining sensible experiences and isolating phenomena from which one intuited simple constitutive elements. Through pure mathematics one then deduced demonstrations which had to be true of every other similar instance. For certainty, demonstrations would be developed whose conclusions could be potentially verified through experimentation. The work of Galileo would have far-reaching impact. The procedures of modern science have distinctive features that are traceable to him (Willis, 1957):

- Crude differences in quality are replaced by quantitative variation which shifts from classification in kind (category or class) to exact measurement.

- The idea of experiment is emphasized and scientific instruments become important.

- The demonstration of homogeneity in nature and the assumption of a deterministic universe conforming to causal laws.

In psychology there is an assumption that if the discipline is to be truly scientific it must adopt those same procedures (Willis, 1957). There must be planned experimentation, the use of instruments, and, most important of all, a reliance on measurement.

Francis Bacon (1561–1626), a contemporary of Galileo, was intent on developing a clearly articulated method for doing science. Knowledge at the time tended to be based upon deductive logic and what could be deduced from accepted truths (by the authority of the Church and Aristotle). Bacon would argue against such hasty generalization, favoring an inductive approach (Peters, 1921/1962). In his approach, the data for induction were natural observations and those facts were forced to reveal themselves through experiment (Blake et al., 1960). Such observations were then arranged in tables to give order to the accumulating facts. The first table listed cases of presence (instances where the phenomenon under investigation, say heat, occurred). The table of deviations recorded cases of the phenomenon's absence where it might be expected (such as heat being present in sun rays but not moon beams). Lastly, the table of degrees involved instances of sporadic presence (such as a body generating heat when active but not when at rest).

Bacon's process was a long, laborious passage from concrete instances to increasingly broader generalizations. As inductive generalizations arose, though, they required testing against facts. In this, failure was just as valued as success since it could eliminate further fruitless fact-gathering in false directions.

What makes Bacon significant is his specification of procedures to guide practice. In the end he was not very influential and for one major reason; he rejected the use of hypotheses. Bacon was mistaken in believing the orderly arrangement of data would make a correct interpretation obvious and there was nothing suggesting a method or formula for inventing hypotheses that would coordinate selective fact gathering (Peters, 1921/1962). As Blake et el. (1960) suggested, the critique is fair when applied to his tabular work but, they contest, he was actually using hypotheses in testing generalizations. That is in agreement with Peters' proposition that scientific experiment implies deliberate observations of anticipated results rather than mere fact assembly (remember he sought deviations only where the phenomenon might reasonably be expected to be found).

Bacon was not alone in his rejection of hypotheses. In the next century Isaac Newton (1642–1727) would also find the practice questionable. Unlike Bacon, Newton never communicated his methods in a systematic manner; instead they were scattered throughout his works (Blake et al., 1960). In *Opticks*, though, he did write of his 'method of analysis' which involved observation and experimentation and the drawing of conclusions by inductive reasoning. He followed that by saying that hypotheses were not to be harbored in experimental philosophy (scientists were considered natural philosophers). He frequently expressed serious contempt for hypotheses. At the same time, he used them (such as when he speculated that light rays may be particulate streams). So was he inconsistent? Not really. It was a particular type of hypothesizing that he opposed. He disliked how his contemporaries abused the use of hypotheses by holding fast to a theory and failing to acknowledge exceptions drawn from other research. The true use of hypotheses was not to be dogmatic but to suggest possibilities for investigation.

The job of natural philosophy to Newton was to deduce causes from their effects until one arrived at the first cause (Hall, 1992). Being a religious man, Newton accepted creationism. After divine design and creation (the first cause), Newton expected the universe, or system of the world, to fall under the general principles of mechanical motion. In this there was no place for anything other than determinism. Jevons (1874), in his treatise on experimentation, reflected the continuing belief in a deterministic world by proposing that a belief in chance is inconsistent with knowledge, that everything that happens has been predetermined. Chance only expresses ignorance of causes and an inability to predict results.

3.3 SCIENTIFIC PRINCIPLES OF THE 19TH CENTURY

By the 19th century the practice of experimentation had been further perfected. Jevons (1874) discussed the principles and scientific method of the time, principles that are familiar in current scientific psychology (bearing in mind that scientific psychology did not yet exist). Science, Jevons wrote, came into existence with the discovery of 'identity amidst difference,' that things that are unalike may yet share certain characteristics (a process of induction). That is the basis of inference; the recognition that what is true of something must be true of what is equivalent to it. Identity is the basis of inferential generalization and is what underlies the achievements made through the scientific method. The simplest inference is based on sampling. If the sample is representative of the whole it can stand for, and serve as the basis of generalization to, the whole. That can be done through simple observation, but experimentation goes further by influencing what is observed and forcing outcomes without waiting.

Observation is simply a matter of noting and recording the unfolding of natural events. Experimentation, on the other hand, occurs when the course of nature is altered, due to intervention, producing unusual results. In sophisticated experiments one removes all those conditions thought to influence results, one at a time, while holding all others constant. By thus disentangling natural phenomena, and holding others constant, one can eliminate 'interfering effect' (confounding variables in today's jargon), eliminating sources of error. There were two further reasons for dealing with one condition at a time. First, if two conditions are varied together one cannot tell if the result of one, the other, or both caused the result (the later development of 'analysis of variance' would allow for this). Second, if nothing happens one cannot tell which factor was indifferent, or whether they neutralized each other. At times it is not possible to vary conditions singly and one must adopt Mill's 'joint method of agreement and difference.'

J.S. Mill

John Stewart Mill (1806–1873) proposed a number of methods of induction and experimental inquiry that would support the search for causes (Mill, 1843/1973). The 'joint method' (which harkens back to Bacon's tables) combined the 'method of agreement' and the 'method of difference.' With 'agreement,' when two or more instances of a phenomenon share a single antecedent condition, the single condition is judged the cause. With 'difference' one seeks two instances similar in all regards but one—the presence in one, and absence in the other, of the phenomena of interest. The element present when the phenomenon occurs, and absent when it does not, is judged causal. The 'joint method' combined the two to deal with conditions that are dissimilar in more than one way and, through a process of elimination, identified the antecedent condition that is always present when the phenomenon is there and always absent when not.

Investigators start with known facts and deduce hypotheses from them (Jevons, 1874). These are then tested through observation or experiment. In quantitative experiments one aims to determine the relation that exists between different values of a quantity that one intentionally varies (the 'variable') and another quantity which is caused and varies as a result (the 'variant'). (In this, Jevons was basically introducing what we now refer to as the independent and dependent variables.) If the results are as expected the hypothesis is retained, but unexpected results require adjustment or abandonment of the hypothesis.

A further issue that Jevons discussed had to do the **problem of induction**, which is associated with **induction by simple enumeration**. By inductive logic, one examines all instances of a phenomenon to seek what is characteristic, or holds generally, of every instance. One then concludes that all future instances will have that characteristic. The problem, as identified by David Hume (1711–1776), was that there was no assurance that such generalizations would always hold in the future (Flew, 1964). For instance, until one encounters conjoined twins, one might reasonably conclude that all twins are born detached. The issue was ultimately addressed by the statistics of probability. As Jevons noted, induction does not lead to certain knowledge but, through observation and deductive reasoning, probabilities are estimated of the likelihood that a particular event will be within the margin of error.

The mathematical theory of probability had its beginnings with games of chance. Gamblers in the 17th century France consulted mathematicians to develop means of determining odds (Cowles, 2001). **Blaise Pascal** (1623–1662) and Pierre Fermat (1601–1665), working on the problem, laid the foundations of probability theory. During the 18th century a number of people began to observe that as the number of instances of a phenomenon grew large, their measures, displayed graphically, revealed a smooth curve that was bell-shaped, the 'normal distribution.' Then, in 1812, Pierre Laplace introduced an interpretation of the curve (variation about an average) as the 'Law of Error.' A short time later (1835) Lambert Quetelet extended the gathering of large samples to human characteristics and discussed the 'average man' as nature's ideal, which corresponds with the central value or average of the curve. What variability exists about the average represents 'error.' (In 'analysis of variance,' a once predominant statistic in psychology, the spread of scores about the average, the variability about the mean, is referred to as 'error variance.')

Pascal's wager

Towards the end of the 19th century, Francis Galton (1822–1911) would develop the idea of statistical correlation and, not long after that, Charles Spearman (1863–1945) would extend correlation into factor analysis. Other statistical techniques soon followed and psychologists took hold of them as they became available.

Despite the statistics that were yet to come, the experimental method and probability statistics that were present in the 19th century were influential on what would become modern experimental psychology.

WHAT DO YOU THINK?

Do you think that humans who have not been trained in scientific thinking can think scientifically?

3.4 SCIENTIFIC PSYCHOLOGY VERSUS COMMON SENSE

Before psychology became a science, people put faith in personal experiences of themselves and others. This resulted in the development of everyday notions (theories) of what to expect in the actions of others. With the advent of scientific psychology, that would change; 'common-sense psychology' would be devalued, if not dismissed altogether. In an early introductory psychology textbook, Fryer and Henry (1937) wrote that psychologists, in adopting the scientific attitude, doubt everything until it has been verified. For generations people have passed along attitudes and beliefs on just about everything and such opinions were likely to be wrong as much as they might be right. From the scientific standpoint, unless something is supported by evidence it is to be doubted, and that means rejecting the psychology of common sense until supporting evidence is revealed.

To Fryer and Henry, every person is a common-sense psychologist. Everyone, before they ever study psychology, acquires or develops notions of what to expect of others. They fail to realize that there is a difference between haphazard, uneducated observations and generalizations based on scientific observation. The main distinction between the two is in the methods used to draw conclusions. Common sense is based on casual observations that often lead to false generalizations, but scientific psychology makes observations that are more reliable, being based on the scientific method.

There is an implication that common sense is wholly at odds with scientific thinking, but the distinction may not be altogether absolute. The scientific attitude, Dewey (1910/1960) wrote, can be found in children given their openness, curiosity, and love of experimentation. Even in ordinary thinking abstraction is an essential element. Abstraction emancipates thought from the familiar, ferreting out unfamiliar properties or relations that support inferences that are more extensive. It exists in all analyses, in every observation, in which some quality is detached from the vague and obscure, in which it is absorbed, and made distinct. On the other hand, all ordinary inferences that are not under the regulation of the scientific method, are impaired, the effect of habits of expectation due to regular, co-occurrence of events in prior experience. With this method, when conjunctions have repeated sufficiently, the tendency toward expectation passes into belief. The scientific method contrasts with the empirical (common sense) by replacing recurring conjunctions of isolated facts with the discovery of some comprehensive fact. This is effected by breaking up the obvious facts of observation into processes that are more minute and not directly accessible to immediate perception.

When it comes to the common-sense approach, such **folk psychology**, as it now referred to, might best be considered a particular culture's shared ways of making sense of the world (Fletcher, 1995). That this is not scientific does not mean that these views are necessarily untested. Neither does the lack of tutoring in the scientific methods, nor probability theory, mean that the notions formulated through practical concerns are invalid. There is a prejudice toward non-scientific humans that may itself be invalid. As the personality psychologist George Kelly (1955) complained, psychologists have tended to propose that the aim of the scientist is prediction and control but rarely are the subjects in experiments credited with the same aspiration or ability. They are likened to animals whose aims are hedonistic and whose only concern is the pursuit of shelter and sustenance.

The social psychologist Fritz Heider shared Kelly's higher regard for ordinary people, and common sense, when he wrote that "The ordinary person has a great and profound understanding of himself and other people which, though unformulated or only vaguely conceived, enables him to interact with others in more or less adaptive ways" (Heider, 1958, in Fletcher, 1984, p. 203). It is not that ordinary humans are unscientific; it is that they are naïve in their practice. As Hebb (1966) put it, every human is well accustomed to formulating inferences from behavior about the mental processes of others, and does so with frequency, but without considering what they are doing in those terms. (As will be discussed in Chapter 8, psychology is now being criticized for 'methodolatry,' an overemphasis on methods over subject matter, and it is the lack of methodological acceptability for which common sense is being criticized.)

BOX 3.2
PSYCHOLOGY AND LITERATURE

While there is an aspect of chauvinistic scientism which discounts the insights of common folk (non-scientists), others regard unscientific apprehension of the human condition as a valuable source of psychological understanding. Gordon Allport (1897–1967), for instance, considered literature (biography, poetry, fiction) a valuable source of information for understanding personality and character (Allport, 1937). Whenever a psychologist succeeds in capturing something of personality, he proposed, one can find some great author who had already made that observation. Not to denigrate psychology, scientific analysis can complement such observations, extracting theoretical insights and hypotheses to test.

Scientific psychology and literature, to Allport, differ in how they approach personality:

- Generalization: Literature is concerned with the individual case and generalization is left up to the reader. The psychologist seeks general principles and lawful generalizations beyond the individual.

- Context of investigation: Literature involves complex social settings, in which many factors are operative in the flow of life, whereas the psychologist prefers highly constrained situations in which surrounding complexity is controlled or eliminated.

- Validity: Literature is unconcerned with replication of observations, statement consistency, or whether observations test some theory. Psychologists are concerned with all three.

As an example of the potential source of psychological insights in literature, consider automaticity. Bryan and Harter (1897, 1899) studied the acquisition of telegraphic skills in sending and receiving messages. They identified a process whereby, after sufficient repetition and conscious attention, the function becomes operative unconsciously and mechanically (automaticity). Here is an example I recently found of the same phenomenon in literature. It comes from Mark Twain's (1894/1966) *Pudd'nhead Wilson* and is in reference to a slave mother (15/16ths White) who switched her infant with the child of her master and had to learn to think of him as her master too:

(Continued)

(Continued)

> … he was become her master; the necessity of recognizing this relation outwardly and of perfecting herself in the forms required to express the recognition, had moved her to such diligence and faithfulness in practicing these forms that this exercise soon concreted itself into habit; it became automatic and unconscious; then a natural result followed: deceptions intended solely for others gradually grew practically into self-deceptions as well; the mock reverence became real reverence, the mock obsequiousness became real obsequiousness. (pp. 30–31)

That, in my opinion at least, reflects considerable psychological insight and deserves its due. What do you think? Might this speak as well to prejudice and other attitudes?

3.5 PHYSICS ENVY

John Stewart Mill argued that the social sciences were backward and would only be corrected by adopting the methods developed by the physical sciences (Koch, 1969/1973). The early psychologists were very much concerned with having their discipline recognized as a science and drew upon the methods of the accepted branches as a first step to being 'scientific.' It was believed that the methods of natural science could be directly adopted (Kantor, 1979) (without questioning whether they were appropriate to the phenomena under investigation). As Cattell (1888) put it, there was good reason to believe that the methods of physics, that have proven so useful, may be of benefit to psychology. Of course, the methods of physics were based on Newtonian mechanism. As a result, psychology, in adulation of the physical sciences and their successes, adopted a machine model that had its origins there rather than in social experience (Allport, 1947). As Allport contended, human behavior was fit into such a model while ignoring aspects like future orientation and symbolic activity which are not found at the level of mechanics. In this psychologists succumbed to what has been termed 'physics envy' (Morawski, 1982).

Psychology was influenced in its development by the advances of physical science and by an adherence to 'dogmatic methodism' (Peters, 1921/1962). Subsequent psychology was full of endeavors to apply formulaic procedures, methodological recipes, only admitting what fit the accepted scientific model, and leaning upon the theoretical concepts of chemistry, biology, and physiology to organize its own explanations. What counted as scientifically admissible predetermined what was studied. Central to this, in the early 20th century, was the emphasis on objectivity and public observability that John Watson (1878–1958) and others emphasized. As a result, human subjectivity and experience were excluded from scientific psychology. In doing so, they may have not only thrown out the baby with the bathwater but the tub as well—psychology lost its mind.

3.6 IS PSYCHOLOGY A SCIENCE?

When psychology was conceived as a science, it was unique in that its methods preceded the concern with its problems (Koch, 1969/1973). The program seemed rational; it was pursuing the hypothesis that natural science methods could be adapted to the study of humans and society. It was beyond doubt that no knowledge deserved attending unless it was replete with the symbolism of natural science. Precedence was given to a commitment to science without concern that it be adequate to the study of humans. The path of 'scientific' psychology has been a series of changing doctrines regarding what in the natural sciences to emulate. Each doctrine seemed to serve the purpose of securing the fetish of scientific recognition and assurance of being scientific.

Since its inception, there has been an increasing recognition that, as a result, significant issues and subject matter were being evaded. Unlike the natural sciences, psychology failed to establish a cumulative body of knowledge or a progressive move forward. The knowledge gained by one generation was usually displaced by the next. In that regard, Dunnette (1966) spoke to the history of fads, capricious concepts and practices, in psychology that are popular for a while, run their course, and fade away. The research that was primary in one decade had nearly vanished from the major journals by the next, being replaced by independent topics and resulting in non-cumulative development (Hunt, 2005).

While there is no question that researchers in psychology believe they are engaged in science, not all would agree. There is a prevailing assumption that if one is doing experiments one's discipline must then be a science. Koch (1969/1973), however, argued that in many psychological studies concepts like variable, measurement, control, law, and experiment simply fail to function with the same meaning they have in the traditional sciences. Those who are meticulous regarding what constitutes science deny psychology is or could be a science (Kantor, 1979). To be so it must deal with occurrences in the spatiotemporal field and free itself from the invisible and intangible (sensation, perception, images, consciousness, thought, anything mental). Kantor, you may have surmised, is aligned with behavioristic psychology which excludes what is not objectively accessible.

From the phenomenological perspective, Giorgi (1985) contended that psychology's conception of the scientific is incongruent with its subject matter. Most of the problems confronting psychology, in its attempt to be scientific, can be connected to the disunity in the field (the diversity of incommensurable approaches and notions of what constitutes psychology). Also, there is a discrepancy between the commitment to being scientific (by implication the adoption of natural science methods and assumptions) and faithfulness to the given that is the real person (including subjectivity and experience). The phenomena of human experience cannot be comprehended with the concepts derived from objective things (natural science's subject matter). Psychological phenomena must be understood as involving the relationship of the subjective to the objective, of person to person, and of person to the past and future.

According to Koch (1985c), psychologists have been involved in scientific role-playing as a major preoccupation. It may well be that a strict modeling of psychological experimentation on an adherence to the practices of natural science may be applicable to only delimited areas like physiological psychology and sensory physiology. It becomes more problematic, however, when applied to 'process areas' like learning, motivation, cognition, perception, et cetera. Scientific reasoning may lead one to propose that humans are equivalent to cockroaches and rats, or that humans can be understood as computers, mechanisms, or the hyphen in S-R (stimulus-response) psychology, but that may be a reflection of scientific methodology rather than knowledge of humans (Koch, 1969/1973). The reintroduction of cultural psychology, phenomenology, and the like, on the other hand, is more in line with the humanities than with science (Koch, 1985c). Perhaps, Koch suggested, psychology would be better renamed 'psychological studies.'

To this I would add that psychology needs a better understanding of the evolution of humans, biologically, societally, and culturally. As well, the theory of levels of integration, and recognition of qualitatively different phenomena at each level, require the development of methods appropriate to them (as discussed in Chapter 1). Scientific psychology, in alignment with natural science, has sought universal laws of psychology (Danziger, 2009) but, in that endeavor, human uniqueness and diversity were reduced to average performance, and lawfulness became a matter of average performance. From a different perspective, Allport (1937), addressing the search for general laws, suggested that "*a general law may be a law that tells how uniqueness comes about*" (p. 194, emphasis in original). It may be appropriate to seek universality at the biological level, but when one is dealing with psychological functions, that originate culturally, there is a potential for a great deal of diversity. That suggests a general law would resemble Vygotsky's **general genetic law of cultural development**. According to that law of

General
genetic law
psychological development, higher psychological functions involve the appropriation and **internalization** of sociocultural tools and meanings. The process of appropriation and internalization is general, but what is appropriated and internalized can be unique and of vast diversity.

3.7 HUMAN KINDS VERSUS NATURAL KINDS

Psychologists have been bound to a claim of respectability based on the appearance of scientific rigor bolstered by a restricted view of what constitutes science (Sherif, 1979). The methods of the respected sciences were adopted without considering whether there was a difference between studying chemicals, rocks, and animals as compared to humans. To Koch (1985c) there is something monstrous in treating humans as objects. It is callous to deal with humans as one would the inanimate universe. Such things do not perceive how they have been described, and they do not suffer. Humans do. The explanation of human action and experience, reductively, in physiological, physical, and chemical terms is part of the 'objectivist orientation' (Taylor, 1985). Humans are treated like everything else, as objects among other objects, and characterized by properties that have nothing to do with human experiences. There is a failure to recognize or acknowledge that humans are animals that self-interpret. If one is studying humans that must be considered.

Putnam in 1975 and Kripke in 1981 introduced the concept of 'natural kinds' into philosophical literature (Haslam, 1998). Terms like 'gold' and 'tiger' are natural kinds. They refer to classes of things that are not established by human conceptual abstraction but to their existence independent of human interests and understanding. Natural kinds have an essential sameness that is constituted by necessary and sufficient core properties. They are historically stable and immutable (although evolution by natural selection and gradual transformation challenges that over long time periods). The categories of 'human kinds,' on the other hand, differ from 'natural kinds' since they are considered artifacts of social conventions, labeling practices, and are contingent on historical developments; they are socially constructed.

Hacking (1995) used the concept of human kinds to refer to types of people and behavior, to kinds of action, emotion, and experience—in other words, ways of classifying humans. Human kinds are the subject of social science. Danziger (1993), in that regard, spoke of what he called 'psychological objects' which differ from 'natural objects' since they are shaped by the constructive activities and interventions of psychologists (Danziger, 1993). They are the things that psychologists consider objects for investigation or practice (attention deficit disorder or emotional intelligence, for example). These objects/concepts are constructed rather than found in nature.

The term natural kind was in reference to those phenomena studied by the natural sciences (physics, chemistry, biology) such as atoms, chemicals, rocks, temperature, but such phenomena crucially lack awareness (Martin and Sugarman, 2001). Human kinds, in contrast, *are* aware, and because of that, when they are categorized in some manner, that is, judged by another to possess some quality, they have the power to alter themselves or to challenge how they have been characterized. Hacking (1995) called this a 'looping effect.' A person labeled an alcoholic, for instance, can go through treatment or they can contest the charge or the criteria of diagnosis. A horse or a rock would simply not respond since such a designation is without meaning for them; it is not something they respond to. Given the designation of homosexuality as a psychological disorder and a criminal act in the 1960s, being so labeled had a different impact on people then than it does today (given its being considered simply a variation in human sexuality), at least within some cultures. Given the historical baggage that the concept of natural kind carries, Hacking (1999) proposed changing 'human kind' to 'interactive kind' and 'natural kind' to 'indifferent kind.' Dogs and storms don't care (indifference) if they are called vicious, but humans do (interactive) and they may challenge the classification. Psychology, as a human science, is not dealing with indifferent kinds and must be sensitive to the impact of its theories and practices on people and, hence, must be concerned with matters of ethics.

BOX 3.3
ETHICS IN WATSON'S BEHAVIORISM

When John Watson and Rosalie Rayner (1920) conducted the famous research into conditioned emotional reactions with Little Albert they were aware that creating a fear response in a nine-month-old may be considered immoral. After all, taking an infant that

Figure 3.1   Albert crying upon seeing the rat

Copyright © 2016 by the American Psychological Association. Reproduced with permission.

displays no fear of rats and, by associating it with something naturally fear-inducing, creating such a fear might strike people as just plain wrong. Watson and Rayner were sensitive to that and addressed it as follows:

> The establishment of conditioned emotional responses. At first there was considerable hesitation upon our part in making the attempt to set up fear reactions experimentally. A certain responsibility attaches to such a procedure. We decided finally to make the attempt, comforting ourselves by the reflection that such attachments would arise anyway as soon as the child left the sheltered environment of the nursery for the rough and tumble of the home. (p. 3)

Notice that they comforted themselves, not the infant.

Watson (1928) developed recommendations for raising children based on his research that, for me, raise ethical questions. At the time Watson was considered an authority and his book, *Psychological Care of Infant and Child*, was quite influential. Watson condescendingly dedicated it "to the first mother who brings up a happy child." Apparently, at least to Watson, children for millennia had been awaiting his expert recommendations since, according to him, no one knows how to bring up a child. Watson's program was intended to raise a child who was independent, not clinging, self-sufficient, and who caused no disturbance to adults. Watson did not know what effect would follow his recommendations, but they were aligned with behavioristic principles and that was enough.

Space does not allow a full description of the recommendations but I will mention some highlights. Perhaps surprisingly, Watson addressed the danger of too much love. The mother becomes lovingly connected with the child but that creates unwanted dependence on the mother. Too much attention paid to minor aches and pains would produce an adult who is too-complaining and dependent on others, and could lead to invalidism. Ideally, mothers should be rotated so as not to form close bonds. Leave the child alone as much as possible (watching from hiding) and let them solve their difficulties on their own. When hurt, don't coddle but coldly and dispassionately treat the wound as a doctor would. Instead of pampering them, treat them like young adults. Never hug or kiss them; just shake hands good night. This was how Watson raised his two sons, James and Bill.

Hannush (1987) interviewed James Watson about growing up with his father. While he loved his father, he said he had unhappy thoughts of his childhood, given his being subjected to the principles of behaviorism. His father was unresponsive, emotionally uncommunicative, and was committed to avoiding expressions of affection or tenderness. Closeness of any kind, hugging, kissing, being held, was forbidden. The boys were without an emotional foundation. This led to emotional instability and to attempted suicide by both in adulthood, Bill successfully. James felt the behavioristic principles were the root cause. To state the obvious, psychologists should be careful in the application of their theories without well-founded bases. I am sure that Watson meant no harm to his children but it happened all the same and it renders his approach ethically suspect.

3.8 A CONCERN WITH ETHICS

In the early days, psychology was not troubled by questions of ethics. To Fryer and Henry (1937), all sciences are characterized by being unconcerned with ethical values since they do not involve moral issues. Scientists deal with facts, and the moral issues attendant upon facts are not within their purview. Facts may have immense social value, but for the scientists they are just facts—neither good nor bad. As Burtt (1938), on the application of psychology to advertising, put it, "It is not within the province of the scientist to evaluate the effect of his investigations upon society" (p. 3). Burtt, however, had a social conscience and considered it undesirable to not consider the social implications of advertising. It is difficult, he thought, not to judge it unethical to sell something to a person who has no need for it. While the scientific concern may be with demonstrating how to influence desire for products, psychologists cannot afford to close their eyes to the fact that they have an ethical responsibility in the application of the influence.

The Nuremburg Trials' (1945–1949) exposure of the atrocities and barbarous medical experiments carried out by Nazi physicians during World War II, supposedly done in the name of science, changed things for experimenters (Berg, 1954). This led to the development of ten principles to guide experiments in medicine using human subjects. Their experiment had to produce results that were for the good of society and could not be obtained by other means. There were to be no coercions, force, or deceit; the person should be fully informed of the purpose, methods, and possible hazards. In psychology, problems of ethics had been handled by codes of ethics for teachers and professors (Hobbs, 1948), but in 1938 the Committee on Scientific and Professional Ethics acted informally and without a written code (Bersoff, 2008). By 1947 the range of activities of psychologists had far exceeded teaching and the President of the American Psychological Association (APA) convened a committee to develop an ethical code (Hobbs, 1948).

In the code that was developed, the American Psychological Association (1953) asserted that, as a science, psychology is devoted to serving humans and that a psychologist's first obligation is to people in general, to society. The values a psychologist holds should therefore reflect a commitment to human welfare. Also, and reflecting the principles established for physicians, the only justification for subjecting people to emotional stress is that the problem is significant and can be investigated in that way alone. If there is a danger of serious after-effects, full disclosure is necessary. The APA was not alone in such concerns. The Canadian Psychological Association first used the APA code but developed its own in 1977 (Seitz and O'Neill, 1996), and the British Psychological Society developed a code of Ethical Principles for Research on Human Subjects in 1978 and a Code of Conduct for Psychologists in 1981 (Gross, 2007).

Despite the injunction to not expose people to undue harm, research was still done that raised ethical concerns in that regard. Most disturbing perhaps, some research done by psychologists has been funded by, and in the service of, the CIA, with the purpose of developing methods of mind control (Brown, 2007). Project Camelot, in the 1960s, was a research program sponsored by the US Army to forecast insurgency so that the military could assist friendly governments to suppress revolution, such as in Cuba, to serve American interests (Horowitz, 1966). (Service to the oppressed peoples was not an issue.) On a smaller scale, Bramel (1962, in Kelman, 1967) deceived male undergraduates into believing that they were sexually aroused by pictures of men. Although they were later debriefed, Kelman wondered whether that could remove the harm of the initial assessment. The study that really aroused attention though was Milgram's (1963) study of obedience.

Milgram was interested in examining why people committed the atrocities in Nazi death camps and aimed to mimic 'obedience to authority' as a possible explanation. Participants administered shocks (a ruse) as punishment for failure to learn in a supposed memory experiment. At the high end of the shock dispenser, the punishing shock levels were labeled "Danger: Sever Shock" followed by "XXX." Milgram referred to the participants' "extraordinary tension," "extreme stress," and "agitation." Despite debriefing, many (such as Baumrind, 1964) felt there may have been long-lasting harm in terms of the self-esteem of the participants (the real victims) for punishing to the extreme of possible death.

The use of deception became controversial, ethically, but Milgram (1977) defended it. Labeling the use of misinformation (which was common in social psychology) as deception, he felt, biased the issue. He preferred less pejorative terms like 'technical illusion' or 'staging.' Outside psychology, he pointed out, the use of illusions, like the use of coconut shells to mimic horse hooves on radio, are quite acceptable. Nobody, he noted, cringes at misinforming children about Santa Clause. So why is misinformation so bad? That, I think, misses the point. Having people believe in Santa doesn't quite measure up to making people realize they would obey orders to execute another electrically. Regardless, the use of deception was being judged unethical.

Psychologists do have a responsibility to humanity and must be concerned with ethics and morality. Space does not permit further discussion here but, in subsequent Chapters (8 and 9) these matters will concern us again.

SUMMARY

The development of the scientific attitude, and the perfection of rational methods of inquiry, reflect a gradual cultural evolution in human knowledge-seeking. A major turning point was the 'scientific revolution' of the 17th century.

- A primitive 'science' can be attributed to the prehistoric invention, technological advances, and the appreciation of regularities in nature.

- Rational thinking and mathematics were significant cultural achievements that contributed to scientific approaches to knowledge and understanding.

- In the 13th century, empiricism, based on observation and measurement, began to challenge purely logical approaches.

(Continued)

(Continued)

- The scientific revolution was characterized by an emphasis on mathematics and a standardized method.
- There is dispute as to whether common sense can be considered a valid source of knowledge or whether it is unreliable because it is unscientific.
- Psychology, in adopting the methods of the natural sciences, and longing to be recognized as a science, has suffered from 'physics envy.'
- There is some dispute whether psychology can ever be a science.
- A necessary distinction to be made in psychology is that between natural kinds and human kinds.
- When dealing with humans who are aware and have feelings, psychology has to concern itself with a consideration of ethics.

SUGGESTED READINGS

Blake, R. M., Ducasse, C. J., and Madden, E. H. (1960). *Theories of scientific method: The Renaissance through the nineteenth century.* Seattle, WA: University of Washington Press.

Crump, T. (2001*). A brief history of science as seen through the development of scientific instruments.* London: Robinson.

Hurd, D. L. and Kipling, J. J. (1964). *The origins and growth of physical science.* Harmondsworth: Penguin Books.

Kimmel, A. J. (2007). *Ethical issues in behavioral research: Basic and applied perspectives* (2nd ed.). Malden, MA: Blackwell.

Want to learn more? For links to online resources, examples of multiple choice questions, conceptual exercises and much more, visit the companion website at **https://study.sagepub.com/piekkola**

4
PHYSIOLOGY AND PHENOMENOLOGY

LEARNING OBJECTIVE

Two general approaches to the examination and understanding of psychological phenomena have been in place since the inception of scientific psychology—physiological and phenomenological. In a sense, the distinction has its modern roots in Descartes' separation of mind from body as two distinct realities. As you might expect, physiological psychology is concerned with the body as it is involved in what we refer to as psychological. In particular, the focus has been on sensory and neurological processes. Phenomenology, in contrast, places its emphasis on human experience and consciousness, on one's subjective condition as revealed through self-examination or **introspection**. These two traditions were both represented in the 'new' experimental psychology, but presented a difficulty in that they appeared to be irreconcilably opposed.

What is involved in each of these traditions will be the focus of this chapter. You should have a familiarity with what is proposed, why they are opposed, and whether their divergence can ever be resolved. In particular, we will consider:

- The development of research into physiology in terms of the nervous system and sensory processes.
- The phenomenological tradition and its incorporation into scientific psychology.
- The divergence between these two approaches and possible resolution of their disparity.

FRAMING QUESTIONS

- Can physiological psychology account for conscious experience?
- Can phenomenological approaches to psychology ever satisfy the requirements of scientific objectivity or is it hopelessly subjective?
- Can scientific psychology afford to ignore subjective experience?

INTRODUCTION

When we begin to consider the dichotomy of phenomenology and physiology we are faced with the issue of appearance versus reality. Our experiences of the objective world are mediated by sensory processes but sensory physiology seems incompatible with the reality of subjective experience. My experience of the color red appears to me as qualitatively different from the chemical processes and organic matter that is its physical basis. Is the phenomenological presentation in any way a reflection of how things actually are (realism), or is it a construction that at best represents reality without resembling it (representationalism)? Or is it misleading and irrelevant? These are questions the ancient Greeks struggled with. Our current consideration, however, will begin with Descartes' absolute separation of mind (phenomenology) from body (physiology), discussed in Chapter 6, and the course followed from then to the emergence of scientific psychology.

4.1 THE PHYSIOLOGICAL TRADITION

Put simply, René Descartes (1596–1650) distinguished mind from body based on the qualitative differences between them. Matter was located in space and was divisible, but mind was non-localized and indivisible. Most importantly, mind had the property of thought which the body was lacking. That would be an issue that psychologists would have to struggle with (the mind–body problem), but physiologists had no real concern with that. In their efforts they aimed to account for mental functions materialistically, and were concerned with the functions of the nervous system and brain, and with sensory systems, often dismissing any question of mind as mythical or irrelevant.

In France, Julien de La Mettrie (1709–1751) laid the groundwork for the reduction of mind to body and a shifting of attention to physiological processes (La Mettrie, 1748/2004). Descartes' speculations and philosophizing were brilliantly useless, as far as he was concerned, and should be pushed aside by the work of physicians and an examination of physical evidence. Doctors' reports were demonstrating the dependence of mental processes on physiology through the effects of drugs, and by the losses in mental functioning associated with brain injuries. Evidence further suggested that the body is mechanical in its operation. Headless chickens were known to run about; and muscles separated from the body mechanically contract when stimulated. Such evidence, as La Mettrie could draw upon, was crude, but more sophisticated procedures would be developed to understand better the mechanics and processes of physiology and which were of importance to psychology, neurophysiology and sensory processes. Around the middle of the 18th century experimental work on the nervous system began to move in three general directions (Brazier, 1959):

- The differentiation of the peripheral nervous system from the muscles and investigation of its constitutional physiology.
- Identifying the function of the spinal cord and developing the theory of reflex action.
- Developing knowledge of the brain free of dogma about the soul.

Peripheral nerves

Descartes, in initiating the idea of reflexive responding (to be addressed shortly), revived a theory about the operation of the nerves traceable to Galen (129–199). Galen, who had identified the brain as a center for sensory and motor activity, proposed that the soul had an intimate connection with the brain, through which it communicated with the nerves by psychic pneuma or breath (Quin, 1994). In time the soul would no longer be considered necessary to explain the functioning of the nerves and brain, but not until after Descartes. For Descartes, the functions of nerve, brain, and musculature were to be explained in terms of 'animal spirits' which were produced by the transformation of fine particles in the blood upon reaching the brain. From there the animal spirits passed from the ventricles (fluid filled chambers at the center of the brain) to the nerves and muscles. The nerves he conceived of as tubes, containing animal spirits, which had threadlike fibers that could open access to the ventricles when stimulated, allowing transmission of animal spirits to the musculature.

In Figure 4.1, Descartes has drawn a fire (A) which stimulates the foot, moving the skin of the foot (B) it touches. This pulls a small thread (C) extending from the foot to the brain. The small passage at the brain is opened (D). Animal spirits pass from the ventricle (F) into the nerve and are transported to the muscles, producing foot withdrawal by inflating the muscle. The sensory impulse is conveyed to the brain and is then 'reflected' to the muscles, producing the reflected (reflexive) movement (Hodge, 1890). In this, Descartes laid out a rudimentary conception of what would become reflex theory of automatic, mechanical responses to stimulation.

Figure 4.1   Descartes' drawing of reflex action

The notion of nervous fluid or animal spirit did not last long after Descartes put it forward. Glisson, in 1677, demonstrated that such influx was not involved in muscle contraction (Brazier, 1959). A person's arm was immersed in water and, when contracted, there was no rise in its level—no increase in volume from sprits streaming in to fill it. Other experiments further discounted the idea. Newton, in contrast, speculated that the nerves were solid, rather than tubes, and that a vibratory motion of some ethereal medium was propagated along the fiber. At the time people could not conceive what such a medium might be, but electricity would soon be suggested. Initially, when electricity was suggested, people were unconvinced. At the time, the transmission of electricity through a wire required that the wire be insulated to counter loss; nerves were not insulated (the myelin sheath was unknown back then). Nonetheless, the idea kept cropping up.

In 1781, Alexander Monro addressed the notion of the passage of fluids within the nerve. First, no channel was observed to exist for the flow. When a nerve was cut, no fluid could be seen to escape. Finally, ligating or tying a nerve caused no swelling (from fluid buildup). Munro also resisted positing electricity because of the insulation issue. Eventually, the application of electrical charges to exposed nerves began to turn the tide. Luigi Galvani (1737–1798), at the end of the 18th century, showed that if electricity was applied to the nerve of a frog's detached nerve–muscle preparation, the muscle would contract. The matter was decided with the invention of the galvanometer, which could detect the presence of an electrical current (Groves and Schlesinger, 1982).

Emil du Bois-Reymond (1818–1896), in the mid-1800s, used more sensitive instruments that could detect weak bioelectric currents in nerve bundles (Lenoir, 1986). Then, in 1868, Julius Bernstein proposed that the membrane of an inactive nerve cell was polarized positively while the interior was negative. Furthermore, the cell, when active, propagated a depolarization along the membrane—the now familiar action potential (Brazier, 1959). Bioelectric theory was established. Soon, Richard Caton, in 1875, applied the galvanometer to activity of the exposed brains of rabbits, and then Hans Berger in 1929 applied electrodes to human scalps and reported brain waves (Groves and Schlesinger, 1982). That brain activity involved electrical activity was no longer in question.

Concurrently, another issue was being decided: How fast was the transmission of a pulse in the nervous system? Johannes Müller (1801–1858), in 1844, made the case that the time needed for a sensation to pass through the central nervous system to the musculature was so fast as to be beyond measurement. Six years later, **Hermann von Helmholtz** (1821–1894), his student, was able to calculate the velocity of signal transmission in the nerve of a frog. Helmholtz
A muscle and its attached nerve were extracted and the nerve was stimulated at various points away from the muscle (Hergenhahn and Henley, 2014). The distance from the muscle and the time until contraction allowed for the rate to be assessed at 90 feet/second. The work of Helmholtz, du Bois-Reymond, and other physiologists marked a shift away from metaphysics in neurophysiology, away from vitalism to mechanism (Brazier, 1959). Müller, whom Helmholtz and du Bois-Reymond studied under, was the last major physiologist to advocate vitalism (see Box 4.1).

BOX 4.1
VITALISM VERSUS MECHANISM

As a theory, vitalism proposed that living things are inherently different from the non-living and must be due to some substance which imparts powers—some vital force, called life, that is inexplicable in physical or chemical terms (Beckner, 1967). To some it meant the existence of something that was separate from the organism and was reflected in expressions like 'lifeless' or 'loss of life' in reference to corpses. While the theory can be traced to Aristotle, in its modern form it arose in response to Descartes' mechanism. The debate went back and forth with mechanism eventually winning the day. Giovanni Borelli (1608–1679), in a 1680 publication, established muscular mechanics, the operation of

(Continued)

Harvey

(Continued)

muscle and bone, through analogy with the engineering mechanics of levers and pulleys (Singer, 1931/1950)—see Figure 4.2. Of greater influence was the coincident demonstration by **William Harvey** (1578–1657) of the circulation of blood due to the heart acting like a pump—see Figure 4.3.

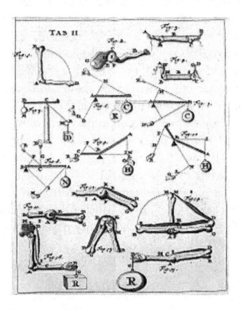

Figure 4.2   Borelli

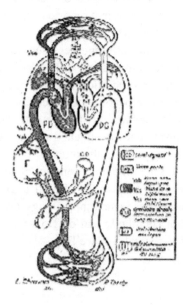

Figure 4.3   Harvey

An alternative to these mechanistic views was advocated by Georg Stahl (1659–1734), who argued that physical laws did not apply to living organisms, that in fact the sensitive soul ruled over the chemical processes of the body. Regardless, the efforts of the defenders of vitalism, evidence was gradually that eventually whittled away at the vitalist position. They had to withdraw from more and more processes as those were explained in natural science terms. John Mayow (1640–1679), for instance, demonstrated a connection between respiration and combustion (Partington, 1937/1960). A candle was placed inside a container, wherein it was floated on water, and was covered by a globe. By this means he demonstrated the consumption of air by the rising water level in the globe. A mouse was then placed in a container sealed by an elastic membrane which stretched inward by the consumption of enclosed air. Finally, a lit candle and a mouse, sealed in separate chambers, expired as the consumable air was depleted. Antoine Lavoisier (1743–1794) demonstrated later that it was oxygen that was essential to each case. A material process had been connected thereby with an organic process.

Most devastating was the work of Friedrich Wöhler (1800–1882) who, in 1828, created an organic substance from inorganic materials (Yeh and Lim, 2007). Instead of analyzing organic molecules into their constituents, which had been the standard procedure, Wöhler synthesized artificial urea (a natural organic compound) without needing a kidney (the organic source). Previously, but no longer, it was believed that vital force was required for the transformation of inorganic materials into organic forms. The artificial creation of urea was most damaging to the vitalist assertion. Over the following decades hundreds of organic compounds were created.

While some question Müller's adherence to vitalism in physiology, Mayr (1997) considered this to reflect his opposition to extreme mechanism and the notion that all biological phenomena could be explained by the laws of chemistry and physics. Living things, after all, have properties not found in inorganic phenomena, and that is the rub. Neither rocks, air, water nor machines adapt to environmental conditions, reproduce, or procure their own sources of energy. Many modern biologists (and psychologists) still find mechanism and reductionism lacking as explanations of biological (or psychological) processes and, as was discussed in Chapter 1, for some of them emergentism replaced vitalism as an alternative explanatory scheme.

The spinal cord and reflex action

Our consideration of the spinal cord begins with the efforts to establish the connection between it and the peripheral nervous system. In 1811, Charles Bell (1774–1842) published the results of his research into the spinal nerves (Brazier, 1959). Although the spinal cord had already been dissected, it was unclear what its functions might be. Through surgical procedure Bell exposed the spinal nerves and spinal cord of live animals. Then, with a knife, he touched the anterior portion and muscle convulsions resulted; but nothing occurred when touching the posterior portion. He concluded the spinal nerves served dual functions, one being motor, but he did not suggest the sensory role. Working with puppies that survived the exposure operation, Francois Magendie (1783–1855), in 1822, (A) severed the posterior roots and found a loss of sensation and (B) noted a loss of movement when severing the anterior portions. Sensory and motor nerves had been identified. It was established that different nerves may serve different functions.

Identification of sensory and motor pathways opened the door to an account of reflex theory physiologically. Since Descartes, David Hartley (1705–1757) had explained how some movements were involuntary, automatic responses to stimuli, and offered a reflexive account of neuro-muscular processes (Herrnstein and Boring, 1965). Soon after, Robert Whytt (1714–1766) suggested that in a reflex, one is dealing with a process whereby a stimulus acts upon a nerve and that leads to a muscular movement proportional to the strength of the original stimulus. Shortly thereafter, George Prochaska (1749–1820) liberated reflexive action from volition, or the action of the will, as an independent process; he was not prepared, however, to deny the existence of voluntary movements that were governed by will. Prochaska judged that between stimulation and movement, in reflexive processes, there were natural laws operative independent of will. Prochaska was not a materialist though, since he continued to believe the nervous system was governed by a rational soul (Quin, 1994). At the time, Bell and Magendie had not yet discovered the sensory and motor roots at the spinal cord, but Prochaska was already referring to impressions being conveyed, by a sensory nerve, to a point where they are 'reflected' and pass into a motor nerve, and then muscle. What was lacking was the actual physiology of the reflective mechanism—enter Marshall Hall (1790–1857).

Hall (1833) conceived of the function of the spinal cord as something more than a mere channel for connecting the brain with sensory and motor systems, and he would make his case experimentally. Hall began by pointing out that in the organism, as an organized whole, it is difficult to determine how sensation and voluntary movement combine with cerebral, brain stem, and spinal cord functions, in order to determine what functions are specific to each. The trick would be to isolate those functions and examine them separately. To that end, a snake was beheaded and went from constantly moving with vigor to motionless. It would remain so without further external stimulation but, if so acted upon, it again displayed movement. Hall concluded that volition had been annihilated by decapitation, given the absence of spontaneous movements, but not the power to move as demonstrated by reactivity to stimulation. Sensation, volition, and movement, he thought, could be considered three links in a chain; and that the removal of volition destroyed the connection between sensation and movement. Nonetheless, the provocation of movement suggested the operation of a different principle and demanded further inquiry.

In another experiment, a turtle was decapitated. Its tail and limbs were stimulated by flame and pointed instrument. Immediate movement was evoked. Going further, if the operation was performed and the spinal cord removed as well, no response to flame or point was forthcoming. This demonstrated the necessity of the spinal cord to reflexive activity (spinal reflexes had been discovered). This was supplemented by evidence from infants born with only a spinal cord and brain stem who also displayed such reflexive processes. The reflex, as he named the function, was an arc (stimulation → spinal mediation → movement) which, at one point, he referred to as the "reflex arc" (1833, p. 655) which was the phrase that took hold.

Hall had introduced a clear distinction between voluntary action and reflex action and established the reflex as an unlearned movement, automatic, and not requiring consciousness. Ivan Sechenov (1829–1905), father of Russian physiology, in 1863 replaced the voluntary activity, that Hall preserved, with reflexes of the brain (Rahmani, 1973). According to Sechenov, organisms depend on the environment for their existence and it stimulates them to action. Mental functioning is not some spontaneous activity, but the result of the continuous stimulation that the nervous system is subjected to. So-called willed movement was simply movement that lacked the first link in the reflex arc (Brazier, 1959). Without the afferent input—the external stimulation—movement could be initiated by memory traces from previous input which could be activated by the recurrence of any portion of the prior input. Just as the spinal cord mediated between stimulation and movement, so too did the brain, only its reflexive activities were more complex.

Expanding knowledge of the brain

The third general direction of research into the nature of the nervous system was the development of knowledge of the brain free of dogma about the soul, in other words, in terms of materialist explanations. Knowledge of the structures of the brain had been attained already during the 16th and 17th centuries but, by the 19th century, there was still a lack of understanding of what functions were performed by the different structures (Brazier, 1959). By the mid-19th century there was a shift away from metaphysics (notions of the soul and vitalism, for instance) among neurophysiologists.

It was not enough to know that the brain regulates behavior; what mattered was how, and research into 'localization of function,' the proposition that different parts of the brain perform specialized functions, was directed at that (Kolb and Whishaw, 1990). This work was initiated by Franz Gall (1758–1828) in the late 1700s. While what was proposed would ultimately be judged laughable and tarnish his reputation, Gall was a serious scientist. Prior to Gall, the cerebrum was considered to be just an inert cover that protected the brain from injury. Gall, however, considered it an important functional part of the brain involved in higher mental functions (Groves and Schlesinger, 1982). Besides his emphasis on the grey matter (the apparent cover) Gall also discovered the white matter tracts (Brazier, 1959). These connected the cells of the cortex with subcortical structures and the two hemispheres with each other (the corpus callosum). He also identified the white and grey matter of the spinal cord (Kolb and Whishaw, 1990). Unfortunately, all of this has been overshadowed by his method for research into functional localization.

Gall (aided by Spurzheim) proposed that human faculties were localized in the brain and these might be determined indirectly by examining the skull (Hergenhahn and Henley, 2014). It was assumed that

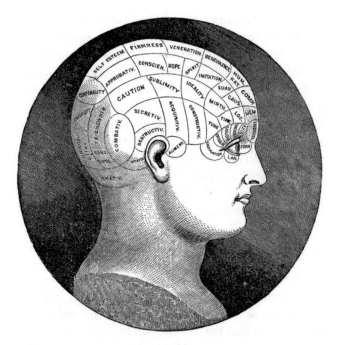

Figure 4.4   A phrenological chart

- People vary in the degree to which they possess a particular faculty—reason for instance, and that these faculties are innate.

- Particular faculties are associated, physiologically, with specific areas of the cerebral cortex.

- A person high or low in a faculty would have a brain region that reflected that by increased or decreased size.

- After birth, as the skull hardens, this would be reflected by bumps and depressions.

The science (so-called) of 'phrenology' would identify those specialized areas by examining people who were high or low in a faculty and then the skull was examined to determine where bumps and depressions existed. People high/low in a function were expected to have bumps/depressions at the same place on the skull, which reflected over- and under-developed brain regions. In the end phrenology failed because the presumed faculties, like faith and veneration, had no relation to actual behavior (Kolb and Whishaw, 1990). The breakthrough for research into human functional localization arose when behavioral losses, specifically the incapacity to speak, began to be connected to areas of brain damage. If one ignores Gall's questionable method, he can also be judged to have anticipated modern neuropsychology.

Gall's theory was attacked in the mid-1800s by Jean Pierre Flourens (1794–1867), who argued against discrete localized brain action in the cerebral hemispheres (Brazier, 1959). Flourens identified three major structural units—the medulla (basically the brain stem) the cerebellum, and the cerebral hemispheres which differed from each other in their functions. Unlike Gall, Flourens' conclusions were based on experimentation (Kolb and Whishaw, 1990). He introduced the procedure of 'ablation'—the destruction of brain areas in live animals and the observation of associated functional losses. He concluded that the seat of intelligence was the cerebrum, that the cerebellum coordinated movement, and that the medulla was involved in life-maintaining processes like breathing. There was no localization to be found in the cerebrum (as Gall suggested) and intellectual functions were coextensive. What loss of function occurred was correlated with the amount of tissue destroyed, not the specific location. If the destruction was total, loss was complete, but, if enough remained, recovery of all functions occurred. In this, Flourens rejected the possibility of sensory and motor functions at the level of the cortex, but that would, in a short time, be disproved.

Localization studies went in a new direction with a report delivered by Jean Bouillaud in 1825 on a patient who had lost the speech function after damage to the frontal lobes. A little later Marc Dax demonstrated speech disorders associated with damage to the left hemisphere and Ernest Auburtin reported that a person whose brain had been exposed lost the ability to speak when pressure was applied to the anterior lobes. Another Auburtin patient lost the ability to speak, but could understand speech and use signs intelligently.

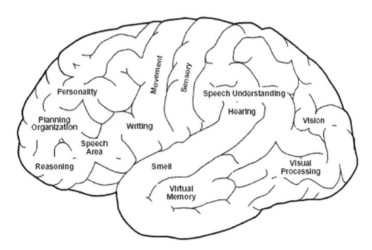

Figure 4.5   Functional areas of the brain

Auburtin predicted the lobes would be found damaged at autopsy. At the meeting was Paul Broca (1824–1880), who had a similar patient without speech beyond uttering 'tan' (so he was referred to as Tan). Tan died soon thereafter and was found to have a lesion at the left anterior lobe (now known as Broca's area). As a result, Broca proposed that specific brain areas control behavior and selective destruction of that area obliterates the behavior. Localization was taking off.

BOX 4.2
THE CASE OF PHINEAS GAGE

The case of Phineas Gage (1823–1860) is one of the most famous in the history of neuropsychology and has been used to demonstrate the functional localization of higher mental functions, specifically personality. Gage, as reported by his physician, John Harlow (1868/1993), was working as a foreman for the Rutland and Burlington Railroad in 1848, blasting rock to build a new railway bed. A hole had been drilled in rock for an explosive charge to be implanted. Gage (pictured below with the iron) was using a tamping iron to pack the explosive in and, having been distracted, dropped the rod, which caused a spark to ignite the gunpowder.

Figure 4.6   Phineas Gage

A blast sent the rod through his lower jaw and out the top of his head. Miraculously, he recovered, but he was not the same. Gage, as Harlow wrote, was a man of iron will who was considered capable and efficient by his employers. He was judged shrewd in business and considered to be possessed of a well-balanced mind. All that changed. His intellectual balance and his ability to hold his animal inclinations in check had diminished. He was irreverent, uncharacteristically given to profanity, had little concern for others. He no longer found it easy to commit to an activity, flitting from one plan to another. He was so changed that his employers would not rehire him. People who knew him well said his mind was changed radically. For a while he and his rod were a circus attraction with P. T. Barnum and then he went to South America to work on a ranch. He returned some years later and died in 1860. The Gage case is regarded as clear evidence of the involvement of the frontal lobes in personality.

Carl Wernicke (1848–1905) opposed localization. Wernicke found that language was involved in more than one area of the brain (he identified an area associated with speech comprehension—Wernicke's area). Second, he determined that damage to one area not associated with a function, the white matter connecting speech comprehension to speech production areas, could make it appear as though the area associated with the function had been damaged when it had not. In other words, a person could understand what someone said but not repeat it, making it seem as though Broca's area was compromised. In this he introduced the possibility of serial processes involved in a function and also the notion of disconnection between functional areas.

While ablation studies were demonstrating losses of function due to damage, an alternative approach was also being developed which involved applying electrical stimulation to the brain to evoke activity. Gustav Fritsch (1838–1927) and Eduard Hitzig (1839–1907) in 1870 wrote that the electrical stimulation of the cerebrum could selectively excite different actions. Depending on where stimulation occurred, on the exposed cortex of a dog, muscular movements were discharged; different movements were initiated by different areas being stimulated. Still there was dispute.

Towards the end of the 19th century a debate ensued over the cerebral localization hypothesis and the 'holistic' theory—that the brain acted as a unitary whole (Tyler and Malessa, 2000). On one side of the debate was Friedrich Goltz (1834–1902), a holist, and on the other David Ferrier (1843–1928), a localizationalist. They confronted each other at the International Medical Congress (1881) in London. Goltz addressed the results of Fritsch and Hitzig, saying there was a flaw in their method since they could not determine how far down into the brain their electrical stimulation went, or whether lower regions were activated or not. Even though they addressed the problem by performing ablation research, he was unconvinced of localization. Goltz supported Flourens and the notion that all cortical areas served the same function. In his own work with dogs he tested the hypothesis that if a specific portion of the cortex had a localized function, that function should be lost if the entire cortex was removed (Kolb and Whishaw, 1990). One of his dogs, that lived for 18 months, was more active than normal, shivered when cold and panted when hot, walked on even ground, regained lost balance, responded to light and sound, and would accept meat soaked in milk but not in bitter quinine. Decortication reduced functions but failed to eliminate them—localization was rejected. At the conference he mentioned the 'phenomenon of restitution,' the finding of Flourens that regions of the brain have the capacity to take over functions after destruction of a brain center (Tyler and Malessa, 2000). The ability of the brain to recover lost functions, due to damage, by reorganizing itself and making new connections between neurons, is now referred to as 'neuroplasticity.'

Goltz was not disputing that such destruction was without effects. His dogs were intellectually deficient compared to normal animals; they behaved more like a reflexive eating machine. Ferrier responded to Goltz, accepting his findings but not his interpretation. It was entirely possible that lower structures served the functions retained and that portions of the cortex might have remained after surgery. Furthermore, he contended that results from more than one species were needed. Using more refined surgical procedures that carefully restricted lesioned areas, Ferrier demonstrated localized motor functions in fish, frogs, cats, rabbits, pigeons, and monkeys (Kolb and Whishaw, 1990). At the conference he presented his research on monkeys. Their presentations were followed by both of them offering demonstrations with live, lesioned animals, which were subsequently killed and their brains examined (Tyler and Malessa, 2000). Goltz emphasized the decreased weight of the dog's brain, but the injuries to the brain were not as extensive as he had contended, and Ferrier's were more precise and convincing. In a short time more localized areas were being identified and localization maps were being drawn up that neurosurgeons came to depend on. Such maps became a part of neurological textbooks from the mid-1880s onward. Localization won out.

Sensation and perception

Another area of physiological research that would impact psychology was research into sensation and perception. By the 19th century it was quite apparent that physical stimuli and the perception of the same were discordant. Central to the concern was the distinction made by Galileo (1623/1957) between 'primary qualities' and 'secondary qualities' (as mentioned in Chapter 3). Primary qualities referred to those properties that reside in matter inherently, for example shape, quantity, and motion. Secondary qualities are those qualities that appear after

WHAT DO YOU THINK?

Do our senses give us access to the world and, if they do, can they inform us of the world as it actually is or only as we experience it?

primary qualities have impinged on the senses—the sights, sounds, and other sensory experiences. Galileo (1623/1957) placed no value on secondary qualities. Tastes, colors, smells, and so on, only reside in consciousness and have no bearing on objects in the world. Newton concurred; whatever primary qualities may be, the only contact with them is indirect, through organs of sense (Burtt, 1952/1980). Colors are just phantasms that are produced in us by the action of light. Such secondary qualities have no existence outside of the brain; they are simply the potential consequence of light acting upon the body. This, of course, brings into question knowledgeable access to objective reality.

In terms of psychology, the expression of this primary/secondary distinction had its roots in John Locke (1632–1704) and his example of the 'paradox of the basins' (Flew, 1984). If one hand is placed in a basin of hot water and the other in one of cold, when they are transferred to the same basin of lukewarm water, one hand will yield qualities of hot and the other of cold for the very same physical stimulus. The temperature, as primary quality, was experienced as two different secondary qualities; the perception of heat was in the experiencer not the object. This contested any ability to know the object world beyond the perception of it (and leads to a solipsistic stance). Without going into the details, David Hume (1711–1776) would deny any access to an objective realm and, furthermore, denied the possibility of knowledge of any order or causality. Immanuel Kant (1724–1804), Hume's contemporary, accepted the unknowability of the object world but believed there was order to experience which, in his estimation, must be provided to chaotic sensations by the organizing capacity, the innate 'categories of the mind,' or conceptual organizers.

Specific nerve energies

Of significance to the emerging theory of sensation and perception was the **doctrine of specific nerve energies** of Johannes Müller (1838/1997). Building on the work of Bell and Magendie (on the specificity of sensory and motor nerve functions), Müller further differentiated sensory nerves. Basically, he proposed that sensory impressions, as experienced, depended on the particular sensory nerve stimulated, not the physical stimulus, and the area of the brain that the stimulation was relayed to. The idea was actually suggested by Charles Bell in 1811 when he proposed that an impression made on two different sensory nerves with the same instrument produces two sensations that are quite different (Carmichael, 1926).

According to Müller (1838/1997), what we perceive is the not actual physical stimulus but the changes effected in the nerves, and each sensory nerve, no matter how stimulated, results in a subjective experience specific to it. The same stimulus, electricity for instance, can produce sensations of light when acting on the optic nerve, sound with the auditory, and sensations of taste and touch with their respective nerves. This demonstrates "the impossibility that our senses can ever reveal to us the true nature and essence of the material world" (Müller, 1838/1997, p. 71). We are thus left with an indirect realism since an inaccessible, but existent, world is proposed, which is known through sensory impressions (secondary qualities) that do not resemble that world.

Unconscious inference theory

Newton had demonstrated that what is perceived as white light is a composite of all the colors of the visible spectrum even though they are not perceived (Hergenhahn and Henley, 2014). Also, Pieter Van Musschenbroek (1692–1761), in 1760, had found that if complementary colors, like blue and yellow, each occupy half of a disc, and that disc is set to rapidly spinning, people perceive the disc as a uniform grey color. It was apparent that what was perceived may not closely match an actual physical presentation—grey is not blue or yellow. The relation between sensation and perception was becoming an issue.

In other experiments, Newton found that mixing lights of different colors could result in the perception of a different color (Levine and Shefner, 1981). By projecting lights of each color onto a screen so that they superimposed, new colors were produced by the intermingling. Three colors (red, green, and blue) stood out as primary in such research, since their mixing produced all perceived colors. Without actually investigating the receptors in the eye, Thomas Young (1773–1829), in 1807, hypothesized three types of tissues must exist that are maximally sensitive to different primary lights (not paints), and that the mixing of those colored lights acted on such tissues to produce the perceivable range of colors. Helmholtz later drew upon Young to develop what is known as the 'Young-Helmholtz' or 'trichromatic theory,' that three types of receptors (cones) in the retina respond differentially to light of different wavelengths. The receptors encode stimulation into activity in the nervous system that signifies the full range of colors.

What concerns us here is not the physiological mechanisms. It is the theory, **unconscious inference theory**, that Helmholtz put forward to account for perceptual experiences which were at variance with the input at the level of sensory receptors. Besides color perception, Helmholtz was confronting an old problem—how do we perceive the visual field in three dimensions when the retina of the eye is two-dimensional (horizontal and vertical but not distance)? Both in terms of specific nerve energy and the perception of depth, the sensory report was inadequate to account for knowledge of objective reality, or of the complexity of perceptual experience. Sensory input, in terms of receptors, is impoverished relative to subjective experience. According to Helmholtz, sensory input is merely a mental representation, not an actual reflection of things as they are: "the sensations have been described as being simply *symbols* for the relations in the external world. They have been denied every kind of similarity or equivalence to the things they denote" (Helmholtz, 1867, in Southall, 1925/2000, p. 18).

The sensory report was inadequate to represent the external world. More than that, what one perceived was inconsistent with sensory stimulation. The percept therefore required mediation from within, between it and the sensory presentation, some sort of subsequent processing of the sensory input, before it was delivered to consciousness as the completed percept. This is what Kant had done in supposing mental categories that processed sensory information, but Helmholtz was an empiricist and believed all knowledge came from experience. He rejected Kant's nativism. These mediating mechanisms would be derived, therefore, from accumulating experience, and would eventually serve as signs of external agents and events. That this was so was demonstrated by the many illusions being discovered at the time. The Necker Cube, (Figure 4.7) is a powerful example. Stare at the cube for about 30 seconds. You should find that it changes its orientation. What appeared to be the back portion shifts to the front, automatically, and without your conscious intent. Your brain is trying out different interpretations and the end result is your perception.

With accumulating experience, the mind—a physiological, or brain process—builds up a store of experiences and, as a consequence, expectations are built up. One such expectation could be the possibility that the recurrence of a previously experienced sensory collage is most likely due to the same stimulating object producing those same impressions. It was upon that basis that one acted with respect to the inaccessible world. The adequacy of the expectation was determined by acting upon current input and, in consequence, receiving the expected bundle of sensations. In the end, despite Helmholtz's vowed materialism, we are locked inside a phenomenal reality. What we know are our experiences after the sensory input has been processed outside of awareness.

Psychophysics

Another area of research that emerged during the 19th century also addressed the relation between the world of objects, sensory processes, and subjective experience—**psychophysics**. The concern was with the correspondence between objective reality and subjective experience. According to Gustav Fechner (1801–1887), psychophysics was aimed at establishing the functional relation between body and mind, of the physical and psychological worlds (Fechner, 1860/1997). Nowhere was this more evident than in the research, initiated by

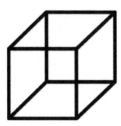

Figure 4.7   The Necker cube

Ernst Weber (1795–1878), into 'just noticeable differences,' the ability to detect differences in magnitude between different stimulus presentations (Hergenhahn and Henley, 2014). You can probably distinguish between the weight of one ounce versus two but not between 1,000 and 1,001 ounces. As magnitude increases, larger differences are needed to notice a difference subjectively. What Fechner hoped to achieve from work on psycho (experiential)-physics (material) was a mathematical function that related changes in one with the other, and to establish a basis for connecting mind and body or "the empirical relationships of body and mind" (Fechner, 1860/1997, p. 130).

4.2 PHENOMENOLOGICAL PSYCHOLOGY

As noted with Helmholtz and Fechner, the subjective realm of mental experience was central to their considerations. This was a concern among the 'new' experimental psychologists too. Wundt and his students incorporated introspection (attending to inner experiences) into their experimental methodologies. For Wundt this was more than the casual examination of private subjective experience (Blumenthal, 2001). In line with Fechner, he preferred controlled experimentation whereby participants were presented with a stimulus of some sort and reported their subjective impressions. Traditional research on illusory perception also relied on such procedures. **William James** (1842–1910) too, in his discussions on the 'stream of consciousness,' was drawing on internal observation (James, 1890/1950). Introspection was a common methodology in early psychology. In fact, James (1892) referred to the psychology of the day as "a mass of phenomenal description" (p. 146). There was in all of this a concern with connecting experience with physiological processes. Not all shared that concern though.

James

Act psychology

The concern for phenomenological psychology is to develop an understanding of lived experience (Langdridge, 2007). In a sense this is an old philosophical concern but, in psychology proper, Franz Brentano (1838–1917) is the figure with whom this is most closely associated. Brentano proposed that the ultimate data of concern for psychological analysis were the manifestations of consciousness (Giorgi, 1970). Furthermore, to explain conscious phenomena in terms of physiology did not do justice to the phenomena of which one was conscious. They were irreducible. More than that, what do we know of physiology really? According to Brentano (1874/1998), there is no basis for believing that the objects of external perception, so-called, are themselves anything more than mere phenomena; and we don't know that they are the same as they appear to us—the old problems of appearance versus reality and subjectivism.

'Act psychology,' Brentano's approach, was in contrast with 'content psychology,' which goes back to Hobbes, Locke, and Hume. The English philosophers espoused the notion that the contents of mind are made up of simple sensations which combine to form complex mental experiences. Among Brentano's contemporaries, notably Edward B. Titchener (1867–1927), the aim of psychological science was the identification of those elements constituting consciousness and the laws of their combination. That involved an analysis of subjective experience but was very much at odds with Brentano's understanding of the analysis of experience. Act psychology was more concerned with processes and mental activity than with elementalism. What was important about the mind was not what its contents were but what it does.

Act psychology stresses mental processes not as mere thought, memory, feeling, judgement, in and of themselves, as mental structures, but as processes having **intentionality** or 'aboutness.' A concern with experience was a concern with ways of acting and what those actions were about (Sahakian, 1975). It was about acts of experiencing. It is not experience, a noun, but experiencing, a verb; not a thing called experience, but a process that has temporal extensions. Mental processes were classified as of three types: feeling, sensing (and ideating), and judging. In this, intentionality is important since there is no thinking without something thought about, or feeling without something the feeling was in reference to, or judging without some circumstance under judgment. "In idea something is ideated, in judgment something is affirmed or denied, in love something is loved, in hate hated, in desire desired" (Brentano, 1974, in Sahakian, 1975, p. 187). The focus is upon the phenomenally given, on conscious experiencing. To examine this, Brentano drew upon 'phenomenological introspection,' which focused on mental phenomena rather than abstracted and isolated mental elements. This contrasted with Titchener, who had people hold a percept in mind and analyze it into constituent elements, like separate sensation.

Würzburg School

The approach of Brentano had been empirical (observational and descriptive) rather than experimental. Oswald Külpe (1862–1953) and the Würzburg School were intent on increasing the power of introspection in its application to higher mental processes and, like Brentano, were discontent with mere analysis of structural–elemental content of people like Titchener (Sahakian, 1975). They went beyond Brentano by introducing experimentation into phenomenology and the adoption of 'systematic experimental introspection,' whereby people were set to complex mental tasks and asked to reflect on what was involved (Hergenhahn and Henley, 2014). The effort was systematic in that the whole experience, which was temporally extended rather than immediately reactive, was broken down into segments and transformational phases were noted in the engagement with assigned tasks.

This could be done retrospectively through recollection or through the introjection of questioning during performance.

In their experiments the Würzburg psychologists identified new types of mental processes. Karl Marbe (1869–1953), for instance, identified 'imageless thought,' thought processes that did not involve conscious content (Sahakian, 1975). People were given similar-looking weights and asked to determine which of the two was heavier. While the participants reported being aware of the weight of the objects, they were unaware of how they came to the judgment as to which weighed more—it just came to them. Another finding, by Narziss Ach (1871–1946), was that of 'determining tendencies,' the finding that the establishment of initial conditions set up a regulating tendency that directed the subsequent engagement in the task, but outside of conscious determination. Subjects were told to add, subtract, multiply, or divide and then were presented with two numbers (Fancher, 1990). Reports were that the instructions did not play any conscious role in the performance. Reflect for a moment on this: You determine to go home. Is the decision enough for you to follow through without any further thought of your intent, or do you keep repeating to yourself 'go home,' 'go home,' 'go home'?

Gestalt psychology

Another approach relying on reports of conscious experience that is connected with the phenomenological tradition is Gestalt psychology. The tradition built upon the work of Christian von Ehrenfels' (1859–1932) idea of 'form quality.' This was the observation that, in perception, sensations are organized and collectively have qualities that are not attributable to the individual sensations (Hergenhahn and Henley, 2014). The overall form is 'emergent' upon the elements and is qualitatively different from its constituents. It forms into an organized whole (a gestalt). Max Wertheimer (1880–1943), who had studied under Ehrenfels, founded the Gestalt tradition with the demonstration of the 'phi phenomenon.' If two fixed, stationary lights are so coordinated that the turning off of one light is followed by the on-turn of the second, despite their immobility, a perception of movement will arise. The whole, as consciously experienced, was more than the sum of its parts (the perception of movement was more than the fixedness of the individual lights).

In the final analysis, the phenomenalism of the Gestalt approach excludes access to any objective reality. Wolfgang Köhler (1887–1967), another founder, proposed that the 'Gestalt Laws of Organization' are functions of the nervous system that take up individual sensations and arrange them into meaningful units that are what is perceived, and that the end result makes no reference whatsoever to objective reality (Köhler, 1947). In other words, epistemologically, this is an indirect realism; objective reality is posited, but access to it is only as it is represented in perception, not as it actually is.

Phenomenological irrelevance of the reflex arc

While not usually categorized as phenomenological, John Dewey's (1859–1952) critique of the reflex arc concept rests upon phenomenal experience. In it Dewey (1896) is addressing the difference between a physiological stimulus and a psychological stimulus.

As discussed earlier, under the physiological tradition, the reflex became a central explanatory concept for mental processes among physiologists. The core of the concept is that of an initiating stimulus, a mediating internal linkage, and a mechanical response. Physiologists saw in this a means whereby psychological processes could be explained. Theodor Meynert (1833–1892), an Austrian neuroanatomist, developed what James (1890/1950) called the Meynert Scheme (depicted in Figure 4.8 below from James). The depiction was intended to demonstrate two reflexive sequences that minimally modeled the sequential reflexivity of all action. In the scheme 1) a candle (stimulus) instigates a reflexive reaching to touch (response), which leads to 2) a burning sensation (stimulus) and a reactive withdrawal of the hand (response). James was unconvinced of the validity of this since little children quickly learn to inhibit reflexive reaching. Meynert argued that a purely reflexive mechanism, which could not be modified by learning, would be repetitive; that no matter how many times the child was burned, the flame would elicit reaching reflexively. To James, this was not the case; children learn and, thus, inhibit the reaching tendency.

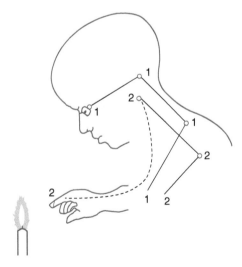

Figure 4.8 The Meynert scheme

Dewey (1896) accepted James' addition of memory mechanisms as modifying reflexive responses. Maynert, however, dismissed the scheme altogether. He considered it completely misleading and inconsistent with the facts as they are found under conditions of concrete behavior. The reflex arc, as a unit, may be appropriate for the analysis for physiological processes, but it was woefully lacking in terms of human conscious experience. The conscious level of activity involved operations and phenomena that were qualitatively different. The reflex arc was an inappropriate importation from a different scientific tradition dealing with qualitatively different phenomena.

The Meynert scheme, and the reflex arc hypothesis that it was based upon, were both defective. The scheme was an abstracted moment from the child's ongoing life process. There was a failure to appreciate that the living person was engaged in a continuous process of exchange with the environment, one that entwined both person and environment (stimulus conditions in the scheme). According to Dewey (1928), the scheme represented a cross-section of ongoing behavior, frozen in time for purposes of analysis. Actual behavior is uninterrupted and unbroken. It is longitudinal, having a history that is written in the active engagement with the environment. It is not a series of discontinuous, stimulus-response sequences—it is a smooth flow, not isolated jerks. Such discrete entities are created in the process of analyzing ongoing behavior, and their existence is an intellectual one, an interpretation. Most importantly, such cross-sectional analysis strips conduct of its psychological qualities of feeling, intelligence, and purposefulness. Human activity involves the intelligent pursuit of ends or goals and these are lacking in the scheme.

The question of purposeful engagement with the world was significant in another regard since, for Dewey, it was involved in the determination of what a stimulus to action may be. There was a tendency among those who assumed the stimulus-response dichotomy, without justification, to consider all physical conditions as stimuli. If everything is stimulus, nothing is stimulus, since all are equally potent. Consequently, we need to justify why some singular aspect from the field of potential stimuli arises as significant. We need to determine why some aspect of the overall scene has those properties that cause it to be singled out as significant. For Dewey the **act**, not the reflex arc, should serve as the unit of analysis for human engagements with the world.

Psychologically, the stimulus for an activity is the end or goal being pursued, and that determines what conditions will be attended to, or stand out as significant, as one works towards completion. It is a question of reasons, not causes. Consider this: When you go shopping, perhaps for shoes, do you respond to every item in the department store, all of which are potential stimuli, or do you go to the section of the store where the item you are seeking is to be found? If you are a woman, do you notice or attend to the men's shoes (the reverse question to men)? Is your behavior under the direction of your purpose or do you mechanically respond to everything? Are you purely reactive in your engagement with your environment or are you active and intentional? These are phenomenological questions that physiological concerns may not apply to.

I should emphasize that Dewey was not discounting the physiological. The psychological rested upon the biological but it had its own characteristics that explanatory reduction to the physiological did not capture.

4.3 TOWARDS RESOLVING THE DICHOTOMY

Lev Vygotsky (1896–1934) recognized what he called a 'crisis' in psychology (Vygotsky, 1927/1997). The field was divided into two basic camps: 1) the natural scientific, materialist; and 2) the spiritualist, or phenomenological, which appeared to be hopelessly opposed. The natural scientists sought to explain the basic mechanisms of psychological processes, such as reflexes and sensory biomechanics, but they failed to provide explanations of higher mental processes like beliefs and purposes. The other side had little interest in the scientific investigation of elementary processes, focusing instead on complex mental processes like abstract thought, will, or subjective experience. Their approach, though, tended toward description without explanation. It seemed as though they were in agreement that their separation was beyond resolution.

The solution to Vygotsky was to trace the origins of psychological phenomena and to discover their characteristics (Leontiev and Luria, 1968). What was required was a move beyond the naturalistic study of psychological phenomena, its biological basis, to interpret it as a product of social history and sociohistorical development. Vygotsky's solution was the basis of Chapter 1, so I will simply refer you back there.

SUMMARY

From the time Descartes' two general approaches to explaining humans have been the materialist and the idealist which were represented in the 'new' experimental psychology as physiological psychology and phenomenology.

- While Descartes had distinguished between mind and body, the natural scientists gradually moved away from metaphysics to scientific examination.
- Three trends were evident in the transition to the move to physiological psychology: (A) the differentiated activity associated with specific nerves; (B) identification of the functions of the spinal cord and of spinal reflexes; (C) specifying the localized functions of the brain.
- Mechanism ultimately displaced vitalistic assumptions.
- Studies of sensation and perception brought into question the possibility of direct knowledge of the objective reality.

(Continued)

(Continued)

- Phenomenological approaches questioned the dismissal of human experience and emphasized the role of consciousness in human life.

- The reflex arc was challenged as a valid model of human activity.

- The crisis of opposition between physiology and phenomenology required consideration of species, and cultural, evolution.

SUGGESTED READINGS

Brazier, M. A. B. (1959). The historical development of neurophysiology. In J. Field, H. W. Magoun, and V. E. Hall (Eds.), *Handbook of physiology. Vol. 1: Neurophysiology* (pp. 1–58). Washington, DC: American Physiological Society.

Dewey, J. (1896). The reflex arc concept in psychology. *Psychological Review, 3,* 357–370.

Dewey, J. (1928). Body and mind. *Mental Hygiene, 12,* 1–17.

Vygotsky, L. S. (1997). The historical meaning of the crisis in psychology: A methodological investigation. In R. W. Rieber and J. Wollock (Eds.), *The collected works of L. S. Vygotsky. Vol. 3: Problems of the theory and history of psychology*. New York: Plenum Press. (Originally unpublished manuscript written 1927.)

Young, R. M. (1990). *Mind, brain, and adaptation in the nineteenth century: Cerebral localization and its biological context from Gall to Ferrier.* New York: Oxford University Press.

Want to learn more? For links to online resources, examples of multiple choice questions, conceptual exercises and much more, visit the companion website at **https://study.sagepub.com/piekkola**

5

NATURE AND NURTURE

LEARNING OBJECTIVE

This chapter has as its concern a debate that begins with Charles Darwin's cousin Francis Galton (1822–1911) around the degree to which human psychological functions, especially intelligence, is a matter of biological inheritance or whether experience makes any contribution. It is known as the argument over **nature** versus **nurture**. More specifically we will consider:

- Galton's dismissal of nurture in favor of eugenics and biological determinism.
- Intelligence testing and the elimination of human defect.
- **Evolutionary psychology** and the explanation of human activity as adaptations to ancient environmental challenges encoded in brain mechanisms.
- Cultural psychology's explanations of human conduct in terms of historical, cultural developments and processes.

You should become sensitized to the potential harm that can come from, and is associated with, biological determinism as an explanatory paradigm and of its limitations.

FRAMING QUESTIONS

- Do you believe that some people are naturally superior/inferior to other people and that there is nothing to do to alter innate biological influences?

- Can the mental behavior of modern humans be explained in terms of basic cognitive mechanisms of the brain that solved problems in the evolutionary past?
- If we can understand the differences between groups of people in terms of cultural influences might there be a basis for recognizing our common humanity in that?

INTRODUCTION

The terms nature and nurture were introduced by Richard Mulcaster (1531–1611), an educator, in reference to what he believed were the two influences that acted together in promoting the development of the child (West and King, 1987). Parental inheritance and experience thus worked together in establishing the capabilities of the adult. Galton, as will be explained, tended to treat these terms, and what they represent, as opposed. He favored an **hereditarian** explanation of mental faculties. Galton's arguments led to the intelligence testing movement, which in turn led to the identification of 'mental defectives' or the 'feebleminded' who would be subjected to sterilization programs upon the basis of test results. In modern times the attempt to account for human psychological functions in terms of innate capacities (nature), which were adaptive in the evolutionary past, has been taken up by evolutionary psychologists. In general, while they acknowledge that culture has a role, the tendency has been to explain human cognition as based in evolved psychological mechanisms. Cultural psychologists on the other hand believe that differences between groups are more a matter of adaptations to immediate cultural conditions (nurture) than to biological differences between people. They emphasize the importance of the appropriation of cultural products and customs to the functioning of mature psychological activity.

WHAT DO YOU THINK?

Do you believe that, regardless of your life experience, your biological inheritance is largely what determines your intellectual abilities?

5.1 GALTON: HEREDITARIANISM AND EUGENICS

Whether intentional or not, arguments in favor of biological determinism, which hereditarianism is a version of, tend to support the preservation of the status quo and class structure since superiority of position is equated with superior inheritance and that, it is contended, is as nature intended (Rose, Lewontin, and Kamin, 1984). The cream, as the old saying goes, rises to the top. Galton was one of the lucky biological specimens, a member of a long line of successful people, and he set out to prove the naturalness of the social order as being due to superior inheritance. He was also much concerned that the ranks of the inferior were rising at a much larger rate than those of eminent stock. To correct this, he would present arguments in favor of public control over reproductive activity in order to eliminate the less desirable and promote increases in the favored group for the good of society.

Hereditarianism

Galton came from a distinguished family. Among his accomplished relatives was his cousin Charles Darwin (1809–1882), from whom he derived inspiration for his own thinking. At school and university, he became aware that disposition and achievement seemed to be passed across the generations to descendants, and that one could identify pedigrees of excellence. He thought, therefore, that biological transmission or inheritance must be a contributor to superiority (and inferiority) and set to establishing empirical evidence. He searched through biographical information and concluded that families who possessed a member of 'eminence' (one of the 250 per million that attain positions of high ability—Galton, 1869/1979). He gathered further evidence on people of excellence in various fields (judges, politicians, scientists, writers) and sought the incidence of relatives with similar talent. He concluded that the incidence of excellence within families was clear evidence of the role of nature, and hereditary transmission, independent of the influence of education. Success in life was predetermined by their inherited faculties:

> I came across frequent instances in which a son, happening to inherit somewhat exclusively the qualities of his father, had been found to fail with his failures, sin with his sins, surmount with his virtues, and generally to get through life in much the same way. The course of his life had, therefore, been predetermined by his inborn faculties. (Galton, 1884, p. 180)

That was not to suggest that a person with some degree of innate talent could not benefit from education, but that people exposed to the same social influences would have their rank order determined by their nature. It further implied that the person lacking inherited capacity would derive no benefit. The laws of heredity apply to the body and to mental powers and one cannot train what one lacks. Social advantage is no aid in raising those of mediocre ability to higher attainment.

Galton's proposition of mental heredity was criticized on the grounds that he failed to consider that the people like himself had the benefit of superior social circumstances that the less fortunate lacked (Galton, 1875/2012). Galton had considered it. In fact, he

(Galton, 1869/1979) had attempted to address this by considering the effect of papal adoptions. Popes and other church dignitaries offered social aid and education to nephews, or less close relatives, and to others from less fortunate circumstances. Despite the social advantage of superior education few achieved positions of eminence in society. The social advantage was the same but the lack of hereditary gifts rendered that of no help. Since his detractors were undeterred, Galton (1975/2012) developed a new methodology to examine the effects of heredity. The **twin method**, a now standard method of estimating heredity, involved comparing monozygotic (identical) and dizygotic (fraternal) twins to assess their degree of similarity. He expected and found identical twins were more alike than fraternal twins. It should be noted that Galton had no means of determining the twin's actual type (identical or fraternal), beyond being the same sex. He simply reasoned that the results were as to be expected if character and physique were determined by heredity as opposed to the environment (Fancher, 1985). In this he failed to consider the impact of being treated alike due to looking alike, and how that contributed to subsequent similarity.

Behind Galton's efforts was the hereditarian doctrine and the belief that the notion of the natural equality of humans was erroneous (Dennis, 1995). There was considerable variability in the possession of innate intellectual ability and Galton (1885) aimed to examine the distribution of intelligence in the population. He established a research station at the International Health Exhibition in London (1884) to test his ideas. He assessed keenness of eyesight, color vision, hearing, and muscular strength, among others. Galton, in these investigations, established the 'mental testing movement' and it established him as the founder of experimental psychology in Britain (Burt, 1962).

An underlying assumption in what Galton tested was that intelligence was an inherited property of the nervous system and, since the senses were related to the nervous system, sensitivity was correlated with intelligence (Fancher, 1985), which explains the tests of sensory acuity. As he expected, Galton found that sense-discrimination was greatest among those who were highest in their intellectual ability—members of the Royal Society (although academics proved poor at visualization compared to the lower classes). The 'sensation-as-indicator-of-intelligence' proposition was somewhat implicit in Galton, but Charles Spearman (1863–1945), another early contributor to the intelligence testing movement, would make it explicit. He believed intelligence was unitary—a 'general intelligence'—and was best determined by measures of sensory discrimination. The main point is that intelligence is biologically based, inherited, and variable in the population.

Eugenics

What would become **eugenics** was already anticipated in Galton (1869/1979), where he noted that, just as could be done with the selective breeding of animals, certain characteristics could be promoted in humans through judicious mating (marriages) of consecutive generations of humans. He put it thus:

> I argue that, as a new race can be obtained in animals and plants, and can be raised to so great a degree of purity that it will maintain itself, with moderate care in preventing the more faulty members of the flock from breeding, so a race of gifted men might be obtained, under similar conditions. (Galton, 1869/1978, p. 64)

The elimination of faulty members would also be part of the program. The point of eugenics was the scientific improvement of a race's innate qualities (Galton, 1904). This would increase the frequency in the population of the higher ability that was represented in the upper classes. Where nature is slow and blind, humans can act intelligently and quickly. Actually, Galton wrote 'man', not 'humans', since male chauvinism was prevalent at the time (to be discussed in Chapter 9).

Galton (1905) fully appreciated that his proposed science of, and control over, people's mating opportunities by social agencies would be resisted. In order to counter interference, he presented a history of different social customs that had put a check on natural instincts by regulating breeding practices. Galton gave examples: Monogamy was favored by some cultures, but others, like Muslims and Mormons, advocated polygamy (simultaneous multiple spouses). For some, polygamy is outlawed. Then there were the religious and legal sanctions exercised in favor of endogamy (restricting union upon the basis of ethnicity, class, caste, or other social category) or exogamy (marrying outside one's group). There were also a multitude of taboos that enculturate repugnance for acts like incest. Yet at one time, in ancient Egypt and Greece, incest was acceptable. His point was that what has been enforced has varied historically and culturally yet the people complied.

Based on his review of these socially regulated practices, Galton concluded that the future regulation of non-eugenic unions would meet with little loathing by the public. There may be initial resistance, but people who were born into such imposed customs would offer no resistance. Furthermore, public opinion was arising in support of regulating the propagation of criminal offspring. Then there were the people who were incapable of caring for themselves. The ranks of the feebleminded could be reduced in the population, however, by removing social institutions that helped them survive or enabled the production of offspring. Indiscriminate charity to those who could not cope with life circumstances, like today's food banks and soup kitchens or welfare programs, were non-eugenic and should be curtailed. Ultimately, Galton envisioned the provision of eugenic certificates granting breeding rights to those possessing socially valued qualities. This would speed up the course of human evolution in a positive direction. Galton's views on this were in line with the social theory known as **social Darwinism**.

5.2 SOCIAL DARWINISM

The idea of social Darwinism originates with Herbert Spencer (1820–1903), a contemporary of Galton and Darwin, who asserted that "Society advances where its fittest members are allowed to assert their fitness with the least hindrance, and where the least fitted are not artificially prevented from dying out" (in Wiltshire, 1978, p. 197). Not only should the demise of undesirables not be guarded against, the best government would be one that increased hardship to accelerate their elimination. They must be impervious to their suffering. Spencer, not Darwin, introduced the idea of **survival of the fittest**, the proposition that species move towards perfection by struggling to adjust to environmental challenges to existence. Those best able to adapt, to compete against others, would defeat and eliminate the less capable (less fit) before they can breed and disseminate their maladaptive natures through the population. Through such natural struggle perfection might be approached. So, by banishing hardship, society would be supporting its own degradation.

Malthus

Darwin wrote the *Origin of the Species* in 1859, but Spencer introduced the 'survival of the fittest' in 1852 and the idea of 'struggle for existence' came from Malthus in 1798 (J. A. Rogers, 1972). **Thomas Malthus** (1766–1834) proposed that populations eventually reach a multitude that cannot be supported by environmental resources and that the excess would be weeded out through the struggle to survive. These ideas, often attributed to Darwin, became central to the dogma of social Darwinism. Darwin was not responsible for these social doctrines and, originally, he did not apply his theory of natural selection to social evolution. He (Darwin, 1874/1998) took up the matter in *The Descent of Man*. There he wrote that among savages (the vernacular of the time) those who were weak in mind or body would be eliminated. Civilized people, by contrast, guarded against that by introducing asylums and other supports for the poor, that allowed the unfit to survive and reproduce offspring—a practice injurious to the race as a whole. Only the ignorant farmer would allow his worst animals to continue to breed and, even though he didn't state it, the implication is that this holds for humans as well. The unfit should be eliminated for the betterment of the whole.

Eugenics and social Darwinism would be taken up wholeheartedly in Nazi Germany under the goal of racial hygiene and the purification of the German people (David, Fleischhacker, and Hohn, 1988). Blaming the post-World War I woes of Germany on the inferior races in German society, Hitler established a program of racial purity. This would eliminate racial impurities, defectives and imbeciles. Millions of people were sterilized or put to death in the cleansing operation. Eugenic programs, you should know, were not restricted to Germany. During the 1920s and 30s eugenic sterilization laws were passed in the United States, Canada, and Sweden (Kevles, 1999), but they were not the only ones. In Britain, the attempt to introduce sterilization laws through the Mental Deficiency Act of 1913 was defeated as a matter of human rights. In North America, the favorite tool for identifying defectives for sterilization was the recently invented Intelligence Test. As the British eugenicist Cyril Burt (1883–1971) put it, psychological testing is of extreme importance to the eugenicist movement (Burt, 1914). So it was.

5.3 THE IQ CONTROVERSY

Mental testing

As mentioned, Galton (1885) inaugurated the mental testing movement with the tests he administered at the International Health Exhibition. Although his own tests would prove to be inadequate to the task, he was inspirational in other ways. Charles Spearman, in Britain, took up the notion that differences in sensory acuity would correspond to differences in intelligence. In particular, he accepted that intelligence was a characteristic that was primarily inherited (Fancher, 1985). He also proposed that intelligence was a singular something he would call **general intelligence** that manifested in various forms of intellectual ability. He created a mathematical procedure called factor analysis to show how different intellectual indicators were interrelated by some underlying, common thread that could be identified mathematically. As Spearman was a member of the Eugenics Society, he hoped his work would spur governments to regulate reproduction. As mentioned, in Britain the effort failed, but North America was a different matter.

Galton's measures were brought to North America by James McKeen Cattell (1860–1944), his student, who called them 'mental tests.' Cattell also accepted that intelligence was inherited and related to sensory acuity. Devising tests of weight discrimination, touch sensitivity, reaction times, and others, he assumed that since they were all measures of the same phenomenon, expressed differently, they should correlate with each other (Hergenhahn and Henley, 2014). Furthermore, he proposed that they should correspond with indicators of academic success (thus introducing the testing criteria of **validity** and **concurrent validity**). The hypothesis was put to the test by his student, Wissler (1901), who found that the individual measures correlated neither with each other nor with college performance. That put an end to Galtonian tests but not intelligence testing.

The Binet test

Mass education was introduced during the 19th century and, in France, an issue arose regarding children who were mentally deficient and how best to educate them (Hergenhahn and Henley, 2014). The intent was benign in that they aimed to identify children who were not profiting from ordinary schooling and in need of placement in special classes, to receive special education outside the normal school (Binet and Simon, 1905/1916a). How, though, was one to identify those children? Alfred Binet (1857–1911) and Theodore Simon (1872–1961) were appointed in 1904 to devise a method to accomplish that. Fundamental to intelligence and everyday life, they believed, was the faculty of judgment or practical sense, and an ability to adapt to circumstances. Binet, in this, was in opposition to Galton, Spearman, and Cattell, since he questioned the notion that measures of sensory acuity would tap into intelligence (Burt, 1914). Even deaf-blind people, like Helen Keller (1880–1968), can display extreme intelligence; that indicates that the senses are not a factor in mental functioning, and that they were not equivalent to judgment (Binet and Simon, 1905/1916c). More direct tests of intelligence had to be devised. In the end, the test they developed assessed skills that would be needed for schoolwork, along with the practical knowledge needed to function in the everyday world, in other words judgment.

Binet and Simon set out to design tests that could distinguish between 'normals' and 'subnormals' in terms of intellectual functions. To do so they devised a series of tests of increasing difficulty (Binet and Simon, 1905/1916b). They identified two factors that had to be considered: intellectual age and age since birth (now termed mental age and chronological age). William Stern made a ratio of the two (mental age/chronological age) and called it the **Intelligence Quotient** or IQ (Fancher, 1985). The Binet-Simon tests were arranged in groups such that each series corresponded with a particular 'mental level.' They examined motor coordination and motor skills, attention, immediate memory, recognition, comparison and differentiation, abstract thought and reasoning, and other abilities. As they emphasized, however, their measures were not assessing intelligence since intellectual qualities do not superpose (map onto exactly) linear scales; they were not actually 'measurements' of something quantifiable. It was simply a means of classification of what is a diversity of abilities (not a single, unitary something called intelligence). What the measures would do was indicate how far ahead or behind an individual was compared to others of their age. That would eventually support the determination of where on the scale the idiot, imbecile, or moron may be found and, later, identified.

Goddard and feeblemindedness

The Binet-Simon test was found in Europe (1908) by the American Henry Goddard (1866–1957) who brought it to North America, and translated it, for use in identifying children of different levels of defect (Goddard, 1916a). This he did at the Vineland, New Jersey, Training School for Backward and Feeble-minded Children, but he (Goddard, 1910) recognized an inherent difficulty in applying the test in the United States. There were differences between civilizations (cultural differences) in terms of what enters into the child's life conditions. American children may well be unfamiliar with questions pertaining to France, like who Marie Antoinette was or what the Eiffel Tower was. Lewis Terman (1877–1956) would correct this in 1916 by standardizing the test for Americans in his Stanford-Binet version (Fancher, 1985). Goddard (1910/1991), in the meantime, introduced gradations of defect based on test scores: low- and high-grade idiots, imbeciles, and, at the high end, the feebleminded whom, since the term had been used previously to refer the whole range of mental defectives, he labeled morons. The test was about to serve eugenic purposes.

The feebleminded were becoming an issue of social concern, since they were becoming a burden on society, and it was feared they may spread their defect throughout the population. Goddard (1911) intended to do something. He proposed that if feeble-mindedness could be eliminated then it should be. What good, after all, did idiots, who cannot care for themselves, serve? The feeble-minded were a drain on society; they became criminals or dependent on charity. In Goddard's estimation, a large percentage of criminals, prostitutes and paupers were feebleminded, and, while unproven, it was highly likely that the condition was hereditary. Humanity, he speculated, would not support putting them to sleep (like a sickly animal), but it might be possible to obtain support in putting an end to their propagation. Two possibilities offered themselves: sterilization or segregation and placement in colonies that could replace the prisons and almshouses. Sterilization, he pointed out, was already being performed in two states.

By Goddard's estimate, probably one in every two hundred people was feebleminded and they were likely to make up the ranks of paupers, drunkards, prostitutes, criminals and other ne'er-do-wells (Goddard, 1913a). Diagnosing these people would be a first step in dealing with the problem and, to that end, family histories would help. If a person, already identified as feebleminded, had a family history of relatives with an incapacity to care for themselves or their family, there may be strong evidence of hereditary defect. Goddard was, in this, pointing to his study of what would become an infamous case—the Kallikak family (Goddard, 1912).

Deborah Kallikak came to the Vineland school for the feebleminded in 1898 at the age of eight. She came from an almshouse and was an illegitimate. Her mother could not support her and she was trouble in school, so she was brought to Vineland. She could wash and dress herself, understood commands but was disobedient, knew a few letters but could not read or count, was destructive and obstinate. At age 22 she was assessed to have a mental age of nine years—moron grade. Goddard asked why she was like that. His answer: "heredity" or bad stock. He traced her family history through a long line of 262 defectives— illegitimates, criminals, drunkards, prostitutes and madams. The sire of the breed, going back to the revolutionary war, started the lineage by a dalliance with a barmaid of ill fame. They produced an illegitimate son. He then married a woman of good stock which led to a line of valued citizens.

Goddard used the **Mendelian law** to account for the defective line. Gregor Mendel (1822–1884), as he wrote, had discovered a law of hereditary transmission of unit characters,

Mendelian
law

Figure 5.1   Deborah Kallikak

now known as genes, that are transmitted through reproduction. Dominant units always manifested their effects but recessive units only manifested irregularly (a recessive gene from each parent is required for the characteristic to manifest). Goddard surmised that feeblemindedness was the product of a recessive inheritance (since it manifests irregularly in offspring rather than always). Such hereditary defect was a social problem since, as Goddard claimed, society was being depreciated. Slums, he wrote, are created by individuals not individuals by slums, and "not until we take care of this class and see to it that their lives are guided by intelligent people, shall we remove these sores from our social life" (2012, p. 71). Segregation or sterilization were solutions that intelligent people should consider.

Feeblemindedness was an apparently new phenomenon and people were asking how it came to prominence so suddenly. Goddard (1913b) explained that it was there all along but, in the past, had been subject to the law of the survival of the fittest. Their stupidity eliminated them through accident or incapacity to provide for themselves. They had only come to attention through the introduction of compulsory education which led, through compassion, to institutions for their care and training. Kindness aside, something had to be done since they were becoming a menace, having reached a population of 300,000–400,000 (Goddard, 1916b). They reproduced at a rate up to six times that of intelligent people. Something had to be done. They should be sought in almshouses, insane hospitals, juvenile courts, reform schools, almshouses, asylums for the blind, or wherever dependent people may be found, and, if laws would permit, identified and sterilized—they should be 'hunted' for in every place possible.

In the United States there was growing concern as well with the entry of undesirables from other countries. A report in 1888 had raised concern about what it referred to as "nameless abominations," arriving from Asia and Europe, the "sewage of vice and crime and physical weakness" (Gelb, 1986, p. 325). In 1912 Goddard was invited to Ellis Island to offer suggestions about incoming immigrants and the detection of defectiveness (Goddard, 1917). Of course, mental testing was introduced. The underlying rationale was that the country was producing enough defectives of its own without importing more. It was recognized that some immigrants were handicapped by not having been to school and developing the necessary skills to pass the tests, such as holding a pen. Nonetheless, testing to identify the congenitally defective proceeded; the country had to be protected.

Among the nationalities tested by Goddard many were feebleminded and in need of deportation. The figures vary but Snyderman and Herrnstein (1983) put them at 83 percent for Jews, Hungarians (80 percent), Italians (79 percent), and Russians (87 percent). Goddard, in fairness, did not intend to generalize to those populations as a whole, but many of the immigrants tested were deemed undesirable. As Terman (1922) suggested, "No nation can afford to overlook the danger that the average quality of its germ plasm (the inherited component) may gradually deteriorate as a result of unrestricted immigration" (p. 660). Whether influenced by the intelligence testers or not, the United States passed the Immigration Law of 1924 that severely restricted immigration on the basis of nationality. The eugenicist movement also succeeded in getting sterilization laws for the feebleminded passed in many states in the name of national preservation. As of 1966, nearly 70,000 people were sterilized for feeblemindedness in the US (Kendregan, 1966).

Goddard (1920) summarized his position in the following:

Stated in its boldest form our thesis is that the chief determiner of human conduct is a unitary mental process which we call intelligence: that this process is conditioned by a nervous mechanism which is inborn: that the degree of efficiency to be attained by that nervous mechanism and the consequent grade of intelligence or mental level for each individual is determined by the kind of chromosomes that come together with the union of the germ cells: that it is but little affected by any later influences except such serious accidents as may destroy part of the mechanism. (p. 1)

So intelligence is unitary, due to an inherited nervous system (nature) that fixes the level of intellectual functioning, and is little effected by experiences (nurture). It had to be distinguished, though, from what was acquired through learning, knowledge in other words. Knowledge and

Figure 5.2 A eugenics poster from the 1920s warns of the scourge of mental defectives. A light flashes every 16 seconds to indicate another birth. Every 48 seconds another flashes to indicate the birth of a mental defective. Every 50 seconds a third indicates someone going to jail (usually not normal people). A final light flashes every 7.5 minutes to indicate the birth of a valuable citizen

With permission from The American Philosophical Society.

intelligence should not be confused. Being determined by heredity, dependent on the brain, mental level was expected to be stable throughout development. Much money, he proposed, was being wasted trying to alleviate their intolerable conditions (such as the special schools the French desired). The best education should be provided therefore to those most likely to benefit from it—those superior in mentality. Education, no matter how good the intention, was not going to change innate intelligence.

Intelligence tests were also applied to people of other races. They were assessed based on the norms set by White people on the intelligence test. I won't go into that literature, but Terman (1922) was reporting that only 15 percent of Black folks, native Americans, and Mexicans were equal to or exceeded the White average. During the 1960s it was being reported that Blacks, in comparison to Whites, had an average IQ that was 10–15 points lower (Lerner, 1976). Arthur Jensen, a hereditarian, interpreted such findings as reflecting genetic differences and argued that supplementary education would do nothing to ameliorate the difference (to be hereditary is to be fixed). More recently Herrnstein and Murray (1994) restated the hereditarian position by proposing that

- intelligence is a single quality that is heritable

- people of low IQ are having more babies than people of high IQ—the nation's intelligence is dwindling, declining (Goddard's concern)

- the US may be divided soon into a huge, low IQ, underclass and a small, high IQ ruling class—a cognitive meritocracy (stratification based on merit)

- educational programs can do little to raise IQs.

The hereditarian argument has been quite durable.

BOX 5.1
"RACIAL DIFFERENCES IN MENTAL TRAITS"

During the 19th century, as a result of increasing contact with so-called primitive peoples, attempts were being made to scientifically demonstrate Caucasian superiority. Nott and Gliddon (1868, in S. Gould, 1981) compared the shape of a Negroid skull with

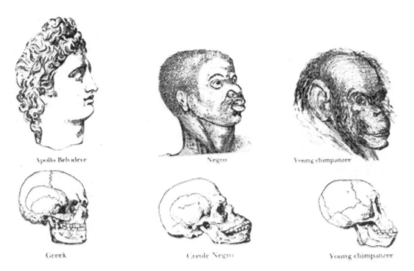

Types of Mankind, 1854

Figure 5.3   Racial skull comparisons

(Continued)

(Continued)

chimpanzees and found similarities; he judged those humans to be at a primitive level of evolutionary development. Down's Syndrome (or trisomy 21), a mental disorder resulting in varying levels of retardation, was called Mongolism by the 'good?' doctor Down because of facial similarities (associated with the disorder) to people from Mongolia. The conclusion, in a paper entitled "Observations on an ethnic classification of idiots," was that White, congenital idiots were typical of the Mongol. I won't offer more examples; I think you get the idea.

Not everyone back then was a racist. Robert Woodworth (1869–1962), who wrote the 'Bible' (Woodworth, 1938) for how to conduct psychological research, was unconvinced by the racial typologies of the day (Woodworth, 1910). He wrote that it is often satisfying intellectually to identify clear distinctions in phenomena that seem to be superficially alike, and to distinguish them from those that are unalike. That done, lines of separation are drawn between them and they are presented as wholly unrelated. Looked at more closely, the differences are actually a matter of degree rather than exclusion. To find two groups whose averages vary on some performance measure is an inadequate basis for demarcation. Going beyond the average, and considering the complete distribution, the within group range of variation may reveal much overlap that the averages conceal. Woodworth meant that, while there is a difference between the averages, the distributions overlap a great deal—a lot of the people in each group were alike. Examination of brain weight, which seems closely related to intelligence and civilization, shows much overlap between Black folk and Europeans, despite an average weight that is two ounces lower for Blacks. To transform such 'differences in degree' into 'differences of kind' is ludicrous when there is so much overlap. The same applies to the mental processes that psychologists recognize (sensation, memory, imagery, emotions, discrimination, comparison, reasoning, and inventiveness); all are within the capabilities of every human race and none are excluded.

To Woodworth, one must dismiss the notion that the powers of 'savages' (sorry, that is the vernacular of the day) for abstraction, reasoning, and foresight are lacking. If the savage differs in that regard from the civilized person, it is, again, a matter of degree. People differ from each other not so much in their power to attend, reason, or remember, as they do in the materials to which these powers are applied. The ability to deal with a particular subject matter is certainly determined in part by native endowment, but training too is very much involved. To assume that what we test for, which is familiar to us, is familiar to other peoples may be unfair given different cultures and ways of life. Without actually studying mental powers, folk psychology (non-scientific) turns to a comparison at the level of civilization and achievements. 'Primitive societies,' those that are lacking in civilization and advanced technologies, do not fare well in comparison to more advanced human groups. The assumption that follows is that a lack of civilization implies a lack of intelligence in the less developed group. To Woodworth, differences in material civilization do not necessitate the conclusion that the difference is due to differences in intellectual potential. The modern German (of 1910) has, on average, greater natural inventiveness or business acumen than the German of sixty generations past, but that does not mean they are a different race. Levels of achieved civilization are not an indicator of the intelligence of a group. Progress depends on invention and the dissemination of acquired knowledge, and on population since larger populations have greater numbers of inventive individuals.

Woodworth offered a thought experiment: Imagine two habitats, as similar as possible, completely isolated from all other communities. Next, imagine populating those habitats with groups of children from highly civilized nations, and that each child has a child equivalent to it in the other group. Place the children in their habitats, without any human technologies or culturally-generated intellectual tools (language for instance), at infancy. Further assume that the infant groups survive to maturity. Now, ask yourself if you think that, over a number of generations, these two groups, initially equal in heredity and environment, would be similar. Differences in mating will produce variability in offspring from the start, but that would not affect average performance. Then consider accidents of invention, since they would be unlikely to invent the same things, despite equal intelligence. After a thousand generations there would likely be divergences in language, culture, customs, and so on. Accidental factors affect the rise of civilization and the differences in culture could be explained without having to infer different mental endowments of the two races. Evolutionary psychologists do not believe that 10,000 years is enough time for evolutionary change (Bereczkei, 2000) so the differences are likely not biological. Of course, Woodworth's point was that the level of civilization or high culture is not an indicator of intellectual defect or superiority.

Before proceeding I should mention that there is little agreement as to what intelligence actually is. Spearman, using factor analysis, believed, and demonstrated mathematically, that it was an underlying general capacity—general intelligence. Thurstone (1938, in Hilgard, 1987) developed a new type of factor analysis that yielded multiple scores instead of Spearman's one. Based on that he identified various 'primary mental abilities' which are basic units that collectively make up overall intelligence (verbal comprehension and fluency, memory, numerical, perceptual speed, reasoning, and spatial skills). Gardner (1999, in Galotti, 2014) examined intellectual losses due to brain damage, and studies of people with exceptional talents, and proposed that Western societies have placed an emphasis on logical-mathematical and linguistic competence and ignored other forms of intelligence (musical, spatial, kinesthetic, interpersonal, intrapersonal, naturalist, and existential). Rather than assessing innate 'general intelligence,' Richardson (2002) proposed that performance on IQ tests is actually a reflection of sociocognitive-affective factors that prepare people for the areas tested (and not something independent of experience) and is more a function of class values than ability for complex cognition. The debate continues.

BOX 5.2
THE FIXITY OF INTELLIGENCE ASSESSED AS IQ

An essential idea of the eugenicists was that intelligence was inherited, uninfluenced by experience, fixed and unchanging. This assumption was soon challenged by research into the IQ. Gordon (1923/1970), for example, examined the 'canal boat people' of Britain. They were born, lived and died on boats moving goods through the inland canals. They, compared to people of their class in cities, were of good health and well-being. Their 'intelligence,' however, as measured by IQ, decreased with age and was not fixed. Every year of increased age was correlated with a decrease in IQ. These children seldom attended school and, when they did, it was at a different location, wherever they happened to dock. This decline is not that surprising when one considers that IQ tests are most valid for the assessment of skills associated with schoolwork—verbal comprehension and abstract reasoning (Bernstein, Clarke-Stewart, Roy, and Wickens, 1997). Wheeler (1932) too found a decrease in IQ with an increase in age among East Tennessee isolated mountain dwellers. Schools had only just been introduced, and when he returned a decade later (Wheeler, 1942) IQ still decreased with age but the 1940 group had gained about nine months in average mental age. I suspect that if they were tested today they would be at a normal level. Flynn (1987), in what has been termed the 'Flynn Effect,' found that IQ has increased 5–25 IQ points in 14 nations, including some European nations, Japan, India, Latin America, and Canada, in one generation. If intelligence is fixed, the Intelligence Quotient is not the means for its demonstration.

Studies of children in institutions have also demonstrated a decrease in intelligence (IQ) with age. Skeels and Dye (1939), due to overcrowding at an orphanage for mentally retarded children, reported increases in intelligence in the presumed mentally retarded children upon transfer to a more stimulating environment. It is unclear how they were judged mentally defective. If you consider the impact of the eugenicist arguments, and the fact that many of these children were born illegitimate, a factor may have been an assumption of parental retardation since one would have to have been retarded to have children out of wedlock. A group of twelve children from the overcrowded orphanage were transferred to an institute for feebleminded children. There, young girls doted on them, played with them, and basically gave them the stimulation they would be deprived of in the orphanage. The orphanage operated on what might be called a horticultural principle—they were fed and watered and that was considered sufficient. Social stimulation—nurture—had been lacking.

Two years later the transferred children were shockingly different. They were vibrant, active, bright young kids who were deemed suitable for adoption (it had been assumed they would be institution-bound, unadoptable due to retardation, like those left at the orphanage). At transfer the children had an average IQ of 64 which increased to 92 after two years. A comparison group of children who remained behind showed average decreases of 26 points from the original 87. In a follow-up nearly 30 years later, Skeels (1966) found that the transferred children were thriving, well educated, and successful, but the comparison group remained mostly institutionalized. Skeels concluded that institutionalization may itself be a retarding influence.

5.4 EVOLUTIONARY PSYCHOLOGY AND CULTURAL PSYCHOLOGY

Evolutionary psychology

Evolutionary psychology, a relatively recent approach, falls on the nature side of what we have been considering. Its aim is to identify the selection pressures (recurring challenges from the environment and interpersonal interactions) that shaped the human mind, its mechanisms, and functions, and to demonstrate their operation in modern humans (Barrett, Dunbar, and Lycett, 2002). In a sense, the approach is aligned with cognitive neuroscience since its conception of mind is in terms of the brain and the functional systems that evolved for specialized adaptive purposes. The focus for evolutionary psychologists is on the mind as a product of the environment of 'evolutionary adaptiveness,' dating back to pre-agricultural, hunter-gatherer times (Lewin and Foley, 2004). The models suggested are speculative since the archaeological record has not provided the information needed to test the hypotheses. As a result, the tendency is to speculate about what the environment must have been like had it yielded the adaptations now embodied as processing mechanisms in the brain.

The essence of this position is that natural selection, during the Pleistocene era (around 2 million–10,000 years ago), led to the development of information processing systems that were adaptive, especially those concerned with social exchanges or interpersonal activity (Cosmides and Tooby, 1989). Such social adaptations include parental investment in off-spring, kinship, friendship, cooperation, selective aggression, and status hierarchies (Confer et al., 2010). Historically these evolved because they supported survival and reproduction and, even though we no longer live in the environment adapted to, they are regarded as determinative in social interchanges today. Human beings continue to live in groups and how they interact with one another is determined by the information they are provided with, and assess, in arriving at an appropriate behavior (Cosmides and Tooby, 1989). Such behavior patterns reverberate or are repeated throughout the group and this results in the production of culture. The study of culture is, therefore, the investigation of how environmental infor-mation, especially social, may be expected to have an effect on the behavior of individuals. To understand cultural processes is to discover the innate mechanisms for processing social information. Such a conception of culture ignores the realm of historically evolved meanings that we inhabit, emphasizing instead what of it fits their evolutionary concerns.

The mind is an assembly of psychological adaptations that are specialized for producing solutions to particular problems, problems that originally had to do with survival and repro-duction, which made them adaptive (Confer et al., 2010). An adequate, mature psychology is required to consider psychological adaptation as indispensable to understanding rather than optional. Psychology, in the past, has tended to focus on **proximate explanation,** or how the mechanism works, rather than **ultimate explanation,** or why the function exists (what adaptive function it serves). By adopting an evolutionary perspective, it is claimed that the dichoto-mies of nature versus nurture, and biology versus culture, are dissolved. Mechanisms evolved phylogenetically due to natural selection and, ontogenetically, the environment continues to influence development because processed input is needed to activate evolved mechanisms.

Socialization is acknowledged, but socialization theory is judged more complete when informed by evolutionary analysis (presumably speculation as to how current social conduct is ultimately an expression of evolved mechanisms). Learning, socialization, or culture, are not explanations, nor are they alternatives to evolutionary explanations; they are ultimately designed by evolved psychological mechanisms (Buss, 1995). Culture is apparently con-ceived of as independent of psychological functioning by evolutionary psychologists who adopt an assumption of 'methodological individualism' (Bereczkei, 2000). Rather than being embedded within a cultural milieu that conditions individual consciousness, individuals evolved mechanisms that allow them to choose from the alternatives a culture provides. What a culture offers is weighed for value, in terms of costs and benefits, to personal behavior (presumably in terms of survival and reproduction). Individuals are not passively molded by their society, but selectively partake of it.

Transmitted culture can itself impose selection pressures if active over many generations (Buss, 1995). Presumably, cultures exist because of their relevance to survival and reproduction. So, I assume, in thousands of years our brains may develop mechanisms adapted to social media, if social media are adaptive. Actually, the usual strategy is to propose that current practices are an expression of more basic evolved mechanisms for social interaction. As Crosier, Webster, and Dillon (2012) explained, our lives are dominated by social networks but these have always existed throughout the history of the species. What has changed is merely the venue (electronic) for their expression. Modern communication devices are a new way of engaging in ancient human sociality.

Perhaps the most familiar theory in evolutionary psychology is Buss' (1989) theory of sex preferences in mates as evolved strategies for ensuring reproductive viability and success. Preferential mating practices likely resulted in successful progeny who transmit those characteristics to subsequent generations and evolve into cues that signal mate viability. Those males and females who possess the preferred characteristics will make mating more likely but will differ based on **parental investment**. Given that human females typically rear children, they may be choosier in whom they mate with; seeking out the most likely, committed provider. Males, by comparison, are freer to impregnate and move on, seeking fertile partners to maximize offspring. Reproductive value drives choice. Despite variability over cultures regarding standards of beauty, it was expected that there are species-typical sex differences among all humans. Thus, Buss reported evidence from 37 cultures suggesting that males seek out females who display characteristics of reproductive capacity and females prefer good providers.

Kanazawa (2010) has applied evolutionary thinking to the question of 'general intelligence,' which was thought to be a problem for evolutionary psychology. The difficulty had to do with the contention that the brain is composed of domain-specific, psychological mechanisms, designed to address particular problems of survival and reproduction. Specificity, however, is not generality, so what is to be done? General intelligence, Kanazawa suggested, may have evolved originally as an adaptation to evolutionary problems that were non-recurring and novel. To the degree that such novel challenges confronted our ancient ancestors with sufficient frequency, they would have developed a biologically rooted mechanism that is general intelligence (the specificity of variability). William Stern (1914, in Fancher, 1985) defined intelligence as "a general capacity of an individual consciously to adjust his thinking to new requirements, … a general mental adaptability to new problems and conditions of life" (p. 101). Do we really need to specify some dedicated mechanism, or is a general function sufficient?

It should come as no surprise that evolutionary psychology has had its detractors. One such issue was recognized by Confer et al. (2010): we are limited by a lack of comprehensive knowledge of the numerous selection pressures faced over the ages of evolution. Buller (2009), in line with that, proposed that we need precise knowledge of the actual conditions, not speculations about conditions, if we are to figure out strategies that may have been used, and, for now, the evidence is scant. In line with that, we also require knowledge of what traits were possessed by these archaic humans since natural selection modifies pre-existing material in effecting adaptation. When it comes to social interactions, this is particularly difficult to assess since the paleontological record is mostly silent in that regard. As a result, evolutionary psychologists have been charged with relying on **just so stories** or offering unverifiable explanations (Holcomb, 1996). To Rose (2000) this results in a **circular argument**. Current behavior is examined, an inference or speculation is offered as to why it was adaptive in the past, and the speculation is transformed into a cause of the very phenomenon it was inferred from. To put it more concretely, I see someone who is combative and infer a combative disposition from that. I then explain the original combativeness as being due to the combative disposition (behavior → inference → behavior which is actually behavior → behavior).

Mayr (1997), from the perspective of biology, accepted that the brain achieved its current capacity around 100,000 years ago, when humans were quite primitive, but it is the same brain that has designed computers. In that regard the extremely specialized mental activities that humans perform today do not require positing particular brain structures. There is no doubt that certain areas are rigidly programmed for particular functions, like breathing and sight, but that does not mean that all of the brain is so programmed, or that everything that can be done must have a related, rigidly specified brain mechanism. The brain appears to have areas that are specified beforehand and are available for 'open programs' that can accommodate specificity after birth through experience and learning. As Rose (2000) proposed, the path of evolution led to a human brain that is exceedingly plastic and adaptable.

Dewey's (1898) thoughts on the notion of 'fitness,' as in survival of the fittest, are relevant here. The term fit, he argued, had been used widely to refer to an environment from the past which no longer exists. Fitness, he contended, can only apply to contemporary conditions and human life has changed drastically since the era of biological adaptations—civilization and later industrialization create their own demands:

> The environment is now distinctly a social one, and the content of the term "fit" has to be made with reference to social adaptation. Moreover, the environment in which we now live is a changing and progressive one. Every one must have his fitness judged by the whole, including the anticipated change; not merely by reference to the conditions of to-day, because these may be gone to-morrow. (p. 328)

Not only do people need to be adjusted to today, they must be able to adjust to changing conditions. What is adaptable and fit is flexibility.

Cultural psychology

In addressing **cultural psychology** I must first distinguish it from **cross-cultural psychology**. Cross-cultural psychology is inclined to conceive of culture as being outside of an individual and acts upon individuals like an independent variable producing differences in thought and behavior (Triandis, 2000). Cultural psychology, in contrast, is more likely to conceive of culture as being inside a person (think 'internalization'). In effect, the person is in a mutualistic relation with their cultural environment where the two are interpenetrating.

In dealing with evolutionary psychology there was an emphasis on biological evolution. Here, we are dealing with the impact of cultural evolution. It is worthwhile therefore to compare biological evolution and cultural evolution (see Figure 5.4).

Cultural evolution includes technological evolution; it refers to the changes over time in technology that give humans increased control over their environment.

The tradition of cultural psychology has its beginnings in 19th-century German *Völkerpsychologie*. The *Volk* (people) were conceived of as sharing in the pervading *Geist* (spirit) which leads to the idea of *Völkgeist* (group spirit), a lawful, objective, and subjective activity of a people which corresponds to the English word 'culture' (Kalmar, 1987). This was the **ethos** of the group as it was objectified and materialized in its institutions and practices, reflecting the group's values, concepts, beliefs, and understandings. It existed on two planes or as two forms of existence: internally, within the individual as dispositions, attitudes, and beliefs, and externally, as embodied in material forms—books, monuments, institutions, et cetera (Jahoda, 1993). The aim, therefore, of *Völkerpsychologie* was to reveal the ways

Biological Evolution	Cultural Evolution
Transmission is from parents to biological offspring	Transmission is social and may involve people unrelated biologically
Transmission is to the successive generations	Transmission is within and between generations (separated by time and space)
Transmitted through genes	Transmitted by communication
Occurs slowly—many generations of reproduction	Occurs rapidly without biological, genetic transmission
Genes are not a personal choice	Cultural traits can be chosen or rejected

Figure 5.4   Comparing biological and cultural evolution

that common activities in a group or nation created objective cultural forms and how these, subsequently, had the ensuing individuals as their product (Danziger, 1983). Through common social activity the group develops cultural organizations and norms which are objectified mental products that, in turn, condition the subjectivity of following generations. Wundt was discussing *Völkerpsychologie* as early as 1863 (Danziger, 1983) and was a psychological concern from the start.

Dewey's cultural psychology

Cultural psychology would not be an issue in North America until the 1960s but, much earlier, **Dewey** had already laid out an intellectual framework. Opposing biological determinism, Dewey (1939/1989) rejected the supposed fixity of human nature. He accepted that certain human needs remained constant but the consequences that follow from them are subject to the conditions of the prevailing culture (laws, customs, morals, industry, institutions, religion, art, and so on). Dewey suggested that if one were to take all of the peoples, classes, tribes, and nations, throughout history, what is relatively constant is innate, native human nature (our biological given at birth). Such constant constitution could not then be appealed to as an account of the vast diversity of practices, beliefs, and values that different social groups have displayed. Organic behavior is transformed into behavior that is psychological and intellectual as a result of life in environments that are cultural (Dewey, 1938/1998). Given life conditions, individuals are compelled to take up into their behavior the beliefs and meanings, customs and institutions, of their social group. That should not suggest that the social community is necessarily homogeneous. Clubs, gangs, fellowships of great variety exist as specialized modes of social association and these have an influence on an individual's active dispositions. The child's mind (based on but not reducible to the brain) is formed by the beliefs and understandings brought forth by the group and provides a center for personal experiences, interpretations, and conduct. Obviously this contrasts very much with nativist theories, but it does not imply a dismissal of the biological basis of human psychology.

SUMMARY

Nature and nurture are two contributing forces to the development of the mature psychological person. The degree to which either is emphasized varies across theorists.

- Galton was an hereditarian who emphasized natural inheritance who emphasized eugenics as a means to improve the race.
- Social Darwinists believed that life was a struggle for existence, a survival of the fittest, and that social controls should be exercised to make life difficult for, and ultimately eliminate, defective humans.

- Hereditarianism and social Darwinism led to the initiation of the intelligence testing movement.
- Binet developed the first useful test to identify children in need of special education and this resulted in the idea of an intelligence quotient.
- Goddard used the test as means to identify mental defectives with the aim of eliminating them from the reproducing population for the betterment of the nation.
- Hereditarians tend to discount the ability of education to compensate for low intelligence, it being largely inherited and fixed.
- Evolutionary psychologists hypothesize the existence of specific cognitive mechanisms in the brain/mind which were established as adaptations to environmental challenges in the evolutionary past.
- Cultural psychologists emphasize the adaptation to cultural conditions and the appropriation of cultural meanings (tools, technologies, symbol systems) as significant to the development of the individual mind.

SUGGESTED READINGS

Fancher, R. E. (1985). *The intelligence men: Makers of the IQ controversy.* New York: W. W. Norton.

Gould, S. J. (1981). *The mismeasure of man*. New York: W. W. Norton.

Rose, S., Lewontin, R. C., and Kamin, L. J. (1984). *Not in our genes.* Harmondsworth, UK: Penguin.

Sterelny, K. (2001). *Dawkins vs. Gould: Survival of the fittest.* Cambridge, UK: Icon Books.

Want to learn more? For links to online resources, examples of multiple choice questions, conceptual exercises and much more, visit the companion website at **https://study.sagepub.com/piekkola**

6

THE MIND–BODY PROBLEM

LEARNING OBJECTIVE

Since the mind–body problem is one of the most basic problems that psychology has to deal with, you will be introduced to the problem in its initial philosophical forms. As a result, you should be familiar with the following:

- The intellectual progression from Descartes' **interactionism**, alternative dualistic solutions were offered: **occasionalism**, **Double Aspect Theory**, **psychophysical parallelism**, and **epiphenomenalism**.
- Monistic materialist solutions based on reductionism or emergence will be considered.
- Dualistic accounts from psychology along with the dismissal of the problem altogether in favor of some form of reductionism.
- Lastly, you will be introduced to possible solutions and the possibility that there is no problem beyond an intellectual one.

In the end you should have sufficient insight to decide for yourself which of the possible alternatives is the one that you most favor, if any.

FRAMING QUESTIONS

- Do you believe that you possess a mind and, if so, do you believe it is separate from your body?
- If you do not believe in a mind, do you believe people can be adequately explained in bio-mechanical terms?
- Will it ever be possible to solve the mind–body problem without having to deny human subjective experience?

INTRODUCTION

The resolution of the mind–body problem has been one of the enduring challenges that has confronted psychology since its inception. Basically there are two aspects to the problem. First, does the mind exist? Second, if the mind exists, in what way, if any, does it relate to the body? The starting point for us will be with the birth of modern philosophy, usually considered to have begun with René Descartes (1596–1650). It was he who made a clear distinction between mind and body in the modern era of philosophy (A. Rogers, 1910). In doing so, Descartes formulated a problem that psychology would have to address. Psychology, when it first arose, was defined as a science of the mind and consciousness. It was obvious to early psychologists that they had minds and bodies and that there was an apparent correspondence between mental experience and bodily activity. So, it was natural that the mind–body problem would have to be considered.

You receive a blow to the eye, for instance, and experience pain. So? What's the problem? The problem is that mind and body are qualitatively different, so different that they could be conceived as two separate 'substances.' That was Descartes' conclusion. If that is so, it becomes difficult to explain the correspondence of occurrences in the two separate domains. According to **psychophysical parallelism**, which Wundt upheld, mind (psycho) and body (physical) run parallel courses (parallelism) in complete independence, never intersecting (like parallel lines) but which, somehow, are in concurrence.

We begin with the philosophers who addressed the problem and then proceed on to how it was dealt with by psychologists. After that, I will introduce you to some solutions that may render the matter resolved. You decide.

6.1 THE MIND–BODY PROBLEM IN PHILOSOPHY

The introduction of the problem

If you reflect on yourself, your deliberations may lead you to form two general categories based on distinctions having to do with body-like or mind-like qualities. You walk and run, eat and defecate, drink and urinate, have bad breath or an appealing scent, are male or female, tall or short, and so on. As well, you notice that you have emotions and thoughts, beliefs, values, and purposes; you have experiences, a personal history, and a sense of self and not-self. If so, you have made a distinction between the mental and the physical. This does not require, however, that you conclude that they are completely separate phenomena as Descartes did.

To personalize this, I want you try an experiment offered by Allport (1955). First, if you would, swallow your saliva. Now, spit into a glass (or imagine it). When you have an inch of saliva in the glass drink it. Are you revolted by the thought? If so you have probably worked from the assumption that as long it is in your body it remains identified with your selfhood. As Allport expressed it, "What seemed natural and 'mine' suddenly becomes disgusting and alien" (p. 43). You've made a conceptual distinction that can be quite powerful. It was the power of such a conceptual distinction, and Aristotelian logic, that led to Descartes' separation of mind from body.

Descartes (1641/1993) reported that it was clear to him that he possessed a body that was close to him and yet it was not him. He had a clear idea of his body as an extended thing in space that was non-thinking, and of himself as thinking but non-localizable in space. As he wrote, "I am really distinct from any body, and can exist without it" (p. 51). The body can be located in three-dimensional space but not mind; the body is divisible but not mind. The essential property of mind, not body, was thought (perceiving, thinking, imagining, willing). He had clear and distinct ideas of body and mind and—given the rules of logic—the laws of identity and contradiction and the excluded middle necessitated their complete separation (see Box 6.1).

BOX 6.1
LOGICAL PRINCIPLES

While logical thought was engaged in prior to Aristotle it was he who began to codify rules for thinking rationally, according to logical principles. Three such principles—the **law of identity**, **law of contradiction**, and the **excluded middle** have been applied to conceptual thinking. As principles they are considered to be self-evident.

- The 'law of identity' refers to 'sameness' and is represented by an equals sign (=) in logic and mathematics (Flew, 1984). It is represented symbolically as A = A.

- The 'law of contradiction' holds that something cannot both 'be' and 'not-be' (A ≠ not-A). Opposites are mutually exclusive.

- The 'excluded middle' allows for nothing in between. The very same thing must be either one or the other; it cannot simultaneously both.

(Continued)

(Continued)

Being near death, for instance, one continues to 'be.' There is no intermediate state—one is either dead or alive, not dead-and-alive. In categorical or conceptual thinking opposites are wholly opposed, segregated, and unrelated. So, in terms of the mind–body problem, mind and body are completely separated from each other by the excluded middle and cannot be related or in contact.

To establish his dualism Descartes offered three logical arguments (Flanagan, 1984).

- First there was the certainty of thinking. In order to arrive at some certain truth Descartes had doubted all that he could and dismissed it on that basis (this 'method of doubt' is developed more fully in Chapter 7). Sensory experience could be deceptive (illusions) or he could be dreaming. Sensory experience, as empiricists would have it, was not a basis for certainty. Doubting everything that he could, he arrived at the certainty of his doubting, and of his thinking. It was further clear, at least to him, that his thinking was completely independent of his body.

- In accordance with the 'excluded middle,' mind and body had to be completely separate. They possessed unique properties like extension in space and divisibility (body) versus non-localization and indivisibility (mind). Given the principles of 'identity' and 'contradiction' they were completely differentiated and unrelated— two distinct entities.

- Mind and body must be considered incommensurable (having nothing in common).

Given that mind and body are completely separate, Descartes was left with a difficulty. Mind and body appeared to be related. When I stub my toe (physical) I experience pain (mental). How is that so? Descartes' solution was **interactionism**, which proposes that mind and body are two separate substances which are subject to mutual influence—each affects the other (as depicted in Figure 6.1). For Descartes, the interface had to be in the brain and he selected the pineal gland as the point of contact. In the end, he found this unsatisfactory; if they were completely independent that should rule out their interacting. Regardless of his dissatisfaction, he had, in this, set up the modern mind–body problem.

Responding to Descartes

Alternative dualisms

While not contesting mind and body as separate substances, others were dissatisfied with Descartes' explanation of their correspondence through interaction and developed

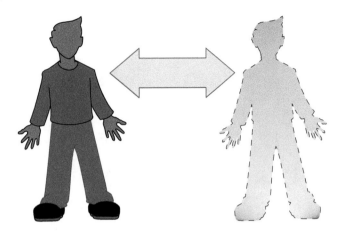

Figure 6.1 Descartes' interactionism

alternative solutions. In this, these individuals reflected prevailing social beliefs that were treated as given, which may no longer be so. I am referring specifically to Malebranche, Spinoza, and Leibniz, who relied on the Christian God as part of their solutions. At the time, people were pervasively religious and explanations that relied upon God would have been seen as completely rational. Later dualisms, as you will see, would have no need for God.

We begin with the solution called **occasionalism**, which is associated with Nicolas Malebranche (1638–1715), a French priest (Hasker, 1998). He based his solution on the assumption that God was the cause of the universe and no created being could be causally efficacious. That meant that neither body nor mind could causally impact the other. So the answer was that God causes the mental and physical occurrences and accounts for their apparent interrelatedness. Furthermore, it was impossible for something to be done without knowledge of how to do it (Nadler, 1998). Mind, given that Descartes had established its complete separation from the body, could have no knowledge of the physiological processes that are the basis of movement and could not, therefore, direct its movement. God, on the other hand, created and sustains the existence of both and is the only causally-effective agent. Mind and body exist but cannot influence each other and must, therefore, depend on God for any correspondence between them (in Figure 6.2, God is represented by the puppeteer adjusting mind to body). Thus, if one desires to swing a club, that is the 'occasion' for God to intervene and cause the physical swinging. Alternatively, if one is hit by a club, that is the occasion for God to initiate the experience of pain. Mind and body are completely separate and independent, and what agreement exists between them is due to God maintaining the correspondence.

A different explanation, **Double Aspect Theory**, was developed by Baruch Spinoza (1632–1677) and also had a religious foundation. Whatever exists, he argued, cannot be

Figure 6.2 Occasionalism

conceived to exist without conceiving of God (Allison, 1998). All that exists depends on God for its existence (God is thus conceived of as a substance). Mind and matter were God-created substances for Descartes, but for Spinoza, God was the only substance and the qualities of thought and extension, the mental and the physical, were attributes of God (in Figure 6.3, God is depicted by the encompassing hands; the human figure is half body and half mind). In the single person, mind and body are expressed as the attributes of thought and extension. They are of the same substance that, looked at in one way, is comprehended under one attribute, say matter, while looked at from a different perspective the other attribute is comprehended. The same thing is expressed in different ways depending on the point of view. Humans are thus conceived of as unified beings having correlated aspects which are qualitatively different. Nonetheless, there is still a dualistic conception since the attributes were not interacting (Fancher, 2000). Thoughts could only give rise to other thoughts and physical events could only effect other physical events. They were associated (corresponding) with each other because they were both under the influence of natural laws that affected them alike.

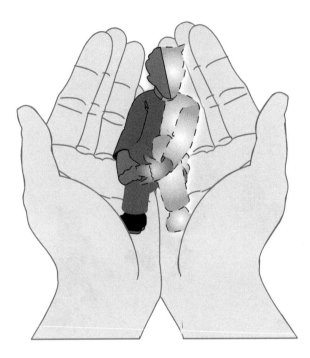

Figure 6.3   Double Aspect Theory

In a sense Spinoza conceived of body and mind as running parallel courses in their corresponding with each other despite separation. This idea would be developed by Gottfried Leibniz (1646–1716) in his psychophysical parallelism and the concept of **pre-established harmony**. Leibniz's explanation involved a form of elementalism in that the universe was composed of atom-like entities called monads. These monads were, to varying degrees, material and mental although mind and matter were completely independent (A. Rogers, 1910). Monads do not act upon one another, but they are related somehow in that they reflect the actions of other monads. Leibniz resolved this apparent contradiction by proposing pre-established harmony. A correspondence exists between monads because they depend on a higher reality—God—that unites them in their separateness and coordinates them. Leibniz offered the example of numerous choirs, separated spatially from each other, whose performances were in harmony, despite not hearing each other, because they performed from the same musical score. It was this idea of pre-established harmony that led to the solution to the mind–body problem: psychophysical parallelism (in Figure 6.4 the top portion, with thought balloons, represents mind, is separated from body by the excluded middle, but corresponds with bodily activity). Mind (soul) and body are separate and follow their own laws, but

Figure 6.4   Psychophysical parallelism

correspond with each other (events in one, parallel events in the other) because they were harmonized with each other from the start.

Mechanistic materialism

For Descartes, only humans had minds and were capable of rationality. The body, on the other hand was physical, of the material world, and to explain its movements he turned to the principles of mechanics, or **mechanism**. Through analogy with clocks and other mechanical devices Descartes reasoned that bodies operated by similar principles. The human body was a kind of mechanism that was equipped with nerves, muscles, and bones, whose motions were independent of any thinking aspect (Descartes, 1641/1993). Based on his observations of hydraulic automata in the royal gardens (stepping on plates released jets of water that caused figurines to move), he conjectured that the nervous system was similar in its operation (Descartes, in Skinner, 1931). It could be thought of as similar to tubes filled with water and the muscles and tendons like springs and engines. Movements were not due to voluntary action but to outside forces acting on them. The sole exception was with humans, given the possibility of mind interacting with body. It was a small step though to simply eliminate mind and offer completely materialistic accounts of humans.

To Descartes' contemporary, Thomas Hobbes (1588–1679), the entire universe was matter alone and mechanical in its operation, a stance known as **mechanistic materialism**. Humans were merely bodies in motion, subject to mechanical laws, and psychological phenomena could be explained by the same principles as bodies (A. Rogers, 1910). Consciousness was explained in terms of motions and changes in the nervous system, as the feeling of change in the brain, and was reduced to sensations and combinations of sensations. To Hobbes, all that exists is matter-in-motion; there was no mind, only internal physical motions.

A more sophisticated mechanistic materialism would arise out of physiological research in the 17th and 18th centuries and was reflected in **Julien de La Mettrie** (1709–1752). While humans were recognized as unique, their uniqueness was not attributable to an immaterial soul but to the complexity of their biological processes, especially of the brain (La Mettrie, 1748/2004). The brain is the mainspring of the body and influences all of its operations, including mental. This was supported by reports from doctors on the effects of illness and drugs on mental functions which suggested their dependence on the body. Sometimes in the throes of bodily disease the soul is nowhere to be found. It sleeps when the body does. Opium alters the will. Sometimes in disease of the body the soul is hidden, lifeless (possibly what we might now consider a coma). In short, the states of the soul are correlated with those of the body.

de La Mettrie

The dependence of the soul on the body, La Mettrie believed, could be shown as well through comparative anatomy. Humans differ from animals in degree, not type. The brain of quadrupeds has similar form but the human brain is the largest and most convoluted. It was because of the bigger, more complex brain, better education, and richer experience that humans were superior. What differences existed were due not to original design (creationism) but to changes over long reaches of time (he was, in this, anticipating evolutionary theory). The smallest beginnings have, by increments, increased. When the universe was nearly dumb, the soul (or mind) was in its infancy. Over time changes occurred that were important to intellectual development: the use of signs and the invention of language (in this he was anticipating cultural evolution). The soul or mind is nothing other than an enlightened machine.

Experimental findings further confirmed his mechanical conclusions. For instance, animals' flesh palpitates after death (and doesn't require a soul). Muscles detached from the body contract mechanically when stimulated; an injection of hot water can re-animate the heart. A man convicted of treason was opened alive and his heart was thrown in hot water; it leapt several times. A chicken with its head cut off continues to stand, walk, and run. Subsequent work in physiology (as discussed in Chapter 4) would develop this.

The discovery of the spinal reflex by Marshall Hall established the existence of physiological mechanisms for responding to stimulation. There was no need to invoke notions of voluntary movement. The **reflex arc** was a purely mechanical, biological process and it would serve as a means for some to attempt to eliminate altogether mental, voluntary activity. As it was employed by Hall, the reflex did not discount the existence, or operation, of non-physical phenomena; what it did do was exclude it from reflex activity (Skinner, 1931). A clear distinction was made between the reflex as unlearned and voluntary action.

The next step was to remove the notion of voluntary behavior and account for all behavior in terms of an assemblage of reflex mechanisms. Ivan Sechenov would do that in postulating a reflexive basis for both involuntary and voluntary behavior (Herrnstein and Boring, 1965). The mind, so-called, in its operation, was not voluntary but was due, instead, to constant external stimulation upon the nervous system (Rahmani, 1973). Acts of consciousness were no longer associated with an immaterial soul or mind but with reflexive processes (Petrovsky, 1989). The operation of the spinal reflex was extended to include the whole brain as intermediary between external stimulation and response. Mental phenomena were just the reaction of the brain to environmental stimulation and to internal stimuli (physiological states of the organism). This was a thoroughly materialist conception of the mental operations.

Epiphenomenalism

An alternative account to the mind–body problem that drew upon the findings of physiologists was **epiphenomenalism**. While accepting the mechanistic conception of the universe, the epiphenomenalist could not deny the subjective experience of consciousness and felt compelled to fit it into the mechanistic model as an irrelevant addendum. Consciousness was a mere by-product of physical events which was causally ineffective or inert (in Figure 6.5 mind is depicted as lagging behind body as a passive observer of the causal activity of the body). Only physical states have causal power and it is they which produce mental states (Campbell and Smith, 1998). The mental realm is just the shifting states of consciousness that are the product of the changes occurring in the nervous system. Mind is robbed of the causal efficacy it possessed in Descartes' interactionism, but it is still dualist because the mental is acknowledged and not reduced to the physical.

According to James (1890/1950), the first person to develop a full epiphenomenalist position was Hodgson in 1865, but it was Thomas Huxley (1825–1895) who developed the standard account (which James dubbed 'automaton theory'). As Huxley (1874) conceived of it, consciousness 'might' be regarded as a function of some entity called the soul and distinct from the brain. Sensation was the means by which soul is affected by motions in the brain. One 'might' think that, but, as Huxley advocated, the soul is a fiction and sensation is just a form of motion in the brain, and consciousness is a mere by-product of the operation of the brain.

Huxley based his conclusions on spinal cord research done on frogs. Removing frontal portions of the brain resulted in an incapacity to eat and starvation ensued, even when food was placed in the mouth. Severing of the rear portions of the brain resulted in spontaneity of movement being lost. Behavior was attendant upon prodding from outside. Walking and jumping awaited external provocation; that stimulation, acting through the spinal cord, could produce complex integrated movements. Severing the spinal cord of frogs near the

Figure 6.5   Epiphenomenalism

brain removed certain reactions from voluntary control. The operation of the brain had been removed, but certain mechanical responses to external stimulation remained intact, such as a foot being withdrawn upon the application of irritants. From such findings Huxley concluded that animals are purely mechanical entities whose actions are not under the guidance of reason. In humans, injuries to the spinal cord also resulted in losses of function below the level of damage, and a loss of consciousness for the associated bodily regions. As long as the brain was not damaged, consciousness remained. Let the brain suffer injury, however, and there was concomitant loss of consciousness. Ravage the brain and consciousness disappears.

Huxley concluded that, even if the unimpaired frog displayed what might be called volition, there was no reason to suppose it to be other than mechanical brain activity. In humans, so-called consciousness of volition was the mere accompaniment of bodily processes, and had no impact on the causation of action chains. Consciousness was merely passive registering of what was going on. Huxley offered an analogy: "the steam-whistle which accompanies the work of a locomotive engine is without influence upon its machinery" (1874, p. 575). There was no evidence, he insisted, to justify the belief that states of consciousness produce movements in a material organism. Humans are just automata that are conscious.

Dialectical materialism

There is one version of materialism, **dialectical materialism**, which does have a place for mind and consciousness. I will not spend a lot of time on this because we have already considered a version of this previously in the theory of 'levels of organization.' The proposition is that matter, which is primary (substance), has undergone a process of evolution which has resulted in ever-greater complexity, and with increases in complexity there have been emergent, qualitative changes and new phenomena like life and mind. Mind here is considered a property of highly-developed matter in the form of a nervous system and brain. Mental processes themselves have evolved to the point where consciousness appears. While consciousness is dependent upon the underlying biology it has been further conditioned by cultural evolution such that higher forms of mental life are the result of the appropriation of culturally developed and transmitted tools and sign systems. I refer you back to Chapter 1 for any further development of this.

6.2 THE MIND–BODY PROBLEM IN PSYCHOLOGY

Dualism in psychology

When psychology appeared as a separate science its practitioners could not avoid the mind–body question, although it was not necessarily of central concern. Since the interactionism of Eccles has been mentioned already in Chapter 2, I will pass that over except to remind you that he suggested the point of contact between mind and body was the hypothesized 'liaison brain.' Occasionalism was the first alternative to interactionism but we will not consider it any further since I am unaware of any occasionalist psychologist. Instead, we will commence with psychophysical parallelism since that was the preferred explanation of the so-called father of psychology—Wilhelm Wundt.

Psychophysical parallelism

The mind–body problem was not something Wundt was particularly concerned with. When he did address the issue he stated psychophysical parallelism to be his preferred explanation since he desired theoretical and conceptual coherence (Robinson, 1982). He accepted that mind and body existed but could not conceive of how two such disparate phenomena could interact. Being so different, neither could be reduced to the other. While it may have seemed as though they interacted, what was actually taking place was that identical conditions prompted both physical and psychical processes. As Wundt put it, "The connection can only be regarded as a *parallelism* of two causal series existing side by side, but never directly interfering with each other in virtue of the incompatibility of their terms" (Wundt, 1861, in Robinson, 1982, p. 137). This was reinforced by **psychometric** research in his laboratory. Among Wundt's research associates it was reported that the psychometrical research (measuring changes in the brain alongside changes in consciousness) revealed "the complete parallelism of physical and mental phenomena" (Cattell, 1888, p. 45).

Double Aspect Theory

The adoption of Double Aspect Theory by a psychologist is evident in one of the founders of comparative psychology—**C. Lloyd Morgan** (1852–1936). Comparative psychology grew out of Darwin's (1874/1998) proposition that higher animals possess attention, memory, some reason, and imagination, and it was not improbable that more complex powers like self-consciousness and abstraction evolved from these. In his investigation of the mental functions of animals, Morgan (1894/1998) seemed to be adopting a materialist stance. He maintained that psychical states should be considered to be associated with the cerebral activity in higher vertebrates. Morgan, however, was a religious man and, despite being committed to naturalism, wrote that "I for one, still retain, and am confirmed in, my belief in God" (Morgan, 1926, p.1). That is the basis of his double aspectism.

Morgan's canon

While Morgan supported evolutionary theory, he had to reconcile that with his belief in God and turned to Spinoza. Any organism, he maintained, had a fundamentally dual nature that could be interpreted in terms of two attributes. For Spinoza and Morgan both, God was substance, and thought and extension were derived therefrom. From the lowest to highest, all was an expression and manifestation of God. Life and mind, while not of spirit, were manifestations of it. Life and mind accompany each other and neither exists without the other. An organism, therefore, has to be looked upon as physical with respect to its life and psychological with respect to its mind.

Epiphenomenalism

Epiphenomenalism can be found in Wegner and Wheatley (1999) in their argument against the possibility of free will. In humans, they wrote, there is a pervasive consciousness of personal causation and willing, but that, they declared, should be judged an illusion. Even when there is no causal connection between thought and action there may be an experience of willing. Such an experience is real enough but the belief in willed action is not. In actuality, both the action, and the idea of performing the action, are due to the very same cause—an event sequence in the brain which produces both. Our belief in willing and causing action depends on three factors—the thought of intent corresponds with the action, the thought occurs just prior to the act, and there are no other potential causes connected with the act.

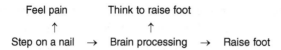

Figure 6.6   The experience of will as epiphenomenal

Under those conditions we falsely conclude that the consciousness of intent had casual force. Thought, as a cause of acting, is only an inference and one that must be questioned. It is merely a by-product of the neural process that actually caused the action along with causing the thought of the action about to be performed.

Ideas of intent, such as raising one's foot (Figure 6.6), are epiphenomenal, by-products of the actual physiological cause, and lack causal efficacy. Experiences of conscious do not indicate an actual connection between the mind and action (but there is an acknowledgement of the physical and the mental).

James (1890/1950) found epiphenomenalism of questionable merit. If there is a consciousness, he asserted, it makes no sense that it has no part to play in those processes it reliably attends to and reports on. James (1879) believed consciousness had utility and considered that to be the basis of overturning epiphenomenalism. Looking at the comparative evidence, as Huxley had, he concluded that consciousness appeared to be most needed in organisms with highly developed nervous systems. The actions of those with a less-developed system were certainly of a mechanical and fixed nature. Nonetheless, the introduction of the cerebral hemispheres introduced an element of unpredictability, especially in humans. There is a vagueness of responding, rather than inalterability, and that is an advantage since conduct is adaptable to slight environmental change.

A close study of consciousness will find, besides adaptability, an increased range of responsiveness and evidence of interest and selective attention. From the multitude of experiences some are chosen for accentuation and the remainder ignored. As he suggested, "we are all seeing flies and moths, and beetles by the thousand, but to whom, save the entomologist, do they say anything distinct?" (James, 1879, p. 12). The mind is selective, tearing things out and breaking them apart (engaging in abstraction). Reasoning takes the totality and draws those aspects that have practical or theoretical importance and point towards possible conclusions. Consciousness thus guides action in the world. Introspecting upon his own mental processes James found consciousness was most intense when the nervous processes were hesitant, or held in check, and minimal when nervous action proceeded with the certainty of instincts or habits. Such a difference demonstrated the efficaciousness of consciousness in that it is most needed when conditions are undecided. To suggest, then, that it is a mere by-product, a spectator, without causal power or role to play in affecting action, must be false.

WHAT DO YOU THINK?

Even though James may have established the role of consciousness he did not, in that, resolve the mind–body problem. Do you think a resolution is possible?

BOX 6.2
PROBLEM—WHAT PROBLEM?

John Dewey considered the mind–body problem an intellectual fabrication. Rather than designating some aspects of human experience and conduct as mental and some as physical, and considering such distinctions to be a reflection of ontological substances, Dewey rejected the absolute disunity. The problem, he argued, was the result of what he called the **tradition of separation and isolation** (Dewey, 1928). In the intellectual analysis of phenomena, it has been customary to identify qualitative differences, to abstract them from the concrete whole of which they are a part, stripping them of context, and then treating them as though they had an independent existence. For instance, in personality psychology there is a tendency to treat person and environment/situation as separate entities that mechanically interact (see, for example, Phillips and Orton, 1983). It then became necessary to explain how, as independent, they are related. May this be a conceptual, rather than an actual, separation? Can people really be considered completely separate from their environment? Try getting by without air. Respiration connects organism and environment.

The separation of mind from body, to Dewey, involved distinguishing qualities of action as being more body-like or more mind-like and then intellectually abstracting them from action, from the immediate conditions of existence and function. They are rendered wholly separate and turned into things rather than descriptive terms referring to qualities the organized whole—the organism. The abstractions are **reified** and treated as discrete. Given the laws of identity, contradiction, and the excluded middle in conceptual thinking, we are left with the problem of how they relate. The problem is not in how could they relate but in how they were separated. Such abstractions can help organize thinking but become problematic when left in the abstract. The difference between them is just a matter of emphasis on this quality rather than that quality, a conceptual distinction. Any absolute separation between them, and consignment of one set of segregated qualities to one substance and the remainder to the other, is in error and distorts what is given—the organized whole.

From the perspective of acting, some functions appear more mental and some more physical, but the distinction exists in the analysis, not the person engaged in living. The person who consumes and digests food is the very same entity that desired and enjoyed it. The physical and mental exist in unity in the individual. To be primarily mental is not to

(Continued)

(Continued)

be disembodied. To be primarily physical is not to be purely mechanical, without capacity to register and evaluate the effects of movement, and incapable of judging what to do. The habit, crystallized in mentalistic and physicalistic language, of regarding them as separate is rooted in thinking of them as substances rather than as qualities and functions of action.

Monism in psychology

Neutral monism

William James felt a need to develop a theory of conscious mental life that would treat mental phenomena as adaptations, produced through natural selection, and which had causal efficacy in confronting life challenges (Robinson, 1982). In 1904 he wrote that he had struggled for two decades over the problem of consciousness, mistrusting the idea that it was an entity of some sort, and had been considering its nonexistence. Nonetheless, he could not escape personal experience; his capacity to think made it an absurdity that consciousness should be denied. Instead of considering consciousness as an entity, it should be considered a function. It was not some stuff that thoughts are made of, present from the beginning, and to be contrasted with that of which bodies are made. The world, as he now conceived it, was composed of one primal stuff he would call 'pure experience' (later labelled **neutral monism**—Myers, 1992). This was metaphysically neutral in that it rejected the proposition that reality is composed of mind or matter but, instead, is of a single something (neither mental nor physical). (The modern concept of 'energy' might have been acceptable to James.)

While James (1890/1950) had dismissed the idea of emergent qualities, his later work moved toward what Flanagan (1984) called 'naturalistic emergentism.' The world is made up of natural objects and events, their properties, and the relations between them. All novel qualities or features are conceived of as emerging lawfully from complicated interactions among natural processes, events, and objects. Conscious mental life is a feature that emerges through natural selection as an emergent property, a function, no different from breathing or walking. Humans, to James (1905), evolved from prehuman ancestors that had sensory processes that supported responding to the environment and avoiding annihilation, but lacked a capacity to reason.

The mental has evolved and is rooted in biological changes. The brain conditions the mental but the mental also influences the physical, in directing movement for instance. The mature mind, in this treatment, was not innate although dependent upon biological mechanisms; what was given required training. The individual had to be educated and their natural powers organized to better fit the current physical and social world. It was that which provided flexibility and adaptability to changing circumstances. Without education the person would be confused, even overwhelmed, by situations other than those that allowed habitual adjustments. The social education and formation of the mind of the individual is central to our next consideration.

Naturalism

In adopting evolutionary thinking, including mental evolution, Dewey was struggling against dualism and mechanism, and emphasized in its place **naturalism** and **organicism**. His adoption of organicism aligned him, as a result, with the theory of levels of organization. That would seem to suggest that Dewey was a materialist but, when asked if that was so, he contended that, if by materialists one meant reductive materialism, naturalists were not materialists (Dewey, Hook, and Nagel, 1945). Such base materialism rejected the mental and was consequently invalid. Naturalism is a version of materialism that acknowledges thoughts, feelings, emotions, and a capacity for rational inquiry. Mental events cannot be doubted, but it would be 'undisciplined speculation' to suggest that mental events did not depend on physical processes. Mental events are contingent on particular physical-chemical-physiological events and their accompanying structures. If there were no organized bodies, there would be no mental states. That did not mean that there were only physical states, but rather that the mental was contingent upon the physical, and not reducible to it. It would seem that **Dewey** was a 'dialectical materialist,' which he rejected. The term materialism carried too much metaphysical baggage, suggesting mechanism and reductionism, which he discarded. Nonetheless there are strong parallels (see Cork, 1949, 1950).

Dewey & Marx

    One of the main reasons for rejecting the materialist stance was the failure to acknowledge the role of the social and cultural in the development of particular minds and consciousness. A child, he believed, is equipped at birth with a capacity to engage the environment (such as with reflexes), but the human, sociocultural environment modifies native abilities and molds potentialities (Dewey, 1916/1961, 1917, 1922). Each infant from its very first breath is subject to the attention and demand of others and to the force of **socialization** and **enculturation**. The directing of native impulses (tendencies to act in a certain way, rather than fixed and invariant like instincts) within a social arena accounted for the development of the mind and its level of sophistication.

    Mind was not present at birth; it was something to be formed and acquired through **sociogenesis**. The child at birth is without language, beliefs, ideas, values, understanding, and purposes, but in the process of interacting with others and through education becomes a member of the group, developing a mind that accords with the community. What the child becomes, and the quality of mind that forms, depend on the social conditions adapted to and not on innate tendencies. Innate potentialities open the door to sociocultural experience, but once that door is opened a realm of non-biological possibilities becomes paramount.

Dialectical materialist psychology

Vygotsky, along with Luria and Leontyev, developed the **'cultural-historical'** approach to psychology, which is rooted in dialectical materialism. It is based on the proposition that mind is an emergent property of highly developed matter—a complex nervous system, and forms in the individual as a result of embeddedness in, and appropriation of, a system of sociocultural relations. The development of this approach had its beginnings in what Vygotsky (1927/1997) identified as a crisis in psychology. During the 1920s there were two general approaches to psychology that were irreconcilably opposed, leaving the field divided and dualistic. The natural science approach of the psychophysiologists was essentially a reductive materialism, and the phenomenological approach, which focused on subjective experience, was basically idealist. Psychology as a field was entrenched in dualism and its practitioners saw no way out.

Vygotsky aimed to develop a general psychology, a third approach that was more than an addition to the other two. The solution was to go beyond the naturalistic approach and to interpret human psychological activity as a product of sociohistorical development. In this he rejected the widespread acceptance of **individualism** and the assumption that the psychology of the individual was independent of social circumstances. This seemed paradoxical at the time since he was proposing that to explain complex human consciousness one had to go beyond the organism, seeking the origins of human conscious activity, and conceptual thinking, neither in the brain nor spirit but in the relations to social life (Luria, 1982). The subject matter of psychology was not just the person's inner life, but the degree to which the sociocultural world is reflected internally as a result of interacting with external reality.

Vygotsky's basic premise was that a distinction had to be made between levels of psychic processes—the natural and the cultural (Leontiev and Luria, 1968). Human psychological activity, unlike animals, is based on the material and social mediation of behavior and the use of means like tools, symbols, and language, all of which carry meaning. Appropriating such means, young humans become liberated from the demands of the immediate environment. While animals are almost totally dependent on their inherited traits, humans learn to master cultural products, acquired through social interaction, which free them from enslavement to nature (these issues are discussed in detail in Chapter 1 if you need to review them). The evolution of the human psyche was therefore conditioned by both biological evolution and the historical development of social organization and culture. It was in the evolving social activity that humans created non-biological, artificial connections through a complex system of symbols which made a new regulatory principle possible (Vygotsky, 1977).

Behaviorism

John Watson (1913a) had no place for consciousness and preferred to leave such issues to philosophers. Even subjectivity was rejected because science demanded phenomena that were publicly accessible. In advocating his **anti-mentalism** he believed that he was free of the mind–body problem but, if it remained, he was content to be ignorant of it. Regardless, he still had to contend with **mentalism** within psychology. He did so by translating mental processes into behavioristic terms like conditioned responses and habit formation. Sensation and perception, for instance, became discriminatory responses to different stimuli (Boring, 1929). Instead of proposing that an animal perceives a difference between a red light and a green light, the animal is said to respond differentially (discrimination) to them. The old psychology was simply being rewritten by translating it into categories of observable responses.

Aiming to emulate the other sciences, specifically physics and psychophysics, a serious problem remained—the **method of impression**. This was an introspective method that rested upon conscious awareness of subjective states and reports on those conditions. Physicists used it to determine the range of visual and auditory stimuli that humans could subjectively perceive (Woodworth, 1931). That meant that people would introspect and give a verbal account of their experiences of perceiving light and sound. The psychophysicists also used the method to determine the detected presence or absence of faint stimuli (**absolute threshold**) and of perceived differences of magnitude between stimuli (**just noticeable difference**). This was problematic because introspection was unacceptable to the behaviorist's emphasis on objectivity and dismissal of consciousness. Watson, supposedly, overcame this by redefining the process and transforming it into the **verbal report**. Rather than a statement conveying meaningful information about subjective experiences, the verbal report (speech) was a verbalization, an utterance of meaningless sounds in response to stimulus conditions.

In a similar manner, memory became the return of a conditioned response when stimulus conditions were repeated (Watson, 1924/1966). Thought was just talking to oneself—subvocal, laryngeal responses. Yet there was a problem. The emphasis on objective knowledge, nonetheless, involved public observability and 'observation.' Well enough, but as Price (1960) asked, what can 'observing' be if it does not involve being 'aware' of something? The behaviorist, engaged in observing behavior and environmental stimuli, is 'aware,' and to be aware is to be conscious. Despite denying mental processes, experience was the cornerstone of Watson's objectivity, and experience implies a subjective agent and an act of knowing (Tolman, 1992). Consciousness may have been dismissed as an object of study, but it was not disposed of. It was central to its method of observation.

Eliminative materialism

Research into neuropsychology led to an alternative materialist theory—**identity theory**. Mental states, in this account, are nothing other than states of the brain (Borst, 1970). Mind is just a term that refers to the brain and its activity (Kolb and Whishaw, 1990). That is reductionism. To others, such a position still left a hint of unacceptable mentalism since the mental remained as a physical process. As a result, a more extreme stance known as **eliminative materialism** arose which sought to be rid of the mental as mere fiction and eliminate it altogether.

The position was first articulated by the philosophers Richard Rorty (1931–2007) and Paul Feyerabend (1924–1994) in the 1960s and is basically a reductionistic, physicalist (materialist) answer to dualism (Dupré, 1988). The argument as originally set forth was a linguistic issue. To Feyerabend (1963) everyday language, unlike the language of science, is based on age-old unwarranted beliefs. Unlike scientific language it is not based in fact. Just because everyday self-observations suggest that thoughts are immaterial does not mean that they are; it proves nothing. An appearance of difference is no proof of difference.

In the end, no mentalistic language has demonstrated its superiority in describing the world. To strengthen his point, Feyerabend (1967) offered the example of the 'geocentric theory' of planetary movement which was based on the misleading observation that the sun and moon circle the earth. The appearance of mind, similarly, does not prove its existence. Mentalistic language has to be replaced by a better one built upon a more sensible basis, one whose explanatory basis is physiological. Mentalistic language should be eliminated and replaced by developing materialistic terms that are testable. Rorty (1965) argued that as our empirical inquiries proceed we will move closer to demonstrating sensation-brain (mind-brain) identity and the outdated nature of mentalistic language. It is no different from the removal of superstitious language (demons and evil spirit) from the explanation of mental illness that psychiatry accomplished.

The idea was taken up in the 1980s by the neurophilosophers Patricia Churchland (1943–) and Paul Churchland (1942–) who were intent upon the eliminating '**folk psychology**,' or common-sense theories of human conduct, in favor of neurophysiological explanation. This did not entail the reduction of the mental to the physical. Reduction and elimination are not the same (Rey, 1998). To reduce a theory does not mean that the phenomena so reduced disappear (Churchland and Sejnowski, 1990). No, the mental had to be wholly eliminated. Folk theories of human conduct, developed over thousands of years, misrepresented the activities and internal states in terms of delusional non-entities called mind and mental. It was a muddled explanatory framework lacking reality; there was nothing to be reduced.

Common sense has generated an explanatory theory of cognitive activity that is basically defective (P. M. Churchland, 1982). That it has so long influenced people does not mean that it is any less misleading. To it we owe such concepts as fear, desire, belief, pain, and sensitivity (P. M. Churchland, 1988). The point and aim of eliminativism is to resolve the mind–body problem by removing mind, and therefore dualism, altogether, and to explain what was deemed mind with neurophysiological explanations. Folk psychology is just a theory and an erroneous one (P. S. Churchland, 1986). Its inadequacies demand substantial revision or complete replacement (elimination) by neuroscience. Neuroscience is our best hope for making sense of how cognitive (neural) beings connect with their environment without invoking some mythical mind (Churchland and Churchland, 1983).

The eliminativist solution is to deny the reality of such phenomena as mental images, experiences, pains, desires, beliefs, and so on (Everitt, 1981). This is irrational since the eliminativist must not just eliminate mental states in others but personally too. Other states to be eliminated include judging, questioning, inferring, and asserting, but these are implied in the assertions made for their removal. The concept of belief is retained in proclamations of the truth of eliminativism. If the proposition were really true, no one would be in a position to believe it to be so.

It is difficult to get around experience as the basis of knowledge and, once you admit that, you have opened the door to awareness and subjectivity. Even the brain, the bedrock for elimination of the mental, requires that it be known in order to be investigated. That, for the Churchlands, is not a problem (actually it is) since, epistemologically, they adopt a solipsistic position (Churchland and Churchland, 1983). A neuron is without knowledge and incapable of knowing what caused its activation or to where its output is going. The brain as a whole adjusts to input but not to what is behind the input and causing it.

Emergent interactionism

Sperry

Concurrent with the Churchlands, **Roger Sperry** (1913–1994), Nobel Laureate (1981) for his work on the 'split-brain', would go in an opposite direction to elimination. In the split-brain work Sperry studied the effects of the severing of the corpus callosum to alleviate severe epilepsy, and what that revealed of hemispheric independence and specialization. This led him to move away from reductive materialism, which he had been aligned with, to an emergent understanding. Arguing that mental states were emergent, Sperry (1980) contended that they were irreducible and their elimination was unacceptable. Subjective experience for Sperry is dependent on the brain but it also has properties that are unique and resist identification with the brain. Churchland (P. S., 1986) argued that, while the current state of neuroscience has not successfully identified subjectivity with brain, that does not mean it will not be forthcoming. Sperry, however, was in a position to respond from a position of deep insight into the workings of the brain and found emergentism more feasible then eliminativism.

Originally, Sperry (1952) conceived of mental activity as cerebral activity, but in time he (Sperry, 1969a) began to shift. It was becoming clear to him that mind or consciousness had an active part to play in ongoing engagement with the environment, directing and shaping the flow patterns of excitation in the cerebrum. Subjective experience, he announced, had to be conceived of as an emergent property of cerebral excitation, inseparable from the material brain, but different from, and more than, the totality of its physiochemical constituents. Properties of consciousness are **molar** in contrast with the **molecular** nerve processes that they incorporate but transcend. Mental processes supervene (see **supervenience**) on the physiological-neurological, but a full understanding of conscious events will be lacking if left to electrophysiological and biochemical data alone. Conscious awareness is a dynamic, emergent property of brain processes, yet distinct with respect to physiological aspects (Sperry, 1969b). Rather than being elemental and molecular, the conscious properties of the brain are holistic and molar.

Conscious awareness, to Sperry (1984), is not going to be found in the nerve cells of the brain or in their constituent parts. The brain processes that underlie and account for unified conscious experience do not have to be unified or have their properties match the properties of unity and continuity of subjective experience. Its properties transcend nerve impulses in the same way that the properties of an organism transcend the properties of cells. An electrical impulse may have a temporal order of milliseconds but a thought can take much longer. Besides that, while mental properties supervene on neural physiology, mental phenomena can themselves act to govern the nerve impulses. The mind can act upon the matter within the brain, affecting and activating regions and processes, in bringing about changes in the physical realm. That does not, however, imply some sort of dualism since the mind is itself a material process—an emergent one.

Conscious phenomena are not epiphenomena either (Sperry, 1970). They can act upon cerebral processes and alter them in directing activity. The mental has directive power over the physical. Wholes and their properties are real and they have causal potency (Sperry, 1976). What one does is influenced by knowledge, values, beliefs, memories, reason, a sense of self, and these have 'downward control,' or 'downward causation,' over lower-level processes (Sperry, 1980). By an act of deciding, one can impel oneself to locomotion, or change direction, or read a book, or whatever. This does not mean that control from below is no longer possible; it is just not the sole source of control. Causation is both upward and downward, interactive without being dualistic. Sperry concluded that mental phenomena were real and had to be recognized. More than that they had causal efficacy and influenced the physical not as a separate substance but as an emergent property of organized matter.

Psychosomatics

While Sperry did not draw upon the evidence of **psychosomatics**, the findings in that area alone support the notion of downward causation, of the influence of the mental on the physical. The idea is not new. During the late 1800s, physicians began to investigate a disorder known as 'hysteria' (now conversion disorder), which involved apparent symptoms of a neurological disturbance like blindness or paralysis without any organic basis. **Jean-Martin Charcot** (1825–1893), a French neurologist, began to suspect the issue was mental in origin or **psychogenic**. This was because through hypnosis he was able to remove hysterical blindness and restore sight.

Charcot

Hypnosis, imagery, biofeedback and other mental techniques all work from the assumption that mind can affect body, that conscious mental actions or suggestions can be utilized to produce physical results. Placebos (inert substance without curative effects) have been shown to be effective in eliminating pain after surgery or in preventing colds (Rosenthal and Frank, 1956). They have also been used in the treatment of ulcers, headaches, and high blood pressure.

Suggestion has been used to produce changes in the state of the skin and skin disorders (Barber, 1984). People whose eyes were closed were told a harmless leaf touching their skin was poison ivy. They developed itching and blistering. Conversely, when told the leaf was neutral (actually poison ivy) no effects resulted. In a different demonstration, soldiers were told a small piece of metal brushing the skin was a piece of molten shell. Having suffered such an injury, it was readily visualized. In four of the soldiers the suggestion produced blistering.

BOX 6.3
A DEMONSTRATION OF DOWNWARD CAUSATION

Bresler (1984) suggested a demonstration of the influence of thought on physiology: First, command yourself to increase the flow of saliva into your mouth (do it now). Tell yourself to increase your level of salivation. Bresler expected that would not be very effective because the division of the nervous system that regulates that physiological mechanism is not normally responsive to verbal commands or under voluntary control.

Now, try this: Imagine holding a very juicy lemon in your hand. Go ahead. Really! Try imagining each step as vividly as possible. Think of its qualities—its aroma, its taste. Imagine cutting it open. The vapors waft into your nostrils. Imagine biting into it. Think of the tartness, the sourness of the juices. Swirl the bitter juice in your mouth. Taste the sourness. Are you salivating more now than when you gave yourself the verbal command to? If yes, your mental state has affected a physiological process.

SUMMARY

In this chapter we have considered past and recent perspectives on the mind–body problem.

- Descartes introduced the problem and offered a dualistic solution—interactionism.
- Those who followed found Descartes' solution unacceptable and offered alternative dualistic conceptions—occasionalism, Double Aspect Theory, psychophysical parallelism, and epiphenomenalism.

(Continued)

(Continued)

- Mechanistic materialists turned to the evidence from physical and physiological science to account for human behavior and reject mind.
- Medical and physiological evidence was demonstrating a close connection between mind and body.
- Work on the physiology of the nervous system, especially the identification of the spinal reflex, promoted explanations based on reflexive mechanisms in the spinal cord and brain.
- Dialectical materialists proposed the mental was an emergent property of highly organized matter—the brain, conditioned by sociocultural forces.
- Reflexivity, in turn, led to behaviorism and the rejection of the mental.
- Other early psychologists adopted dualistic explanations or monistic solutions (neutral monism and naturalism).
- The whole problem was designated artificial and a product of the tradition of separation and isolation.
- Eliminative materialism aimed to eliminate the whole problem by discounting it as a mere linguistic tradition and one that would ultimately be resolved by advancing neuroscience.
- Emergent interactionism proposed the mental was emergent upon increased complexity in the nervous system and the appearance of properties not found in the neurophysiology that depended on it and had causal efficacy over it.

SUGGESTED READINGS

Erneling, C. E. and Johnson, D. M. (2005). *The mind as a scientific object: Between brain and culture.* Oxford: Oxford University Press.

Robinson, D. (1998). *The mind.* Oxford: Oxford University Press.

Searle, J. R. (2004). *Mind: A brief introduction.* Oxford: Oxford University Press.

Want to learn more? For links to online resources, examples of multiple choice questions, conceptual exercises and much more, visit the companion website at
https://study.sagepub.com/piekkola

7

PHILOSOPHY OF SCIENCE

LEARNING OBJECTIVE

The philosophy of science, excepting Francis Bacon, is a relatively modern branch of philosophical inquiry, having been subsumed within theory of knowledge in general that deals with issues specific to modern science (Harré, 1967). The scientific method, as discussed in Chapter 3, is rooted in natural philosophy and the development of a means of rational inquiry. It involves issues of epistemology (theory of knowledge) and ontology (the nature of existence). Philosophers of science have been concerned with the nature of reality and how best to inquire into it, including identifying what are considered fruitless avenues of exploration (such as metaphysical questions regarding reality and truth). As we delve into the issues we will consider the following:

- Empiricist philosophy as a basis of subsequent practice and debate.
- The problem of induction.
- Positivism and scientific inquiry.
- Logical positivism.
- Popper and falsification.
- Kuhn and Feyerabend—paradigmatic relativism and anarchy.
- Lakatos—research programs.

FRAMING QUESTIONS

- Does philosophy have any role to play in scientific practice and inquiry?
- If something is unobservable, like gravity or mind, should it be excluded as metaphysical and therefore anti-scientific?
- Does science deal with an objective, independent reality which is the basis of inquiry and its ultimate test?

INTRODUCTION

As was discussed in Chapter 3, Galileo (1623/1957) distinguished between **primary qualities** (properties inherent to matter) and **secondary qualities** (the product of primary qualities acting on the senses). Newton, borrowing from Galileo, considered the human soul to be locked within the body, without contact with the outside world (Burtt, 1952/1980). The soul, to Newton, exists in a part of the brain called the *sensorium*. Whatever primary qualities may be, contact with them is indirect, through sensory organs. Colors, he noted, do not exist in light; they are phantasms produced in us by the action of light. Such secondary qualities have no existence outside of the brain; they are the consequence of light acting upon the body.

This distinction was taken up by a group of British philosophers known as the Empiricists (John Locke, George Berkeley, and David Hume). Whereas epistemologically the rationalists emphasized reason, the Empiricists proposed that whatever is known comes from experience, which was largely sensory experience. While psychology may have asserted its independence from philosophy, the explanations offered by the empiricists, and the attendant difficulty with the senses as a barrier to objective things, continue to dog psychological explanation, mostly implicitly. Before dealing with the Empiricists, there is one rationalist argument that bears consideration since it served as a foil for some of Locke's initiating arguments.

Descartes' method of doubt

Skepticism regarding certain knowledge was rampant during the 17th century. Descartes' contemporaries despaired of the impossibility of certainty given the history of opposing viewpoints, each of which had been asserted as definitive (Flew, 1984). To resolve his own uncertainty, Descartes turned to rationalism. He aimed to establish a rational basis for certain incontestable truths by using his **method of doubt**. He determined to examine various beliefs and to reject all but those that were incontestably certain. If something could be established beyond doubt, skepticism may be overcome and a **foundation** established for subsequent knowledge.

Descartes began with sensation, since that was commonly considered the basis of knowledge of objective reality. He found it wanting. It was already apparent that the senses were deceptive given the evidence of perceptual illusions and the delusions of insanity. Sensory experience may be just a dream or the deceptions of an evil demon (an acceptable idea at that time). After considerable doubting he realized that when he thought, no matter how, or on what, he could not doubt the thinking itself (Pappas, 1998). Thinking was self-evident and, as a corollary, if he was thinking, he existed as a thinker. This led to his famous proclamation of *Cogito, ergo sum* or "I think, therefore I exist." Without going into the details, Descartes reasoned from the certainty of his own existence, and his thinking, that he was innately endowed with ideas that did not come from sensory impressions (nativism). These included mathematical theory and the idea of a perfect being or God. Now, since God is a perfect being, God's perfection would not admit to an imperfection such as His deceiving humans. One was free, therefore, to have confidence in the existence of the external world and in the **reliability** of one's senses. Locke, in response, would challenge the existence of innate ideas.

7.1 THE EMPIRICISTS

John Locke

According to John Locke (1632–1704), what we know comes from experience; we are not endowed with any innate ideas. The supposed inborn ideas, he claimed, do not exist in children, savages, illiterate people, or idiots (A. Rogers, 1910). To Locke, the mind at birth was a *tabula rasa*, a blank slate, upon which the experiences of the world were written (Brennan, 1982). Nothing in the mind exists that was not first in sensory experience. Whatever knowledge we have only comes from experience. Through sensation one attains immediate knowledge of things, external to the senses, that cause the idea of them (Ayers, 1998). We know of things through their power to produce ideas in us. Such ideas only suggest the existence of things beyond the senses but not their actual nature, their essence, what makes the thing what it is. Our ideas are 'representations' of what has acted upon us. **Representationalism** contends that the sensing mind lacks direct access to objects but understands them through the medium of ideas; ideas represent objects (Flew, 1984).

Locke developed his ideas based on 'corpuscular theory' of the chemist Robert Boyle (1627–1691). To Boyle, the physical world was composed of atoms that possess position in space, motion or rest, size and shape, and without the properties of color, hardness, odor, or sound (Stroud, 1980). Locke accepted that what happens, including perception, is due to the action of physical particles. While that is essentially Galilean, Locke differed from Galileo since primary qualities became ideas produced in us by physical phenomena, mental representations of the physical particles. 'Primary qualities' became the power of physical particles, when acting upon the senses, to produce in the perceiver ideas that resemble the qualities of physical particles (Flew, 1984). In agreement with Galileo, 'secondary qualities' do not exist in the particles but are the product of primary qualities acting upon sentient beings. They are the power of primary qualities to produce ideas that do not resemble their cause. The qualities of experience do not correspond exactly with object properties. This was demonstrated with the 'paradox of the basins' (mentioned in Chapter 4), wherein the same temperature may be experienced as both hot and cold.

In the end, what we know are our ideas (mental representations) of the world, not the world itself. That, however, raises skepticism about any objective existent. Whether the world is the same as it is experienced did not really concern Locke (Stroud, 1980). He simply supposed that the qualities that are referred to in physical explanations actually exist in those objects. One could be certain that 'simple ideas' (basically individual sensations) are produced by something real beyond oneself; they could not be produced at will or derived from ideas one already possessed (Popkin and Stroll, 1993). They must therefore represent something external to oneself. With respect to secondary qualities, even though they did not resemble their causes, they had to be the result of the power of external things. (This marks the beginning of modern perception theory and the proposition that perception is an interpretation of sensory input rather than direct knowledge of objective reality).

George Berkeley

Bishop George Berkeley (1685–1753) considered the notion of an unperceived existent, some object beyond immediate experience that produces our ideas of things, an unintelligible proposition (Stroud, 1980). If what is known is known through perception, what is known must be of perception. The essence of sensible things is their being perceived. Sensible qualities cannot exist in something unperceived (like physical particles and primary qualities) since that something is just an idea perceived through the senses. Berkeley was referring to all qualities without making a distinction between them as primary or secondary. His point was that all qualities are perceived qualities and, being objects of perception, are 'ideas' that only have existence in being perceived.

Berkeley was not questioning whether ideas of primary qualities resemble objects, but whether any idea can resemble a non-idea, like the unthinking substance called 'matter.' According to Berkeley, "it is evident ... that extension, figure and motion are only ideas existing in the mind, and that an idea can be like nothing but another idea" (Stroud, 1980, p. 153). Berkeley was a thorough-going idealist or **immaterialist**. Whatever qualities exist they depend on mind for their existence.

In proposing that all we know are ideas, Berkeley was in danger of 'solipsism.' What he knew were his own ideas. Certainly he had the capacity to produce ideas but, just as Locke proposed regarding primary qualities, certain ideas appeared to be outside his control, which suggested an objective reality. Yet since something non-ideational could not produce ideas (remember the excluded middle), what was objective had to be of mind or spirit. The solution was God (Thomson, 1964). Some ideas, which we share with others in common, come to us due to a universal mind within which such ideas are maintained. They thereby continue to exist whether or not any individual currently perceives them. Objective reality exists because it is maintained by God's ongoing perception. Objective reality is not of matter but of mind or spirit (this is known as **objective idealism**—objective because it was external to one and idealism because it was of mind or spirit).

David Hume

David Hume (1711–1776) is a significant figure for the philosophy of science since he formulated one of the major problems that scientists have to deal with—the problem of knowledge by induction. Hume accepted Berkeley's judgment that Locke's primary qualities were known as experienced and that what we know is limited to ideas and impressions (Flew, 1964). He rejected, however, Berkeley's objective reality since sensory experience could not be a basis for knowledge of anything beyond sensation. All one can examine are the experiences and the beliefs one forms on that basis, including beliefs about the supposed objective world. To Hume, the basis of any science was observation and experience, and that demanded examination of the human capacity to know and of what it is possible to have knowledge about.

Locke, Hume believed, had overworked the term 'idea' and replaced it with 'perceptions of the mind' which were of two sorts—primary and secondary or derivative (Hergenhahn and Henley, 2014). 'Impressions,' equivalent to sensations, were primary, resulting from sensory stimulation, and 'ideas' which were the residual images left by impressions. That is all that is presented to mind, not objects or connections to objects. Hume did, at the same time, retain Locke's distinction between 'simple ideas' and 'complex ideas.' Simple ideas were former impressions and complex ideas were amalgams of simple ideas (which need not correspond with complex impressions since mind can rearrange simple ideas). While ideas were open to any recombination, Hume observed that how ideas become associated reveals similarity over individuals, which suggests lawfulness.

Associations were the forces that united mental atoms (ideas) and created compounded ideas. Hume identified three laws of association: 1) the 'law of resemblance'—the tendency of certain thoughts to shift from one event to a similar event; 2) the 'law of contiguity'—the tendency towards recall together events that were experienced together, the one calling up remembrances of the other; 3) the 'law of cause and effect'—the tendency of mind to infer that if, in experience, one event always preceded another, the first event caused the subsequent event. With this third law Hume would introduce a vexatious problem for science and epistemology.

When one examines the different impressions presented to mind, there is nothing to suggest the cause of those impressions, only that they are immediately present. Nor is there anything in the ideas, based upon them, to suggest causality because there is nothing in immediate experience to suggest a necessary connection between them (Baier, 1998). Instead of evidence of causality, what one has is a 'habit of mind' to associate those events that always occur together in experience, in close and regular succession, and to infer a causal relation from it. As Hume (1739–1740/2003) put it, the notion of cause and effect is based on the experience of certain impressions as always being conjoined (separate entities experienced together) and in regular order of succession in past experience. As a result, in thought, the idea of the first evokes the idea of the second. These two are then inferred to be a cause and its effect. Their constant conjunction produces a mental habit that joins them in thought and infers the occurrence of one from the other.

In 'classical conditioning' depicted below, parts 3 and 4 can be used to demonstrate the false assumption of causality based on contiguity, succession, and constant conjunction. Contiguity (nearness in time or space) is represented by the food following closely after the bell has rung. Succession involves the food following the bell. Constant conjunction means that sequence repeats: 1) Bell…Food / 2) Bell…Food / 3) Bell…Food / et cetera. The food reliably follows the bell but there is no necessary (causal) relation between them. The dog, salivating in anticipation, has developed the habitual expectation of food following bell, but bell-ringing does not cause the appearance of the food (the experimenter does).

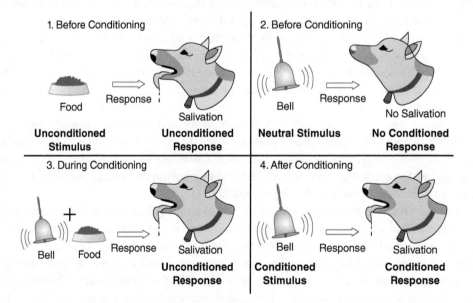

Figure 7.1   Classical conditioning as misinterpreted causality

Hume's argument (represented in Figure 7.1) is that the idea of 'necessity' is essential to causality but that cannot be derived from observations of immediate experience. All we observe is 'constant conjunction' (appearing together) and 'succession' (one always follows the other). There is nothing in succession and constant conjunction to suggest necessity, but necessity is required for judgments of causality. The inference of causation, due to imagination, is projected to where it will not be found—the world as experienced. Just as causality was a product of imagination, so too were other metaphysical entities like God, matter, and self, since none appeared at the level of impressions (Hergenhahn and Henley, 2014).

A further problem Hume introduced was the **problem of induction** associated with **induction by simple enumeration**. Through inductive logic various instances of a phenomenon are compared and the general proposition, lawful regularities true of them all are identified (Flew, 1964). It is then assumed that this generalization will apply to all unexamined instances. Upon the basis of 'all-known-examples,' assertions are made about 'all' possible cases. The problem is that there is no certainty that contradictory occurrences may not be encountered in the future. Just because every snake I have ever seen has but one head does not mean that every snake has one head. Hume showed there is no basis for certainty and introduced an epistemological problem for science. No matter how many observations of recurrence are made, absolute certainty is unfounded.

WHAT DO YOU THINK?

Given the denial of access to an objective reality, and the removal of causality and order, do you think that science, including psychology, can benefit from Hume or is there something unreasonable with this? Why?

Immanuel Kant and Herman von Helmholtz

Immanuel Kant (1724–1804) took up the problem set forth by Hume's skepticism, his denial of order or causality in experience. He agreed that Hume was correct in concluding that order could not be derived from experience (Flew, 1984). What order is experienced must be derived, therefore, from the operation of the mind since order does exist in phenomenal experience. Kant also accepted that there were no innate ideas. There were, however, innate operations of the mind, organizing conceptual tendencies called 'categories of the mind,' that organized sensory input and provided order to the chaotic sensory impressions. Causation, for instance, did not come from sensory impressions, but it did enter conscious experience. It must therefore be due to mental operations. The object world beyond the senses was inaccessible and unknowable, but it was responsible for sensory experience. The 'thing-in-itself' (the objective realm) was not the world as experienced, as it 'appears-to-us' or as 'phenomena' (Lamprecht, 1955). In this, Kant is a **subjective idealist** (since all one knows is of inner mental experience), phenomenal and solipsistic.

Hermann von Helmholtz (1821–1894) was a famous physiological psychologist who developed the 'trichromatic theory' of color perception, the 'place theory' of auditory perception. His theory of perception, 'unconscious inference theory' (previously discussed in Chapter 4) was his response to Kant and underlies modern perception theory. Whereas Kant is considered a rationalist for his emphasis on reasoning processes (categorical organization) in knowledge, Helmholtz was an empiricist. He found Kant's position untenable and rejected innate mental categories. He accepted organizing principles, but was intent on establishing an empiricist account of how they were a product of experience.

It was well-established that humans, in their perceptual experiences, are susceptible to illusions. The false experiences that were the basis of the 'doctrine of specific nerve energies,' such as a blow to the ear producing a ringing experience, seemed to suggest that whatever is acting upon the sensory receptors need not result in an experience that is consistent with it. Furthermore, the information available at the level of sensory processing was impoverished with respect to the richness of conscious experience. The retina, for instance, is composed of three types of color receptors whose stimulation translates into the full color spectrum of experience. Also, the retina, a two-dimensional structure, could not provide the basis for the perception of three dimensions, specifically depth/distance (Helmholtz, 1867, in Southall, 1925/2000). Perception did not correspond with input at the level of sensory registers.

Just as perception and sensation were inconsistent, the qualities of sensation did not correspond with the qualities of external excitants (Helmholtz, 1869/1971) as the doctrine of specific nerve energies demonstrated. The sensory report was inadequate to give a report of the external world. The percept therefore required mediation from within, internal processing acting on the sensory presentation, like Kant's categories, which delivered its product to consciousness as the completed percept (Helmholtz, 1867, in Southall, 1925/2000). These mediating mechanisms were acquired through experience. The mind/brain is empty initially, but as a result of accruing sensory impressions, builds up a store of experiences. These serve to symbolize the inaccessible and unknowable objective reality. So, instead of innate categories, one builds up a store of experiences that are drawn upon in processing current sensory input. Our ideas of things, our perceptions, are not the things as they are in the realm beyond the senses, but inferences, made unconsciously, about those things. The impoverished stimulus input is compared with the store of prior experiences, outside of consciousness, and from that a speculation called the percept is produced and appears in consciousness. Upon that basis, one is able to act correctly in the inaccessible world. Correctness of perception is determined by acting and then receiving a new set of sensations that confirmed one's expectations regarding what sensations should follow from acting in the unknowable world. The store of acquired experiences thus replaced Kant's categories in analyzing sensory input.

Consistent with Locke, Hume, and Kant, Helmholtz accepted that what is known is not objective reality but ideas about that reality. The world was simply unknowable. With Locke and Kant, he believed in an unknowable world beyond the senses that produced sensations. These would become epistemic problems in later philosophy of science. What Helmholtz

The world of objects		The world as it appears
Galileo Primary qualities	S	Secondary qualities
	E	
Locke Objects		Primary/secondary qualities (ideas)
	N	
Berkeley Objective idea		Secondary qualities
	S	
Hume Objective world (unknowable)		Perceptions of the mind (impressions, ideas)
	E	
Kant Thing-in-itself (unknowable)		Categories of mind
	S	
Helmholtz Unknowable objects		Acquired experiences Unconscious inferences

Figure 7.2   Stages in the empiricist debate

advocated, as would later philosophers and psychologists, is known as **indirect realism** (see Box 7.1 for a discussion of indirect realism in experimental research into perception). Figure 7.2 summarizes the trends discussed to this point.

BOX 7.1
INDIRECT/DIRECT REALISM IN PERCEPTION RESEARCH

Traditional perception theory has been based on the experimental demonstration of the inconsistency between perception and objective reality, as perceptual illusions demonstrate. Physiologically, it is concluded that too much processing mediates between object and percept (object → light → retina → optic nerve → occipital lobe → conscious percept) for the percept to reflect the world as it is—see Figure 7.3 below. This leads to an assumption of

(Continued)

(Continued)

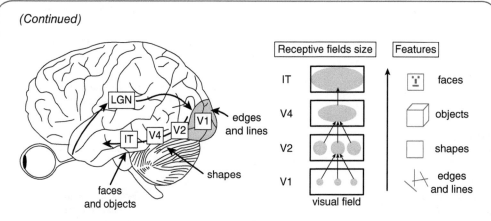

Figure 7.3 Stages in visual processing

© 2011, IOVS Online by the Association for Research in Vision and Ophthalmology

indirect realism, but Wilcox and Katz (1984) contend that there is a contradiction in this—a confusion of two epistemologies since **direct realism** is relied on in proving indirect realism.

How, asked Wilcox and Katz, can one 'know' that a perceiver's reconstruction of current sensory input is in error or not? In experimental proofs it is the psychologist who judges the discrepancy between the world as it is (experimental stimuli) and the world as perceived (by experimental participant). Wait a minute! In order to make judgments of correctness/incorrectness, the psychologist must have direct access to the world as it is. This assumes direct realism for the psychologist in order to prove the indirect realism of the participant. It is logically absurd to hold one epistemology for psychologists and another for non-psychologists. Both are human perceivers. They either both perceive indirectly or both perceive indirectly. Being a psychologist does not establish a privileged epistemological position.

Wilcox and Katz proposed a thought experiment: Imagine that the psychologist and the experimental participant switch places. Now the experimenter only has access to sensations and representative knowledge and the former participant has direct knowledge. Obviously, nothing has really changed—changing roles does not alter perceptual processes. Human is human, psychologist or not. Being humans all, we cannot have two epistemologies, one for the psychologists and another for everyone else. Either both are direct realists or both are indirect realists. If judgment favors indirect realism, the psychologist can say nothing because s/he cannot pass beyond sensation to the external world and that leads to solipsism. If one accepts realism, on the other hand, as a basis for knowledge, one can justify reference to the objective world, other people, and accumulated human knowledge. While Wilcox and Katz did not address it, even the argument from stages in brain processing assumes actual access to, and knowledge of, the brain in order to make the case for the inaccessibility of objective reality.

7.2 POSITIVISM

Auguste Comte

Auguste Comte (1798–1857) conducted a historical analysis of the development of the sciences and identified three stages they passed through as they progressed towards what he considered the positive approach (Mazlish, 1967).

- The first, the 'theological' stage, was characterized by a projection of human qualities onto nature, and supernatural explanations, as with gods of thunder or sea, reflect the period (anthropomorphism and animism). These were human inventions not based in fact, not observed directly (Acton, 1951).

- During the 'metaphysical' stage, gods were replaced by metaphysical, conceptual abstractions, that were not within immediate experience (Mazlish, 1967)—Hume's issue. Ideas of natural laws, human nature, substances, and so on, prevail in speculative explanation but they are not present in immediate experience.

- The final 'positive' stage abandons laws, metaphysical first causes, and absolute knowledge claims. Positive knowledge rests upon observation alone. Observation was not restricted to sensation though. The scientific task was to observe and formulate hypotheses regarding the invariable relations between phenomena, verified in subsequent observations. What conceptions are used have to refer to phenomena only (Acton, 1951).

Positivism rejects metaphysical speculation and focuses on observable, verifiable facts (Abbagnano, 1967). That meant excluding traditional philosophical concerns that were outside empirical investigation—causality and objectivity, idealism and materialism, and religion were dismissed (Naletov, 1984). What was beyond the limits of experience did not accord with positivistic empiricism (Hume's point). They were speculative, senseless, and non-scientific. In place of speculations Comte emphasized observation, experimentation, description of observations, and generalization based on observation. Unlike Hume, a fact is not in reference to sensations; Comte is aligned more with French 'common sense realism' which opposed subjectivism and believed knowledge was of the world (Acton, 1951).

Ernst Mach

Whereas Comte was associated with common-sense realism, the physicist and philosopher Ernst Mach (1838–1916), was aligned with Hume's empiricism and phenomenalism. All one can know of anything is through sense experience; sensations constitute the world, including oneself and others (Mach, 1890/1897). What we know are sensations: "the world consists only of our sensations" (p. 10). Actually, Mach preferred to speak of 'elements' rather than 'sensations' because the term sensation carried vestiges of a one-sided theory (presumably the inherent subjectivity of traditional empiricism). Whereas Kant had posited an inaccessible realm beyond the senses, different from phenomenal existence (the 'thing-in-itself'), Mach considered that notion "monstrous" and 'superfluous." Both outer and inner world are composed of these elements and the purpose of research is to determine the connections between them. Sensations are not produced by bodies; bodies too are complexes of these elements (the body is a 'concept' derived from sensations). Bodies are symbols of thought based on particular sensation complexes. According to Mach, physicists are mistaken in considering bodies real, abiding existences, rather than transitory sensations. Matter, too, is just a mental symbol for a complex of elements that are sensuous. All are concepts based on recurring sensation complexes.

The subject-matter of all the sciences was the same to Mach. Where they differed was in terms of which set of sensations, and relations between sensations, they attended to. When our gaze shifts from the sensations that one science focuses on to those of a different science, nothing has actually changed, they all form a whole. When dealing with color as a physical object, a light source, one is within the field of physics and when dealing with it in terms of the retina and optic nerve it is physiology and psychology. Mach conceives of the sciences as unified, given sensation is the common object of study. The world of sense belongs to both the physical and psychical domains; there is only one kind of element. Due to this common subject matter Mach, and others, would posit a unity of the sciences.

The aim of every science is to describe its observations in terms of sensations. What we call laws are merely descriptions of the relations between sensations. Laws summarize past experiences; they mentally represent the sensuous facts in general, and support prediction of future experiences. Descriptions are what constitutes explanation in science and explanation does not invoke metaphysical concepts like causes. There is no need of unknown, unknowable processes behind the interdependence of sensations (Mach, 1905/1976). An isolate ego (self, mind) is a provisional fiction, as much as the isolated object, given that both are different aspects of element complexes. They are objects of experience that enter consciousness and are identical in that they are element complexes. By restricting oneself to the description of the functional relations that existed between sensations, there would be no need to introduce unnecessary metaphysical notions like causes (Winston, 2001). The goal of science is to seek the most economical description of the largest number of observations rather than explanations based on unobservables (Robinson, 2000a).

Within psychology Edward B. Titchener (1867–1927) and Edwin Boring (1886–1968) were supporters of Mach's philosophy of science (Winston, 2001). Titchener accepted that description was the aim of science (Danziger, 1979). He had adopted a form of positivism in basing his subject matter on the direct experience of what is given to consciousness.

Skinner

To Tolman (1992), John Watson, the arch-behaviorist, in emphasizing a science based solely on what was observable, was emphasizing immediate experience too, and in that he was a phenomenalist and **presentationist** like Titchener (and Mach). **Burrhus F. Skinner** (1904–1990) wrote that his "debt was to the empiricism of Mach" (1987, p. 208). Having read Mach's *Science of mechanics*, he (1979) began to deal with the reflex in Machian terms. Skinner (1953/1965), rejected the terms 'cause' and 'effect' and replaced them with changes in independent and dependent variables; what were cause-effect relations became functional relations (akin to Mach seeking functional relations between sensations). Skinner, however, replaced Mach's sensations with 'stimulus,' 'response,' and 'reinforcing stimulus' but, after that, their philosophy of science was basically the same (Kitchener, 1996).

7.3 LOGICAL POSITIVISM

Positivism has been influential in biological and physical science but, by the 20th century, scientific findings, such as Einstein's 'relativity theory,' were challenging the approach (Hilgard, 1987). The assertion that science must be restricted to observables constrained scientific work. It was becoming clear that a number of theoretical concepts, unobservables, were essential (Hergenhahn and Henley, 2014). In physics and chemistry, concepts like gravity, valence, electromagnetic fields, atoms, and electrons could not be bypassed. Such unobservables were crucial to their explanations of what they observed and had to be retained, while still avoiding unverifiable metaphysics. A group of philosophers, called the 'Vienna Circle,' proposed **logical positivism** as a solution. Theoretical terms (referring to unobservables) would be accepted if they could be connected to observations, but empirical observation was the ultimate authority.

Precursors

Henri Poincaré (1854–1912), a mathematician, considered himself an empiricist who disallowed reference to an objective reality, only sensory impressions (Alexander, 1964). Lacking access to what lies beyond, mathematics and geometrical principles were not derived from experience but they should be given privileged status, like Kantian categories, independent of experience. This is known as **conventionalism**, the positing of certain truths from the start (like mathematics or logic). Rather than proven, these truths were a matter of agreement among adherents—by convention. Theories based on conventions were not meant to yield 'truths;' they served as aids in coping with empirical data as given (Hung, 1997). That certain statements could be asserted, simply upon the basis of convention, was accepted by logical positivists.

Poincaré's influence was further evident in his distinction between **theoretical statements** and **observational statements** (Hung, 1997). Observational statements were propositions that could be checked for truth or falsity by direct experience. Theoretical statements, on the other hand, were propositions that could not be checked for truth or falsity against direct observation; they were speculations upon, or summaries of, observations. The positivists had rejected theoretical terms as belonging to Comte's metaphysical stage of explanation in terms of non-observables. Regardless, practicing scientists found theoretical terms like 'gravity' useful. As a correction, the logical positivists allowed for theoretical terms but only if they could be connected to observational terms.

Physicists like Mach and Albert Einstein (1879–1955) were also influential. Mach (1872, in Lenin, 1947) believed the job of science was to determine the laws behind the connections between sensations, of ideas with ideas, and between sensations and ideas. The notion of an external reality made no sense to him (Klee, 1997). The function of theories, therefore, was to coordinate the collected sensory data, not 'explain' events (Hung, 1997). They organized data from observations of sensations, not material objects, and rendered those facts economical. An objective, independent reality, composed of things, was excluded from Mach's scientific realm.

To Einstein (1936/1996), establishing the 'real external world' required formulating concepts of bodily objects derived from the mass of sensory experiences. From repeatedly recurring complexes of sensations, interpreted as signs, one attributes those sensations to bodily objects. Two major physicists, Mach and Einstein, asserted that the data they worked with were sensations and the logical positivist would base their philosophy of science on the proposition that only statements referring to direct observation had any meaning.

Logical positivism as neo-positivism

During the 1920s the Vienna Circle met to discuss the state of philosophy (Urmson and Rée, 1989) and the new role for philosophy in science. Their aim was to improve theorizing in the sciences and to establish a positive base for it. Metaphysics had to be purged and unobservables disavowed as empirically empty, unless connected to observables, in order to clarify and perfect the language of the sciences. Hypothetical statements were irrelevant scientifically unless connected to observations. Notice that, as philosophers, their focus was on linguistic statements, not scientific practice. To accomplish their end, they drew upon the Empiricist tradition, Kant, and recent developments in mathematics and logic.

According to the Vienna Circle, apart from formal statements of logic and mathematics which were a priori (conventionalism, nativism), only statements based upon direct observation had any meaning (phenomenalism). Combining Hume's empiricism with Kant's nativism, one arrives at logical positivism. In this, the role of philosophy was to examine the statements made by scientists and perfect the rules governing scientific language (Stevens, 1939). Rudolph Carnap (1891–1970), a leading figure, thought it would be possible to join mathematical logic with empiricism (Creath, 1998). By doing this, the logical positivists believed that they could resolve the problem set by Poincaré when he distinguished between theoretical terms and observational terms.

The logical positivists proposed that science deals with two languages—theoretical and observational—and that it took place in three steps (Hung, 1997):

- First, record observations (sensory experience) in observational terms.

- Second, data is generalized into statements about anticipated empirical observations.

- Third, explain generalizations in theoretical terms.

There were two components involved in proper scientific theory: First, internal principles (theoretical statements) which explained the thing-in-itself (things beyond the senses); second, 'bridge principles' were statements that mixed both theoretical language and observational language to establish the relation between the thing-in-itself and the thing-as-it-is-experienced (observations). By connecting theoretical terms with observational terms it was thought metaphysics would be bypassed. The bridge principles would be explicit definitions that combined the two, but this proved too difficult, so the idea of **correspondence rules** was introduced (Flew, 1984). These rules logically connected the two languages and, once connected, the theoretical terms were admitted as acceptable. An **operational definition** which defines theoretical terms according to how they are detected or measured is equivalent to a correspondence rule. The theoretical terms referred to what was unobserved, but measurement and detection were. The connection to them justifies the theoretical terms.

Linguistic expressions are thought to convey meaning, and the meaning of statements also had to be addressed. Meaning could be assessed on conventional grounds (logically) or else empirically by connecting statements to observations (Urmson and Rée, 1989). Thus, according to the **verifiability principle** (or verificationism), the meaning of a proposition is determined by how the statement is verified. This was intended to serve as a basis for discounting metaphysical propositions. Unfortunately, this would eliminate what they wanted to retain. In principle, natural laws could not be verified since that would require every instance to confirm the generality (the problem of induction).

The logical positivists also continued Mach's **unity of science** proposal. The core idea was that there are no special sciences whose fundamental principles and concepts cannot be equated with those of at least one other science (Klee, 1997). In the end, the logical positivists believed that all of the sciences formed an interconnected network and that higher-level sciences like sociology and psychology could be reduced to the more basic science of physics. Remember that they share a common data—observations. This results in a further theory generated by the logical positivists: **physicalism** (Flew, 1984).

Physicalism takes the view that all propositions having to do with existences and facts can be expressed as statements that refer to observable occurrences and objects using physical language. In terms of psychology, all sentences used to refer to psychical states are translated into physical language sentences (what is observable). Given that, the psychology that the logical positivist recognized was behaviorism since it emphasized the observable (Stevens, 1939). According to Carnap (1932–33/1959), the laws of psychology, as generalized sentences, are translatable into physical language and are, ultimately, physical laws. Psychology may use its own terminology, but its definitions of those terms in psychological language have to be linked to physical language. That is what Watson had been doing by turning mentalistic terms into behavioral terms.

We end this section with **operationism**, the doctrine that, to be scientific, terms used should be subject to **operational definition**. While rooted in logical positivist thinking, specifically correspondence rules, the proposition actually came from physics (Stevens, 1935). In 1905, Einstein reported a problem with the term 'simultaneity' (Hung, 1997). Two nearby events can be judged for simultaneity quite readily, but when separated by vast amounts of space the matter is not so easy. To solve the problem Einstein proposed an operational definition based on how the two events would be measured. Bridgman (1927, in Plutchik, 1970) extended Einstein's solution to all theoretical terms. Each term's meaning was identical to the set of operations by which it was determined. Stevens (1935) introduced the notion to psychologists and it became a cornerstone of psychological methodology and theory.

WHAT DO YOU THINK?

Even though it is based on subjective experience, do you think that logical positivism has anything to offer psychology?

7.4 KARL POPPER AND FALSIFICATIONISM

Karl Popper (1902–1994) took issue with the belief that the cornerstone of empirical sciences was the inductive method, moving from particular instances or singular statements, to universal statements, hypotheses, or theories (Popper, 1934/1959). Hume had shown the inherent problem in induction and Popper drew upon that. No theory could ever be proven. He therefore rejected **justificationism** as an epistemological ground for belief, the notion that something is true or verified through agreement with immediate experience. The verificationism of the logical positivists was an example. According to Popper, scientific theories could never be justified, or proven, but they could be tested and subjected to disconfirmation. If a theory passed a test it was not judged proven or true, it was merely 'corroborated' (not yet falsified) but expected at some point to be discredited. After all, the greatest scientific theory—Newtonian mechanics—was found faulty by Einstein after centuries of success.

The **pragmatist** philosopher Charles Peirce (1839–1914) took up the problem of induction and accepted that absolute certainty could not be established. Nonetheless, as a realist he believed knowledge of the independent, objective world was attainable, and that the validity of our beliefs could be determined through use in practice (Hookway, 1998). Theories, and the people who formulate them, could be fallible, but knowledge grows through debate and objective demonstration (a social and objective affair). In response to the problem of induction, Peirce proposed the notion of 'warranted belief.' Reality, the final arbiter, could be approached, not with certainty but with increasing levels of probability. Inductive thinking is prone to error but in the long run it is self-correcting. As the number of observations increases and remain in agreement, one is justified in speaking of likelihood (probability) of correctness. While there was always the possibility of future refutation, until such time belief was warranted. Popper (1934/1959), however, rejected probability as a corrective; it was no basis for universal statements or certainty.

The positivists and logical positivists allowed for inductive reasoning but Popper rejected it. It was not a suitable means for demarcation of the scientific, for identifying what was legitimately scientific. The theoretical systems of scientists could never be verified empirically. What renders a theory scientific, then, is not that it can be verified but that it can be falsified. To be scientific the theory must be of a form that leaves it open to **falsification**. No theory can be proven true but it can be shown to be false. Once falsified, the theory should be eliminated.

Willard Quine (1908–2000), in 1951, resurrected the proposition of Duhem that failure to support hypotheses cannot defeat a theory because hypotheses are not tested in isolation from related aspects of the overall theory (Hung, 1997). According to the **Duhem-Quine thesis** all statements are essentially theoretical and are not by sense experience (Urmson and Rée, 1989). Hypotheses exist within a web of related assumptions, any of which can be adjusted to protect the failing hypothesis. Falsification is an impossibility because the scientific predictions are not based upon simple hypotheses but on whole sets of assumptions, and the inferences that went into the testing procedure (Stam, 1992). Popper (1934/1959) had argued that evading falsification by introducing auxiliary hypotheses, or redefining terms after the fact, was mere evasion and inadmissible as proper science.

Not only did Einstein incorporate Newtonian theory, he accounted for its inconsistencies, and also predicted possibilities that exposed his theory to falsification; that impressed Popper (Magee, 1973). When comparing competing theories, preference should be given to the one that has demonstrated its fitness by surviving disconfirming tests. Such a theory must be compatible with what was already known (not disconfirmed?), but succeed where it had failed.

Science, despite the expectation that all theories will face disproof, was progressive to Popper, since false theories can be improved upon (Tichý, 1974). In the 1960s, in response to concerns that this leads to skepticism, given the expectation of eventual falsification, he introduced the notion of **verisimilitude**. This meant that a theory was not true but truth-like.

Popper was developing standards for scientific theories (statements) and not taking a position regarding objective reality. Scientists put forward statements and test them against experience (Popper, 1934/1959). He, however, had no intention of defining 'observability.' His concern was with 'basic statements' (closely connected to perceptual experience) regarding some observable event. When he used the terms 'objectivity' and 'subjectivity' the usage was similar to that of Kant. To be objective meant scientific knowledge was independent of personal whim, and open to being tested and understood by anyone. Scientific statements were neither justified nor verifiable but referred to regularities in observation and were repeatable and testable—tested inter-subjectively (within experience).

In the end, science does not go beyond basic statements: "Every test of a theory, whether resulting in corroboration or falsification, must stop at some basic statement or other which we *decide to* accept" (p. 104, emphasis in original). It is not a matter of agreement with reality. The aspect of science that concerned Popper was not realism but theoretical statements and hypotheses. Nonetheless, Popper did influence psychology. The American Psychological Association (APA) Board of Scientific Affairs (Wilkinson and the Task Force on Statistical Inference, 1999), for instance, emphasized the need to precisely define variables so that they would be open to empirical falsification; and Ferguson and Heene (2012) proposed that science depends on theory falsifiability.

7.5 THOMAS KUHN AND SCIENTIFIC PARADIGMS

Thomas Kuhn (1922–1996) was interested in the history of research activity as a basis for understanding scientific practice and explanation (Kuhn, 1962). Kuhn opened with a criticism of the notion that the history of science has demonstrated **incrementalism** or 'development-by-accumulation.' The evolution of knowledge has not been continuous and belief in incrementalism may be an instance of **presentism**. Concepts, methods, and theories are discovered in older texts and current science is projected backward to them as though continuous with them (Hoyningen-Huene, 1998). This, to Kuhn, was the basis of the fallacious notion of continuity in scientific advances. By attending to the history of actual research practices it became apparent that what actually happened was the emergence of **paradigms** which were dominant for a time and then displaced by new, competing paradigms.

As a new science emerges, facts are gathered and various approaches compete with each other as explanatory accounts (as with the 'new' psychology and the competing approaches of Wundt, Charcot, and Galton; see Chapter 8). Eventually one approach becomes dominant and a paradigm is established that attracts the greatest adherents. In time, anomalies, errors and failures accrue, and the paradigm is displaced. This is what happens over time, not incrementalism. One may therefore speak of stages in the development of a science:

- Pre-paradigmatic Stage: A period of competing factions struggling to define the subject matter and methods. Consensus is lacking. What needs to be explained and what the relevant data are is unclear.

- Paradigm Stage: A period of 'normal science.' Fundamental problems have been identified and procedures established. There is a shared theoretical perspective and a paradigm-specific jargon that guides and informs the research community. Larger issues are settled and fundamental principles direct further inquiry. Findings accumulate internally. Anomalies (inconsistent findings) arise but are largely ignored. Such anomalies represent falsification to Popper but not to Kuhn (Worrall, 1998).

- Revolutionary Stage: Anomalies accumulate and are taken seriously by new generations of scientists (Kuhn, 1962). Amendments and adjustments may be made to the paradigm. When anomalies reach a critical mass, alternatives to the paradigm are put forth and a period of crisis emerges. In time a new paradigm may be sought which marks a revolution.

The old and new paradigms are **incommensurable**, lacking a common standard for comparison. The revolution represents a change in world-view; the world is perceived differently and entails a new observation language. Paradigms have different standards and definitions; their terms exist in different conceptual webs. To Kuhn, science is a matter of producing a socially-constructed image of the world, but to others (Hung, 1997; Klee, 1997) this is relativism and a form of idealist anti-realism. Science, to Kuhn, does not model an objective reality and the notion of 'truth' does not make sense (Hung, 1997). Kuhn rebuts that. He is not a relativist because relativism implies the possibility of truth (which he denies—truth has no part to play in assessing theories). The stages he described had nothing to do with truth—a term he avoided, or progress toward any goal like a true account of nature (Kuhn, 1962).

Kuhn was influential in psychology and was referenced with some frequency (Driver-Linn, 2003). This was likely due to the fact that psychology is a splintered discipline, comprised of numerous divisions encompassing traditions in both natural science and social science, which have differing perspectives on truth and what constitutes progress. The disunity, to some, suggests that psychology is in a state of crisis and seeking a unifying paradigm.

Perhaps Kuhn's greatest influence has been on the **postmodern** turn in psychology. Gergen (1990) credits Kuhn with the attack on **foundationalism** by proposing that what appears to be incrementalism is really changes in perspective or viewpoint. Truth is merely a matter of perspective, not some immutable truth. To Gergen, beliefs are just social conventions; they do not refer to an independently existing subject matter. Gergen's position is known as 'social constructionism' in psychology (see Gergen, 1985) and it shares in Kuhn's relativism.

7.6 IMRE LAKATOS AND PAUL FEYERABEND

Imre Lakatos

To Imre Lakatos (1922–1974), Kuhn, in rejecting justificationism and falsification, failed to provide a rational explanation of scientific growth and his correction led to irrationalism (Lakatos, 1970). Popper, too, failed to provide an account of the actual practice of scientists. Falsification did not lead to the immediate rejection of theories. Instead of discarding falsified theories, the theory was maintained and efforts to support it continued. In fact, highly successful scientific theories forged ahead despite numerous anomalies or counterexamples—they were simply ignored. Instead of scientific practice being guided by theories, or successions of theories, 'research programs' directed ongoing practices.

The 'game' of science begins with a research program, not falsifiable hypotheses, and, because of that, there are no Popperian 'crucial experiments' that immediately disconfirm a theory and eliminate it. The overall program was the basic unit for assessing scientific progress, not corroboration or falsification of sub-aspects. This was because programs have a 'hard core' that is immune from falsification by single experiments. Only 'auxiliary hypotheses' derived from it are tested, and that insulates the core. Auxiliary hypotheses may be falsified but they form a 'protective belt' about the core. It is auxiliary hypotheses that are adjusted or dropped, but the core remains unchallenged and safe from refutation. This is consistent with the previously mentioned Duhem-Quine Thesis.

Besides the core, research programs have 'positive heuristics' and 'negative heuristics' that direct research activities. The positive heuristic determines the research paths to pursue. It moves forward regardless of refutations or anomalies. Anomalies are sidestepped with the hope that they will eventually be disproved or incorporated into the programme. The negative heuristic, in contrast, determines the research paths to avoid because they would challenge the hard core.

Kuhn's 'normal science' is just a dominant research programme; these are seldom long-lived. In the history of science, one finds simultaneous, competing research programs, rather than successions of paradigms. In the struggle between programs, the successes of competitors do not eliminate programs. Defeats are allowed; a comeback from defeat is always possible. As long as 'heuristic power' is sustained (new facts are being produced, empirical content is expanding, and refutations are being explained) there is staying power. After prolonged effort, if no comeback is achieved the program dies. It is then that, in retrospect, the original challenging experiment is deemed crucial. The successful alternative must explain what the competition did and supersede it with greater heuristic power. That is what is revealed by the historical record. Neither falsification nor revolutions are behind scientific advances. By examining actual scientific practice, Lakatos (1974) concluded that the philosophy of science has greater impact on historians of science rather than guiding scientific practices.

Paul Feyerabend

Paul Feyerabend (1924–1994) liked controversy. In a monograph (1970) and a book (1975/1988), he declared himself an anarchist and advocated an 'anything goes' attitude. Anarchy, he wrote, was an excellent foundation for the philosophy of science and epistemology. The notion that there is a method for conducting science, with obligatory, fixed principles was inconsistent with the history of science. Some singular method may alleviate intellectual insecurity, but a better principle is to be open to anything. Methodological pluralism is preferable. In fact, he advocated challenging accepted views by inventing hypotheses inconsistent with well-established viewpoints (like Copernicus promoting the heliocentric, sun-centered view of the inverse). You never know what surprises may be in store. Step outside; replace induction with counter-induction. Proliferate theories. No idea, whether ancient or absurd, is incapable of improving knowledge. Science is just one method, an all-too-powerful yet fallible method, invented by humans to deal with their world. It is one tradition among many.

Feyerabend was attracted to Dadaism in art. Dadaists rejected conventional, cultural values; they lacked a program and opposed all programs. Anarchistic, anything goes pluralism did not mean that science could be dismissed (it is, after all, part of anything going). To Feyerabend, science is not grounded in 'objective facts.' Rather than stating how things are, it manufactures ideas about laws and facts. The traditional image of science is a 'fairytale' (Feyerabend, 1975). There are no special methods guaranteeing success. Natural magic, primitive medicine, witches, Voodoo, and other approaches have all helped people deal with their circumstances. As he admitted, the epistemological anarchist is not opposed to defending the outrageous or the absurd. Science and its methods are no answer to anarchy. Anything goes, except universal standards, universal laws, and ideas about truth.

As Tibbetts (1977) rightly argued, I believe, it is difficult to know when to take Feyerabend seriously or judge him intentionally absurd. Certainly methodological pluralism is to be valued over dogmatic commitment to 'the' method. That does not, however, mean that all methods are equal in pursuing knowledge. The value of scientific methods is their provision of reliable knowledge, subject to the scientific community's criticisms and corrections. Over time, fallacies are recognized and removed. Such self-corrective measures are not apparent in magic and myth-making. As a result, science has a better chance of separating the credible from the incredible. Medical science has learned from shamans and primitive medicine. They have revealed healing herbs, for instance, but it is the chemists and doctors who can determine what the healing properties are and why they work. That is something more than a mere fairytale.

WHAT DO YOU THINK?

Do you think science, let alone psychological science, can contribute any real knowledge or is it doomed by subjectivity to be a matter of personal belief?

7.7 AN APPEAL TO REALISM

Perhaps, due to the problem of induction, philosophers of science, and some scientists, have emphasized empiricist philosophy and its attendant antirealism. Cognitive psychology and perception theory, asserting sensory input as their starting point, are forced into some sort of indirect realism. We need to ask, however, whether the fact that we cannot have certain knowledge commits us to deny the possibility of useful knowledge however imperfect? Science is based on testing ideas against experience, against observations, but the question that remains is what is observed—our perceptions or the objective world?

According to Vladimir Lenin (1870–1924), in our transition from ignorance to understanding, we have been increasing our store of relative truth (Lenin, 1947). We may not have absolute knowledge of the universe but, relative to earlier historical periods, we have expanded our grasp of how things are. Two hundred years ago our knowledge of gravity confined us to the planet surface, but increased inquiry into aeronautics and propulsion has taken us to flight and into space. Planes crash and spacecraft fail, so we have more to learn, but that does not negate what we have come to know reliably. The key here is that our ideas are tested in '**practice**,' not in passive observations or disavowal of reality.

Practice

The experimental side of the pragmatist tradition was Dewey's instrumentalism, or 'knowing through doing.' To know something is to act on that knowledge and to test in practice. Untested belief is mere conjecture. Verification depends on active experimentation (Dewey, 1916). The consequences of acting in the world determine the value of an idea. The history of cultural evolution, especially as reflected in technological advances, is a testament to the effectiveness of the methods of inquiry that humans have developed (Dewey, 1929). Nature has its secrets, but careful inquiry and research may reveal them. Absolute truth is an unattainable idea and all assertions of truth are provisional, but some provisional truths have been verified so often that one is justified in treating them as absolutely true (until disproven). Knowledge exists in the realm of practice and engagement with the world, not in rational debates that are ultimately anti-realist.

> The requirements of continued existence make indispensable some attention to the actual facts of the world. Although it is surprising how little check the environment actually puts upon the formation of ideas, since no notions are too absurd to have been accepted by some people, yet the environment does enforce a certain minimum of correctness under penalty of extinction. (Dewey, 1920/1948, pp. 34–35)

SUMMARY

Psychology, despite its exhortations to the contrary, has been under the influence of philosophy. In this chapter we have looked at the philosophy of science and ways in which it bears on psychological practices. We have noted the following:

- The primary/secondary quality distinction has had far-reaching impact.
- Empiricist philosophy set the stage for subsequent debate regarding knowledge—what can be known and how best to achieve it.
- Hume's problem of induction has had an enduring impact on notions of certainty of knowledge.
- The Empiricists and Kant, through Helmholtz and Mach, have brought access to objective reality into doubt.
- Experimental demonstrations of indirect realisms have relied on direct realism.
- Positivism introduced observational fact as the sole basis of scientific subject matter.
- The distinction between observational statements and theoretical statements has been taken up by psychology, especially through operational definitions.
- Popper's falsificationism has served as a directive for scientific research.
- Kuhn's paradigmatic theory of science was relativistic and is reflected in post-modern psychology.
- Lakatos' theory of research programs, and the Duhem-Quine thesis, may reflect actual scientific practice.
- Realism, rather than anti-realism, allows for the possibility of 'truth,' or at least a basis for action in the world, however uncertain.

SUGGESTED READINGS

Dewey, J. (1916). *Essays in experimental logic.* New York: Dover Publications.

Hung, E. (1997). *The nature of science: Problems and perspectives.* Belmont, CA: Wadsworth Publishing.

Klee, R. (1997). *Introduction to the philosophy of science: Cutting nature at its seams.* New York: Oxford University Press.

Want to learn more? For links to online resources, examples of multiple choice questions, conceptual exercises and much more, visit the companion website at **https://study.sagepub.com/piekkola**

8

MAINSTREAM AND ITS CRITICS

As the above heading suggests, in this chapter our concern is with mainstream (the main stream) psychology, the dominant approach within academic psychology. The term 'mainstream psychology' is often used in criticisms but goes undefined, so to be clear, to be mainstream is to hold a position of pre-eminent influence and command. In that sense, mainstream psychology is 'experimental psychology' (Much, 1995). There may be disagreement on other issues but there is broad consensus regarding the role of the experiment; the manipulation of independent variables to note the effect on dependent variables, while holding confounds constant (Winston and Blais, 1996). It is the basis of psychology's 'scientific method' as represented in textbooks since the 1970s.

As an expression of that dominance, the British Psychological Society and the American Psychological Association define psychology as a science. The websites of Oxford and Harvard Universities describe psychology as a science and an experimental discipline. The *Publication Manual of the American Psychological Association* is itself an expression of the dominance of experimental psychology (Budge and Katz, 1995). The manual socializes neophytes into its core, empiricist values, attitudes, and the preferred epistemology—the empirical method (Madigan, Johnson, and Linton, 1995). It is the conception of psychology as an experimental science that pervades academia and represents what is mainstream. To be the main stream, though, implies that there are alternative streams or approaches. Much of the criticism of the dominant approach comes from there, but it also comes from within. That psychology is a science is not at issue, but what the nature of a psychological science should be is, especially as that is reflected in its methods.

Mainstream psychology has achieved the status of what Fleck (1935/1979) referred to as **vademecum science** (handbook science). In a sense this is comparable to Kuhn's 'normal science.' In the evolution of a science, after an initial period of struggle and fractious debate, one approach rises to supremacy. Its viewpoint and methods are established as definitive, the challengers are dispatched to oblivion or marginality, and it becomes the basis of training initiates into accepted principles, procedures, and basic concepts. As the system becomes more formalized its assumptions become ever more implicit and are passed on to novices as accepted canon. It is treated as given and no longer questioned. Blind faith sets in and training becomes proselytizing and embodied in condoned texts (a sort of catechism and cookbook of methodological procedures as exemplified by chapters and texts on the scientific method in psychology). By committing to one method the contemporary psychologist, often unknowingly, eliminates significant issues that do not fit within that framework (Robinson, 1981). The critics of the mainstream approach question the assumptions and accepted practices, and challenge their authority and validity.

LEARNING OBJECTIVE

Mainstream psychology has been challenged on many fronts, more than a brief chapter can convey. The intent is that you be a competent, critical consumer of psychological doctrine and sensitive to possible dogma. The discussion will be selective and focus on the following themes:

- The path to dominance.
- Value-free objectivity.
- The search for universals.
- The problem of meaning.
- The ecological validity of research.
- The subject-object dichotomy.

FRAMING QUESTIONS

- Should psychology be modeled after the natural sciences?
- Can you identify yourself in experimental findings? Does individuality matter?
- Does psychology capture the 'humanness' of being human?
- Does psychology have any bearing on everyday life?

INTRODUCTION

As a discipline psychology is heterogeneous, composed of multiple sub-disciplines (biological, neurological, social, cognitive, motivation, abnormal, personality), and yet homogeneous in its natural science aspirations. Method and measurement have pervasive and privileged status (Smith, Harré, and Langenhove, 1995). Central to this is the separation of a phenomenon into, or reduction to, variables (independent and dependent) and the identification of relations between them. This leads to a neglect of alternative modes of inquiry and different conceptual formulations of the object of investigation. In fact, the literature leaves one with the impression that many things are excluded from discussion, including what constitutes the subject matter for the discipline (Langenhove, 1995). By drawing upon the natural sciences model there is a tendency to treat human beings as material objects and, often, only in terms of those aspects that are publicly observable.

Explanations based on such models become akin to those of the physical sciences (such as Newtonian mechanics and inorganic chemistry). The purpose is to identify lawful relations and to make successful predictions, and that leads to the dominance of experimentation. Elementalist reduction to constituents (variables) becomes common in explanations. Such a view also promotes assumptions of mechanistic determinism and ignores the fact that human conduct is meaningful and intentional, subject to modification through social communication, and done for reasons rather than mechanically caused.

8.1 THE EMERGENCE OF THE MAINSTREAM MODEL

As psychology was struggling to find itself it was caught in a rift between the humanities (history, linguistics, religious studies, literature, art) and the social sciences versus natural science (Danziger, 1990b). The difference between the natural sciences and the social sciences, according to Kagan (2009), rests on the generalizations of natural science transcending current historical conditions, whereas those conditions seriously influence social science. The successes of the natural sciences, at the time psychology was emerging, led to beliefs that its methods were the only ones suited to securing useful knowledge. At the beginning, three general models emerged that would shape early research (Danziger, 1990b).

In Germany, Wundt drew upon the experimental practices of physiology to study elementary processes like sensation and immediate perception. At the same time, he believed that higher mental processes would require a non-experimental methodology that was *Völkerpsychologie*, roughly folk or cultural psychology. This was because the experimental method unduly separated the subject from the sociohistorical context of their lives. The object of research and knowledge were the basic processes of the generalized, normal adult mind. Given the commonality of the processes involved—sensation, perception, attention—a single individual could be representative of the population.

In France, Jean Charcot (1825–1893) favored the clinical method which extended a physician–patient relationship into an experimental situation (a demonstration). The knowledge object was that of abnormal behavior and processes of inter-individual suggestion. Charcot famously demonstrated the effectiveness of hypnosis in removing hysterical symptoms. A person who subjectively was blind, for instance, but whose visual system was perfectly functional, could have sight restored through hypnosis. In Germany the people tested had social relations with each other, but the relationship in France was less personal; the roles of doctor and patient were clearly defined. In Britain, the relation between the researcher and the researched was the most impersonal—that of strangers meeting in brief encounters.

The interest of Francis Galton (1822–1911) was in the performance variability within the population on various measures thought to be related to intelligence, like sensory acuity (as discussed in Chapter 5). The individual mind was of little consequence; what mattered was the person's rank within the pool of people tested, as part of an aggregate or distribution of scores for a particular measure. The knowledge object that was created was that of individual performance within the group and normative data (the average and range of scores). The characteristics studied were deemed abilities of independent, socially isolated individuals (hence biological and innate).

The rise of the Galtonian model

In time, the Galtonian model was the one that became most influential. There were three main reasons for that:

- Radical individualism: The claim was that it was dealing with individual characteristics that were uninfluenced by social conditions. That provided grounds for assuming that test performance would generalize to natural situations beyond the laboratory.

- Relative standing: The idea of individual differences as a means of comparing and ranking individuals relative to each other meant a move from the study of individual performance to the population as a whole.

- Statistical information: Quantitative values were applied to performance and the individual became a statistic (a score within a collection of performance measures).

Given psychology's aim to be scientific, the statistical rendering of findings was significant. Quantification had been taken to be a key element characterizing a discipline as scientific; but Kant had denied psychology that possibility (Hornstein, 1988). Quantification, as Boring (1961) pointed out, was desirable for the prestige it conferred.

Between the two world wars the original tradition of attributing results to specific individuals by initials or numbers progressively declined (Danziger, 1990b). Munsterberg (1894), for instance, in the first issue of *Psychological Review*, gave individual results for participants A.P., Bi., Bu. E.P., and W. Gradually there was a shift to group data within which individuality was submerged and diffused. Psychological research no longer was interested in the individual mind. The significance of each individual became that of a contributor to collective performance on some abstraction of interest (the characteristic being assessed). Psychologists sought to establish statistical norms of response around which individual responses (human uniqueness) were deviations from average performance and called error variance. This led to knowledge claims about laws of behavior that applied across individuals and situations. Psychological characteristics were no longer attributable to individuals but to collectives.

The presentation of average results, rather the results for each individual, suggested that the function under investigation was comparable to a scientific law that held for everyone. Bills (1938) proposed, quite succinctly that "Psychology as a science is necessarily abstract and general, dealing with the ways in which persons obey general laws or differ quantitatively in respect to general traits" (p. 384). The procedure itself, however, may limit what generalizations are possible (Allport, 1942). Group research inevitably selects one, or a few, characteristics from concrete persons' lives; the more individuals that are selected, the fewer common aspects are available for comparison. The resulting laws of human nature become, in the end, rather narrow as one singles out what is universally applicable.

Ultimately, it becomes necessary to distinguish between 'personal identity' and 'experimental identity' (Danziger, 1990b). The characteristics under investigation may become abstractions, the trait of anxiety for instance, constructed by the researcher's investigative practices, and may not even coincide with the participants' individual and social identities. In personality psychology, for example, there has been a concern with 'common traits' which are measurable aspects of personality shared to different degrees by many people (Allport, 1937). Tests, such as the Taylor Manifest Anxiety Scale, are developed to measure these common traits in the population. Whoever takes the test will get a score and appear to be anxious to some degree even if they are not. The trait frequently has but a faint resemblance to the person who received a score. The common trait is an intellectual abstraction—since traits only exist in individuals—that reflects something about the group, not any individual. I believe it was Allport who once wrote that there is no such thing as 'anxiety,' only anxious people.

Artificial groups versus natural groups

In everyday life there are traditional categories by which people may be grouped, such as children versus adults or females versus males (Danziger, 1990b). While Danziger does not mention it, there are also natural groupings represented by affiliation with social collectives such as political parties, religions, occupations, boy's and girl's organizations like Boy Scouts and Girl Guides, criminal organizations such as the Mafia and the Yakuza; one could go on and on. Psychologists, given their interests, tended to create their own categories for grouping people that were independent of traditional classification schemes (Danziger, 1990b). These artificial grouping procedures provided a basis for a science of psychological abstractions. An abstraction, to be clear, is some quality or characteristic that is considered apart from the thing in which it is found (like individual persons). Dealt with in the abstract, those characteristics could be considered independent of any real contexts (individual, social, or historical).

There were three ways in which psychologists created artificial groups. First, the responses to an experimental treatment could be pooled and mean performance discussed. The average finding is not expected to be demonstrated, necessarily, in the performance in any one, or even any, individual. As **Carl Jung** (1875–1961) argued, the ideal average abolishes the exceptions that exist at the lowest and highest ends of the distribution (Jung, 1958). There is a saying that a statistician can have his head in an oven and his feet in ice but will, on average, feel fine.

Jung

A second grouping can be based on the division of participants into different treatment conditions or experimental conditions (different independent variables) for comparison (Danziger, 1990b). The patterns of individual responses, under this purpose, are not as interesting as the differences between the groups, the inter-group comparison. Lastly, people can be grouped by performance on some measuring instrument like a test—the psychometric group. The psychologist, by developing some construct like anxiety, intervenes to create the group. The artificiality of these groupings is due to their being created in the investigation rather than found in the everyday world.

The psychological 'group' is consistent with the definition of English and English (1958): "several items or cases, recognized as individually different but assembled, or thought about and treated, for some purpose or purposes as if alike" (p. 231). In contrast, the 'natural group' is one that requires no outside pressure for their formation. Neither does 'group' reflect the 'social group' which is a collective that acts as a unit to some degree (Drever, 1952). The psychological group is artificial, a collection of strangers that are unaffiliated, other than having been gathered for someone else's purpose.

BOX 8.1
QUALITATIVE DIFFERENCES BETWEEN SOCIAL GROUPS

Social groups are hardly homogeneous in their qualities. Petrovsky (1985) identified two dimensions around which they can vary—the degree of personal relations and whether pro- or anti-social. Five classifications follow from that:

1 Highly cohesive, interpersonal, and prosocial, such as 'doctors without borders' or 'free the children.'

2 Highly cohesive and antisocial, like the Mafia or the Hells Angels.

3 Insignificant interpersonal relations, but prosocial like protest marchers against war or climate change.

4 Insignificant interpersonal relations, but of an antisocial nature like sports hooligans rioting.

5 Groups that are neither prosocial nor antisocial and without any connection personally, like people on a bus (excluding people traveling together).

Group '5' represents the people who constitute the artificial grouping of the psychology experiment. Not only are there no interpersonal relations, members are often unaware of each other, having been tested one at a time.

The illusion created

Given the conditions established by the experimental method, the end result was a conception of humans that was illusory (Danziger, 1990b). Experimental results were not the product of social interaction between people at a particular period in history, or in a particular socio-historical context, but were the manifestation of processes that were abstract, transpersonal, and transhistorical. The abstract laws and not the carriers of the abstractions became all-important. Individual identity became irrelevant and the choice of subjects (those who were 'subjected to' conditions not individual persons) became a matter of convenience—undergraduates were readily available.

Laboratory research is aimed at isolating some behavior or characteristic of interest from extraneous contaminants (the confounds or variables that exercise an unwanted influence) in order to confine it to the experimental manipulation (Riger, 1992). It is assumed that participants, upon entering the laboratory, leave behind their beliefs, values, social status, personal history, their life experiences, and, when not, that this can be mitigated as an influence by random assignment in order to diffuse their impact. Actions are thereby abstracted from the social being and behavior is stripped of its social context. Sociocultural factors are ruled out and whatever the person does in the experiment is attributed to internal factors independent of life history. Experiments themselves usually take place as brief encounters between strangers in unfamiliar settings. All of that raises questions about the generalizability of the results.

Regularities in research had nothing to do with individuals-in-life-contexts (Danziger, 1990b). They pertained to an individual in isolation whose assessed characteristics existed independently of any social involvement. Yet the actual persons investigated are not social blanks; they enter the experiment with established social identities. Experimental psychologists were intent, however, on establishing a type of knowledge regarding humans that would be universal, acultural (unrelated to, uninfluenced by culture), and ahistorical. That means that the assessment of the obtained results applies to the experimental, not the social, identity of participants. Danziger referred to this myth of the isolated individual as the 'Robinson Crusoe assumption' after the 18th-century literary character who is shipwrecked alone on an island.

WHAT DO YOU THINK?

Do you believe that the experimental method can rightly be applied to all domains of psychology, or should it be restricted to areas that are obviously universal to all humans? What might those domains be?

8.2 VALUE-FREE OBJECTIVITY

The positivist Ernst Mach (1838–1916) was influential in the development of a scientific framework for both physics and psychology (Marr, 1985). His emphasis on the observations of facts and descriptions congruent with the facts, free of metaphysics and unwarranted speculation over unobservables, would be influential. The ideal positivist scientist never allowed personal preferences in theory to intrude on their practices (Baker, 1992). Facts were to speak for themselves without beliefs or biases impinging on fact-gathering or fact interpretation. Science was to be made objective by eliminating the scientist's subjective side and was restricted to procedures and methodologies that prescribed good science. Completely objective observers, who could be separated from the phenomena under consideration and objective in their reporting of results, was the ideal. The myth of science as value free and atheoretical was created.

The method depersonalizes the experimenter and the subject matter. Experimental subjects were to be treated as just another object rather than as persons with their own predilections. Individuality became a deviation from the sought-after general laws. This would lead to describing psychological phenomena in terms of variables because it allowed for an apparently objective language that could bypass individual subjects. During the era of positivism psychologists rejected persons as valid sources of useful psychological data (introspection was devalued). The neurotic need to be ranked as scientific, like the much-admired physics, led to the subjective world being publicly rejected as unobservable. As a result, what is the quintessential domain of psychology (subjective experience) was dismissed.

Karl Pearson (1857–1936), a follower of Galton and the person who formulated the correlation coefficient, was also a positivist and supporter of objectivity. Pearson (1892, in Cantril, Ames, Hastorf, and Ittelson, 1949b) contended that knowledge of the scientific method could train the mind to engage in an impartial and exact analysis of the facts. That meant the individual scientist would be freed of bias in forming conclusions. This contributed to the proposition that true inquiry in science takes place in a world that excludes personal judgments. The ideal of objectivity became an ideal for psychologists that remains influential. For example, McBurney (1997), in a text on research methods, indicated that science is a means of obtaining knowledge that has objective observation as its basis. The 'canons of method' restrict what is scientifically admissible to what is public (observable) and communicable (Levine, 1974). By such requirements, any qualified observer could make the same observations if told how to replicate the observation (what goes in a scientific report describing methods and procedures). That standard, however, has been questioned as to both its possibility and its worth.

Cantril et al. (1949b) contended that it was becoming clear that the thought process involved in scientific investigation is not a mere matter of 'impartial analysis' of a set of facts. Value judgments on the part of the scientist are involved in recognizing problems with current explanations, identifying relevant functional relations to the matter at hand, deciding upon those features of the phenomenon (variables) that can be used in an experiment, and designing the experiment. (Recall here the concept of **theory laden**, the proposition that observations are initiated by some theory.) Then there is the interpretation of the results—all of this involves judgments of value or importance. Beyond that, not only is objectivity, or the removal of personal bias, an illusion, it is also undesirable. While one must be aware of personal attitudes, preconceptions, and interests, they are essential to scientific investigation. They shape the whole investigatory practice.

Objectivity is an ideal that may be inconsistent with actual scientific practice. Mitroff (1974) conducted interviews with the prestigious scientists studying moon rocks from the Apollo mission. Inconsistent with the idea of emotional neutrality and objectivity, these people were extremely competitive and emotionally involved with their ideas, resisted letting go, and did all they could to confirm them (remember Lakatos, Chapter 7, and the idea of research programs and protective belts). They were committed to their theories and tests of their hypotheses. In fact, they argued that scientists should have strong commitments and that it was naïve to think that scientists are objective and uninvolved emotionally.

To conceive of scientific activity as independent from life experiences, purposes, values, and personal world view denies what is a fundamental aspect of human activity, including scientific psychologists (Bevan, 1991). Scientific activity is not free from the power of some ideology. It may consider itself value-free and objective, but scientists are produced by their societies and that shapes their world view and values (Spence, 1985). These belief systems influence research in all of its phases from problem selection to result interpretation. For example, in the West, especially the United States, there is a cultural **ethos** of self-contained **individualism** (Sampson, 1977). Success or failure is the personal responsibility of the individual, not the community or society. Despite the social conditions supporting poverty and social injustice, personal suffering and misery are treated by psychologists as individual matters.

By promoting this ideology (whether conscious or not) the practitioners have a value bias that interferes with effective solutions, except at the level of the individual. That creates more problems, instead of resolving them, since it is all up to the individual internally to cope and adapt (ignoring the possible source of misery as social in origin). Psychologists tend to reduce conflicts to subjective conditions, to internal psychological factors, eliminating the conflicts between real people (Sampson, 1981). There has been a process of psychological reification—the social-historical process is turned into a basic psychological process (internal to the individual) which loses connection to the social, historical, life conditions. If psychology ignores its reifying approaches it will support current social arrangements while purporting to discover and describe human realities. According to Sampson (1977), psychologists need to be concerned with human welfare and that means they need to focus on persons as social beings in specific sociohistorical contexts (a focus of the next chapter).

8.3 THE EXPERIMENTAL METHOD AND THE SEARCH FOR UNIVERSALS

A goal of mainstream psychology has been the search for universals or lawful generalities. The discipline of being 'scientific' came to imply the formulation of universal truths; truths free of particulars (individuals), of history, and from local meanings or culture (Danziger, 1988). Group data supported this cause because the results were attributed to the aggregate rather than particular individuals (individuals became anonymous). The new types of studies were called 'statistical' and dealt with the distribution of a characteristic within a population.

Both the experiment and its findings were deemed separate from the historical context of any particular, individual life (from whom the characteristic was abstracted). It was the abstraction that led to universals and, since they were liberated from sociohistorical contexts, they were often identified with the biological level.

As a disciplinary ideal, the formulation of general, universal laws necessitated context independence as a necessary feature (Mishler, 1979). This was because freedom from the constraints of any context meant that findings could be applicable to all. The standard experimental method thus has 'context-stripping' as a central feature of design and measurement. For a hypothesis to be tested for generality, subjects had to be removed from ordinary social relations, roles, and circumstances. This was a logical step since social contexts are extremely variable and historical contexts undergo rapid change, and both make universality unlikely given the inconstancy introduced. Consider, for instance, how the internet has created a global environment, or how international terrorism has affected government policies and personal freedoms; this affects people's lives and alters behavior in ways that are unique compared to the past. While the variables abstracted for investigation may not be context dependent, the lives, experiences, understandings, and activities of the persons from whom they were abstracted are not. The issue of the generalizability of findings to real-world contexts becomes problematic on that count.

Human universals has been a foundational assumption of scientific psychology but the issue remained largely an unexplored assumption that was taken for granted (Norenzayan and Heine, 2005). The assumption is apparent in the method of sampling used in research. In the *Journal of Personality and Social Psychology* participants are mostly undergraduates, 92 percent from the United States (US) and Canada. Rather than general human nature being studied it is young, middle-class, educated Westerners. Yet American psychologists have implied that their results apply to all humans even though 95 percent of the human population have not been considered (Arnett, 2008). Largely lost in this was the fact that, from the beginning, an alternative approach was advocated by people like Wundt, Dewey, and Vygotsky (as well as Rivers and Bartlett in Britain) who recognized the importance of attending to contexts and cultures.

The universalistic assumption is challenged by the growing evidence of cultural diversity in psychological phenomena (Norenzayan and Heine, 2005). As Danziger (2009) expressed it, the pervasive belief that psychologists were studying universals remained implicit until cross-national and cross-cultural differences began to be explored. The assumption has become especially problematic given the rise of 'indigenized psychologies' (approaches to psychology that are appropriate to different ethnic or cultural groups) that are adapted to specific local conditions by psychologists from those regions. What was assumed to be universal has been found to be quite variable, and cultural specificity is becoming ever more apparent.

BOX 8.2
THE PROBLEM OF IGNORING INDIGENOUS PSYCHOLOGY

The United States has been highly influential in exporting its brand of psychology around the world and of being **ethnocentric**. Not only have American psychologists been largely US-centric, they have been mostly unaware of how their own culture has shaped their research practices and theory (Christopher, Wendt, Marecek, and Goodman, 2014). Each psychology is culture-bound and therefore indigenous, including the American brand. Ignoring that, however well-meaning, American psychologists have been criticized for insufficient attention to local traditions and values when attempting to help other cultures. After the devastating Indian Ocean tsunami of 2004, for instance, some psychologists rushed to Sri Lanka to lend a hand. There was concern that widespread post-traumatic stress, depression, and suicide would be evident. Traditional Western therapies (cognitive behavior, debriefing, stress counseling, and exposure therapy) were instituted. Their assumptions and priorities were unfortunately at variance with those of the local peoples.

Often their recommendations clashed with local ideas of appropriate conduct around social interaction, privacy norms, and emotional displays. Their group therapy techniques failed to consider segregation practices around caste, sex, and religion. Others sought to engage in individual therapy without considering the intense shame, personal and familial, associated with mental illness. Attempts were made to release intense emotion, for catharsis, without considering Buddhist and Hindu strictures against public displays of emotion. In fact, the local people saw no need for alleviating personal suffering. More than that, the psychologists ignored or devalued local practices of ritual healing, meditation, and other community networks. In the end their efforts were wasted and even brought about negative consequences. Culture is far from a nuisance variable and challenges notions of universality, at least at some levels.

The experimental situation in psychology is established by choosing a method that is a-personal; the subject is forced to limit their involvement to a response to objective events established by the experimenter (Romanyshyn, 1971). Subjects do not enter the situation as persons and the experimenter's interest in them is as a data source. The procedure results in generalizations that describe the relations between variables, which is not a problem so long as that is all one is interested in, but problems arise when going beyond such modest purposes (Danziger, 1985). If the essence of scientificity is the methodology, there will be pressure to accommodate psychological theory to the structure of the methodology (such as asocial, ahistorical, and impersonal). For instance, there was a broad belief that aggregate data from many people was the only acceptable basis for rendering general theoretical assertions about people. That involves an implicit assumption of an isomorphism (one-to-one correspondence) between the structure of group data and the structure of the psychological processes in the individual. To Robinson (2000b) the data sets that are generated by large samples do not model anything beyond themselves—the large data set. Harré (2005) believes it is an error for one to infer the propensities of individuals from the statistical distribution of a population. Individuality and subjectivity are eliminated from experiments; persons become anonymous (Morawski, 2007). Perhaps that is why, as Mishler (1979) pointed out, it is generally known that research subjects have trouble recognizing themselves in the reports of the research they were a part of.

The logic of experimental design and statistical inference required that each 'subject unit' be independent and neutral, and thus interchangeable—one is as good as another (Levine, 1974). Humans' social nature, however, renders the interchangeability assumption suspect. Even when they come from the same social system, there are many ways in which people have differentiating life experiences that preclude the assumption that the experimental conditions will be interpreted in the same way. Being poor or rich can lead one to consider a new vehicle costly or a mere pittance—same vehicle, different value. That people are not interchangeable may be one of the reasons that there has been a lack of replication in psychology. People, given different life experiences and learning, are not uniform and that enters into experimental situations and can alter results as the subject sample changes; hence non-replication.

The historical and social nature of individuals and individuality, as was mentioned earlier, is dismissed when the concern is with abstractions and not individual persons. A published report on experimental findings reveals little to nothing of the persons involved. The individual is eliminated from psychological writing through statistical procedures like averages (Gigerenzer, 1987, in Billig, 1994). This is so even where it might be expected to not be so. In a review of research into personality entitled "Where is the person in person-ality research?" Carlson (1971) found little knowledge of anyone in particular—personality without persons. An examination of current literature on personality will demonstrate this by examination of the Methods section under Participants, for instance Giacomin and Jordan (2016) mention their participants were undergraduates, their age range, and their ethnicity. Presumably that is all one needs to know in order to develop a matched sample in replicating findings.

The American Psychological Association (2009) *Publication Manual* states that in order for results to be properly generalized it is critical to properly identify participants. An adequate description would include demographic information (age, sex, sexual orientation and gender identity, ethnicity, educational level, socioeconomic level, immigrant or disability status), and anything topic-specific to interpreting the results. Too much information provided about participants would introduce the problem of heterogeneity and non-generalizability, but a total lack of information would suggest procedures that were unscientific (Billig, 1994). Of course, avoiding the problem of heterogeneity by excluding too much detail just buries the issue by non-disclosure. The disregarded details were still present, just not mentioned. What we end up with is journal text that is mostly devoid of individuals; the materials are 'depopulated' (Billig, 1994). Abolishing concrete individuality, psychological states are depicted as disembodied abstractions. As Martin (1996) indicated, the data of psychology seldom describe 'anyone' and the statistical regularities reported do not correspond with any particular person's experiences or actions. The strategy represents the victory of statistical methods over real psychological understanding. In contrast to physical objects subjected to idealized situations in laboratories, humans fail to respond in predictable ways to life circumstances. As a result, the finding that generalizes from research in psychology is that what is found does not generalize.

8.4 THE PROBLEM OF MEANING

When Hermann Ebbinghaus (1885/1964) did the first research into memory, he recognized that stimulus meaning was a potential confound (some materials may be more memorable by being personally meaningful). To counteract that, he developed 'nonsense syllables' (consonant-vowel-consonant combinations that were not words) to be learned and remembered. Sir Frederic Bartlett (1886–1969) found the assumption that meaningfulness had been eliminated absurd (Bartlett, 1932). If stimuli can arouse human responses, he argued, meaning cannot be gotten rid of. Furthermore, there is no guarantee that simplicity and uniformity of structure in stimuli corresponds with simplicity and uniformity of response. When confronted with supposedly meaningless presentations there is what he called 'effort after meaning.' This was a fundamental process whereby patterns are connected to some personal setting or scheme (organized memory structure). Every cognitive reaction from perceiving, thinking, to remembering is an attempt to makes sense of what confronts one, and one draws upon already formed knowledge structures to do so. The immediately presented, meaningless material, is interpreted in terms of what is not immediately present, and therein is the origin of meaning (which is socially and personally tinged and can be quite idiosyncratic). That is why meaningless Rorschach inkblots have something personally meaningful projected onto them. 'CIN' could serve as a nonsense syllable, but it makes me think of 'sin' or an abbreviation of Cynthia or Cincinnati; it may, of itself, have no meaning, but I can provide it with some.

Researchers have traditionally assumed that a stimulus is a stimulus and that it will evoke homogeneous responses, that it will mean the same thing to all. Sometimes, however, that assumption is challenged. Krause (1970) argued that a person's behavior in a social situation is influenced by the definition of the situation and that, when using situations as experimental stimuli, that has to be considered. Within personality research, Magnusson and Ekehammar (1978) proposed that situational similarity cannot be determined objectively since people perceive situations differently. The situation must be defined by the individual perceiving it. According to Endler (1984), how participants perceive a situation may not be consistent with the experimenter's interpretation. It is necessary therefore to ascertain the subject's interpretation of the environment if one is to understand their reaction to it. To take a simple example, to Nazis and racists the swastika may evoke feelings of pride and superiority, but to many it is a repulsive symbol. The same thing may awaken different meanings, depending on the individual, and that means that subjectivity cannot be ignored, or shouldn't be.

Of significance here, bearing in mind that mainstream psychology tends to ignore subjectivity and historical and cultural conditioning, is the work being done by cultural psychologists to examine how culture affects basic psychological processes like perception and cognition. Depending on one's cultural background, how something is experienced, and what it means, may be quite different. For instance, in Figure 8.1 below, Hudson (1960) expected that Westerners, using standard depth perception cues like 'relative size' (a far-away object produces a relatively small retinal image), would perceive the tiny elephant as a large one at a distance. The drawing would be perceived as an attempt to spear a Gazelle. The Bantu people of Africa, if they had not been to school and had no experience with two-dimensional representations of three-dimensional depth, thought the hunter was attempting to stab a baby

Figure 8.1   From Hudson (1960)

elephant. The schooled Bantu, familiar with pictorial representations, perceived it in the conventional manner. Despite being the same stimulus, the pictorial representations were not equivalent perceptually.

An example that may be easier to relate to, particularly if you are not a wine aficionado, concerns the qualities that experienced wine tasters can identify, and categorize, based on 'mouth-feel sensations.' Personally I can tell whether a wine is red or white, sweet or dry, but that's about it. My crude experience pales in comparison to expert tasters. To red wine experts there are multiple sensations interacting with each other in producing overall taste; these include sweetness, acidity, warmth, viscosity, and bitterness (Gawel, Oberholster, and Francis, 2008). There are 53 terms that could be used to identify the possible qualities of red wine for thirteen categories (such as weight, surface smoothness, and flavor). The expert and I (and maybe you) may take the same wine into our mouths but our perceptions would be quite different. Personal experience matters.

Cross-cultural research has challenged the precaution that 'hard-headed, American experimental psychologists' have entertained since the 1920s regarding the 'objectivity' of experimental materials (Toulmin and Leary, 1985). When the materials used in experiments are stripped of their context, in order to eliminate or insulate from extraneous associations and meanings (like nonsense syllables), their efforts may have been futile. All they achieved was to force their participants back to their unexamined assumptions about normal contexts in everyday life in order to give meaning to objects. This makes it compulsory for experimentalists to reintroduce materials they had long excluded (meaningful stimuli, contexts, persons, and personal meaning, for instance).

Traditionally, the experimenter doesn't ask what one thinks or feels, or what one's responses mean (Jourard, 1968) but, as Levine (1974) put it, even when subjected to uniform conditions, personal histories may result in unknown, unexamined factors interacting with those conditions and affecting the results. To Jourard (1968), subject status should be changed from that of an anonymous object to a fellow seeker of knowledge and a collaborator. Participants should be allowed to reveal what stimuli mean to them and, furthermore, the experimenter should explain what their results mean to her/him and request feedback and authentication. As Carlson (1971) pointed out, our participants are a rich source of untapped knowledge.

8.5 ECOLOGICAL VALIDITY

Clinicians and people working in the community have bemoaned the failure of the scientific method to fit problems that confront people in their daily lives (Levine, 1974). The research is artificial and irrelevant to the context of actual living. There are important psychological problems that have to do with whole events occurring in social-historical contexts, and they cannot be addressed by being severed from that context. Research that is based on isolated variables interacting with each other in antiseptic, highly controlled conditions, simply does not reflect real-world conditions and does not generalize to that context. These experiments lack **ecological validity**.

Koch (1971) proposed that psychology, since it arose as a discipline, has been unique in the fact that the institution of its methods preceded its problems—the application of the method of natural science to the study of humans and their society. Holt (1962) went so far as to propose that "Science is defined by its methods, not its subject matter" (p. 397). As Koch expressed it, the "stipulation that psychology be adequate to *science* outweighed his commitment that it be adequate to man" (p. 684, emphasis in original). Such idolatry of science, Koch believed, has generated spurious knowledge. Mainstream psychology paid insufficient attention to the nature of its subject matter and failed to develop methods appropriate to its investigation. As a result, a lot of psychology has been 'scientistic role-playing' that either trivializes or evades significant problems (Koch, 1981).

According to Robinson (2000b), scientific progress is not achieved by choosing problems because they fit an adopted method. When this is done, knowledge becomes a simple and automatic matter of processing via methodology—'method fetishism' (Koch, 1981). Under such procedures it may even appear as though the object of investigation is irrelevant (remember the question: "where is the person in personality research?"). This reflects the concern of Bakan (1967), who proposed that the scientific enterprise has turned method into idolatry or 'methodolatry' (a term used by May, 1958). Further back in time, Peters (1921/1962) wrote of 'dogmatic methodism' as the prescribing of certain methods for the sake of being scientific in psychology. When methods take priority over that to which they are directed, methods become idolatry (Bakan, 1967). That is where issues of ecological validity arise.

Working in their laboratories, psychologists create the reality that they impose on their subjects (Braginsky, 1985), but the integrity of psychological scholarship depends on being situated in the real concrete world as lived in and experienced (Bevan, 1991). This is what Bartlett (1932) proposed regarding Ebbinghaus' exact recall of nonsense syllables as largely irrelevant. According to Bartlett, literal recall is quite unimportant; remembering almost always occurs in a social setting that is constantly changing and it is to those circumstances that memory is serviceable. Exact recall of stimulus materials in experiments does not address everyday memory.

Neisser (1978/2000), decades later, proposed that naturalistic, ethological study of memory may be more fruitful than its counterpart—the laboratory study. Neisser (1996) identified three characteristics of everyday memory: it is purposeful (serving some end), it is personal (affected by experience), and it is particular (influenced by context). 'Everyday cognition' has since become a concern, at least for some, in naturalistic research (see, for instance, Rogoff and Lave, 1984, and Hutchins, 1995). Also deserving mention here is Roger Barker, who set up a field station in 1947 for naturalistic research, or 'ecological

WHAT DO YOU THINK?

How are we to conceive of people in the context of their everyday lives? Are people wholly independent of their environments, as Cartesian thinking would have us believe, or are they embedded in a web of relations with their physical and cultural environments?

psychology,' in Kansas that was carried on for two decades. According to Barker (1968), some of the conditions of everyday life are not created experimentally; the experiment excises important environmental properties, but naturalistic experiments are going on all the time and they are instructive. The laboratory cannot mimic the complexity of ordinary life. Mainstream psychology fails to take on difficult matters like actual lives, situated culturally and directed toward goals (Robinson, 2000b).

8.6 THE PERSON–ENVIRONMENT DICHOTOMY

Since the time of Descartes, an opposition has been set up between the subject and the object, or the person and the environment, a distinction that has been adopted within mainstream psychology. Certainly it manifests most clearly in those positions which maintain mind/body dualism (as discussed in Chapter 6), but it occurs in various forms throughout psychology. In cognitive psychology it is reflected in the distinction between input and internal processing mechanisms. In perception theory it exists in the distinction between the distal stimulus and the percept. In motivation theory it exists in the distinction between internal causation and external causation. Even the distinction between the independent variable (as external stimulus event) and dependent variable (as organic response) bears that distinction. An early manifestation in psychology can be found in the reflex arc scheme—the basis of the stimulus-response (S-R) distinction of behavioristic psychology. This represented organism and environment as separate entities that mechanically interact and posits environmental determinism. The matter, as it concerns us here, is the degree to which, if at all, one can correctly separate the organism from environment as discrete entities, both the physical environment and the sociocultural.

As mentioned in Chapter 4, the first person in psychology to mount a challenge to the S-R dichotomy was Dewey (1896) and, as was mentioned, he contended that what constitutes stimulus and response depends on what an organism is doing and why. In acting in the world the organism and its environment are **coordinated**, they are interconnected and interpenetrating, a unity. When activity is running smoothly the organism and environment are coordinated, but should a disruption occur in that engagement (a blockage, say, to free movement) the relationship has to be reconstituted. That is when it is necessary to determine the conditions and the resolution—a matter of determining the stimulus, and once the stimulus is identified, so too is the response. It is a matter of adjusting the organism to its environment in order to re-establish the **coordination**—the inter-relationship was strained, not broken. It is the idea of adjustment, or adaptation, and coordination that is of particular relevance to our current consideration.

BOX 8.3
COORDINATION AND DRIVING

In an attempt to bring the concept of person–environment coordination home to you, I will use the example of driving a car. When you first approach the vehicle you have little knowledge of its operation. You have to learn about its instrumentation and what to monitor. You have to learn about the gas pedal, clutch, brake, steering wheel, turn signals, wipers, and the like. You have to learn the rules of the road, the signs and signals. You have to put it all together into a singular activity that connects your movement towards your destination while you monitor your progress and anticipate what is going on around you. Once you have mastered it all, it requires little conscious attention as it has become automatic and coordinated—you are one with the machine and the road, so much so, you may find yourself thinking 'I don't remember driving the last couple of miles.'

Psychology, especially evolutionary psychology, has made much of evolutionary theory but, in doing so, has tended to focus on processes that were evolved in our evolutionary past and which, supposedly, account for current behavioral patterns. Missing in this is the appreciation of the fact that evolved organisms are fitted to, into, and throughout their environment; they are matched to their 'niche.' Expanding on that, for humans this includes their cultural niche, or at least those aspects that any particular individual functions and acts with regards to. Individuals must adjust to the current life circumstances if they are to successfully survive. These are the conditions of existence (Dewey, 1884). Given that, the concept of the environment is a necessity to the idea of the organism. Without an environment there would be no organism. For the individual human this includes an organic relation to the physical environment and to social life lest the individual remain mentally inadequate to meet current demands. There is a large literature that demonstrates the debilitating effects of social deprivation, in terms of inadequate social and intellectual skills (see, for instance, Mason, 1942, and the case of Isabelle, or Skeels and Dye, 1939, on institutional deprivation). The whole point of our educational system is to develop the necessary skills to function effectively in one's societal environment. To consider evolution in terms of ancient adaptations alone leaves something significant out of consideration.

Biologically, as evolutionary theory stresses, an organism that is not coordinated with its environment, adapted to its conditions now and in the future, is an organism that is subject to elimination. If an organism could truly be separated from its environment it would cease to be viable. There must be what is termed **mutualism** (discussed in Chapter 1). Humans, as much as we may conceive of ourselves as apart from nature, are intimately connected to it and subject to its vicissitudes. Consider, for instance, what we have done to the atmosphere in depleting its filtering effects of ultraviolet radiation and increasing our susceptibility to melanoma; or what impact global warming is going to have on the survival of our species. We are natural, not supernatural, beings, and our reliance on our environment has to considered.

Where, as psychologists, should we draw the line between organism and environment, or person and environment, or should we? According to Sumner (1922), the organism constitutes an inseparable whole with its environment; were the environment to be detached, no organism would remain. Some consider the skin to be the line of demarcation—the organism is inside the skin and the environment outside. Palmer (2004) called this the 'morphological conception of the organism.' Angyal (1941/1958), on the other hand, challenged that in asking at what point does the food we consume transition from being of the environment to being part of oneself. The organism and environment are two poles of the singular process called life and whatever division exists between them is conceptual, not actual. Dewey and Bentley (1949) concurred but extended the connectedness to culture. Organisms, they wrote, will cease to 'be' without food, water, air, or radiation. They live across the skin as much as they live within. The environment, including cultural conditions, is the medium and milieu for human activity. In this Dewey (1938) was not suggesting that the entire world is that which any individual is coordinated with. There is obviously a natural world whose existence is independent of the organism and only parts of it become an environment when it enters into the life functions of the organism.

The person–environment and person–culture relation is one of adjustment in the course of engagement and, in those adjustments, the individual grows and develops psychologically. Humans, from birth, occupy what Super and Harkness (1986) called a 'developmental niche.' This is the setting, both physical and sociocultural, of a child's everyday life, involving the mutual interaction of child and culture. Culture, as Angyal (1941/1958) proposed, is an abstraction that only becomes a reality as the individual is connected with it. It is the physical, social space which one inhabits (in-habituates) and within which one acts and becomes a person. Not all aspects of a culture in general, culture in the abstract, are equally important to personality development; they are differentially incorporated into the system of meanings of the individual (Sapir, 1932). Some cultural patterns may only become a reality for some members and non-existent for others. Specialized trades and occupations have their attitudes, values, and concepts, a restricted world of meanings (class, ethnicity, religion, and so on, selectively differentiates positioning in the whole). Allport (1937) proposed something comparable in judging 'personality' as the mode of adjustment that an individual establishes, either consciously or unconsciously, given their life conditions.

Traditional personality theorizing has tended to dichotomize, rather than mutualize, person and environment. Two general approaches existed when personality psychology appeared in the 1930s. These might be simply termed the 'environmentalists' and the 'internalists.' The environmentalists were basically the behaviorists who rejected internal causality and argued for the complete environmental determinism. It was expected that whatever consistency was evident in behavior over time was a matter of environmental similarity—the more similar the circumstances the more similar the behavior. Personality was thus conceived of as thousands of independent, specific habits. Personalists, in contrast, believed that whatever stability existed over time and circumstances was due to some sort of inner determinants or dispositions like needs or, most often, traits of personality. Over three decades each side mustered evidence to support its position. Eventually, Raush, Dittmann, and Taylor (1959) suggested a resolution: "Which is more important for behavior, the individual personality or the situation? The question is a meaningless one. Neither component can be uncoupled from the other" (p. 373).

Endler and colleagues (1962) took the suggestion of Raush, Dittmann, and Taylor but decoupled individual and environment to satisfy methodological and statistical demands. Using the concept of statistical interaction, they proposed, and found, that the interaction of person and environment accounted for more of the variance (the overall variability of individual scores from the average) than did either factor alone. With that, they introduced their theory of 'interactionism' into personality theory (that behavior is determined more by the interaction of personality traits with environmental situations than either situation or trait alone).

As the theory was developed, a distinction was made between 'mechanistic interaction' and 'dynamic interaction' (Endler and Edwards, 1978). Mechanistic interaction was aligned with the standard experimental model and investigated unidirectional causality between independent variables (trait and situation) and the dependent variable (responses). Dynamic interaction, which reflected a process, rather than mechanical interactions, was what was ultimately of interest. In that model, person and environment were considered inseparable, a unified system undergoing change and flux over time and situations, involving acting, receiving feedback, and adjusting. In concrete reality one cannot abstract persons and situations at any moment in time since, in real-life conditions, they are entwined in an interwoven, ongoing process. As Endler (1983) put it, regarding mechanical interaction, "We are dealing with static snapshots rather than movies" (p. 192), but it is the process, the movie, that we need to understand. The appropriate unit of analysis was therefore neither the person nor the environment alone, but the person-in-the-situation as a dynamic mutualism extending through time (Magnusson and Allen, 1983).

It is a matter of getting to know one's subject matter. In the final analysis, it appears that the experimental method has come up against everyday existence and proven wanting. It is lives in context, lives as lived, whole and complete, that we want to grasp and that entail a reconsideration of the significance of human activity, human subjectivity, and human experience. That is why issues of meaning, indigenous psychology, and ecological validity arose. These themes are continued in the next chapter.

SUMMARY

Psychology, in its attempt to be a legitimate science, mimicked the model of the natural sciences and subjected humans to object-based procedures which have been subject to criticism.

- Three investigative models competed (Wundt's, Charcot's, and Galton's), but the Galtonian approach gained dominance due to its radical individualism, relative standing, and statistical formulations.
- Gradually there was a shift from the study of the individual to that of the group and psychological abstractions.
- The group average and individual differences displaced the individual person.
- The psychological group was itself an artificial creation that did not resemble real-world groups.
- Individualism, and the asocial, ahistorical, acultural person, was the psychological image created.
- The positivist ideal of the value-free scientist has been challenged as inconsistent with the facts.
- The scientistic aim of experimental psychology became the psychological universal, or general law, which yields knowledge claims far removed from individual persons.
- Individuality and subjectivity were removed but slipped back in with the recognition that variability in personal interpretations could not be ignored.
- The experimental paradigm is being critiqued for its lack of ecological validity.
- The person–environment dichotomy, the absolute separation of person from the environment, is now being questioned.

SUGGESTED READINGS

Angel, R. and Thoits, P. (1989). The impact of culture on the cognitive structure of illness. *Culture, Medicine, and Psychiatry*, *11*, 465–494.

Koch S. (1971). Reflections on the state of psychology. *Social Research*, *38*, 669–709.

Koch, S. (1981). The nature and limits of psychological knowledge: Lessons of a century qua 'science.' *American Psychologist*, *36*, 257–269.

Ratner, C. (2008). *Cultural psychology, cross-cultural psychology, and indigenous psychology*. New York: Nova Science Publishers.

Want to learn more? For links to online resources, examples of multiple choice questions, conceptual exercises and much more, visit the companion website at
https://study.sagepub.com/piekkola

9

CRITICAL PSYCHOLOGY AND FEMINIST PSYCHOLOGY

LEARNING OBJECTIVE

In the previous chapter we considered some of the criticisms that have been made of mainstream psychology. This chapter continues that theme but differs in that the criticisms are levied, not by individuals, but by collectives of scholars who share a common concern. Overall they may all be included under the banner of 'critical psychologies.' According to critical psychologies, psychology has to include historical and social analysis (Billig, 2008). As a product of their age, their culture, and the web of social relations, by which individuals are constituted as psychological beings, the context of life cannot be ignored. Individual psychology, rather than explained in terms of 'individualism,' is situated socially and historically.

According to the ethical standards of the American Psychological Association (2002), "Psychologists are committed to increasing scientific and professional knowledge of behavior and people's understanding of themselves and others and to use such knowledge to improve the condition of individuals, organizations, and society" (p. 1062). From the perspective of critical psychology, that responsibility has been shirked as the mainstream practices have tended to support the status quo (probably unwittingly) and have failed to address areas of social injustice. Those who align with critical psychology, on the other hand, tend to have as a central concern the well-being of people and the elimination of various forms of oppression and exploitation (Sloan, 2000). In that sense, critical psychology is necessarily political since its intent is to change sociopolitical systems to the betterment of the disadvantaged—to identify, analyze, and work to effect positive change for the citizenry. The aim is to empower and liberate. By advocating a theory of individualism that is asocial and ahistorical, mainstream psychology can justify, at least to itself, its failure to concern itself with sociopolitical issues, but to critical psychologists the social generation of human suffering cannot be ignored. As it is taken up here, we will examine three general areas:

- Critical psychology—German and Danish.
- Other critical psychologies including liberation psychology and community psychology.
- Feminist psychology.

FRAMING QUESTIONS

- In your studies have you ever felt there was something woefully amiss in psychology?
- Have you ever wished psychology could address issues having to do with real life, issues that you could relate to and that pertained to you?
- Do you believe that psychology, by designating itself a science, and therefore value free, has failed to concern itself with real people and real problems?

INTRODUCTION

A hallmark of science has been its social nature, that findings and theories are shared with fellow investigators and subjected to rigorous debate and criticism. Psychology is no different in that regard. The introspective method of reporting on subjective experiences, as used by Wundt and others, was ultimately challenged for inconsistent results and the lack of objectivity of its phenomena. Objective methods would eventually be favored, but they, in turn, are now being criticized. Vygotsky (1927/1997) saw the dichotomy of physiological and phenomenological psychology as a crisis in psychology. During the 1920s and 30s, a group of psychologists, including Gordon Allport, formed a science of personality since, in their opinion, general psychology was neglecting the organized, unique whole that was the individual person (Woodworth, 1931). The 1960s and 70s was a period of crisis in social psychology over the lack of social relevance of its research, given the problems of racism, sexism, drugs, and environmental degradation (Altman, 1987). My point is that there has always been debate and it has often come from within the mainstream.

So why, you might wonder, have a special chapter on critical psychology? Well, the simple fact is that a tradition emerged in Germany during the late 1960s that had as its focus the possible reform of psychology and its transformation into something socially relevant (Tolman, 1994). To that end reformers, under the central figure **Klaus Holzkamp** (1927–

Holzkamp

1995), engaged in an in-depth critique of the methodological and theoretical problems of psychology and sought to reconstruct psychology as a science of human subjects (not objects), for people rather than about people. Their approach was called *Kritische Psychologie* or *Critical Psychology*. Since the 1990s another 'critical psychology' has developed independent of that of Holzkamp (Billig, 2008). A major goal for many within the 'critical psychology' tradition has been to change psychology into an emancipatory discipline that resists the status quo and seeks social justice based on the recognition that much of what is psychological occurs, historically, within particular political, economic, and cultural contexts (Teo, 2013). The United Kingdom has been a center in this movement; and in North America many who identify themselves as critical psychologists come from community and clinical settings.

9.1 KRITISCHE PSYCHOLOGIE

After World War II, psychology in West Germany became Americanized and method-centered; by the 1960s its defects were becoming apparent (Teo, 1995). At that time there was a student movement in Germany which was critical of society as a whole—the status quo, politics, and academia—and this impacted Holzkamp (Teo, 1998). He began a critical analysis of traditional methods and assumptions and was led to question the relevance of psychology for practice in the everyday world of concrete life. In the real world, all those variables that are highly controlled in the laboratory intermingle and display their effects collectively. The field of psychology was a proliferation of competing theories and theoretical fads. Knowledge had suffered stagnation as a result of the accumulating, statistically significant, but theoretically insignificant, findings and a failure to progress scientifically. Traditional psychology was criticized for using investigative procedures that were prescribed by methods, rather than subject matter, and which determined how the subject matter was conceptualized. Even problem choice for investigation was dominated by method. Method dominance was part of the problem since it excluded, rather than embraced, human subjectivity. Subjectivity may not be an issue for atoms and plants, but it did matter to humans and psychology was dismissing it.

Variable psychology

As part of the standard curriculum, students of psychology are taught how psychology is done (Tolman, 1994). Issues of measurement, reliability and validity, and the analysis of the relation between variables are introduced as the means whereby general statements are produced as genuinely scientific psychological knowledge. Holzkamp (1984/1991a) referred to this experimental-statistical method as **variable psychology**. Its focus is on the relationships between variables and the exclusion of the relation of the person, as a conscious, subjective being, to their life contexts in society. In this approach the psychological subject matter becomes 'variables' and virtually excludes the possibility of understanding actual connections of individual lives within societal activity. It leaves one with a science of abstracted individuals who have been reduced to measures of responses (dependent variables) as they are correlated with a world that has been reduced to independent variables.

Research consists of assumptions about experimentally created initial conditions (independent variables), response measures, and the connections (determined mathematically) between them. Individuals become mere switchboxes that transform the initial conditions into patterns of behavior that are taken to reflect general laws. The person's actual 'life-world' and 'life conditions' are represented only to the degree that they exercise their immediate influence (as variables) on the individual. From the start, the individual's societal nature is excluded and the relationship of personal subjectivity to societality (the functioning of society) is made inaccessible. Traditional psychology acknowledges this and considers it a matter of division of labor in science. Psychology is restricted to a concern with individuals and not with societal conditions. The societal is partitioned into the domains of political science, economics, anthropology, and sociology. Aspects from these disciplines, when they do enter, are translated into variables, like economic status or culture, which suggests that they are meaningless for psychological explanation. Individuals are isolated, discrete, and distinct.

Holzkamp (1984/1991a) wrote of the opening speech that his institute's director would deliver to incoming students up to 1968. They were told to forget everything they had heard about psychology and abandon any notion they might have that psychological study would have anything to do with them or their life experiences and personal problems. Psychology was a science, and as a science it was concerned with what was objective; human subjectivity was not an issue. Nevertheless, for many students and psychologists the necessary precondition of ignoring or denying the subjective was problematic. Certainly it is a cornerstone of clinical approaches to the person. Nonetheless, for variable psychology, subjective consciousness is considered inaccessible—a 'black box,' and it becomes necessary to either exclude subjectivity or control it. Where it does enter it is treated as 'intervening variables' (intervening between stimulus and response; hypothesized internal processes).

To render unobservable intervening variables acceptable, they were operationalized (as to how they are identified or measured) and rendered 'surface phenomenon,' not subjectivity. If you recall the discussion from the last chapter, the need to understand the participant's subjective interpretation of a stimulus had to be considered, and that was a concern for Holzkamp. Having consciousness means the participants in experiments relate consciously to the objective stimulus arrangements and that these enter into the black box. There is no guarantee that instructions are being followed as directed, and one cannot conclude whether the subsequent observed behavior actually tests the hypothesis under examination or whether

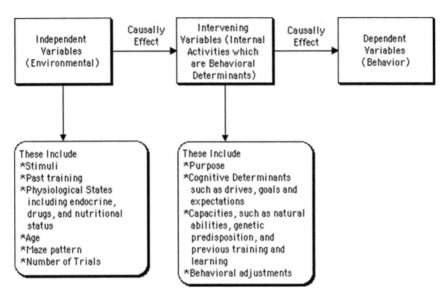

Figure 9.1   Independent, intervening, and dependent variables

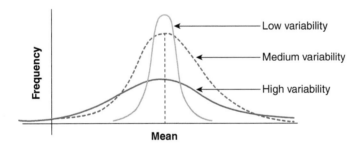

Figure 9.2   Variability

a different hypothesis exists in the experimentee. That means that subjectivity has to be considered the most significant error factor for variable psychology and improvements in experimental techniques will not resolve it.

Hypotheses in psychology are unconcerned with individual subjectivity. Their focus is on distributions of scores within a population and the statistics which reduce distributions to arithmetic descriptions, like averages and variability (how much individual scores deviate from the average—see Figure 9.2). Information about personal, subjective experience only appears as isolated particulars within a distribution (a score that encompasses the effect of the subjective and contributes to deviations from the average) and it disappears into the data and statistical tests of the data. It is overlooked in the service of statistical generalization. Statistical averages are produced by treating individual characteristics (the variable of interest) as comparable elements abstracted (extracted) from each person, then quantified and placed in a distribution. The mean or average is a statistical artifact that does not correspond to psychological reality; nonetheless the results are discussed as though they refer to subjective experience. There would be no psychological interpretation otherwise. There is no sense in discussing anxiety without presupposing an anxious person in some situation. After all, there is no statistical person, the artificial average, and no person unrelated to their life context.

Science of the subject

An alternative to variable psychology's external standpoint is psychology from the perspective of the conscious, self-experiencing person—the personal standpoint (Holzkamp, 1984/1991a). There is no solipsism to this since every person expresses **intersubjective** social relations and can relate to each other given the common grounds of experience. Personal perspectives interconnect from different standpoints. While Holzkamp did not assert it, this is obviously a realist position which enables individual subjects to appreciate each other because of those common grounds for action. According to Holzkamp, solipsism has to be rejected, as does the notion of subjective self-experience as the impenetrable black box of variable psychology. The actions of other people, and their grounding in subjective situations, are the realization of 'action possibilities' in society. To the degree that they are meaningful for the person, they have meaning for others due to reasons and meanings of the intersubjective context (shared experiences). As humans we live within an objective web of meanings (cultures) that we share with others and appropriate (Tolman, 1994). The meanings that become the basis of our acting in the world are originally found in objective meaning structures (language, literature, tools, human activities) of the person's societal world. What is done with them personally can be quite variable but that doesn't change their basic societal nature.

Unlike variable psychology, generalization is not based on statistical generalizations from samples to populations. Generalizability is based on the relation of each particular individual to immediate experience, but such experience is of objective societal conditions and possibilities. Personal subjective experience in the immediate moment is only accessible to the individual, but there is more to it than that. The subjective aspect of actions in the world is just a variant of general human experience as that is related to the concrete historical action possibilities. Individuals connect with each other through their societal relations and the necessities of acting in the world, and the opportunities afforded by society. Subjective experience can be objectified and generalized 'as subjective experience' given the context of experience as intersubjective (we can communicate and share our experience given a common language and shared system of meanings, and by reference to the common conditions of existence and action). The everyday world is composed of a social network of meanings as **generalized action possibilities**. In realizing their action possibilities, their actions and subjective situation become meaningful to others.

Variable psychology, with its objectivity and statistical generalization, is in stark contrast with therapeutic practices that are unconcerned with statistics, and focus instead on persons and concrete life circumstances. As a method, variable psychology cannot begin to appreciate clinical procedures (or for that matter, everyday intersubjectivity). In everyday life people formulate hypotheses regarding each other's motives, reasons, and subjective experiences. To the degree that their lives can be lived in common those hypotheses may be correct—lives become comprehensible in the context of shared life. From the point of view of the subject, Freudian psychoanalysis may be more relevant than mainstream psychology's scientific, statistical abstractions since Freudian concepts were intended to clarify concrete experience (Tolman, 1989). In that respect, according to Maiers (1987), the science of variable psychology is actually science fiction since it has little relevance to individual subjects in their life-world.

Psychoanalytic theory was problematically individualistic (ignoring the societal) and biological, given the explanatory emphasis on instincts (Holzkamp, 1984/1991b). **Sigmund Freud** (1856–1939) took what were essentially societal conflicts and turned them into issues of early childhood; therapy became an individual task. The person was directed back upon herself as the location of the difficulties. Repressive conditions of society were excluded, as were efforts to struggle against these; social conflicts were psychologized (rendered internal to the individual). On the other hand, Freud was a researcher dedicated to advancing knowledge, and academic psychology, the mainstream, despite its apparent scientific rigor, fails to achieve Freud's level of knowledge and insight into the therapeutic relations and mental dynamics. Freud was seeking to understand not just individual experience, but the expression of themes of existence and conflict that were of a 'general human-social nature.' Freud's concepts function to mediate between objective social relations and subjective experience and represents the classical view of generalization, not the statistical form.

Freud

Generalization-as-abstraction is a recent invention tied to statistical analysis; the older, classical form of generalization that dominated psychology in Germany was the 'typical case' (Tolman, 1994). With Wundt, the subject matter was immediate experience (of a few normally functioning, typical people) of external reality from a particular perspective (Holzkamp, 1984/1991b). Intersubjective accessibility (understanding) was achieved with individual subjectivity as a representation of the experience of objective reality given to everyone. The task of psychology was considered the determination of laws that are generally valid and which account for the real world reflected as subjective experience. Immediate experience can be generalized and comprehended as **intersubjectively homogeneous**. It can be generalized to the degree to which it is apparently an instance of what is general human experience.

Psychoanalysis rejected variable psychology's elimination of consciousness (due to its conception as private inwardness and being inaccessible). Immediate experience was what was being investigated. The task was the clarification of the subjective and intersubjective relation to the world and to oneself. Academic, variable psychology has integrated psychoanalytic concepts like repression, projection, regression, and anxiety, but has operationalized the concepts for purposes of experimental testing. In the process of subjecting the concepts to scientific methods they are altered, and their meaning and function radically changed. In the concern with the connections between conditions and reactions the methods of variable psychology evaporated individual subjectivity (it was operationalized). The subjectivity of each person, and the subject–object connection, were excluded from theoretical reflection, disappearing into the black box as empirically inaccessible. The conception of consciousness as the medium for intersubjective connection with the world was replaced by an external conception of the organism.

The function and structure of psychoanalytic concepts are vastly different from those of variable psychology. The concepts of Id, Ego, Superego, and defense mechanisms were intended for a theoretical framework whose purpose was not to predict a relation between an independent variable and a dependent variable but to clarify for another, and help understand, immediate experience. The purpose was to appreciate one's life situation, its conflicts, dependencies, compulsions, and denials. To put psychoanalytic concepts into variable psychology, and reconfigure them to be scientific, subjects them to criteria they were not intended for (see Box 9.1). Operationalizing repression removes it from the subjective-intersubjective context of experience and places it in a context of external behavioral sequences that extinguish the meaning of the intended use. That some psychoanalytic concepts cannot be operationalized (How do you measure Superego or Ego?) or tested experimentally, and to reject them on that basis, is a failure to understand what they are for. The Superego (as internalized morality) was intended to help understand the subjective appearance of conscience and feelings of guilt. Since it is about experience, which variable psychology bypasses, it is meaningless in the context of variable psychology. On the other hand, many Freudian concepts have been taken up in popular culture, which suggests that they have become part of how people think and communicate (Funder, 2013); and that suggests that they are, as Holzkamp put it, intersubjectively homogeneous (Figure 9.3 is an example of their presence in everyday life).

WHAT DO YOU THINK?

Can mainstream psychology ever appreciate Freudian psychology with its experimental methods? If not, should Freudian psychology be rejected on that count?

"LISTEN— IT'S PSYCHOANALYSIS COMING UP THE RIVER FROM VIENNA."

Figure 9.3 Freudian concepts reach everyday understanding

Source: Cartoonstock.com

BOX 9.1
VARIABLE PSYCHOLOGY DISTORTIONS OF FREUDIAN CONCEPTS

A frequent criticism of Freud among experimentalists is that Freud's theories are hard to test (Mischel, 1986). Defense mechanisms are one part of the theory that have been subjected to experimental verification. One such investigation was that of Davis and Schwartz (1987), which studied anxiety and repression. Participants were given tests of anxiety and defensiveness and were formed into three groups based on their scores. The 'low anxious'

(Continued)

(Continued)

group scored below the average for anxiety and defensiveness. The 'high anxious' group scored above the average for anxiety and below the average for defensiveness. The 'repressor' group scored below average for anxiety but above average for defensiveness. In the test phase they were asked to recall memories of whatever sort from childhood to age 14. They were then asked to recall specific memories that were happy, sad, fear-provoking, angry, and of wonder. Since the memories may be embarrassing or too personal, they were to briefly describe each experience generally. In this they were instructed that the specific details were not required in order to guard against an experience that was recalled not being reported. The average number of memories recalled are represented in Figure 9.4 below.

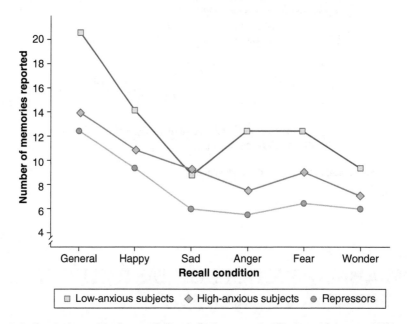

Figure 9.4   Repression and the inaccessibility of affective memories (Davis and Schwartz, 1987)

In psychoanalysis **repression** is an unconscious process that forces memories that are dangerous from entering awareness (Hall, 1954). Davis and Schwartz recognized this in stating that repression involves affective memories being inaccessible. According to their results the repressors recalled fewer memories that were negative, and they saw this as a successful test of Freud's concept. Was it? That is the issue here. First of all, a successfully repressed memory would not be recalled, so does that mean that if fewer memories are recalled that repression is in effect? Well, no. We need to know what life experiences the person actually had that had to be repressed. Whether any of these people were repressing anything is simply unknown since we know nothing of them beyond what they can recall, and which, by definition, is not repressed if recalled. Even at that, we really know nothing of what was recalled since the details were to be omitted. Furthermore, what we know is of the group on average, not any individual in the group. In the end, this may satisfy the demand of variable psychology but it does satisfy the intent of the concept for Freud.

The intent of German critical psychology is to affirm human uniqueness and to preserve subjectivity (Tolman, 1994). At the core of subjectivity is the fact that humans have evolved societally and that our species' history, and individual histories, have to be considered if psychology is to approach adequateness as a science of people. We need to account for subjectivity through the larger theory of society and history; that subjectivity is produced by and reflects it in each individual. Human needs and interests are primarily in reference to, and concerned with, societal-historical conditions (consider, for instance, the impact that cellphones and social media have in creating new needs and interests). Holzkamp wanted to establish a 'context of understanding' of the determinants of the relationship that exists between societality and subjectivity.

Human and societal evolution

In order to appreciate modern human psychology, Holzkamp felt that it was necessary to understand the historical path we followed as we developed to this point. In this, Holzkamp drew from Leontyev's theory of the development of mind. Since this was discussed in Chapter 1, I will not go into it further (see Holzkamp, 1992, and Tolman, 1989, for a summary of Holzkamp's treatment). Of particular significance here is that, while the social relations of humans are biologically rooted, there was a transition from biological **phylogenesis** to historical **sociogenesis** and the emergence of societal modes of existence that come to dominate the biological (Tolman, 1994, 2009). Living in society, their biology even becomes an object of investigation. As a species, humans are characterized by how they control their biology rather than by how their biology controls them (consider medical science and the correction of biological defects). Historical development, rather than evolution, becomes a governing process and the relation to the world is no longer natural (biological). It is mediated by socially-constructed meanings. It is in society that individuality and subjectivity are attained.

The first qualitative transition in the movement toward hominization was the production of mediating instruments—tools (Holzkamp, 1984/1991a). At first the implements were produced when a needed object was present and then discarded once the purpose was served, but, in time, instruments were produced in anticipation of future need. Planned provision enters into the process of maintaining life. As a force in evolution, societal life brought about processes for further evolution to support societal activities and led to inner life becoming more societal. Social labor developed into a process of socially planning appropriation of nature and effecting changes in nature to support satisfying human needs (like farming and irrigation). Humans create an objective world of their own design and establish social relations (economy, politics, religion) which become an independent force in further development.

There was a time, in the very distant past, when individuals satisfied their needs on their own. Specialized labor developed (carpenters and other crafts-persons) and people came to increasingly depend on each other to play a role in the overall satisfaction of the need of the group. As an academic, I depend on farmers and manufacturers to produce the food and clothing I need, besides other people doing other tasks I rely upon to support my existence. Production in modern society is complex; each person performs a small portion of all the tasks involved and has a role, and a position, in the functioning of the whole (Tolman, 1994). To a large degree the person's position is what determines her immediate 'life situation'—the place in the workforce, community, home, and so on. The immediate world one exists within is the source of frustrations, satisfactions, pleasures, and possibilities. Life situations differ, depending on the position occupied, and that affects subjectivity (the subjective situation) and **action potence**.

Action potence

In class society the greater population is excluded from having conscious control over those affairs by which they are affected (Holzkamp, 1984/1991a). A person of great wealth has available, as possibilities for action, a vast range of options that are simply unavailable to a person of limited resources—even to the point of not having access to food. Personal action potence is an analytic concept that emerges in socioeconomic society. It refers to the degree to which an individual can consciously control the societal, individual conditions of life. Depending on one's life situation, the conditions one exists within, there may be obstacles to social development (such as poverty or a dictatorial enslavement) and a restriction of action potence. **Action impotence** results from situations where one has limited control over their possibilities of acting in the world and results in individual suffering due to powerlessness and isolation.

Life demands provide people with alternatives with respect to making a secure existence, the most basic being whether or not to act (Tolman, 1994). Humans are free in that regard. Across the different societies, currently and historically, there are variable latitudes of freedom. Under the current despotic rule in North Korea the people have highly restricted freedom and are subjected to harsh penalties and widespread starvation. Kim Jong-un, the supreme leader, suffers no constraints. This is a case of **restrictive action potence** since the benefits are limited to specific persons at the expense of others. It is upon the basis of such comprehension, of 'consciously-relating-to,' the 'possibilities for action' that one can anticipate, plan, and act. The possibilities for action are also the conditions for need satisfaction.

The development of individual subjectivity occurs within the context of these 'possibility relationships,' of what can or cannot be done. That creates the conditions for two essential characteristics: action potence and 'subjective situation.' Action potence, as the ability of an individual to exercise control over life conditions, can be considered a primary need to acquire meaningful control over the conditions that affect needs (Tolman, 1996). The 'subjective situation' is an individual's emotional, evaluative aspect of the relation to the world and the understanding of needs with respect to the possibilities for action. Subjective states reflect, or assess, the individual's objective situation and gauge the individual's quality of life. Impeding action potence frustrates needs and leads to experiential anxiety (Tolman, 1989). From the critical psychology perspective, rather than being focused on the individual, psychotherapy has to be political and concerned with the societal conditions of individual functioning. Psychology should be in the service of the people.

Science for people

Intersubjectivity is a human reality and psychology has to include it (Holzkamp, 1984/1991a). Psychology has to be a 'subject science' that involves researcher and researched. It has to be not just about the other's subjectivity but about their overlapping subjectivities. Instead of being outside the research, the researcher is completely involved in it. Its procedures should not be 'about people' but 'for people.' The research program of Kritische Psychologie, especially as that is reflected in Danish critical psychology, involves the participants as co-researchers. The role of the researcher is cooperative and participatory rather than a neutral observer of facts (Mørck and Huniche, 2006). Unlike mainstream, with its individualizing personal problems, critical psychological practice aims at engaging with people in confronting oppressive social situations, and approaches the person as a societal being, rather than dichotomizing individual versus society.

The research methodology, called 'practice research,' involves developing methods that are appropriate to the problem under investigation and doing so through consideration of human subjectivity. By getting to know the individual's perspective one can analyze how the societal context of the individual mediates their existence. Analysis is directed at identifying those conditions that are relevant to the life of the subject, what they mean to him or her, and the reasons for their acting as they do. These are considered interrelated and have to be studied together. Holzkamp was criticized for abstract theorizing about how the 'societal action context' imposes conditions and possibilities of action for the individual and is involved in structuring individual subjectivity around thinking, feeling and acting. The Danish group concretizes this in practice research. In conducting such research, one develops a collaborative community based on common interests (Mørck et al., 2013).

The purpose is to develop comprehensive understanding of the complex societal conditions that are involved in **interpellation**, and how that empowers or suppresses individuals. The 'subjects' under study are incorporated into the research program as active contributors whose self-reflections are valued since the project is not only 'about' but 'for' them (Nissen, 2000). The process begins with felt problems identified as important by the co-researchers in order to conceptualize it. Second, that was examined for inherent ideology and reformulated in critical psychology concepts (like restricted action potence). Action possibilities were identified and efforts made to put them into practice. This is followed by an examination of the feedback on what had been done, the identification of subsequent problems, and possibilities for further action. The process continues until, hopefully, it seems no further research is needed. One such project, without going into detail, is 'Wild Learning' that works with at-risk youths, gang members, and attempts to help them find a place and a way into society (see Nissen, 2003, 2012; Mørck et al., 2013). The program involves the youths, social workers, community officials, and other academics since the issue extends through a complex network of social relations and competing values.

9.2 OTHER CRITICAL PSYCHOLOGIES

Since the 1980s a critical psychology separate from Holzkamp has been developing which builds upon diverse theoretical traditions—discourse analysis, cultural studies, feminist theory, and Marxism (Billig, 2008). A common theme is the criticism of mainstream psychology's theories and practices and its contribution to the maintenance of an unjust status quo (Prilleltensky and Fox, 1997). The assumptions, norms, and values of psychology have supported the dominant institution of society since its inception and therefore the social injustices associated with that. This results in a failure to promote human welfare (recall the sterilization of so-called defectives). Critical psychology is concerned with the well-being of oppressed and vulnerable peoples. The mainstream tradition of individualism, in disregarding societal conditions of existence, supports oppressive institutions (organizations, laws, practices, and customs) whether the individual psychologist intends to or not.

British critical psychologists have been concerned with how psychology frequently makes problems worse by convincing people that social problems are actually personal, individual problems (Parker, 2006). During the Margaret Thatcher era in Britain, for instance, Thatcher proclaimed that "there is no society, only individuals" (Nightingale and Cromby, 2001, p. 118). As a result, there was an escalation of poverty and an inculcation of individualistic values; welfare was of the past. This individualizes distress and shifts attention from the social roots of the anguish. The response (excuse) of the mainstream was to claim that it is involved with explaining the individual and that the study of the larger group, of the societal influences, is within the domain of anthropology and sociology (Prilleltensky and Fox, 1997). That merely oversimplifies the sphere of the psychological (and an abrogation of responsibility). Individual behavior only makes sense in the context of social interactions, and of socially constructed institutions, since values, goals, and self-concepts are shaped in social contexts and activities.

Critical psychology is predominantly concerned with examining how certain types of psychological experience and action are privileged, and how the dominant perspective on psychological functioning operates ideologically and serves power (Parker, 1999). A second aim is to examine how different psychologies (indigenous psychologies, for instance) are constructed historically and culturally, and how these alternative approaches may support or challenge mainstream's ideological assumptions. A third purpose is to investigate how power structures affect people through their involvement with societal relationships and institutions. This includes how academic psychology influences the world beyond the laboratory. Psychology involves practices woven into the fabric of social and personal life (Nightingale and Cromby, 2001). A simple example would be the identification of new disorders like 'attention deficit disorder' and how that affects the lives of children in school and at home, including the imposition of corrective drug regimens. Often psychologists are asked by the press to speak on public issues and they thereby influence how these events are understood in the public. Lastly, Parker holds that it is incumbent that everyday activities be investigated in order to develop defenses against disruptive psychological practices (such as ineffective therapies). In effect, Parker is advocating movement against the mainstream, challenging its power and ideology, so that psychology may better serve humanity.

The influence of Paolo Freire

A lot of what falls under the banner of critical psychology (liberation psychology and community psychology) has been influenced by the work of Paulo Freire (1921–1997) with the oppressed and impoverished people of Brazil during the 1960s. According to Freire (1968/1981), to be concerned with humanization leads to the recognition of dehumanization as a fact of history. Furthermore, to be a matter of history meant it was not a question of destiny. Dehumanization is due to unjust social orders that generate violence and oppression against certain members of society. You need only consider the working poor, racial discrimination, genocide, and slavery to appreciate its existence. To Freire, eventually the oppressed are led by feelings of being less human to struggle against those who create those feelings (the 'Occupy movement' of 2011 struggled against economic and social inequality; the 'Idle No More' movement in Canada, 2012, rallied for the rights of indigenous people; 'Black Lives Matter' in 2012 responded to police killing Black folks in the US). To be meaningful, Freire believed, the struggle must not lead to the oppressed becoming the oppressor in their efforts to recapture their humanity. Their task is to liberate both the oppressed and the oppressor.

As a result of being subjected to oppressive conditions, the oppressed internalize those conditions which act from within and make them fearful of their own freedom. This must be excised and replaced by personal responsibility and autonomy. In line with this, Sampson (1983) proposed that when one is confronted with a social system in which a few benefit at the cost to many, one is faced with circumstances in which domination has seeped into the culture's consciousness, into relationships and structures, and demonstrates the operation of ideology. Ideology inhabits the deep structure wherein develops subjectivity and self-understanding. When oppression is internalized 'psychological oppression' occurs; the person establishes a negative self-assessment and a sense of not deserving an increased share in resources, or a role to play in social life (Prilleltensky and Gonick, 1996).

The oppressed, who are immersed in and adapted to the conditions of domination, and who are resigned to it, are inhibited from struggling to be free. They feel incapable of taking the needed risks, possibly fearing greater oppression (Freire, 1968/1981). The 'pedagogy of the oppressed,' the method of teaching, has to be developed with the oppressed, rather than for them, as they struggle to reclaim their humanity. Oppression and the causes of it are made objects of reflection and from that reflection will arise the necessity to be engaged in a struggle to be liberated. The reality of oppression has to be perceived not as a closed world but as a limiting situation that can be transformed. Humans have created social realities and the transformation of that reality is a historical task. It is not how things must be. The oppressor too has to be educated since the oppressor can only be in solidarity with the oppressed when they cease perceiving the oppressed as abstract categories (those people) but are regarded as persons who have been treated unjustly, exploited and deprived of a voice. Oppressors who fail to realize that monopoly on greater ownership is a privilege, dehumanize other people and themselves.

As to the role of the 'teacher,' the person who is committed to the liberation cause but incapable of entering into communion with the people, who regard them as ignorant, is horribly self-deceived. Imposing personal status and not listening to the people (who know their circumstances best) will not work. While the oppressed are characterized by self-depreciation, due to internalizing their oppressor's opinions, and convinced of their inferiority, they have to begin to believe in themselves in order to struggle for liberation. Through the method of dialogue, and using the people's own thought-language, the people are made aware of their own theories, their sense of their reality, and how it is perceived, the limiting situations or barriers, and how these are perceived as insurmountable and enchaining. Humans as conscious beings are aware of their world and themselves in it and that manifests in action and inaction. Through dialogue about their circumstance it is intended that they develop *conscientização* (consciousness-raising and critical consciousness) and a deepened understanding of their situation. They become aware of societal organization and are prepared to act against the repressive elements of that reality. That is the basis of their emergence from submission and active intervention into their life conditions. 'Scientific revolutionary humanism' must not treat oppressed people as objects for analysis and simply prescribe solutions to them. That would be to fall into the ideology of the oppressor—the absolutization of ignorance and the assumption of power through directives. One has no right to accept the myth of the people's ignorance and to fail to dialogue.

True commitment to the conditions of the people involves transforming the reality that oppresses them and that necessitates a theory of transformative activity that gives the people a fundamental role. To merely activate and lead the people is simply manipulation; they must be given the opportunity to reflect and to generate activities designed to overcome their limiting situations. Hope and confidence develop and support efforts at liberation through concrete, transformative action. That is the essence of 'liberation psychology.'

Liberation psychology

Critical psychology assumes the role of raising questions about what psychology will do to alleviate social control and human suffering, and to advocate for social justice and the liberation of the oppressed (Austin and Prilleltensky, 2001). Rather than a laboratory study of oppression, it aims to effect real changes in the world for real people. There is general agreement that critical psychology is directed at efforts after social justice and emancipation (Dafermos and Marvakis, 2006). Thus, critical psychology is intent on the transformation of psychology so that it becomes an agent in the promotion of emancipation. 'Liberation psychology' emphasizes the recognition that oppression is internalized and becomes a further oppressive condition (Moane, 2003). Psychological patterns of helplessness, and a sense of personal inferiority, are connected to social degradation and powerlessness. Liberation psychology emphasizes analyzing the social conditions of lived life, understanding oppression as internalized, and developing intervention procedures to transform the social and psychological patterns connected with oppression. The framework for liberation means standing with the people and working collaboratively with them, in their life contexts, to realize power inequities and to empower transformative activity (Comas-Díaz, Lykes, and Alarcón, 1998). Freire's awakening of consciousness is central to liberation, the awareness of one's place in society, the capacity to analyze situations and possibilities, and instilling a sense of power and agency.

Liberation psychology is most apparent in South America. While there is no actual school of critical psychology in Chile there is a general practice that is critical in nature (Shafir, 2006). The practice is committed to change and is intrinsically political. The aim is to destabilize the domination relationship that exists rather than acting to preserve the ruling order. Instead of helping people adapt to the current social system, they want to produce emancipatory knowledge and give rise to people who want to subvert and transform the dominant social power and its effects. Rather than having the people regard such conditions as inevitable, the social scientist works to create awareness in them of their social construction and of the possibilities of change. Similar movements can be found in Brazil (de Carvalho and Dunker, 2006), Venezuela (Montero and Montenegro, 2006), and Columbia (Valencia and Mesa, 2006).

Community psychology

'Community psychology' is a critical psychology in North America which is a response to the alienation and loss of power in people that the mainstream ignores (Austin and Prilleltensky, 2001). Its focus is the community rather than the individual and it is aligned with feminist psychology and the civil rights movement. It draws together academics and community members to resolve issues affecting loss of power. It can be considered a form of clinical psychology working at the level of a particular geographic locale (Kelly, 1971). The community is considered ecologically to see how persons, roles, organizations, and events are intertwined in order to better meet the needs of the community. There is a focus on the disadvantaged community and issues of drug abuse, violence, minorities, and inner-city decay (Iscoe, 1974). A characteristic of the disadvantaged community is not just economic circumstances, but the psychological disadvantages associated with feelings of powerlessness and helplessness. It intends to be proactive rather than reactive since it is insufficient to treat the victim and not the condition. The ideal of community psychology is the scientific change of social conditions that are degrading by collaborating with the community to effect change and by being accountable to the community (Walsh, 1987).

9.3 WOMEN AND PSYCHOLOGY

Prejudicial psychology of women

During the 1860s the Women's Rights movement was gaining notice and was considered a threat to English social order (Fee, 1979). Social reform groups were being organized by women, making public speeches, publishing journals, and trying to gain entry into what were the professions of men alone. More disturbing to the patriarchal order, John Stuart Mill (1806–1873) introduced a bill in parliament supporting women's suffrage. This was a threat to the privileged position of men. From the time of Aristotle women had been regarded as completely passive and simply incubators for children (Bleier, 1984). To challenge this was a threat to male dominance. According to Bleier, scientists, all people, are reared in specific cultures with beliefs and values, opinions and biases, that will affect their work and what they believe to be true, or want or need to be true. This was quite apparent in the efforts of 'scientists' to refute the demands of women for fair treatment.

In the 19th century there were men who hoped to preserve patriarchal social relationships as they existed (Smith-Rosenberg and Rosenberg, 1973). Biological and medical arguments were employed to rationalize the traditional conception of the sexes as inevitable, as prescribed by anatomy and physiology. The characteristics of the ideal Victorian woman included nurturance, domesticity, affection, and passivity, and they were proclaimed rooted in their biology. The woman's natural condition, according to Allen (1869), was marriage and motherhood. Men, he contended, had been formed to engage in physical labor and prolonged mental tasks, whereas females were formed to reproduce. Let a woman be educated to her full capacity and then compare her with an uneducated man and the man would display greater reasoning power and profundity of views. As for evidentiary support, he noted that the female skull was closer to that of infants and lower races and reflected an earlier stage in the development of her race.

Mill (1869/1988), unlike Allen, was a supporter of women's emancipation and believed the legal subordination of women to men was just wrong. Women, he wrote, were claiming a right to be educated and admitted into professions that were closed to them, and he was on their side. He challenged the efforts being made to repress their aspirations for being against what was proper for their sex. Men were trying to enslave the minds of women, and to keep them in subjugation, by representing their attractiveness to men as involving submissiveness to men's will, meekness, and resignation to that role. So-called woman's nature, Mill judged, was artificial and due to forced repression and distortion by their masters. Were men able to tolerate women as their equals, they would have to admit that there was an injustice in keeping half of the population from higher social roles that were ordained, ideologically, beyond their capacity. There was, he argued, habitual disregard of the external causes of suppressed capacity. The evidence was lacking for any rational determination of whether observed differences were natural or artificial; and the evidence that women have smaller brains, and the assumption of correlated mental insufficiency, disregarded their smaller bodies. Besides, there had been many instances throughout history of women demonstrating the ability to succeed at what men do. Not allowing women to pursue their full powers, Mill contended, may have been robbing society of half of its talent. Mill's arguments fell on deaf ears.

George Romanes (1848–1894), a founder of comparative psychology and a proponent of evolution, reported that the female brain is five ounces lighter than the male and that, therefore, an inferior intellectual capacity should be expected (Romanes, 1887). That noted, Romanes went on to recognize that women had not had the educational advantages of men and that education may be a factor in the differences. Women's education had involved her being sheltered from the struggling and striving involved in the training of the male intellect. Traditional education may have thus constrained women and resulted in their absence from intellectual work. If women could compete with men on fair terms, under altered social conditions, they may yet prove themselves equals. Thus, it would seem Romanes was intent on supporting women, but hold on. He went on to argue that, because of the injustices of the past, the female mind could not be expected to cast off the ages of cumulative disadvantage; that subjugation and neglect leave their mark on the hereditary constitution of mind; that it was unclear how long it would take to recover the lost five ounces but it would probably be centuries before they were made up. In effect he was saying had only things been different millennia ago, and men had been as magnanimous as he, women might be equals; but they are not. Alas, poor women, your biology now is your oppressor, not he.

The brain argument continued with Patrick (1895), who reiterated that the female brain is smaller in weight; however, that is of little significance if one considers the ratio of brain to body mass. Be that as it may, according to Patrick the brain of the female is less modified, and less varied, and that is why they are weak in logical reasoning, and less adapted for the analytical thinking needed for work in science, invention, and discovery. Being less variable mentally, that suggests, but doesn't prove, that women suffer from arrested development. According to Mobius (1901), mentally, women are half-way between child and man in possessing a small brain. Furthermore, women are more captivated by instinctual tendencies. What they do is always the same (ignoring the social sanctions enforcing that) and, if there were only women in the race, humans would remain primitive—progress rests with men. Women live in their children and their husbands, and are uninterested in the world beyond the family (thus ignoring the women's movement that was going on). If women actually had a desire for knowledge, that would interfere with their maternal duties and that is why nature supplied it in slight amount.

Wells (1909) used a novel approach to maintain the status quo—he appealed to women's sense of social responsibility and guilt. For half of humanity to be excluded from having their native talents cultivated, he wrote, echoing Mill, assumes beforehand the inferiority of females, but that may be an economic waste. There are, however, essential differences between the psyches of the sexes and their education should therefore be different. Women should be trained to be wives and mothers despite what they may strive to achieve. Their ultimate value to society is in motherhood. Even if superior women were allowed to receive higher education, and to forgo having children until later, the lower birth rate would be equivalent to sterilizing the superior stock. In fact, among college girls (women were attending college at that point) the marriage rate was expected to be lowered. While he had sympathy for women receiving higher education, heredity (reproductive) could not be bypassed. Even should a superior woman have a child of superior capacity, that would not make up for the losses associated with the restriction in the inheritance of superior inheritance by the large number of superior women avoiding their maternal responsibilities.

By the early 20th century Karl Pearson (1857–1936), a founder of statistics, dashed the hopes of proving female inferiority by craniological studies (Fee, 1979). Pearson (1906) studied 1,000 graduates of Cambridge and 5,000 school children. He found a slight correspondence between head size and general intelligence, which was unaltered by consideration of brain-to-body ratios. It was so small as to be useless in making even rough predictions from it about intellectual ability. Wooley (1910), in a review of the literature, concluded that serious mistakes had been made in the scientific procedures used in difference findings. As she wrote, "There is perhaps no field aspiring to be scientific where flagrant personal bias, logic martyred in the cause of supporting a prejudice, unfounded assertions, and even sentimental rot and drivel, have run riot to such an extent as here" (p. 340). This is apparent in Hollingworth (1914), who pointed out that in 1914 Meckel concluded, on the basis of pathology, that females were more variable than males. He concluded that this made sense since variability was associated with inferiority and males were superior. Then, later, when anatomists found that males were more variable, variability was then deemed an advantageous characteristic—women were devalued again by whatever evidence could be jerry-rigged to suit the prejudice.

The Freudian tradition

Freud was no great defender of women. He believed that women were destined by their biology to an inferior place in the world. Responding to the women's movement, Freud (1924/1977a) argued that the demand of feminists for equal rights would not go far. Psychical development was based on morphology and "Anatomy is Destiny" (p. 320); female character traits are constituted biologically. Although the young girl's clitoris initially behaves just like a penis, when she becomes aware of the male member she inevitably feels cheated and inferior. This prepares her for her reproductive role which compensates for that loss with a baby serving as a penis substitute. Her aims are inhibited and directed toward conduct of an affectionate type. Due to differences in the formation of the superego (internalized moral standards) differing from males, women are ethically moral in ways that differ from men (Freud, 1925/1977b). Their superego is less impersonal and less independent of its emotional origins as required of men. This is why every epoch has noted abiding female character traits: "that they show less sense of justice than men, that they are less ready to submit to the great exigencies of life, that they are more often influenced in their judgments by feelings of affection or hostility" (p. 342).

Karen Horney (1885–1952), while trained in psychoanalysis, found Freud's views on women unacceptable and ignorant of the effects of culture and history. According to Horney (1934/1973a), the attitude that exists towards women is an expression of the patriarchal ideal of what a woman should be—one who should long to love a man, receive his love, and admire

Horney

and serve him. In that, the psychology of women was being considered from the male point of view (Horney, 1926/1973b)—(which, of course, dismisses the women's point of view). What had to be realized was that, from birth, girls are exposed to suggestions of inevitable inferiority, conveyed subtly or brutally, which stimulates feelings of inferiority in women. In various fields, achievements deemed inadequate are called 'feminine,' contemptuously, while the achievements of women that are considered distinguished are called 'masculine' in praise.

Such ideology functioned to reconcile women to subordinate roles by presenting masculine activities as unattainable due to the 'nature of women' being of limited capacity for autonomous thought and independent work (Horney, 1935/1973c). That is further strengthened by women who comply and become the ones to be chosen by males as preferred mates. Such a position to Horney was one-sided in its neglect of social and cultural factors. The influence of culture on women had been neglected. There was a failure, as well, to consider women from different civilizations and from different customs. The importance of this was evident in the changes effected in the role of women in Soviet Russia who had transitioned from patriarchal domination to being self-assertive. Such a woman would be outraged at being subjected to the abuses suffered under the old regime. As of 1971, 33 percent of engineers and 75 percent of physicians in the Soviet Union were women (Bem and Bem, 1971). Female inferiority and superiority were culturally, not biologically, conditioned.

Adler

Alfred Adler (1870–1937) was something of a male dissenter since he was a supporter of women and argued against the deleterious prejudice directed at them. According to Adler (1927), men are continually trying to dominate women and women are appropriately dissatisfied. In the home girls are subjected to indoctrination regarding female inferiority, being of lesser capacity, and unsuitable for essential social activities. The girl is convinced of the fixity of her station and unfortunate fate, and comes to believe it. She is denied preparation in the home and in the larger society. The young female enters a world filled with prejudice against her and actions designed to quash her belief in personal value, destroying self-confidence, and any hope of achieving anything worthwhile.

Male dominance is not natural. If it were, there would be no need for laws to support its maintenance. Such dominance, to Adler, emerged from primitive peoples who engaged in battle, and resulted in the prominence of the warrior. This led to the assumption and retention of leadership. Male privilege was not natural; it had to be fought for. Over time it became encoded in laws and customs that support it, and forms the world female infants must get used to, as they develop. Rather than inborn, traits of character are adjustments to one's life conditions, and as such they can be changed. Change women's opportunities and life possibilities and she will develop character traits suitable to that role, instead of the psychological disturbances that arise from male advantage and female disadvantage. What is needed is to foster our potential for what Adler (1937/1957) called 'social interest,' our innate sense of kinship with, and responsibility for, the rest of humanity. The long-term progress of humanity rests upon it.

Feminist psychology

The 1960s was a decade of liberation for marginal groups (Blacks, Natives, women) and the return of the feminist movement—the first declined during the 1920s upon gaining voting privileges (Dixon, 1971). Women were struggling against institutionalized oppression through sexual and economic exploitation, and psychological deprivation through the establishment of a false consciousness of their collective inferiority. To Weisstein (1971) psychologists had been describing the 'true' nature of women from a male perspective of how they should be; they adopted cultural norms that were men's fantasies of how women should be dependent upon them, and in servitude, failing to recognize the true potential of women. The new feminist movement, to Carlson (1972), could serve as a basis for introducing overdue changes in psychology's conceptualization of human nature. As she suggested, prophetically, it was unlikely to be achieved until psychologists no longer reacted to the movement and experienced it ideologically and politically.

The year before, Carlson (1971) wrote what I consider to be an important paper in psychology (not because of its feminism, which was not even hinted at, but because it represented just good psychology, at least to me). She reviewed articles in the *Journal of Personality* and the *Journal of Personality and Social Psychology* for 1968. Although the main topic of these journals was personality, Carlson could find no evidence of 'persons' and noted that the really important issues were being avoided. It is no wonder she entitled her paper "Where is the person in personality research?" Undergraduates were the preferred subject-group but that left out a broader sample of adults from varied backgrounds and circumstances. They were two-thirds males and male–female differences were largely ignored. Very little was known of the particular individuals and there was nothing to connect the data to their individual lives. The participants' experience was not considered. The interpersonal connection was impersonal and brief. Such research could reveal nothing of personality organization, development, maturity and stability, psychosexuality, friendship and love, or personal goals. What was needed, she argued, was to utilize our subjects fully and to treat them as collaborators, asking what they experience and what they think of what is being done. In many ways, Carlson foreshadowed formal feminist psychology in this paper.

Male–female differences

When women were rediscovered, during the 1970s, by mainstream psychology the focus was on how women differed from men, not how they were similar (Lott, 1985; see Maccoby and Jacklin, 1974, for a review). The research suggested differences in visual-spatial ability and quantitative abilities favoring males, and verbal abilities favoring females (Feingold, 1988) but subsequent analysis found the differences to be quite small (Hyde, 1981). What differences there were diminished in time, suggesting either increased care in research or that the differences were artificial and historical, rather than universal, ahistorical laws (Riger, 1992). Female psychologists pointed out that, in this, there was failure to publish evidence of no differences or to ignore them (Sherif, 1979). Part of the problem is that negative findings are not publishable, and that means a literature on similarities will not develop (Grady, 1981). To Riger (1992) many studies are failing to find differences so 'sex similarities' might be a better designation.

Women's actions and abilities, when studied, are deemed deficient relative to men (Riger, 1992). This, to many feminist psychologists, reflects a bias that favors men. That was recognized by May (1966, a man), who noted that far too often women have been forced, inappropriately, into male categories. As a result, there was a tendency to interpret 'different' as 'deficient.' As Westkott (1979) put it, when the social sciences have considered women they have been measured in terms that are masculine. They interpret the concept of 'human being' as 'man,' with women being a deviation from essential (see **essence**) humanity. The point is that tests developed for use with males (based on male norms—Crawford and Marecek, 1989) are biased against women (Sherif, 1979). As a result, "it is normal for women to feel abnormal" (Tavris, 1993). Typically, women are found to be lower in self-esteem, value their own efforts less, and have less self-confidence. If, however, women were the norm, men would be assessed as deficient for having greater conceit, overvaluing what they do, and unrealistic evaluations of personal ability. As Crawford and Marecek (1989) asked, "If the stereotypical female is problematically unassertive, why is the stereotypical male not problematically overassertive?" (p. 153).

BOX 9.2
EXPERIENCING GENDER STEREOTYPES

In an attempt to sensitize students to their internalization of gender stereotypes, Fahs (2011) developed a simple class exercise. You can try this yourself but, at the very least, pay attention to your subjective reaction to what is suggested. If you find the idea repugnant, you have probably internalized social values about gender-appropriate activities that are operating at a nonconscious level.

The task is simple: Fahs asked women to grow their body hair for ten weeks and men to shave theirs. Norms for women to remove body hair did not arise until the 1920s, but have been supported since then by negative sanctions, even hostility. Students were directed as follows:

1. Attend to your emotional response.

2. Did this effect your sexuality and feelings about your body?

3. How did other people react?

4. Did this cause you to reflect on socially constructed norms of sexuality?

Feminist psychological research

Feminist psychologists challenge the 'supposed' value neutrality of mainstream psychology. In fact, it is obvious from the preceding section that considerable bias has guided research into male-female differences. The experiences of women have been ignored (Westkott, 1979) as have women's issues, such as domestic violence, sexual harassment, reproduction and choices about bearing children (Wilkinson, 1988, 1989), rape, murder, illiteracy, and women in poverty (Kitzinger, 1991). What one looks for determines what one finds (Unger, 1983) and a lot of research has had no relevance to the lives of women (Grady, 1981). Values are important aspects of research and cannot be ignored (Wallston, 1981). They can be found at all stages of research from conceptualizing the problem, selecting design and subjects, presenting and generalizing findings, how results are interpreted, and conclusions drawn. For that reason, feminist research challenges the notion of objectivity (Lott, 1985) and advocates **reflexivity**, ongoing analysis of research and practice to reveal underlying assumptions, biases, and values (Wilkinson, 1988; Eagly and Riger, 2014). One such value in feminist research is to advocate for women (Wilkinson, 1989). Advocacy involves a commitment to political and social change for the betterment of women.

The methods adopted by experimental psychologists have involved 'context stripping' by isolating social phenomena from the normal situations in which they occur (Crawford and Marecek, 1989). Feminist psychologists see that as problematic. The truth is that lives are situated, historically and culturally, and methods should be concerned with dynamic processes, no longer excluding cultural-historical influences as nuisance variables but considering them, instead, as legitimate phenomena for investigation. Context stripping robs human conduct of meaning and ignores the personal history of unique individuals (Bleier, 1984). Not searching for it, little evidence was found of the influence of the cultural-historical nexus, of social ties and personal histories, on individual lives (Sherif, 1979). Feminist psychologists, in contrast, advocate a contextually valid psychology (Fine, 1985). Traditional research has distorted gender through decontextualization so social structures, economic and political arrangements, are not considered as they impact the psychology of women, collectively and individually.

Psychology also abandoned concern with individual experience (Carlson, 1972). Not so for feminist psychology. In order to try and enhance contextual validity, findings are shared with participants to see whether the dates fit, whether they make sense (Fine, 1985). Information is gathered from numerous individuals who are part of the same context in order to examine the social and psychological dynamics affecting individual psychology. Diversity of experience is recorded and gender essentialism avoided. Intersubjectivity, and shared involvement in the work, is emphasized (Grosz, 1987). A new dimension is thus added to psychological knowledge in the form of human experience from the female perspective; that contributes an enriched appreciation of the whole of human activity and possibilities (Wilkinson, 1989). As you might have guessed, experimental methods are not favored since the experiment is considered sterile (Wilkinson, 1999). Rather, in developing research for women, unstructured qualitative methods, like interviews, are employed (Henwood and Pidgeon, 1995; see Campbell and Wasco, 2000, for an overview). Adopting more naturalistic methods is intended to draw upon everyday communicative practices, and social processes, that is consistent with the lives of people (Wilkinson, 1999). Rapport and cooperative relationships are established with participants in order to appreciate their frame of reference and experiences (Henwood and Pidgeon, 1995). Qualitative research, which will be considered in Chapter 10, is the norm.

SUMMARY

Critical psychologies have opposed mainstream psychology for its abstractness and irrelevance to real-world problems.

- A central component of science is critical evaluation.
- German critical psychology finds serious drawbacks to variable psychology, especially the incapacity to deal with human subjectivity.
- Subjectivity is operationally defined away as objective phenomena.
- Societal activity is central to appreciating human psychology and activity.
- Societal activities and meanings are the basis for intersubjective understanding.
- One's freedom to act in the world depends on generalized action possibilities and action potence.
- Variable psychology distorts Freudian concepts and fails to comprehend what they are useful for.

- Psychology must be for people rather than about them.

- All critical psychologies are concerned with injustice and empowering the oppressed.

- Freire's liberation pedagogy has informed many of the practices of critical, liberationist, and community psychologies.

- Mainstream psychology has been chauvinistic with respect to women and has unfairly judged then from the male perspective.

- Feminist psychologists emphasize the empowerment of women and advocate a psychology that is culturally-historically sensitive and rejects context-stripping methodologies.

SUGGESTED READINGS

Bleier, R. (1984). *Science and gender: A critique of biology and its theories on women.* New York: Pergamon Press.

Crawford, M. and Unger, R. (2004). *Women and gender: A feminist psychology* (4th ed.). New York: McGraw-Hill.

Fox, D., Prilleltensky, I., and Austin, S. (2009). *Critical psychology: An introduction* (2nd ed.). Los Angeles, CA: SAGE Publications.

Tolman, C. W. (1994). *Psychology, society, and subjectivity: An introduction to German critical psychology.* London: Routledge.

Want to learn more? For links to online resources, examples of multiple choice questions, conceptual exercises and much more, visit the companion website at **https://study.sagepub.com/piekkola**

10

PSYCHOLOGICAL METHODS AND PRACTICE

LEARNING OBJECTIVE

Over the past couple of decades there has been a burgeoning interest in qualitative methods as alternatives to the standard experimental paradigm. For their part, hard-nosed experimentalists reject qualitative methods as unscientific or soft science (Denzin and Lincoln, 1994). In a sense, qualitative methods are treated as though they are something new, but there have always been advocates of qualitative methods in psychology. They were simply displaced by the rise of quantitative methods. In this chapter we will examine the 'quantitative imperative' in psychology and the eventual call for alternative methods as scientific psychology began to reveal its limitations. In considering this, you should become familiar with the issues and be prepared to take a position on what are the appropriate methodologies and why. Topics considered will include the following:

- The quantitative imperative and the drive towards scientific recognition.
- The influence of statistics.
- Measurement in psychology and psychological testing.
- The experimental versus the clinical tradition.
- Is it objective to dismiss the subjective?

FRAMING QUESTIONS

- Why is so much emphasis placed on quantification in psychology?
- Can quantitative and qualitative approaches coexist?
- Can psychology remain objective if it distorts its subject matter to fit its methods?

INTRODUCTION

Scientific psychology came from the period in human understanding referred to as **modernity** which is associated with the development of the scientific method and rational inquiry. It included an assumption of a knowable reality which was independent of the individual and excluded the investigator's subjectivity as a factor in the knowledge revealed (Shotter, 1990). A central belief was the notion of a knowable world and that the impersonal scientific method would produce truth (Gergen, 1990). During the 1980s, this conception was being challenged by theories of **postmodernity** (Kvale, 1990). The general proposition was that supposed truth is an historical and cultural construction, and that absolute knowledge and realism should be replaced by skepticism and relativism. The departure point for the discussion of knowledge was the belief in 'contextual relativism,' that what one considers to be true arises from the communicative network of which one is a member. Meaning and truth (so-called) are relative to the shared reality of groups of people and not because of access to some knowable, independent, objective reality.

Given the emphasis on communicated understanding, a focus has been on the linguistic construction of reality. Rather than due to an objective science, psychological knowledge is itself judged by postmodernists to be a social construction and emphasis has shifted to subjectivity (not necessarily Holzkamp's 'science of the subject' which is a realist psychology). The fundamental human reality, as represented in Figure 10.1, is conversational (Brown and Stenner, 2009). The construction of meaning, as opposed to the discovery of meaning, is becoming a fashionable proposition in psychological accounts. As a result, there has been a rise in qualitative methods as more adequate than mainstream quantitative approaches in the investigation of the psychological. That is because of their focus on subjectivity and personal meaning. In this chapter we will contrast the two positions, the quantitative and qualitative, but I must emphasize that qualitative methods are not new; they simply went out of favor as what is now mainstream psychology became dominant and they are becoming more popular with the rising criticisms of the mainstream approach.

WHAT DO YOU THINK?

Do you believe that all psychological phenomena can be quantified and, if they cannot, should they be dismissed from psychology for that lack?

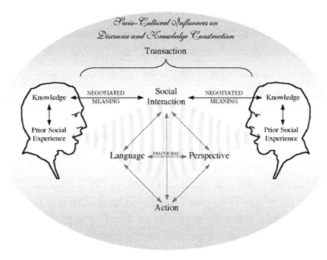

Figure 10.1 Communicative construction of reality

10.1 THE QUANTITATIVE IMPERATIVE

At the beginning of scientific psychology, a question that had to be answered was whether psychology could be a quantitative discipline. The necessity of measurement for science led Kant to question whether psychology could be a proper science (Sturm, 2006). Kant wrote that "in every special doctrine of nature only so much science proper can be found as there is mathematics in it" (Kant, 1776, in Sturm, 2006, p. 355). Mathematics, he contended, could not be applied to internal phenomena and therefore was not within the domain of psychology. The early 19th-century psychologists, as a result, believed that a major problem for psychology was to disprove Kant.

Kant was not alone in this demand. Historically, quantification has been regarded as a key characteristic of any particular discipline being deemed scientific (Hornstein, 1988). To the founders of psychology, measurement was imperative and they contrived ways to quantify (Michell, 1999). Below, unless otherwise stated, early psychologists echo that attitude.

- To Galton (1879), "until the phenomena of any branch of knowledge have been subjected to measurement and number, it cannot assume the status and dignity of a science" (p. 149).

- Cattell (1890) maintained that "Psychology cannot attain the certainty and exactness of the physical sciences, unless it rests on a foundation of experiment and measurement" (p. 373).

- The British physicist William Thomson, known as Baron Kelvin of Largs, put forward what is known as Kelvin's dictum: "when you cannot express it in numbers, your knowledge is of a meager and unsatisfactory kind" (1890, in Michell, 2003, p. 7).

- Cattell (1893) noted that "The history of science is the history of measurement" (p. 316) and that the sciences that are the furthest advanced have the most exact and extensive measurement.

- Boring (1929) maintained that "we hardly recognize a subject as scientific if measurement is not one of its tools" (p. 286).

More recently, and rather succinctly, the historian Crosby (1997) proposed that mathematics is "the native tongue of science" (p. 104.). Michell (2003) has referred to this as the 'quantitative imperative,' by which he meant that the scientific study of something means that it has to be measured. Underlying this commitment to the idea that measurement is essential to science is the Pythagorean idea that all attributes are quantitative at the core. It was to this Pythagorean heritage that Michell traced the commitment to quantification in psychology rather than to the positivists as some recent advocates of qualitative psychology have argued.

The science of calculations

The 'calculators,' or the 'science of calculations,' was a movement during the mid-14th century which initiated a new habit of measuring that would be important to the approach of modern science (Kaye, 1988). The new habit, and the institution of an arithmetic mentality, can be partially traced to the monetization of society. Prior to this, the economic organization of society centered about the manorial estate (Heilbroner, 1993). This was a large land tract, owned by a feudal lord, with a manor house or castle that housed workshops (textile, iron-work, milling). Most of the land was the lord's, although plots were allotted to serfs who were close to being property. The serfs were obligated to work the lord's land and to turn over a portion of their personal production. Serfs were tied to the land and their station in life was fixed. Manor estates were not entirely self-sufficient; they could support the crafts but not every need. In the towns, new production activities arose (masons, glazers, armorers) whom landowners had to turn to. Some slight monetary transactions were enacted but society was not yet fully monetized.

Agriculture began to be capitalized during the 13th century (Kaye, 1988). Production for sale was being emphasized on large estates. Markets, towns, and mercantile classes grew. There was the rise of a monetary economy. By the 14th century the effects of the transition to monetary economics (as opposed to barter and trade) were becoming manifest. There was a shift from payment in kind (eggs, produce, labor) to payment in money (Heilbroner, 1993). Monetization influenced the development of a quantitative approach to phenomena (Kaye, 1988). Money served as an instrument for measurement and established a new way to look upon the world and think about it. That is consistent with Vygotsky's hypothesis that, as a function of the transition from one historical form to another, not only the contents of consciousness, but the structure of higher mental processes that underlie psychological activity, are changed (Luria, 1976). Market items were being measured and quantified and that became the basis of valuation for exchange, instead of subjective estimation of value (Kaye, 1988). Even labor, which had been fixed by social position and regulated by social reciprocities (the serf provides labor, the lord provides protection), was becoming a commodity and monetized as wages. What had been considered unmeasurable and unquantifiable was becoming so.

Duns Scotus (1265–1308), at the beginning of this period, made a revolutionary proposal when he suggested that one could understand qualitative change as analogous to quantitative change (Michell, 2003). He proposed that there may be, involved in qualitative change, an increase or decrease in some unobserved, homogeneous parts. In that he raised the possibility that quantification may be applied to areas previously thought to be unquantifiable. This was taken up at Merton College, Oxford by a group known as the 'Oxford Calculators.' Up to this time the Scholastics (the schoolmen at the universities) upheld Aristotle's absolute distinction between, and separation of, quantity from quality (Kaye, 1988)—recall the 'excluded middle.' Scholastics simply thought of qualities as greater or lesser than each other and that was all (Crosby, 1997). The calculators, on the other hand, began to concern themselves with qualities changing in intensity and the possible quantification of those changes (Kaye, 1988). They attempted to measure increases and decreases in different qualities and to express them mathematically. This was significant, historically, because a precondition for the emergence of science was the quantification of descriptions of physical reality. A particular problem that concerned them was the measurement of motion which, as mentioned in Chapter 3, was quantified by Galileo in the 17th century.

One figure who stands out in this context was the philosopher and mathematician Nicholas Oresme (around 1320–1382) in France (Kaye, 1988). Oresme reasoned that any qualities that could change in intensity were measureable and that a line was a perfect medium for expressing changing values. The line was the basis for the common measure of qualities because it was divisible and it could be expanded to represent a range of varying intensities or qualities (just like a ruler that gets expanded into a measuring tape). As a result, the calculators began to formulate conceptions of things as part of a continuous scale that could be represented by a line indicating different intensities. With this new approach one could reduce what was being thought of, and visualize it, as a line that could be divided into equal portions, or quanta, that could be measured and counted in terms of numbers of quanta (Crosby, 1997). Quality was being redefined as a measurable continuum, an intellectual development that laid a foundation for future scientific thinking (Kaye, 1988). Thus began the rise of quantification in organizing life and thinking, and investigative practices.

10.2 QUANTITATIVE PSYCHOLOGY

From the start it was assumed that psychology, in order to attain the status of a science, should model itself after classical physics (Gigerenzer, 1987a). As Boring (1933) suggested, "Historically science is physical science. Psychology, if it is to be a science, must be like physics" (p. 6). Such 'physics envy,' as it has come to be known, was indicative of a strong inferiority complex to Bills (1938). He identified some of the criteria, in current scientific psychology, that frame research practices (and which suggest allegiance to the physics model): empirical, analytic, mechanistic, nomothetic (seeking general laws), and quantitative. Psychology, to be a science, it was proposed, had to act like a science and in accordance with the scientific method. As Holt (1962) proposed, "Science is defined by its methods, not its subject matter" (p. 397). Of course it is this attitude and assumption that qualitative researchers challenge as inadequate to the investigation of the psychological.

Measurement in psychology

The history of the development of measurement in psychology began with four distinct trends—psychophysics, reaction times, memory research, and individual differences psychology (Boring, 1961). Of course, since quantification was considered a hallmark of science, these efforts at measurement marked the coming into existence of a scientific psychology.

Fechner
Weber

To some, the experiments of **Gustav Fechner** (1801–1887), reported in his 1960 text *Elemente der Psychophysik*, represent the beginning of experimental psychology. Fechner was building on the work of **Ernst Weber** (1795–1878) into the subjective experience of changes in a physical magnitude. This involved an act of discrimination since it addressed the question of how much of a difference was required for someone to be able to identify whether two stimuli were different from each other in magnitude (Coren et al., 1994). This resulted in the concept of the 'just noticeable difference' (JND) which, as the name implies, is the amount of change in stimulus magnitude required for a person to just notice that the two stimuli were actually different. What Weber found was that as the magnitude of the comparison stimulus increased, a larger and larger difference was required for a difference to be 'just' noticeable.

Fechner, for his part, needed to express Weber's findings mathematically and to scale the work of Weber. In **scaling** one attempts to measure how much of something is present, in what quantity (like scales of weight). It refers to the development of rules by which numbers are assigned to events (like noticing a difference) or to objects. The issue that arose for Fechner was how does one measure a subjective experience and relate it to a physical intensity. Fechner started with the assumption that every JND was equal to every other JND. Regardless of how much stimulus change was required to notice a difference, every time one just noticed a difference, subjectively, was the same as every other just noticed difference. In Figure 10.2 below,

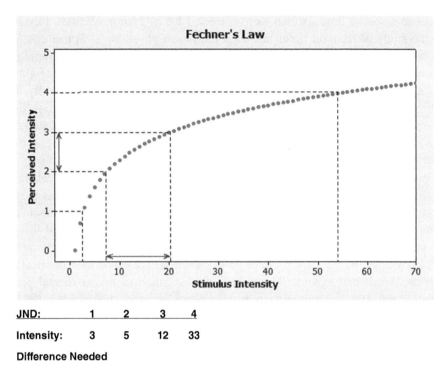

JND:	1	2	3	4
Intensity:	3	5	12	33
Difference Needed				

Figure 10.2   Psychophysical scaling

the change in physical intensity is related to each JND and indicates that there is a mathematical increase in JNDs (quantitatively equal), while the amount of stimulus intensity required for the detection of change increases geometrically (increasingly larger). In this, Fechner was successful in establishing psychology as quantitative because he connected quantitative physics with quantitative psychology (JNDs) and devised methods of measurement (Michell, 1997). At heart, Fechner was a Pythagorean; he believed that reality was basically quantitative and that both physical and mental domains were subject to mathematical determination.

Reaction time research was very popular in early psychology, especially in Wundt's laboratory. The original work stemmed from the finding of astronomers at the beginning of the 19th century (Boring, 1961). It was found that observers differed in their measurement of the time at which a star reached a set point in the sky, an apparent error in observation in different observers or in the same observer on different occasions. That led to the realization that people differ from each other in the speed of their reactivity and that it fluctuates within individuals. That resulted in the identification of the 'personal equation'—individual differences in response times, which were corrected for by taking averages. Physiologists took up the study of reaction times and then the Dutch physiologist Franciscus Donders (1818–1889) turned the approach into a measure of cognitive processing. Simple reaction time was established to a single stimulus—such as pressing a telegraph key to a light turning on. Next, a couple lights were introduced and the person had to respond to one only, discriminating between the false light stimulus and the correct one. The simple reaction time was then subtracted from the time taken to discriminate and the difference represented the time it took to discriminate (discrimination being a mental process)—a mental process had been measured temporally.

The procedure was taken up in Wundt's laboratory and was the basis of what was called **mental chronometry** (Hergenhahn and Henley, 2014). Chronometry, which is the science of accurate measurement of time, was applied to various types of mental processing. In the estimation of Cattell (1886) this type of experimental psychology established the relation between stimulation, sensation, and the time of mental processing and, in doing so, had proven Kant wrong—psychology *could* be an exact science (based on measurement).

Whereas Wundt had rejected the scientific investigation of higher mental processes, Ebbinghaus (1850–1909) attempted to study learning and memory (Ebbinghaus, 1885/1964). Ebbinghaus recognized that memorizing depended on the difficulty of the material to be learned, for instance memorizing a poem verbatim may require numerous repetitions of the material before it was successfully retained (Boring, 1961). Numbers of repetitions before memorization became for Ebbinghaus a measure of learning. In Chapter 5 we looked at Francis Galton's inauguration of the mental testing movement and the 'individual differences' tradition. In his measures of different abilities and sensory acuity Galton not only introduced quantification, he also attempted to assess, mathematically, how different measures (such as head size and height—Galton, 1888) may be related to each other, and invented the concept of co-relation. Not being a professional mathematician, he turned the problem over to Edgeworth, who in 1892 renamed it an 'index of co-relation' and then, in 1896, Karl Pearson (1857–1936) developed the mathematical formula for the 'product-moments method of linear correlation' (Boring, 1961) or, as we know it today, the coefficient of correlation.

For the first half-century of psychology, psychophysics was the main area of psychology in which quantification was attempted, but this was eventually displaced by efforts to measure intelligence (Michell, 1999). It was out of this area of investigation in particular that statistics entered psychology. It begins with the use of correlations, which leads to factor analysis, and eventuates in probabilistic, inferential statistics.

Statistics in psychology

By introducing measurement, psychology gained an independence from philosophy; and when measurement entered so did 'variability', which was key to statistical analysis

(Gigerenzer, 1987b). In experimental psychology, as reflected in the approaches of Fechner and Wundt, variability between individuals, as well as within individuals, began to be thought of as 'error' around some 'true value.' In the tradition of Galton and Pearson, in contrast, variability between individuals was taken as knowledge rather than as error. Individual differences were important to Galton's mental testing and ranking of individuals relative to each other. The correlation coefficient, originally developed to assess hereditary resemblance, quickly became a tool in the mental testing movement. What had been just a summary statistic was turned into a core theory in data analysis (Cronbach, 1957).

The correlation coefficient was the beginning of all statistical techniques (Cowles, 1989). In 1904 Charles Spearman took it and developed factor analysis. Factor analysis assesses the relations between manifest (measured) variables and some latent, unmeasured variable (Mulaik, 1987). Different variables are correlated and then the correlations are examined to see if there is some unexamined factor to which they are all related to some degree. The basic assumption was that the manifest performance variables were to be explained by what does not appear and is known only indirectly. To give an example, in Chapter 5 mention was made of how Spearman, as part of the mental testing movement, developed factor analysis to see if he could identify an underlying 'general intelligence' that manifested in various forms of apparently unrelated intellectual abilities like spelling, arithmetic, and musical ability.

Inferential statistics was another great influence on psychology. William Gosset (pen name Student), a statistician with the Guinness Brewery, was in need of a statistic to help assess the results of experiments with hops (Cowles, 2001). He worked with Pearson on the problem in 1905 and published his results in 1908. In this he provided a new statistic that social scientists would adopt—the T-Test, an inferential test that estimates the degree to which the obtained result is likely to be due to error. The work was largely ignored, but influenced Sir Ronald Fisher's (1890–1962) **Analysis of Variance** (ANOVA). Fisher (1926), conducting agricultural research, asked what a valid estimate of error may be, and Analysis when to judge results to be statistically significant. Significant here does not imply the variance everyday sense of important, but rather that the results are unlikely to be due to chance, that one's experimental manipulations are the likely cause of the obtained results. The answer to when to make that judgment was to be decided by the use of estimates of error (the probability). Fisher decided on the probability level of one in twenty (or $p. = 0.05$, meaning five times out of 100 would such results be obtained due to chance) as the decision point for accepting the results. He wrote that if that was not high enough, however, one could choose one in fifty, or 2 percent (it is a subjective determination). Fisher's 0.05 was the level of significance that psychologists have adopted by convention. After World War II, Fisher's ANOVA became experimental psychology's dominant instrument of research (Gigerenzer, 1987a) and theories of inference later became part of the required methodology (Gigerenzer, 1987b).

Psychological tests

The coefficient of correlation proved important to the psychological testing movement as attempts were made to establish tests that could be considered adequate measures of the characteristic of interest. Given the significance of measurement to conceptions of 'the scientific' it is no wonder psychologists placed great emphasis on perfecting their measurement tools. Almost from the start issues of reliability and validity arose. Cattell and Farrand (1896) introduced the need for what is now called 'interjudge reliability' by noting that whenever different judges were to be used in scoring tests, the level of agreement among judges should be established and, ideally, should be strongly correlated. They also noted a need for 'test-retest reliability' (correlating performance on two separate occasions) which they referred to as a measure of validity but which also introduces the idea of 'temporal stability' (stable over time). Wissler (1901) introduced the concept of 'criterion validity' (relation of scores to a related outcome), or, more specifically, 'concurrent validity' (relation of scores to a separate measure of the same thing). Wissler found that the Galtonian tests of intelligence did not correlate with each other or with college grades, thus lacking concurrent validity.

The Journal of Educational Psychology convened a symposium on the measurement of intelligence and what to do next (Thorndike et al., 1921). Colvin surmised that tests of intelligence were also tests of character and Thurstone called for tests of character. This opened the door to personality testing. Symonds (1924) discussed what is now known as 'cross-situational consistency' (the stability of a trait over different situations). Hoitsma (1925) introduced 'split half reliability' (correlating the first half of a test with the second) and what became 'discriminant validity' by demonstrating a lack of relation between intelligence and introversion. The term 'validity' as we understand it today had achieved consensus, which is reflected in Skaggs (1927), as the measure's degree of success in testing what it was intended to test and nothing more.

An issue that arose in personality testing was trait independence. The general idea was that if a trait truly existed it had to be shown that it could be measured independent of any other characteristic. Towards that end, Kelley (1928) wrote of the need to test independent mental traits since "any trait not discovered and not separately measured will always be a source of uncertainty and confusion" (p. 32). Thorndike (1934) recognized the demands that trait tests should measure 'unitary' traits (forming a single unit unrelated to any other) that were therefore 'pure.' The issue was considered by the Unitary Trait Committee from 1931–1935 (Holzinger, 1936). Alexander (1934) recommended the use of factor analysis since it could demonstrate independent traits or at least independent factors (the currently popular **Big Five Personality Traits** are based on this). Lorge (1935) argued that for a trait to be useful it had to be freed from the influence of other traits, and Flanagan (1935) maintained that an ideal personality theory would consist of independent elements. McClelland (1951) suggested the study of personality should study parts before proceeding to comprehend

Big Five

the whole. This singling out of pure traits led Campbell and Fiske (1959) to develop the 'multitrait-multimethod matrix as a means of demonstrating 'construct validity' (evidence that the construct—the conceptual abstraction—is empirically useful) by showing both 'discriminant validity' (two different traits, like 'anxiety' and 'pugnacity,' are uncorrelated) and convergent validity (separate measures of the same trait are correlated, like an anxiety test and galvanic skin response).

BOX 10.1
DOES MEASUREMENT TAKE PRECEDENCE OVER SUBJECT MATTER?

An assumption that has been central to research into personality has been the **fundamental lexical hypothesis** (Goldberg, 1990). The basic idea is that if there have been individual differences of sufficient importance in the life of a group, those differences will be represented linguistically. It is further assumed that trait terms reflect underlying regularities in personality (which trait psychologists seek evidence of). The idea, although not referred to as the fundamental lexical hypothesis, was first put forward by Galton (1884). He contended that the character that determines one's conduct is a 'durable something' and that it is quite reasonable to try to measure it. He cautioned, however, against supposing that the separate names we use to refer to moral 'faculties,' like courageous or sociable, refer to separate entities. So integrated were they in actual persons that it would be wrong to assume that they ever act singly—they intermix. To that end, he examined Roget's Thesaurus and found 1,000 words that were expressive of character and, further, that each had a different shade of meaning that overlapped with others. Allport and Odbert (1936) updated his count to almost 18,000 terms referring to behavior and personality.

Following the recommendation to study character by the symposium on studying intelligence (Thorndike et al., 1921), **psychometricians** began to pursue the study of character (personality in modern terminology) by assessing individual traits, drawing upon trait language to identify traits of interest. The effort was accompanied by recommendations of caution. Symonds (1924) wrote that before a trait was measured it should be determined whether they operate independently of the situation the person is in and, furthermore, that one must guard against **nominalism** and the error of thinking that because there is a name for 'something' that the 'something' actually exists. Trait terms,

(Continued)

(Continued)

for instance, which refer to regularities in observed behavior, may be presumed to reflect an independent something, a trait, that accounts for the observed pattern. There was a danger of **hypostatization** or **reification** (Allport, 1928; Symonds, 1931). As Campbell (1960) wrote, the introduction of construct validity (which his multitrait-multimethod matrix contributed to) encouraged trait reification.

Besides hypostatization, there was the added issue of elementalism. Allport (1928) accepted that every supposed trait would have to be established separately, but he (Allport, 1924) had earlier judged that, while there were gains to be had from the study of single traits, one must not lose sight of the organized whole, the personality undivided, in which traits function as part of an ensemble: "the traits are there but the personality is lacking" (p. 133). This 'spuriousness argument' also applied to factor analysis: "By seeking independent (non-correlating) factors, a further abstraction is committed. Traits are not independent of one another; they overlap" (Allport, 1934, p. 170). Rather, "'pure' traits are not to be expected in mental organization, for in fact nothing in mental life is altogether independent of other influences" (Allport and Odbert, 1936, pp. 12–13). "Such an assumption," Allport (1937) wrote, "is highly artificial. So interwoven is the fabric of personality that it seems almost impossible to think of any patterns that are wholly unrelated to others" (p. 245). Personality, as it presents itself to us in living beings, as the integrated person, was being lost sight of and distorted.

Recall the words of Holt (1962), who proposed, "Science is defined by its methods, not its subject matter" (p. 397). The need for adequate, scientifically acceptable methods, in this case tests, took precedence over the subject matter. People as persons, in everyday life, do not appear as dismembered or disarticulated, unless, of course, one is encountering someone with dissociative identity disorder (formerly multiple personality disorder). The precedence of method over subject matter is also readily apparent with the so-called Big Five personality traits or factors. The list of terms in Allport and Odbert (1936) had long been subjected to factor analysis to identify the structure (the common core basis) of human personality. During the 1970s and 80s factor analysis was consistently producing five factors from data sets that led to their being referred to as the 'Big Five' (Piekkola, 2011). Costa and McCrae, the creators of the modern influential Big Five, originally arrived at three factors but, under the influence of the widespread discovery of five, added questions to their test bank that were designed to produce two more factors. As they (McCrae and Costa, 1985) wrote, "one could argue that an openness factor emerges in the analysis of the extended set only because the selection of items had been biased in that direction" (p. 719). It was the results of the application of the method that propelled their decision, not a concern with concrete humans. There is an acronym labeling factor analysis that may apply here: GIGO (garbage in, garbage out), or what you get depends on what you select to include.

Since mental life gives no evidence of separate compartments, Allport and Odbert (1936) proposed—and it is applicable to the Big Five—that "we must dispense with the methodological ideal of pure or independent traits" (p. 15) as promoted by factor-analytic approaches. Thorpe (1938) summarized it best:

> It may be that the statistical tools so essential to an analysis of the data of the physical sciences will prove to be a source of oversimplification in an attempted quantitative treatment of the psychological data of personality organization. The point is well exemplified by the factor-analysis method by means of which Thurstone has been able to reduce the wide variety of specific traits usually associated with the personality of a normal individual by divesting him of many of his more intangible but nevertheless essential and unique qualities leaving merely four or five mathematically distinguishable components as a sort of personality skeleton. (p. 523)

What we end up with is that individual differences, which are real differences between real people, become an annoyance, instead of a challenge, and are cast aside as 'error variance' (Cronbach, 1957). To deal with error variance, characteristics that can influence results, other than the variable of interest, have to be eliminated through the rigorous control of conditions (Adams, 1930). Personal impressions, expectations, memories, emotional values are all sources of error. Scales are more objective the more they are freed from subjective influences: "the greater the extent to which the scale can be freed from the 'human' element, the more objective it becomes" (pp. 122–123). What we end up with is a psychology without individuals (Gigerenzer, 1987a).

10.3 THE QUANTITATIVE AND QUALITATIVE IN EARLY RESEARCH

The quantitative imperative advocated by the mainstream has led to qualitative methods being summarily dismissed by what appear to be a priori conclusions (Michell, 2003). Not all agreed with such a position. According to Cantril, Ames, Hastorf, and Ittelson (1949a) the quantitative and the non-quantitative procedures are interdependent in scientific work, and creating a dichotomy between the two actually creates an artificial barrier to progress.

The researcher should be led by whichever procedure is best suited to the matter at hand. Regardless, the qualitative approaches would be dismissed. This was apparently due to the rise to prominence of the experimental method and ANOVA, after 1945, as the way to be scientific in psychology. After all, qualitative work had been done all along to that point in time. Wundt, for instance, had relied on introspection as part of his experimental approach, as had Fechner. So too did James (1890/1950) in his description of the stream of consciousness.

Galton (1879) discussed a qualitative experiment in which he analyzed every object that captured his attention. He maintained focus on it until he had one or two thoughts directly associated with the original attention-catching object. He then created the 'word association test' by selecting a list of words and timing (quantitative) how long it took for each word to evoke at least two direct associations in mind. Jung (1981) reported on word association experiments during the first decade of the 20th century, some of which were designed to identify underlying psychological complexes. Freud's (1924/1953) method of free association, in which a person reported whatever came to mind without censure, was a further variation on this, and his interpretations of dreams were also qualitative investigations. Of course, within the therapeutic community, case studies qualify as well.

Perhaps the best demonstration of the significance of qualitative research in early experimental psychology was Titchener's (1901/1971) manual for training psychology students in laboratory practices. Volume I was devoted to qualitative experiments. In this, he included work on perception which required reports on subjective experiences and perceptual illusions. Bartlett (1916), from a different perspective, examined the processes involved in perceiving ambiguous stimuli like ink-blots (prior to the famous Rorschach ink-blots) and found that when presented with meaningless stimuli people internally engage in an 'effort after meaning' trying to make sense of the unfamiliar or ambiguous. Bartlett (1920) followed this with an investigation into the effects of repeated reproduction of stories, the well-known War of the Ghosts (a west coast Canadian First Nations' tale). He found that when people are confronted with repeated recall from memory the recollection undergoes significant transformations. In particular people would take unfamiliar material, from an unfamiliar culture, and reconstitute it so that it fitted into a framework consistent with their already established, mental representations.

Even up to the 1930s one can find evidence of the acceptance of qualitative research within the mainstream. For instance, Reymert and Hartman (1933) applied quantitative and qualitative methods to the assessment of mental tests. As they pointed out, at the time there was a trend toward mental testing being lost in statistical treatments. Beyond the quantitative results, they were interested in the actual methods employed in solving the problems presented in the 'Knox Cube Test.' So they asked their participants how they went about solving the task. They found a broad array of procedures that the quantitative method simply bypassed but which were relevant to fully comprehending how the individuals solved a problem, and how they differed in their approaches. Nonetheless the tide was turning. Psychology was becoming a science of variables and statistics.

As a technical term, psychologists had been familiar with 'variables' from statistical procedures (Danziger and Dzinas, 1997). In his 1911 textbook, Yule introduced psychologists to correlational techniques and discussed them within the context of the 'theory of variables.' According to Yule (1912), numerical measurement applied to cases involving quantity and that meant more than a single numerical value but a varying quantity or 'variable.' Consistent with that, the original distinction between independent and dependent variable did not originate in experimentation. It was introduced in 1883 by John Young in his *Elements in Differential Calculus* in reference to mathematical functions (Winston, 2004). The phrase 'independent variable' also appeared in both Heidbreder and Cullen in 1927, but not in reference to experimentally manipulated conditions, but to elements that were independent of each other (Winston, 2004). Allport (1927) also referred to an independent variable as a reliably measured trait that is considered independent of all other variables. It would be another decade before the terms achieved their modern usage and began to dominate psychological discourse.

Woodworth, in the 1921 edition of his widely adopted introductory psychology text 'Psychology,' discussed experimentation as simply the systematic varying of conditions (Winston, 1988). In this, he did not exclude introspective research or correlational procedures as experimental. In line with behaviorism, he also proposed that environmental and organismic phenomena could be broken up into discrete units called stimuli and responses (Danziger, 1996). In the third edition (1934), for the first time in a textbook, manipulated conditions were referred to as independent variables and dependent variables (Winston, 1988). Boring (1933) had already proposed that in an experiment there were a minimum of two terms: the independent variable and dependent variable. The independent variable is manipulated and changes in the dependent variable are noted, the intent being to identify causal relations. In 1938 Woodworth published the influential *Experimental Psychology*, the long-awaited 'Columbia Bible' which would define experimental psychology for future psychologists (Winston, 1990). The terms stimulus and response were replaced by independent and dependent variable and they became part of the language that was common to psychologists across all sub-disciplines (Danziger and Dzinas, 1997). That noted, it was E. C. Tolman (1886–1959) who, in his 1932 *Purposive Behavior* in *Animals and Men*, demonstrated how variable language could be interdisciplinary and used in comparing different systems of psychology (learning theory, perception, Gestalt). What the variables represented didn't matter just so long as the investigative units were variables. As a result, the official psychological language was impoverished. Variables and statistics became the core around which psychological research and communication orbited. Qualitative research did not fit that conception of the psychological.

10.4 THE HOLISTIC AND ATOMISTIC DISPUTE

The experimental approach to psychology has tended to be elementalistic in its approach by taking the complex whole and breaking it down to parts or elements that could be investigated independently. It also tended to be individualistic in that persons were separated from the cultural-historical contexts of their lives. From the beginning, however, there had been an alternative approach towards understanding human existence, practice, and the psychological as embedded within a dynamic relation with the psycho-cultural milieu of personal being. It was an approach that dealt with whole persons rather than parts.

Völkerpsychologie

To set the stage we begin with German Völkerpsychologie. While Wundt had argued that beyond the elementary psychological functions, which could be subjected to experimentation, knowledge of higher mental functions had to consider sociocultural and historical forces as they impacted individuals. The idea did not originate with Wundt. While, by tradition, psychology begins with Wundt's 1879 creation of an experimental laboratory at the University of Leipzig, some twenty years prior Moritz Lazarus (1824–1903) was appointed chair of the Department of Psychology and Völkerpsychologie at Bern (Kalmar, 1987). The next year, along with Hermann Steinthal (1823–1879), he published a journal devoted to the topic of völkerpsychologie. The approach was based on the concepts of volk (people) and völksgeist (group spirit) and joined volk to geist (spirit). This was not in reference to some supernatural being, but rather, refers to what is the prevailing ethos through which the group's values, understandings, and beliefs are objectified through its institutions. Such 'objective spirit' had two forms of existence—embodied in material forms like books, monuments, laws, and the like, and within individuals as dispositions, attitudes, and thoughts (Jahoda, 1993). Lazarus and Steinthal were the first to develop a psychology on social/cultural influences. In this they extended the realm of the psychological beyond the individual person. An influential figure who would develop this understanding was Wilhelm Dilthey (1833–1911).

Wilhelm Dilthey

To Dilthey, psychology had to be redefined as a 'human study' or human science and distinguished from natural science (Dilthey, 1894/1977a). Natural sciences and human studies differ in that natural science deals with objects that are presented to consciousness from outside, whereas human studies originate in, and are approached from the perspective of, a real, living continuum. Psychology, as such, deals with the original connectedness of the immediately lived experience, as a coherent whole or nexus (a connected series). Human studies have a qualitatively different subject matter from the natural sciences and have to establish their own methods, methods that will correspond with the object of investigation. In human studies these are understanding and interpretation (Dilthey, 1927/1977b). The basis for this was that individuals are understandable given the interrelatedness of people to what is common (Dilthey, 1894/1977a). Social (societal) life provides insight into an individual's inner life and establishes what can be expected from them.

The affairs of daily life require the development of individual capacities and character. Inductive inferences are made from each person's expression of life to their entire life context. Understanding, in its initial forms (in people in general, not psychologists), arises in the interests of practical life and the interactions between people. People have to make themselves understood to each other; we need to know what the other is up to and what to expect. Growing up in families, sharing with other people and learning from their instruction, individuals absorb the common context. The child is immersed within the medium of common context. The child learns facial expressions, gestures, words and word combinations, because they are confronted by them as constantly the same and bearing a constant relation to what they signify. The child becomes oriented to the realm of objective spirit as it is ordered and organized within institutions—a 'sphere of communality.'

Dilthey opposed the natural science approach to psychology, which he called 'explanatory psychology.' Explanatory psychology aims to account for mental life in terms of elements and laws, like chemistry and physics explain the natural world. This was represented by associationistic psychologists. By this, Dilthey was referring to the tradition from British Empiricism that assumed the existence of elementary sensations which combined with each other, upon the basis of associationistic laws (like contiguity, similarity, opposition, and repetition), to produce complex mental configurations. Helmholtz's theory of perception and Wundt's and Titchener's elementalism would be examples. Explanatory psychology subordinated lived experience to elements in a system of components (Dilthey, 1894/1977a). According to Dilthey, one has to question whether it is legitimate to transfer the assumptions and methods of natural science (like reductionism, atomism, and elementalism) to an appreciation of psychic life. Explanatory attempts to break apart the totality of the content of consciousness into elements and seeking some corresponding physical stimulus were inadequate. Explanatory psychology was bankrupt since it handed over its affairs to physiology.

Psychic life to Dilthey is not an assemblage, not a construction built of component parts; it is not a composite of collaborating atoms of sensation or affect. From the start, the psychic life process is a comprehensive unity, comprised of an inner connectedness of psychic life within an organized whole. Over the course of development psychic functions may be differentiated but they always remain connected with the nexus. One can distinguish cognitive, affective, and volitional characteristics (the traditional categories of psychology) of consciousness but they are interdependent rather than opposed (Teo, 2003). Development tends toward establishing a 'stable nexus of psychic life,' an interconnectivity that is harmonized with life conditions (Dilthey, 1894/1977a).

In the developed psychic life of the adult there are three formative conditions: bodily development, the physical environment, and the environment of the spiritual world (objective spirit, ethos). Collective history is continually present for the individual in objective spirit, and the self is nourished from early childhood by it. Those conditions act upon the 'structured nexus of psychic life.' In the beginning instincts and feelings constitute the agency moving the person onwards. With development, feelings and instincts are subordinated to intellectual and volitional processes, giving the emerging psychic developments and transformations the quality of adaptation to individual life conditions. Movements are adapted to instincts and the will becomes habitually oriented, connections are made between means and ends. Perception becomes more fully developed (knowledge enriches perception). Concepts or mental representations are formed more purposefully. While always an organized whole, psychic life is undergoing qualitative changes, moving from a life-unity that is governed by stimulus changes to one that inhibits and controls reactions by will and idea, and adapts needs to reality. To be clear, Dilthey is not proposing that psychic life is wholly internal, since psychic life is an aspect of life as a whole, and life-unity involves reciprocal interplay with the objective world. Reciprocal action is an adaptation of the 'living-psycho-physical unity' with lived circumstances.

Gradually, with experience, a stable nexus is formed of values, reproducible representations and intentional activity—a living, historically formed organization. Psychic life is structurally organized into a coherent whole that can be differentiated as attention, memory, perception, and will—not as separate entities but as functions of the living whole. As one develops and becomes more conscious, one becomes aware of the unity and differences in inner states. They constitute perception and form memories, ideals, and goals, which are all aspects of living, vibrant connections with the entire psychic life.

Explanatory, natural science approaches to psychology usually avoid the development of the living psyche, restricting its interest to psychic elements. While experimental psychology has been driven by an ideal of prediction and control, to Dilthey one cannot predict how psychic life will unfold. Only afterwards can reasons (not causes) for what has occurred be disengaged (abstracted intellectually) from the concrete nexus. In place of explanatory psychology, Dilthey offered 'analytic' or 'descriptive' psychology. Its aim is the analysis and description of adult psychic life in all its developed aspects as components constituting the unique nexus. Developed psychic life had to be grasped, described, and analyzed as a whole. The apprehension of psychic states had to originate in lived experience, in which the psychic processes were operating together, and continually connected with each other. The whole of psychic life disclosed in experience had to remain the immediate, lived foundation for psychology.

In terms of method, Dilthey (1900/1972) proposed adapting **hermeneutics**, the art of textual interpretation, to human studies. Understanding is supported by common backgrounds (what we previously referred to as 'intersubjectively homogeneous' with Holzkamp, Chapter 9) and conventional ways of living consisting of social networks and cultural practices (Martin and Sugarman, 2009). Other people's existence is provided by words, actions, and gestures, and it is through this that one attempts to apprehend the individual's personal sense of life (Dilthey, 1900/1972).

Other oppositions to elementalism

While I have focused on Dilthey's rejection of atomistic reductionism, I want to briefly mention two other psychologies in opposition to what Dilthey called explanatory psychology. Max Wertheimer (1880–1943), Wolfgang Köhler (1887–1967), and Kurt Koffka (1886–1941), the founders of Gestalt psychology, opposed elementalism in perceptual theory (Heidbreder, 1933). To them, what was perceived was recognized as an organized whole and could not be explained by dissection into presumed, constituent, elementary sensations. Decomposition to elements would lose qualities that were present in the organized percept. As 'holists,' they focused on immediate conscious experience and in that they found no elements. Furthermore, the analysis into elements forced the need for a theory of how elements were joined together (associationism), one that was altogether a product of analysis and intellectual abstraction. Only because it was intellectually torn apart did it need to be glued back together. Likewise, William James (1890/1950), in his discussion of the 'stream of thought,' and what is now referred to as the 'stream of consciousness,' discussed the phenomena of thought as a unity. Consciousness is continuous and indivisible. It is in a constant state of flux, yet an undivided, single state. Associationistic, elementalistic psychology imposes intellectual divisions that do not exist in immediate experience.

10.5 THE IDIOGRAPHIC AND NOMOTHETIC APPROACHES

The philosopher Wilhelm Windelband (1848–1915) noted that the disciplines that have been directed at knowledge have been classified as natural science and the humanities (Windelband, 1894/1998). The distinction, in some ways, reflects the knowledge object that they are focused on and connects to Socrates' concern with the relation between the 'general' and the 'particular.' The empirical sciences, for their part, have either sought natural laws that pertain to phenomena in general, or phenomena in their historically conditioned presentation as particulars. One form is constant and enduring while the other aspect involves unique contexts. Windelband introduced the terms nomothetic (pertaining to the general) and idiographic (pertaining to the particular) to distinguish between the two. Natural science tends to be dominated by a concern with abstraction, with what is general, whereas history tends to be dominated by concern with concreteness (occurrences in context). Extending this distinction to psychology, he professed doubt that the recent conception of mathematical laws, regarding psychological processes, would ever contribute any true understanding of human life. There is in the individual, particular person, historical, personal experience that will not be subsumed under natural laws. The ultimate nature of personality, the whole person, will withstand analytic decomposition to general categories.

Allport

Not surprisingly this distinction found its way into personality psychology, and did so through **Allport's** (1937) *Personality: A Psychological Interpretation*. Allport recognized that psychology was tending in the direction of becoming a fully nomothetic discipline, but he argued that a psychology of the individual (which is what personality psychology is supposed to be—a science of the whole person) would have to be mostly idiographic. At the same time, he did not believe that the two approaches should be completely separate; they should complement each other. That meant that nomothetic psychology, the science of 'mind-in-general,' could not overcome the need for a science of 'mind-in-particular.' Methods suited to the investigation of the whole person, the individual, would have to be adopted.

In his text on personality, Allport argued in favor of case studies as a means to get to know persons. As he noted, psychology (the mainstream in emergence), for the most part, failed to recognize the case study as an appropriate method in psychology, largely because it displayed little concern with the 'complete person.' Reflecting that, Lundberg (1926) argued that the case method was not scientific and, at best, an initial step; that the best method, scientifically, was the statistical which summarized a large number of cases and identified patterns and uniformities. In fairness, Lundberg acknowledged that social workers contended that what is vital about humans is thereby destroyed; that the statistical method reduces humans and social relations to mere component parts which are then counted. Lundberg, nonetheless, did not waver in his preference for the 'scientific' approach. Despite scientific biases, individuality exists, and is never repeated, and a method to capture that is the case study (Allport, 1937). One must become acquainted with the person as much as possible. Certainly, Allport acknowledged, there will be similarities due to shared cultural life, but the circumstances of any individual can vary in the range of possibilities and of avenues pursued. Shared cultural backgrounds, despite internal variability, will support understanding so long as one's mental life is in tune with another.

Allport (1962) pointed out that the ethical standards of the American Psychological Association required that the psychologist be "committed to increasing man's understanding of man" (p. 405), which meant that not only 'man in general' but 'man in particular' has to be of concern (suggesting of course that the battle he had been fighting for 25 years had not been successful). Rather than being impatient with single cases and rushing to generalization, he asked, why not be impatient with generalization and turn to individual behavior to develop hunches, and then look for generalization? Generalization, at best, is 'actuarial' (the use of statistics to predict the future of a population). That may be of use for insurance companies and government but it says nothing of individuals. While 70 percent of boys from disadvantaged circumstances will be criminals, that does not mean any one of them has a 70 percent chance of doing so. To predict the individual, his circumstances would have to be examined to get a basis for prediction. Our knowledge of human nature should begin with knowledge of concrete individuals, understanding them as they exist in their natural complexity (Allport, 1942). Knowledge always applies to single cases when used and nomothetic knowledge has to be particularized to be of value. Any method that contributes to knowledge, he claimed, should be admitted as a scientific method (and not constrained by a narrow conception).

I think it is safe to say that the greatest contention around the nomothetic and ideographic approaches has occurred between clinicians and experimentalists, or more specifically between the clinician and the psychometrician. Vernon (1937) believed the two approaches were legitimate and should reinforce each other, and that the psychometric approach, alone, was unsatisfactory for the needs of the clinician. Psychometricians eliminate subjective judgment in favor of rigid standardization, reliability, and validity. Clinicians, from their perspective, point out that standardizing a test does not standardize subjectivity, the meaning of items to the person tested, and it is that which determines responses. To deal with individuals they must be treated in ways appropriate to them if anything of value is to be obtained, including subjectivity and personal meaning. The proof clinicians seek is of an entirely different type from mathematical consistency, and the psychometrician devalues the clinician's methods by applying an inappropriate standard. The Rorschach Ink-Blot Test and The Thematic Apperception Test (TAT), which use ambiguous stimuli, to serve as a basis for the projection of subjectivity, are examples.

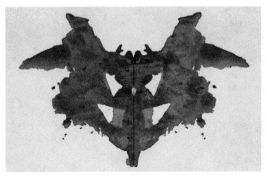

Figure 10.3   Rorschach and TAT examples

The Rorschach and TAT are 'projective techniques' based on the assumption that forms of behavior (actions, statements, even possessions) are expressions of, and reveal, personality (Rapaport, 1942). As such they are 'global' in studying personality in the whole, as opposed to 'atomistic' quantification of component traits, and they are qualitative in that they depend on subjective interpretation (Hertz, 1934; Harrison, 1943). The Rorschach (first reported on in 1921, shortly before Rorschach's death) is a variation on Freud's method of free association, except that the ink-blots act as stimuli for free association about the blots. The basic idea is that what is free associated will serve as clues to the person's personality.

The TAT was inspired by Schwartz's (1932) Social Situation Pictures (Morgan, 2002). The pictures (see below) were used in interviews with delinquents (10–12 years old) in an effort to establish rapport (Schwartz, 1932). It also removes the barriers that can be encountered with direct questions and answers, which provoked evasion, emotional blocking, and fabrication, or because they may not be able to verbalize. They were told each picture had meaning and were asked to interpret it. It was expected that identification and projection may occur, revealing something of subjectivity. The TAT was first reported on in 1933, by Morgan and Murray, as a method for investigating fantasies, but it achieved its developed form in 1943 (Morgan, 2002). In this test the person is asked to interpret what is going on, what preceding events were, and what the likely outcome might be (Murray, 1938/1962). Absorbed in the task, the person is unlikely to be self-aware and defensive. The therapist investigates the responses and identifies relevant unifying themes over the stories created. Relevant elements are identified by symbolic

Figure 10.4 A Social Situation Picture

significance, repetition, uniqueness, interrelatedness over picture series, and the subject's self-involvement (Murray, 1951).

Throughout the history of these tests, and others, which are still used with frequency by clinicians, they have been denigrated as useless by psychometricians because they lack reliability and validity (Lilienfield, Wood, and Garb, 2000). Despite their scientific status, clinicians argue that they are indispensable to their therapeutic practice. According to Harrison (1943), less precision is needed in the clinic than in the laboratory. The issue of reliability is more meaningful, therefore, for psychometric tests. The TAT is not a formal test but more of a probing tool in a task of detection. Furthermore, contrary to the demand for reliability (consistency over time), people are in flux and changing. Just because results are inconsistent over sessions does not invalidate the TAT. It is all rather reminiscent of Holzkamp's criticism of variable psychology for trying to fit Freud's theory to a model it is unsuited for.

By way of closing, I have not addressed the modern approaches to qualitative methods but the issues that have been addressed are the issues that remain. In the final analysis, as Denzin and Lincoln (1994) wrote, qualitative research is naturalistic and interpretive with respect to the subject matter. There is an attempt to study phenomena in terms of the meanings brought to the situation by the participants. Qualitative researchers attempt to understand the phenomenon of interest from the perspective of the person under study: "The aim of qualitative research is to represent the experiences and actions of people as they encounter, engage, and live through situations" (Elliott, Fischer, and Rennie, 1999, p. 216). I leave it to you to judge which is scientific or not.

SUMMARY

Academic psychology emerged during the period of modernity during which there was a reliance on objectivity, realism, and science. The passage into the period of postmodernity challenges those basic assumptions.

- Some conceive of human understanding as a linguistic construction rather than access to objective reality.
- The quantitative imperative is the assumption that to be scientific is to quantify and measure.
- The 14th-century calculators introduced the science of calculations and attempted to measure qualities, setting the groundwork for science.

(Continued)

(Continued)

- Measurement in psychology began with four distinct movements: psychophysics, reaction times, memory research, and individual differences.

- Individual differences research into mental testing led to the statistical procedures of correlation, factor analysis, issues of reliability and validity, and psychometric tests of character or personality.

- Personality research drew upon the fundamental lexical hypothesis and used descriptive terms as a basis for identifying personality traits; this was accompanied by the danger of hypostatization.

- In the early days of psychological research both quantitative and qualitative methods were used.

- During the 1930s, the experimental method and the distinction of independent variables and dependent variables was entrenched, and inferential statistics became conventional.

- Two general trends have coexisted in psychology—elementalism and holism.

- The scientific and clinical traditions have been opposed in their reliance on nomothetic versus idiographic procedures.

SUGGESTED READINGS

Allport, G. W. (1961). *Pattern and growth in personality*. New York: Holt, Rinehart and Winston.

Kvale, S. (1992). *Psychology and postmodernism.* London: SAGE Publications.

Smith, J. A., Harré, R., and Langenhove, L. V. (1995). *Rethinking psychology.* London: SAGE Publications.

Smith, J. A., Harré, R., and Langenhove, L. V. (1995). *Rethinking methods in psychology.* London: SAGE Publications.

Want to learn more? For links to online resources, examples of multiple choice questions, conceptual exercises and much more, visit the companion website at
https://study.sagepub.com/piekkola

11

THE COGNITIVE REVOLUTION

LEARNING OBJECTIVE

In this chapter you will learn about the reasons why cognition, which was basic to early interests in scientific psychology, underwent repression and the circumstances which led to its reinstatement as a valid concern.

- The stultifying influence of the behaviorists will be considered along with the factors that led to the ultimate transcendence of the anti-mentalism and radical objectivism that came to prevail.
- The impact of communications engineering and computers and the subsequent mechanistic modeling of mind will be discussed along with the work in artificial intelligence.
- Questions about whether humans can rightly be equated with computers will be considered, and we will end with a consideration of the problem of individualism in cognitive psychology.

FRAMING QUESTIONS

- Did behavioristic psychology represent an advance in knowledge, or did it hinder psychological growth?
- Are human mental processes mechanical in their operation and can computers effectively model human beings? Will machines ever display human cognitive and intellectual capacity?
- Can humans be fully understood as independent agents, whose thoughts and abilities are uninfluenced by social and historical conditions?

INTRODUCTION

In dealing with the so-called cognitive revolution in psychology, I feel that this appellation is somehow misleading. It might be better termed the 'cognitive revival' or even the 'cognitive revision.' By revival I am referring to the fact that psychologists had been concerned with cognition from the beginning of scientific psychology. Wundt studied sensation, immediate perception, mental reaction times, and attention. James addressed sensation, perception, attention, conception, discrimination, memory, imagination, reasoning, and consciousness. Furthermore, the revolution is a specifically North American phenomenon since cognitive processes continued to be studied in Europe while Behaviorism was dismissing them. Revision might be an applicable term since the revolution was due to the impact of communications engineering and computer processing. Cognition was reconceived as information processing rather than the traditional mental processes, which was more palatable than positing unacceptable 'mentalism.' Lastly, rather than a revolution, the period might be better conceived of as the demise of the behavioristic hegemony since neuropsychology, cultural psychology, and theoretical psychology were coming to the fore as well.

Before considering the revolution itself, brief mention will be made of early developments in studies of cognition and the parallel work that continued while behaviorism ruled. The intention is that you understand that it is a sweeping generalization to propose that the behavioristic hegemony in North America precluded all interest in cognitive processes elsewhere in the world.

11.1 EARLY COGNITIVE STUDIES AND BEHAVIORISM

Early cognitive studies

When dealing with cognitive psychology it may be the case that a specialized subdiscipline did not appear until the 20th century, but there were precursors in the 19th century and earlier. Socrates, for instance, in ancient Greece was interested in **inductive definition**, which involved examining all instances of a concept to examine what they had in common (Hergenhahn and Henley, 2014). This would be the later basis of the **classical view of concepts** that was dominant in cognitive psychology until the 1970s (Galotti, 2014).

Aristotle contributed to memory and recall by introducing the 'laws of association,' whereby ideas are related such that the recall of one tends to elicit the connected ideas (Hergenhahn and Henley, 2014). The law of association due to contrast, for instance, proposes that when one thinks of one thing, one tends to recall its opposite. Thinking of 'hot' may provoke thoughts of 'cold.' He also distinguished between 'remembering' (passive, spontaneous recollection, without effort) and 'recall' (active, requiring effort), which resembles the modern distinction between recognition and recall. If, for instance, I ask you your name that will require no effort and is an example of remembering. Recall, on the other hand, may be involved if I ask who taught you in third grade, since it may not come readily to mind.

The mental processes of sensation and perception were a concern to Helmholtz and Wundt. Wundt also examined **mental chronometry**, which involved having partici- pants engage in simple reaction time tasks (tapping a telegraph key in response to a light) and introducing a mental procedure like deciding how to respond to two different lights (Hergenhahn and Henley, 2014). The difference in time between the two tasks reflected the amount of time to decide. Wundt, however, did not believe higher mental processes could be studied experimentally. This was quickly dispelled by Ebbinghaus (1885/1964) in his study of learning and memory. Galton (1880), in England, studied mental imagery (asking people to form a picture in their head of their breakfast). In France, Charcot and Binet (1893, in Nicolas, Gounden, and Levine, 2011) examined two people who were outstand- ing at mental, numerical calculations (one used words, the other visual imagery); they also studied hypnosis in relation to hysteria.

The range of cognitive issues that concerned early psychologists is also indicated by the publications in the first ten years of the *Psychological Review* (1894–1903). Topics included sensation, perception, language and perception, time perception, illusions, attention, associa- tions between ideas, judgment, imagination, imagery, after-images, music imagery, dreams, memory, amnesia, recognition, hypnosis and suggestibility, read- ing, deductive and inductive logic, problem solving, subliminal consciousness, automaticity, telegraphic language, concepts, and meaning. In short, there was a wide interest in cognitive processes and so when we speak of a cognitive revolution it should not sug- gest that these phenomena were being discovered for the first time.

WHAT DO YOU THINK?

Can a psychology that ignores mental processes effectively deal with the full range of human activ- ity—and should it?

Behavioristic stultification and shortcomings

When Watson (1913a) introduced the 'behaviorist manifesto' he was intent on removing any- thing subjective and unobservable, which cognitive phenomena qualify as, from scientific psychology. Terms like mind, mental states, imagery, and the like, would be banished and psychology would become a science of stimuli and responses, habit formation, and adjustments to the environment. The behaviorists either dismissed or reframed the cognitive functions in order to fit them to their theoretical framework. Thought (inner speech) became habits of speech occurring at a subvocal level (faint, movements of speech musculature). Speech production was a habitual production of meaningless vocalizations. Mental images were rejected and replaced by changes in behavior (Watson, 1913b). Sensation and perception were mentalistic terms that were to be avoided. They were replaced by objective evidence such as discriminatory responses, like 'responding' to a red stimulus but not a green one replacing 'perceiving' a difference between them (Watson, 1919, in Boring, 1929). The mentalistic terms of the old psychology were being translated into terms that applied to observable stimuli and responses.

What the 'ordinary' person meant by memory, to Watson (1924/1966), required a scientific explanation, especially since critics of behaviorism considered this a problem. In defense, memory was deemed merely the return of a previously established habit when the stimulus conditions that last provoked it were reinstated. When a stimulus is re-encountered after an absence, we perform our old habits of repeating the same words or displaying the same visceral-emotional behavior. A further issue that had to be addressed with memory involved the established experimental paradigm of Ebbinghaus (1885/1964) into list learning.

Ebbinghaus explained the acquisition and retention in memory of learned lists in terms of associations formed between ideas. In the hands of the behaviorists the focus would be on a connection between observable events—the words to be learned. According to the '*chaining hypothesis,*' serial learning involves a process of associating adjacent items in a list (Slamecka, 1985). List items were hypothesized to form a sequence of stimulus-response links wherein a response to an antecedent item became a stimulus for the subsequent item in the list, in a chain of successive stimulus-response links. Through associative chaining, connections would be formed only between adjacent items. These would eventually be challenged by subsequent research that indicated that associations were formed between distant items. Even more problematic, '*clustering effects,*' or the grouping of related items based on similarity in meaning during recall or reproduction from memory; 'meaning' mattered (Deese, 1959). Even from within behaviorism there were attempts to introduce cognitive processes. Tolman and Honzik (1930) demonstrated the existence of 'cognitive maps' (a mental representation of a spatial layout) which impacted performance. Razran (1939), from a different perspective, demonstrated that verbal conditioning too was based on word 'meaning' (see Box 11.1).

During the behaviorist hegemony psychology became, as Allport (1937) expressed it, a science regarding meaningless movements of mindless organisms. It was an approach that

BOX 11.1
COGNITIVE FUNCTIONS INTRUDE ON BEHAVIORISM

Tolman

In demonstrating 'cognitive maps' **Edward Tolman** (1886–1959), along with Charles Honzik, had hungry rats wander through an alley maze that involved a series of choice points where turning one way led to a blind alley and turning the other allowed further progress. At the end of the maze was a food box (Tolman and Honzik, 1930). The accepted behaviorist interpretation of learning to find the correct route without error (entry into blind alleys) was that reinforcement (food in the food box) was required for learning to occur. Without reinforcement, there was no learning (change in behavior). Tolman and Honzik had two control groups—one which was always rewarded and one which never was, and an experimental group which only found food on the eleventh day, after ten days of none (when no learning supposedly occurred). What was interesting was that on day twelve, after the switch, the experimental group made fewer errors in reaching the food box than did the group that was always rewarded with food. Apparently, they had learned about the layout of the maze without reward and had formed a mental representation that they drew upon once there was the possibility of food being available. Skinner (1974) would dogmatically dismiss their conclusion, asserting that there were no cognitive maps, no stored knowledge, only changed behaviors.

Razran (1939) used classical conditioning procedures to demonstrate that a conditioned reaction to a verbal stimulus, such as the word 'cent' presented visually, would transfer or generalize to another word that was similar in meaning ('penny') rather than in its visual-auditory form ('scent'). In the conditioning phase four words (urn, style, surf, and freeze) were flashed on a screen while participants chewed gum, sucked lollipops, or ate sandwiches. Salivation, due to such consumption, was paired with the neutral words (which do not naturally elicit salivation). Subsequently homophones (same pronunciation but differing in meaning and possibly spelling) and synonyms (same meaning) were presented and the amount of salivation to each was measured. Generalized salivation occurred at 59 percent for semantic similarity (for example, style and fashion) than for homophones (style and stile) at 37 percent. According to Razran, a person conditions more readily to a word's meaning than to its visual-auditory form. Of course, meaning was something mainstream behaviorists had tried to deny any validity.

(Continued)

(Continued)

Other studies (cited in Kimble, 1961) have also demonstrated 'semantic generalization' (generalization based on meaning). A response that was conditioned to a blue light was found by Osgood (1953, in Kimble, 1961) to generalize to the word 'blue.' Other experiments conducted by Diven (1936, in Kimble, 1961), and later Lacey (1956, in Kimble, 1961), showed that a conditioned galvanic skin response to the word 'barn' generalized to other words having to do with rural settings, for example corn and tractor. Reis (1946, in Kimble, 1961) found that semantic generalization is also influenced by the age of the subjects. Generalizations for seven- to nine-year-olds were made upon the basis of homophones (right and write), but for 10- to 12-year-olds the generalization favored antonyms (right and wrong); for 14- to 24-year-olds it was synonyms (right and correct). So, not only does the capacity for generalization involve meanings, the type of meaning which serves as the basis for generalization involves growth and development in cognitive processes.

Koch (1964) considered demeaning, unfruitful, and just plain simplistic. To Hilgard (1987) it was stultifying and to Dunlap (1930/1961) it impeded development in psychology. The cost to Kimble (1985) was enormous—"Psychology lost its mind" (p. 295). Watson had created an un-psychological psychology.

11.2 THE COGNITIVE REVOLUTION

While North American psychology was suffering a loss of mind, in Europe work on cognitive functions continued. Gestalt psychologists were studying perception and phenomenology and problem solving. Vygotsky and colleagues were examining attention, memory, perception, conceptual thinking, thought and language, abstraction, generalization, and reasoning. Piaget was investigating children's thinking. Bartlett, in Britain, was conducting work into memory and schemas. In fact, an examination of the *British Journal of Psychology* (1930–1950) reveals a broad range of cognitive phenomena under consideration: language and generalization, conceptual thinking, children's thinking, visualization and visual memory, memory and repression, motivation and recall, attention, perception, insight, reading, proofreading, thinking and volition, music recall, hypnosis and suggestibility, and cognition and phantasy. Much of this would eventually find its way to North America.

World War II antecedents

Behaviorists, Skinner for instance, contributed to the war effort. Skinner (1960) discussed his 1940s 'Project Pigeon,' which was aimed at developing a homing device for guided missiles. Basically, it involved pigeons being trained to peck at controls to change the direction of a projectile they were enclosed within. Pecking at buttons for up, down, right, or left, they could alter the trajectory of the missile as it moved toward a target. Although pigeons were successfully trained for laboratory tests, in the end the project was terminated.

For the most part behaviorism offered no help in practical issues of training and human performance, especially in piloting aircraft (Medin et al., 2001). **Human factors engineering** was emerging as a concern. Donald Broadbent (1926–1993), in England, was called upon to improve piloting skills. He found that the organization of the instrument panel made it difficult for pilots to access the information they needed from the multitude of dials displayed. In fact, not all of the information available to them was being used by the pilots and they were limited in their ability to attend to it all (Best, 1999). Furthermore, some instruments were more closely monitored than others. It made sense to reorganize the instruments for ease of processing (placing frequently used dials within easy access for attention). This challenged the behavioristic assumption of humans as passively reacting to impinging stimuli since information was being sought by the pilots. It was becoming apparent that humans should be conceived of as information processors.

In the United States, issues arose with the landing of aircraft; specifically, space (distance) perception at extreme rates of locomotion was proving difficult for novice pilots. **James Gibson** (1904–1979) found that landing depended on the ability to perceive and process visual information regarding the relation between the ground and oneself during descent
Gibson
(Gibson, 1955; Gibson, Olum and Rosenblatt, 1955). For instance, as one proceeds to a landing point, if attention is fixated on that location as a center of the visual field, the ground expands outward from that center. The continuous rate of expansion corresponds with the speed of approach. The changes in these **optical flow** patterns must be read by the pilots in their successful approach and for correct 'judgements' to be made. The flow of information provides continuous feedback to which adjustments are made and, when the flow ceases, movement has stopped and the plane is at rest (see Figure 11.1). The regulation is voluntary and purposive, aiming the plane at an end while avoiding obstacles. Information is obtained and involves active attention rather than passive responding to imposed stimulation (Gibson, 1966). Thus the classical stimulus-response formula was deemed inadequate in the ongoing flow of activity which involves actions, feedback (input produced by action), and adjustments made towards an end.

Another problem was the computing machine (Gardner, 1985). The large-scale operations of the war effort meant that planners were dealing with large data sets that were unwieldy

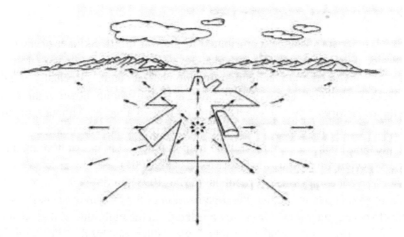

Figure 11.1   The outflow when landing a plane

when dealt with by hand. Calculating machines were needed. Alan Turing (1912–1954), in 1936, envisioned a machine that could engage in sophisticated data processing by using a simple binary code. By the 1950s computers were a reality and notions of thinking machines were abuzz. Norbert Wiener (1894–1964), as a result of his work with guided missiles, began to develop ideas about how machines could be self-regulating, self-correcting systems, ideas that amalgamated communication and control engineering. Something radically new and influential would be the progeny of this union: the proposition that machines could fairly be discussed as 'striving toward goals,' of monitoring ongoing progress towards a future end. Information processing within a machine and the importance of stored information would be a serious challenge to radical behaviorist proclamations regarding the lack of a need to investigate internal processes. If it was important to machines, why not humans?

Communications engineering

If cognitive psychology underwent a revolution it was in how cognitive functions were to be reconceived—as based upon communications engineering and, in particular, the adoption of **information theory**. Communications engineers developed information theory during the war due to the need to design systems for the transmission and reception of electronic signals such as radio transmissions (Gardner, 1985). Encryption and decoding of messages was paramount to the intelligence battle. Code-crackers were confronted with the need to decipher completely distorted enemy messages.

The solution to the problem lay in the realization that any language can produce many more potential messages than any actual message sent. By applying mathematical, probability theory to language production, distorted messages could be turned into probable communications. In any language, English for instance, some letters are more likely to be used than others. The letters A, E, N, O, and T are more common and only A and I can be single letter words. In actual production, words selected are a matter of personal choice but the structure of language constrains their use, and that can be subjected to statistical analysis (Weaver, 1949/1964). The letter J is never followed by a B, C, D, F, et cetera, so there is a zero probability of that occurring. Such probabilities, and your familiarity with English, makes it likely that you can read the following with ease:

> Aoccdrnig to a rscheearch at Cmabrigde, it deosn't mttaerin what order the ltteers in a word are in; the only iprmoetnt thing is that frist and lsat ltteer be at the rghit pclae. The rset can be a total mses and you can still raed it wouthit porbelm. (Kaufman and Klein, 2005, p. 1168)

When I make an error in typing this my computer gives me options when I go to spell-check that I presume is based on information theory. At the same time, I am not suggesting that my computer understands what I write; and that is a key aspect of information theory—it is not concerned with the meaning of a message, only the mathematical probability of letter combinations.

Information theory is a mathematical theory of communication and a branch of probability theory (Shannon and Weaver, 1949/1964). Information, in this context, is not about the conveyance of knowledge or meaning and it does not 'inform.' The term 'communication' is also not the ordinary usage; it is simply the proposition that one mechanism affects another (it is the same idea behind the notion that one neuron communicates with another). Rather than being concerned with the meaning of a communication, information theory is only concerned with the likelihood of what could have been transmitted (see Figure 11.2). In communications, a message is decided upon and sent through a transmitter (telephone, radio, voice) which changes the message into a signal (electrical, radio wave, sound wave). A receiver picks up the signal and converts it into its original form. In dealing with this, communications engineering is concerned with the success of the message transmission and receipt, not content or meaning.

Input → Transmitter → (Signal) → Receiver → Output
(Encoding)   (Decoding)

↑

Noise
(Distortions)

Figure 11.2   A communication system

Sometimes, during the war, some enemy equipment was captured that, it was feared, may include explosive devices rigged to activate if opened (Watzlawick, Beavin, and Jackson, 1967). The internal mechanisms came to be referred to as the **black box**. The idea was taken up by Wiener (1948/1961), who spoke of black boxes as apparatuses that had inputs, which it performed operations on, and outputs that were black because the operations and mechanisms were unknown. These inner mechanisms mattered and, applied to humans, would be of concern to cognitive psychologists. Skinner (1985) allowed for black box mental mechanisms but argued that science must deal with observables; and we do not observe these operations in ourselves or others. Despite cognitive psychologists inventing mental mechanisms, all we observe are inputs, outputs, and consequences. By that time (1985), Skinner had no impact. Also indicative of the influence of communications engineering on humans as information processors, Craik (1948) was suggesting an analogy to engineering by conceiving of humans as elements in control systems composed of sensory devices, computing systems, amplifying systems, and mechanical linkages.

The turning point

During the 1950s, converging forces were coming to oppose behaviorism for its insufficiencies. Previously suspect inner processes were emerging as indispensable. Turing (1936), as noted, anticipated a computing machine that would operate on a binary system of zeros and ones that might compare with humans doing the same thing. It would be 1949 before that became a reality. Turing early on had suggested the possibility that a machine might think and he (Turing, 1950) later suggested the **Turing test**, which involved a human and a computer answering questions and that, if observers could not identify which was which, the machine could be said to think. In line with the binary logic of computers, McCulloch and Pitts (1943) developed what they called a 'logical calculus' that would apply to neural functioning. The production of an 'action potential,' the generation of an electrical signal along the neuron's axon, operates according to the 'all-or-none' principle. If the 'graded potential' over the cell body reaches threshold a signal is generated, otherwise not. It could be conceived of as a binary operation comparable to on–off switches in electronics and true–false in logic. Two conferences were convened which incorporated issues of information theory, computer processing, and neuropsychology, and turned the tide against behaviorism.

The Hixon Symposium. In 1948 the California Institute of Technology held a conference on 'cerebral mechanisms in behavior' (Gardner, 1985). Karl Lashley (1890–1968), a former associate of Watson, argued that before the recent work on computers and the brain could be drawn upon, the time had come for behaviorism to be confronted regarding complex behavior (Lashley, 1951/1967). Any theory that purported to account for human activity would have to explain serially organized behavior, especially speech. The proposition that the elicitation of one word is a stimulus for the next, in simple associative chains, would not do; and the dismissal of intent and meaning was mistaken. Speech production is so rapid that the likelihood of one word eliciting the next was improbable. Even more compelling was the inference to be made from certain speech errors. Sometimes words whose place is later in a sequence intrude much earlier. For instance, a person may say "it was the longest year of the day" rather than "day of the year." Such a mistake suggested planning and intent, antecedent to vocalization, rather than reactivity to a stimulus-word. What the person intends to say guides the production of the subsequent word series.

At the conference McCulloch introduced the ideas he had worked on with Pitts on neurons as binary logic mechanisms. First, he submitted the brain could not be ignored and, second, it may be comparable to a computer in its operation. Von Neumann (1951/1967), a computer scientist, spoke of computing machines or automata and, like McCulloch, spoke of the comparison to the nervous system. He recognized that the computer was much less complicated than one of the brain's systems, but he also believed that there were some similarities between them in terms of their functions. As Gardner (1985) concluded, what made the conference significant was the relentless challenging of behaviorism and the linking of the brain and the computer. That linkage would stimulate a lot of the early research into cognition. Perhaps one reason for this was that if the mind could be conceived of in mechanical terms there would no longer be a troublesome mind–body problem (as discussed in Chapter 6).

Symposium on Information Theory. Although there were other conferences on cognition, the symposium on information theory at the Massachusetts Institute of Technology in 1956 was a watershed in the flourishing of cognitive psychology (Gardner, 1985). Miller introduced the famous 'Magic Number 7 +/– 2' regarding the limits in the 'span of immediate memory' (now 'short-term' or 'working' memory) and proposed humans be considered limited capacity processors of information. Newel and Simon spoke of their 'Logic Theory Machine' that could solve problems in logic. Chomsky, on the other hand, made the case that an information theory perspective on language could not account for natural language.

Miller (1956) reported that human cognitive processing is limited in the amount of information that could be retained (5–9 items). While the limit to capacity was stable, how much each single item contained could be increased by organizing ('chunking') each piece. The magic number remained constant but the magnitude of content that each item could hold increased. The numbers 195619001984 are twelve pieces of information (more than the 5–9 pieces ceiling), but organized into years—1956, 1900, 1984—they become three items, the pieces become chunks. Miller made it clear that his work was based on information theory—the human observer is a sort of communication system with a limited channel capacity. Capacity limits, he suggested, may be due to nervous system design or learning. Miller connected this to memory span and it remains a basic premise regarding the limits of short-term or working memory.

Chomsky (1956) discussed the question of 'linguistic structure' and whether there are grammars (rules for speaking and writing) in English usage. While decryption was based on statistical probabilities (information theory), Chomsky found no statistical procedure that modeled the output of English grammar. Language use and understanding may be based on 'phrase structures' that involve breaking sentences down to syntax—the relations between words, clauses, and phrases. Skinner (1957) would offer an account of language (verbal behavior) acquisition based on the 'three-term contingency' (stimulus-response-consequence) and 'shaping' by reinforcing closer approximations to the desired utterance. Verbal responses are just more conditioned responses. The claim was based on an extension of his work with animals. Chomsky (1959) leveled a devastating critique of Skinner's theory and was a key contributor to the downfall of behaviorism. Skinner, he charged, was just playing at science since he conducted no actual research into language. He just generalized from his work with rat's bar-pressing for food, an astonishingly unwarranted assumption. Not only that, Chomsky went on to point out that evidence from children learning a language suggested the involvement of innate capacities for processing linguistic materials. Of course, staunch behaviorists rejected internal mechanisms.

Newell and Simon (1956) described their 'logic theory machine,' which was a 'complex information processing system' for discovering proofs in simple elementary logic. This system mimicked human problem solving by using heuristic procedures (strategies or shortcuts). The specification of the method was then coded into machine language for use in digital computers. In a couple of years, Newell, Shaw, and Simon (1958) were reporting that Turing's anticipated thinking machines had become a reality since they now had problem-solving machines. Such mechanisms involved a control system, designed to follow rules (programs), which held symbolized information (coded memory) that directed operations in solving problems from symbolic logic. In this they were not suggesting that brain and machine had similar processes but they might have similar functions or **functional equivalence**. That function, as Newell, Shaw, and Simon conceived of it, would involve a system having considerable storage capacity for holding information processing programs. It would also have strategies that could be brought into action by stimuli that determine which program will become active. The behaviorist idea of stimulus control has not been abandoned; digital computers respond to stimuli too (input), but, more than that, they required a memory and inner processing.

11.3 INFORMATION PROCESSING

Miller clearly saw in communications theory a means whereby human cognitive processes could be susceptible to experimental treatment and explanation. Newel, Shaw, and Simon saw in the computer a means of unraveling human problem solving. Neither of the presentations at the Symposium on Information Theory went unnoticed. Research into attention and memory processes would quickly reveal their influence.

Cherry (1953) was concerned with the transmission of acoustic information. In this he was under the influence of communications engineering and looked upon humans as message transmission channels or transducers. Separate messages (recordings from the same voice) were fed into each ear and participants were to attend to and repeat aloud one of the channeled messages. This is now known as 'dichotic listening' and the selective attention with repetition is termed 'shadowing.' The results suggested near perfect shadowing and exclusion of the unwanted message. Cherry likened the results to the 'cocktail party problem' of attending to one speaker in a room of people speaking. That suggested to him that a machine might be constructed with a 'filter' for blocking channels that could do something similar—an idea that would influence Broadbent (mentioned earlier regarding training pilots).

Drawing on Cherry, Broadbent (1957) developed a mechanical model of information processing for attention and immediate memory, assuming that information concepts could be applied to any system—physical or physiological. Just like communications devices, the attentional system of humans is subject to capacity limitations and, of necessity, must select from the broad array of concurrent input from different channels (ears, eyes, et cetera). What got selected for subsequent processing would depend on the nature of the input characteristics and information contained in a permanent store (memory).

In what became 'filter theory' Broadbent (1958) argued that the nervous system can be considered a limited capacity communication channel that requires a mechanism—a filter—to perform a selective operation on the vast array of what could be attended to and further processed. Selection for subsequent processing and access to consciousness is based on physical properties like pitch, spatial location, or intensity. What is not selected would

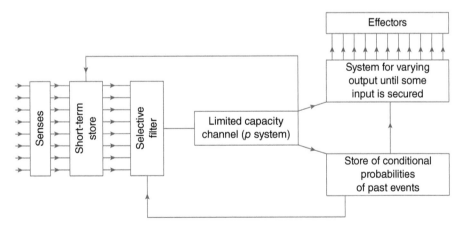

Figure 11.3 A tentative information-flow diagram for the organism

With permission from D. Broadbent (1958, p. 299).

be lost. In order for selection to occur Broadbent hypothesized a temporary information store (now called sensory memory) where information briefly awaits selection. These cognitive processes were depicted, for the first time, diagrammatically as communications engineers did for information flow in communications systems (Gardner, 1985)—with input, encoding, transmission, decoding, and output sequences (see Figure 11.3). Since the selection processing occurred outside of consciousness, selection based on meaning was not involved (others like Treisman, 1964, would assume selection based on meaning would occur at a later stage but only if input could not first be differentiated on base characteristics like voice quality, intensity, or input channel). If it could be done earlier, meaning was unnecessary for selection to occur. This dismissal of input meaning, of course, is consistent with the basic principles of information theory discussed previously. It was the processing mechanisms that were of interest.

The work of Broadbent, and of Miller, convinced some psychologists that 'primary memory' (a concept used by William James, 1890/1959, along with longer-term, 'secondary memory'), renamed 'short-term' and later 'working memory,' was a phenomenon worth studying (Willingham, 2001). A rash of memory research was performed and a larger theory of human memory, drawing from information theory and computers, would emerge. Shiffrin and Atkinson (1969) examined the studies and developed the 'modal model of memory' (based on the statistical 'mode' or most frequently obtained result). This was an information processing system that included stimulus input, memory stores (sensory, short- and long-term), control processes (encoding, transfer, storage, retrieval), and output represented in a flow diagram (see Figure 11.4).

There is a great deal more to cognition than this but space does permit any further discussion. The main purpose of this presentation was to show the impact of information theory and computer technology on the cognitive revolution. There is one point that I have neglected, that I should like to make now, which is that, although behaviorism was being surpassed, there is a certain allegiance to it nonetheless. There remains an assumption of determinism reflected in the terms stimulus and response being replaced by input and output.

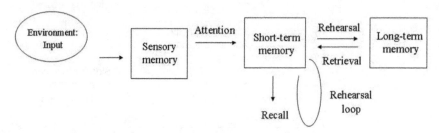

Figure 11.4 The modal model of memory

With permission from http://www.simplypsychology.org/

These early models also reflect the notion of human passivity and reactivity. This would be addressed in time by people like Baddeley and Hitch (1974), who reconceived of 'short-term memory' as 'working memory'—a limited capacity 'work space' with control processes that were more active than reactive.

11.4 ARTIFICIAL INTELLIGENCE

Mechanical functionalism. In their treatment of so-called cognitive processes, the theories of Cherry, Broadbent, Miller, and other early cognitive psychologists came to be known as 'Information Processing Theory' which, given the allegiance to communications engineering, is a version of 'mechanistic materialism.' In this, they clearly intended to preserve mental functions but were not the least concerned with the mind–body problem. Rather than dealing with mind, their concern was with functions like attention and memory. The idea of mental functions would result in a new approach to the mind–body problem called by its proponents 'functionalism.' I will refer to it, however, as '**mechanical functionalism**' since William James and John Dewey, at the end of the 19th century, had developed an approach to psychology they called **functionalism** which proposed conceiving of mind and mental processes as having evolved by natural selection due to their serving adaptive purposes. They functioned to adapt the organism to changing circumstances and deal with problems. Recall here that James (Chapter 6) argued against epiphenomenalism because it made no sense for consciousness to have evolved but to serve no function.

During the resurgence of cognitive psychology, neurophysiological reductionists had been inclined toward an **identity theory** of mind which proposed that mental states were brain states. It soon became apparent that there was no reason for concluding that a mental condition like a pain or a belief would always be realized by, or identical with, a specific neurophysiological process. It was altogether possible that the same mental phenomenon could be realized in different brain areas by different people. This was bolstered by the discovery that people who suffered brain damage and lost a specific mental function may recover the absent function by alternative neural structures performing it—the phenomenon of **brain plasticity** (see Kolb and Whishaw, 1998).

Given the problems that identity theory was running into, suggestions were being made that instead of identifying mental states with brain states they should be identified with functional states. This was the idea behind 'mechanical functionalism.' Mental states, as functional states, could then be realized independent of the physical condition that supported them. That allowed the possibility that animals with differently structured brains may yet possess certain mental functions. More significantly, in our current context, machines may also possess psychological states on that basis. Mental phenomena, then, should be reconceived as functional phenomena and one should be concerned with what service they perform (Moravia, 1995).

Hilary Putnam (1926–2016) drew inspiration from the Turing test, and the notion that non-human, Turing machines may be said to think, in developing the philosophical ground for the new approach (Putnam, 1967, 1967/1975). People may be like computers whose functional states are programs for performing operations. A Turing machine could be realized in any number of ways physically; they were **multiply realizable**. Mental functions, in this conceptualization, are no longer confined to mind or brain. They extend to any functional organization. The initial formulations of Putnam were developed by Jerry Fodor (1935–), who intended to establish the importance of 'functional equivalence' (discussed earlier by the computer scientists Newell et al., 1958) and extend the proposition to psychology (Fodor, 1968). The aim of psychological explanation, he proposed, is to demonstrate how behavior is a function of the environment and mental processes. Suppose, he asked, that an organism's behavior is explicable by reference to a machine that simulates that behavior, organized internally as relays (electrically operated switches) rather than neurons, but that are functionally equivalent to neurons in their operation. In their effects they would be indistinguishable. Further, if human cognition involved mediating between input and output, why not the machine? Machines may have 'psychological mechanisms' (a set of directions) that are functionally equivalent regardless of their constituent makeup. In the language of computer science, they may differ in their 'hardware' (physical constitution) but be equivalent in their 'software' (the program). Thus, he claimed, "it may be argued that understanding the operations of a computer capable of simulating a given form of behavior is tantamount to understanding the behavior itself" (Fodor, 1968, p. 121).

In the foregoing you can see that Fodor has offered a rationale for studying human cognition by studying computer processing models. He (Fodor, 1980) introduced a 'computational theory of mind' which, you might have guessed, proposed that mental processes and states are computational or symbolic and formal. They are symbolic in that they operate with symbols like those used in symbolic logic (such as ⊃ which symbolizes the proposition "if, then"; or ≡ which represents "if and only if") or in calculus (such as the symbol for equality: =). They are formal in the sense that they deal with issues of syntax (the rules by which symbols may be arranged). Now at this point, I should remind you that in information theory (as per communication engineering) meaning was not an issue and it is not here. Mental processes only have access to formal or non-semantic (unconcerned with meaning, truth, or reference to something) properties of mental representations. They are simply rules of thought—a 'language of thought'—that are independent of content. The language of thought is a language of computation, and mental processes compute (remember Fodor wants to establish functional equivalence with computers: 'compute'-ers) or process input according to formal, syntactic rules or programs.

You may be wondering about the non-semantic nature of mental processes and the lack of meaning or reference. Fodor, in establishing the mental as computational, has pushed himself into what he referred to as 'methodological solipsism' and, like any solipsism, makes no reference to external reality. Actually, Fodor is more of an indirect realist in that he does believe there is an inaccessible something beyond. What we have access to are the mental representations (representationalism) provided by the senses. In this, one is blocked from considering the semantic properties of such representations. The computer, in its inner processing, meets the formality condition in that it enacts formal operations (computations based on syntax) and only has access to non-semantic, formal properties. If mental properties are formal too, they apply to the representations provided by the senses, not the things producing those sensations. Neither computers nor humans have access to the representation's semantic properties such as truth or reality, to their having referents, or to the possibility that they may be representations of something environmental. Whatever truth claims, beliefs, or intentions may be held, they apply to an inner realm only.

Artificial intelligence

Artificial intelligence, as it influences psychology, involves the employment of computer programs to serve as theories about thought processes in humans, and tests them by comparing human behavior with the performance of a computer program (Simon, 2000). For the theories to be tested it was necessary to identify the step-by-step procedures that actual humans use. This was done by utilizing 'thinking out loud protocols' or having problem-solvers verbalize their thought activities during on-going problem solving (Simon, 1996). The general hypothesis behind the simulation of cognition by a computer is that the simulated processes are the same as those operations used by a human in learning and thinking. In other words, computers, that are appropriately programmed, can perform as human-like entities.

Examining actual computers, most of the specific artificial intelligence systems demonstrate intelligence for specific tasks. Any one, in that sense, may seem rather limited but collectively they have covered a broad array of tasks. The computers used in these tasks are not human in the sense that they do not pick up information from outside or decide what area of expertise to develop—human programmers do that (Sobel, 2001). Systems have been designed to suggest what the chemical structure of unfamiliar compounds may be. Another was designed to aid physicians to select the best antibiotic for bacterial infections. Computers playing chess were programmed to evaluate every possible move (175,000/sec.), and every ramification, but experts could beat them. The famous Deep Blue, which beat chess master Gary Kasparov, improved on chess-playing by being programmed to not just run through all possible moves (one billion/sec.) before each selection. It had evaluation features built in. Some computers were programmed to do language translations but, because they did not consider context or understand metaphors, translations were not based on understanding and may not capture the essence of the original.

BOX 11.2
THE CHINESE ROOM

The philosopher John Searle (1932–) offered a famous argument against artificial intelligence and functionalism (Searle, 1980, 1990). Computers, he contended, do not have mental states. They mimic them, and are without understanding. To make his case he suggested a thought experiment in which a computer translated text from one language into another. According to artificial intelligence the translating computer would 'understand' what was being translated from and to. Does it?

Figure 11.5   The Chinese room

- Imagine, he asked, that you are locked in a room and provided writings in Chinese, an unfamiliar language, written in a script you cannot differentiate from Japanese.

- After time, a second collection of Chinese writings enters the room along with a set of English instructions which you do understand. The instructions explain how the first and second Chinese texts can be correlated with each other.

- A third set of Chinese writings arrives with another set of instructions (rules) for correlating all three sets. The last set of rules provides instructions for returning Chinese symbols in response to the symbols gathered in the third set.

Unknown to you, people outside your enclosing room are sending the writings in. The first set they refer to as 'script—Chinese symbols,' the second as a 'story,' and the third as 'questions.' The symbols that you return in response are 'answers.' Further, the set of rules for correlating the sets of Chinese writing with each other are referred to as the 'program.' Analogous to a computer, we have a programmer, input, central processing, memory, data, programs, and output to the operator of the computer.

Now, suppose that the people outside send in another story set written in English—your language. This material you understand. Also you are given questions in English that you can answer in English. Imagine further that you, due to continuing practice at matching undecipherable Chinese symbol with Chinese symbol, have become quite proficient at that. A point is arrived at when the people outside cannot distinguish them from a Chinese person doing the same task (think Turing test). The readers outside the room would have no sense that the English-speaking person understood nothing of any of the text, despite answering correctly. While the answers to English questions did involve understanding, the Chinese task was performed mechanically and without understanding.

Based on that, Searle concluded that the processing of the Chinese symbols was analogous to the processing that goes on inside a computer. Searle contested the claims of supporters of artificial intelligence that it was done with understanding and that the processing mechanisms could serve as a model of human comprehension. Just as the English person processing Chinese symbols did not know what those symbols meant, neither did a computer grasp the meaning of what it was processing. A programmed computer has as much understanding of what it is doing as does a toaster, as far as Searle was concerned. While a human and a computer may both pass a Turing test, only the human would possess actual understanding.

The previous systems did what they were programmed to do. **Connectionism**, however, is a computer model that is intended to reflect how neural processing may be taking place in the brain. They have units (called nodes) that are intended to possess neuron-like properties but were not meant to represent actual neurons (Crick and Asanuma, 1986). Nonetheless, Rumelhart and colleagues (1986) were 'neurally inspired' and intended to replace the 'computer metaphor' for mind with a brain metaphor which, it should be noted, remained a computer simulation. Resembling brain physiology, the units receive input and transmit it for further processing. Units interact with neighbors by transmitting signals and the degree of unit activation determines signal strength. The connectivity patterns that exist between units constitute the basis for knowledge and involve different connective weights or degree of influence (inhibitory

WHAT DO YOU THINK?

Will knowledge of the structures involved in general cognitive functions inform us of the cognitive functions of the individual—you for instance?

or excitatory). With subsequent input, activation weights may be altered, and that constitutes learning. While machine memory appears to be involved here, some have doubted whether such connection-making processes actually apply to cognition. As Green (2001) argued, connectionist models do not model cognition, they model brain activity. That brings us back to whether brain activity alone can account for cognition.

11.5 THE INDIVIDUALISTIC FALLACY

Much of the early work in cognitive psychology was based on an assumption of **individualism** and, in an effort to be scientific, adopted **nomothetic** procedures. The aim was to identify the mechanisms and neural structures that were the basis of human cognition. Randomly sampled persons were subjected to experimental designs intended to tease out the nature of the different functions and results were generalized to all humans. Such procedures, based on an assumption of universality, naturally loan themselves to explanation by biological determination and ignore the impact of history, culture, and individual experience which may contribute to idiosyncratic processing. Recall that Charcot and Binet studied mental calculators who were considered arithmetical prodigies and, as the term prodigy indicates, were unusual. Taking social context into consideration, Rogoff (1984) found that cognitive skills are variable and fluctuate depending on the situation and that such skills are limited in their generalizability.

Where individuality enters it tends to be within the context of individual differences, introduced by Galton, which treats individuality as a deviation from the average in a normal distribution—whether the person is below, at, or above average performance levels (Galotti, 2014). There is, in this, an assumption that if a capacity exists it exists in all people to some degree. Such universal assumptions tend to be ahistorical and asocial and lead to presumptions of a biological basis for the structures of cognitive processing. In challenging this, it should not be taken to imply that the brain is uninvolved, but it does imply that the brain is plastic and subject to cultural influences that shape individual performance. We are not born speaking, reading, calculating arithmetically, and so on. Why else would we be subjected to so many years of education in order to function in modern society? Those skills are not inborn. Even something as basic as perception may be influenced culturally.

According to Luria (1976), the **classical view of perception**, in dealing with the apparent universality of perceptual illusions, appealed to innate physiological mechanisms to explain such phenomena. Very few considered the possibility that the illusions may have a cultural basis or that people may differ in the degree of susceptibility depending on their culture's historical development. Rivers, according to Luria, was the first to suggest that optical illusions have cultural origins. In his investigations of the Toda in India, Rivers (1905) found they were not as susceptible as Europeans to geometrical visual illusions like the 'Müller-Lyer' and the 'horizontal-vertical.' According to Rivers, such differences reflected not just physiological processes but the addition to these of experiences derived from 'civilized life' (such as training in geometry); what we would today refer to as differing cultural conditions.

Traditional psychology treated visual perception as a natural process which could be studied by physiological methods (Luria, 1976). It was assumed that the laws underlying such processes were independent of social practice and universal. This was true of the Gestalt psychologists. They failed to consider the importance of sociohistorical forces in developing even basic psychological processes like their '**Gestalt laws of grouping**'. According to Luria, they had what we would call a 'biased sample' since their selection of experimental subjects was restricted to well-educated people, usually with a university background, who had undergone specialized training including knowledge of geometry. Luria tested this in 1932, along with Gestalt psychologist Koffka, with illiterate peasants in Uzbekistan and found they were not as susceptible to illusory perceptions or the Gestalt laws of perceptual organization. Education and experience mattered. Based on subsequent studies of people from different cultural backgrounds and experiences. Segall, Campbell, and Herskovits (1966) put forward the **carpentered world theory**. The general proposition is that people who live in highly carpentered environments (composed of rectangular structures) are rendered more susceptible to linear illusions like the 'Müller-Lyer' due to their experiences in carpentered environments.

I should caution you not to take this point too generally since there have been those who recognize the importance of experience in developing cognitive competencies that allow for greater individuality and specificity of skill. Consider the recognition of expertise. Miller (1956), introducing his 'magic number,' considered possible cognitive differences in processing and chunking of Morse code depending on level of familiarity. Experts were more likely to organize material into patterns instead of single dots and dashes. Simon and Simon (1978) reported differences in solving physics problems between novices and experts. Chi, Feltovich, and Glaser (1981) suggested that such processing differences reflected the use of abstract principles by experts and by novices focusing on surface features. Similar findings of differences between experts and novices have been found for the board game 'Go' (Reitman, 1976), the card game bridge (Charness, 1983) and reading and recall of electrical circuit diagrams (Egan and Schwartz, 1979). I could go on. Nonetheless, the desire to be scientific does push researchers into the nomothetic model, which leads to universalistic assumptions that are asocial and ahistorical, and lead to individualism.

A further issue related to the asocial approach to psychology is the effort by some to remove personal experience from consideration. In an effort to remove the 'confounding' influence of stimulus meaningfulness Ebbinghaus (1885/1964) created 'nonsense syllables' (consonant-vowel-consonant combinations that were not words). The idea was that the

Gestalt laws of grouping

materials would be equally meaningful (meaningless). Bartlett (1932) countered that such materials were irrelevant to everyday memory functions and that even where meaning does not exist there will be 'effort after meaning.' Humans search for meaning. Consider the nonsense syllable CYD. By itself it means nothing, but one might impose meaning by treating it like the name Sid or an acronym for Child and Youth Development. Neisser (1978/2000), echoing Bartlett, believed that laboratory experimentation and the search for a general theory of memory failed to address ordinary, everyday memory. Artificial tasks, like learning lists of words or numbers, do not address how memory is actually used in the context of people's lives, under natural conditions. Rather than recalling exact details required in experiments, we remember, as Bartlett pointed out, the gist, the significance or meaning of circumstances. Such studies lack **ecological validity**.

We are societal beings and our cognitive functions develop socially. They are functional for our life context and what is common among us all, whether in thinking, perceiving, or whatever, is too general and abstract to capture how any particular individual confronts their world cognitively. As Rogoff (1984) put it, learning and thinking occurs in social contexts. Interaction with others, and the appropriation of psychological tools, conditions cognitive potential. Cognitive development is channeled by the social system the child is embedded within. Rather than being broadly general, cognitive skills are highly variable and fluctuate as situations change. That means that studying cognitive functions as pure processes misses the integral nature of context to functioning. Context is not a nuisance variable to be eliminated. Cognitive skills may be both general and situationally specific. Cognition is a practical activity that should be addressed in those terms. It may be useful to study the universal aspects of cognitive functions, but one must bear in mind that these are fitted to the individual situation, and the context of everyday life of the individual, and that demands consideration too.

SUMMARY

In this chapter we have examined the cognitive revolution in psychology.

- Despite the behaviorist hegemony in North America, cognitive processes had never gone out of fashion in Europe and even among some psychologists in North America.
- What led to the increased interest in cognitive processes began with the apparent inadequacies of behaviorism in the war effort and the need to consider perceptual and attentional factors in adjusting airmen to the demands of their tasks.
- The need to decipher encrypted information led to the development of computing machines to process large amounts of data and notions of thinking machines.

- The development of guidance systems introduced the idea of machines operating in terms of goals, which challenged the behaviorist rejection of actions directed at future ends rather than immediate stimulus conditions.
- Communications engineering and information theory added to an increasing interest in internal processing, suggesting material cognitive processes without invoking dualism.
- Ultimately, cognitive psychology emerged under the banner of information processing in humans and drew heavily from communication theory and computer processing mechanisms.
- The assumption of individualism leads to ahistorical, asocial approaches to cognition.

SUGGESTED READINGS

Eysenck, M. W. (1990). *The Blackwell dictionary of cognitive psychology*. Oxford: Blackwell Reference.

Galotti, K. M. (2014). *Cognitive psychology: In and out of the laboratory* (5th ed.). Los Angeles, CA: SAGE Publications.

Gardner, H. (1985). *The mind's new science: A history of the cognitive revolution*. New York: Basic Books.

Rychlak, J. F. (1991). *Artificial intelligence and human reason: A teleological critique*. New York: Columbia University Press.

Want to learn more? For links to online resources, examples of multiple choice questions, conceptual exercises and much more, visit the companion website at **https://study.sagepub.com/piekkola**

12
FREE WILL VERSUS DETERMINISM

LEARNING OBJECTIVE

Since determinism is a basic assumption in science, and psychology aspires to scientific status, mainstream psychology has tended to support the dismissal of free will, or **agency**.

- Quite possibly you have struggled with this, as William James (1842–1910) did. If science was right, he was deluded for believing in his ability to act as he saw fit and was less of a being, a human being, than his life experience suggested to him. In what follows you should come to appreciate his dilemma.
- In understanding the issues involved, and the arguments that have been put forward, you will be armed intellectually to meet this dilemma. It is expected that you will be equipped to establish for yourself how best to deal with this challenge. You should also be able to recognize when one or the other stance is being affirmed. For instance, you may have passed over my belief in free will in suggesting that you decide for yourself, but will be more sensitized in the future.

FRAMING QUESTIONS

- Do you make choices and act on them?
- When people commit crimes like rape and murder should they be held to account?
- Just because physical science has relied on determinism does that mean that all science should be based on determinism?

INTRODUCTION

In this final chapter we will be considering the issue of 'free will' versus 'determinism.' It is the question of whether we are agents in directing and controlling our own action in the world or whether we are merely mechanical automatons driven hither and yon by causal forces that regulate all that we do. In Chapter 2 we briefly considered the notion of determinism as it was first proposed by Leucippus and Democritus. We also noted that Aristotle had made a distinction between voluntary and involuntary action and how people could only be held responsible for those actions within their control. Free will seemed given or obvious to him, but it was Epicurus who recognized the implications of determinism and how it led to 'fatalism' and a rejection of free will. The issue as it concerns us here is with the arguments that stem from natural science and the deterministic assumptions that are associated with it.

Before considering this, it should be mentioned that, as Western society developed, it came more and more under the influence of the Christian religion and the tenet of free will that was espoused therein. It was an issue debated within the church since there appeared to be a paradox. The matter was rooted in the problem of human suffering in life (Barnes, 1984). Tradition claimed that God was omnipotent, omniscient, and infinitely good. How could God then, given His goodness, allow suffering in His creation? Why does God not eliminate it? There must be a reason. For some, that reason would be found in the further belief in human freedom. It is from the human capacity for free choice that human suffering stems. To this was added the concept of original sin and the inherited sinfulness of humans for which they suffer, and from which they must seek redemption.

Teachings of the medieval period (5th–15th century) regarding free choice advised that God had given humans the capacity to choose between good and evil, or what we refer to as free will (Dilman, 1999). An individual's destiny or fate depended upon the decisions that s/he made and, with God's grace, one may obtain salvation. One needed to have faith. Thomas Aquinas (1225–1274) would add to faith the human capacity to reason. Bodies, especially animal bodies, are enslaved by natural necessity and possess little in the way of freedom. If humans were bodily beings only, they would be slaves to natural necessity. Humans, however, are unlike animals and have the capacity to reason which gives us the ability to make choices. Our spiritual side is the source of human freedom. The human person is self-moving—a causal agent having the power to act of one's own accord—and can be held to account for their choices.

As the debate confronts us in the modern era it is framed around the themes of **compatibilism** and **incompatibilism**. For some, the issue of freedom versus necessity (determinism) holds that the two positions are diametrically opposed, an either/or situation (incompatibilism). This would reflect something of the laws of logical thinking (laws of identity, contradiction, and excluded middle). The thinking is that, if determinism is true, every occurrence, every event, is due to antecedent causal conditions, and that precludes free will. Alternatively, one may opt for the stance of the libertarian (see **libertarianism**) and contend that free will is in fact true. Or one may hold that both are true and not logically exclusive but compatible—thus compatibilism. I will leave it to you to decide which best agrees with your understanding and personal experience (bearing in mind the epiphenomenalist challenge that personal experiences of agency are illusory).

12.1 ANTECEDENTS TO DETERMINISM IN PSYCHOLOGY

Descartes and Hobbes

As was previously noted, Descartes was a dualist and on the mental side he allowed for free will and voluntary action. How that was translated into bodily action was supposedly explained by 'interactionism,' but in the end that proved unsatisfactory. On the material side Descartes was a mechanist, and 'mechanism' carries an assumption of determinism. The rules of nature, including the operation of bodies, were mechanical (Grossmann, 2009). Bodily movements, from the musculature to nerves and sensory processes, were all mechanical in nature. A completely mechanistic account of humans was developed by Hobbes, Descartes' contemporary.

Hobbes, in taking up the issue of voluntary human action, was attempting to align human existence with, and interpret in terms of, the 'science of bodies' or physics (Taylor, 1967). Hobbes was influenced in this by Galileo's laws of motion. The principles of matter in motion and of force would be used to explain human conduct and the idea of immaterial entities was rejected. All psychological processes and behavior were just another type of matter in motion. Matter in motion is moved by necessity, and what are referred to as voluntary acts are just movements caused by mechanical necessity. Humans are fully passive and any movements they produce are determined physically. An act of choice may seem to be an immediate cause but it is neither free nor uncaused. The voluntary actions of humans are under the causal influence of alternating desires and aversions that act like physical force. So-called deliberation is just the competition between various appetites (physical needs) and one prevailing as the strongest.

People had long been held responsible for actions that were considered voluntary and Hobbes believed that they should too, even though he considered all human behavior to be determined physically. In what seems like a contradiction he proposed that voluntary acts are caused by acts of will but that the acts of will themselves are caused. The will is itself an effect and like any motion is the result of what preceded it and which was the cause of what followed (Damrosch, 1979). So-called deliberation is merely a succession of opposing appetites of which one is the last and the last is the effective power that moves to action. This last is what is then referred to as will. A free agent is one that does as it wills but what it wills is determined and thus not truly free. So, by Hobbes' account, we have free will but are not free in having it. Determined will is not free will.

Newton's enduring influence

Newton developed the mechanical explanations of Hobbes and Descartes. The whole universe was conceptualized by him as mechanical in nature and subject to complete determinism. Every event was therefore completely explicable in terms of its antecedents. Given that, with complete knowledge of all of the prevailing conditions one could even predict the behavior of individual persons. (There is in that an anticipation of the behaviorist goal of Watson, 1913a, as "the prediction and control of behavior"; p. 158). Besides prediction, and going in the other direction, Newton expected that with future expansions in knowledge, the antecedent links would be revealed to the ultimate mystery which was God, the author of the material world (Hall, 1992).

The job of natural philosophy (science) was to deduce causes from their effects until one arrived at the first cause. It was this first cause (divine design) that set the universe in motion. Once initiated, Newton expected the remainder of the universe, or system of the world, to operate in accordance with the general principles of mechanical motion. Beyond the intentions of God there was nothing other than complete determinism. That was the legacy of Newton to subsequent science, including psychology. In an influential treatise on science and the scientific method, Jevons (1874) proposed that "In nature the happening of an event has been pre-determined from the first fashioning of the universe" (p. 198). Chance for Jevons was merely an indication of the lack of sufficient knowledge and ignorance of the underlying causes. The same sentiment was expressed in psychology. Knight (1946) proposed that "Determinism is a fundamental tenet of all science" (p. 251) and behavioral science has "no place for the fortuitous or 'free will'" (p. 251). Echoing that, Kimble and Perlmuter (1970) contended that "the concept of volition will lose its usefulness and will be replaced by more scientific concepts" (p. 362). To Immergluck (1964) "The notion that *behavior* ... is lawfully related to antecedent and attendant events ... has been indispensable in at once liberating psychology from its metaphysical ancestry and bringing it into the fold of natural science" (p. 270, emphasis in original). The experimental method itself, I should point out, incorporates an implicit determinism since the manipulated, independent variable was interpreted as the cause (determining) of the changes effected in the dependent variable.

WHAT DO YOU THINK?

If natural science is correct in its assumption of complete determinism, do you believe human science has to succumb to its premises as foundational and determining?

Thomas Reid's common sense

In his common-sense philosophy, or what would be now termed **folk psychology**, Thomas Reid (1710–1796) took exception to determinism and the dismissal of human agency. Determinism was simply inconsistent with many of the beliefs of humans and that justified continuing to believe in voluntary behavior, despite philosophies to the contrary (Taylor, 1967). Examined in the light of human experience and conduct, determinism was inconsistent. More weight should be given to experiences of deliberation on possible courses of action and the choices made in the pursuit of ends or purposes. There were also questions of morality and social judgment. If determinism were true, it would bear on issues of personal responsibility and morality and would negate holding people responsible for their actions. As a religious man, Reid (1788) contended that God had endowed humans with the power to be active in the world and had given them the responsibility to manage those powers in securing the best ends. It was that power that was the basis of praise and blame since people could not be held to account for what they had no control over.

Leaving behind the religious and turning to common sense, Reid drew upon human language and the use of words in common language, both vulgar and learned, that refer to 'active powers' in humans. There was in that something more than the trifling of philosophers. Such terms are found in every language and reflect common human experience, and they convey a common meaning and reference. Even children, in the early development of their linguistic capacities, distinguish between acting in the world (agency) and being acted upon (determined). There was no question that external causes affect reactions but that did not negate, nor justify dismissal of, self-causation and self-determination.

Humans are more than individuals; they are social beings. On the social side, how people choose to act is the basis of social indifference, praise, or condemnation. Individual choice is a matter of morality and judgment and that involves a consideration of motivation. The words 'ought' and 'ought not' indicate that certain acts are within the power of the individual and that is why 'responsibility' is assessed. Words like 'decision,' 'responsibility,' 'approval,' disapproval,' 'judgment,' 'guilt,' 'condemnation,' and 'punishment' imply the freedom to act in socially approved or disapproved ways. People are agents of their actions and responsible for them.

The idea of social judgment would recur in subsequent arguments against determinism, especially upon the basis of the existence of the legal system (Popkin and Stroll, 1993). The argument was that if all acts were determined by forces outside of personal control there would be no basis for judgment of guilt or innocence. People are prepared to hold others responsible because of their awareness of their own choices and decisions. No deterministic argument has succeeded in defeating the personal experience of free will, of acting upon the basis of personal intent and the power to exercise control over oneself.

According to Morse (2008), a professor of law, psychology, and psychiatry, the idea of human agency remains foundational in American jurisprudence when ascribing criminal responsibility. Despite the efforts of eliminative materialists and some neuroscientists to get rid of folk psychological concepts in favor of complete determinism, they have not impacted the legal system. Law continues to address questions of personal responsibility, consciousness, knowledge, and intention, and treats people as rational, purposive creatures rather than mechanical automatons. Echoing Reid's distant voice, Morse wrote "Machines do not deserve praise, blame, reward, punishment, concern, or respect because they exist or because of the results they cause" (p. 6). Humans do.

Automaton theory

'Automaton theory' is the theory put forward by Thomas Huxley (1825–1895) in his dismissal of mind as a mere epiphenomenon (see Chapter 6 on epiphenomenalism). Much of Huxley's (1874) argument was based on the work of Göltz on dismembered frogs, decerebration, and reflexivity, and his own replications of those findings. Huxley contended that such findings supported the conclusion that animals and humans were automatons. To extend the conclusion to humans, Huxley drew heavily on a case study of an ill-fated French sergeant who had suffered a debilitating head injury. This man displayed actions that appeared to involve no consciousness and justified the conclusion that "the man is a mere machine" (p. 573).

In many ways the poor sergeant appeared normal—he ate, drank, smoked, dressed himself, and walked about. When in unfamiliar surroundings, in contrast, he would stumble into objects and feel his way around them with his hands. Anyone could alter his course of movement without resistance. He gave no evidence of pain to electric shocks or pins thrust into his body. He appeared to not respond to sight or hearing but did to tactile stimulation. He ate or drank whatever was offered including quinine and vinegar. Having been a café singer, sunlight streaming through a window like a spotlight caused him to break into song. If engaged in writing, the ink could be replaced with water, and no notice was made. Having rolled, lit, and smoked a cigarette he prepared to fashion another, but his tobacco had been absconded. He sought for it in vain. Subsequently, his tobacco pouch was placed before his eyes, and then beneath his nose, but the image and the aroma evoked nothing. Placement in the hand set the act in motion. As he began to light the cigarette the match was blown out. A lit match was placed before his eyes but ignored, as was a lit cigarette. In this abnormal state he certainly appeared bereft of awareness and mechanical.

By 1874, determinism had become axiomatic in science and was at the root of Huxley's automaton theory. Huxley, while accepting Descartes' dualism, chose to ignore the facts of consciousness and treated physical activity as the only phenomena that science should deal with. In this he rejected mental states of volition as causal influences on the body. Not all were convinced. A contemporary of his, the physician/physiologist William Carpenter

(1874/1896) could not accept that consciousness was uninvolved in conduct and ineffective. The performance of frogs that Huxley relied on did not invalidate the human subjective experience of the need to attend to performance in unusual situations. A collapsed bridge, for instance, would require consciously working out an alternative route. Carpenter also found it hard to reject the need for constant attention to, and direction of, precise, delicate operations like those involved in painting miniatures.

Huxley made much of the unfortunate sergeant; Carpenter made little. Where Huxley found reflex actions comparable to the frog, Carpenter believed he was dealing with 'acquired' or 'secondary automatisms' (what modern cognitive psychology refers to as **'automaticity'**, colloquially referred to as 'being on autopilot). Unlike mechanical reflexes, they were acquired habits that no longer required conscious control. It was true that such

Automaticity research

performances could be engaged automatically and without volition, as automation theory proposed, but that did not mean that volition never had a role to play in their execution. That some behaviors have become automatic did not mean that conscious effort and volition were not involved in their establishment. The rolling of a cigarette is not natural, for instance, and requires an exercise of will and attention in the perfecting of the muscular/manual dexterity to become facile in the performance. In time the operation may become mechanical, but that did mean it was always so. Vygotsky (1978) referred to this as the problem of **fossilized behavior**. Fossilized behaviors are those that have undergone a process of development and which, in their final form, no longer display their history or the transformations undergone, such as liberation from conscious control, as they become mechanical and automatic.

The unfortunate sergeant is reminiscent of Luria's (1980) report of the loss of capacity to regulate serial tasks (like cigarette preparation and smoking) due to frontal lobe damage. Such injuries result in a loss of regulatory control over voluntary behavior and disruptions to goal-directed actions. Such unfortunates can be easily distracted and lose focus on an activity. One person went to catch a train and impulsively boarded the first one to arrive despite going in the wrong direction, the immediate situation having provoked the response (the sort of thing behavioristic psychology professes as an account of all behavior). Another person planed a piece of wood but, once started, could not stop, went through the piece of wood and continued through the workbench. Such disturbances in normal voluntary behavior (which Huxley emphasized as evidence of a lack of voluntary control), rather than disproving voluntary control, demonstrated to Luria its importance to normal activity. Were it not for the damage to the frontal lobes those actions would have been under personal regulation.

To Carpenter, many automaton-like behaviors were originally actions that were under voluntary, conscious control. This was especially so during the phase of development and acquisition. (Recall what it was like to learn, if you did, to ride a bicycle or drive a car.) While originally under conscious control and willful effort, they become fixed and can be performed without consciousness. Carpenter suggested the case of the acquisition of translating messages into, and sending, Morse code, by telegraph operators as a possible instance. This was subsequently demonstrated in studies by Bryan and Harter (1897, 1899). In the process of learning the skill, sending and receiving telegraphic messages became easier and underwent qualitative transformations. In receiving there was a shift from identifying single letters to there being no gap appearing between the letters; they had melded into word units. Later the conscious unit became the sentence. In transmitting, much conscious attention was applied to converting the letter into appropriate dashes and dots but eventually it became an automatic translation into muscular movements and increased to the point where no thought was applied to sending whole messages.

Beyond secondary automatisms, Carpenter turned to the common subjective experience of mental intention producing muscular activity (what James 1890/1950 called the theory of 'ideo-motor action'). This was the hypothesis that the occurrence of the thought of an action is followed immediately and unhesitatingly by that movement. The thought is sufficient to engage the unfolding of the action or action sequences. This ability, he believed, was not present at birth but was developed through growth and education. Self-control is acquired, developed, especially through guidance, and becomes habitual. In time, one gains control over one's actions. Carpenter believed the best evidence of this came from the awareness of the power to resist temptations and to act in accordance with duty. He offered the case of 600 soldiers who stood their post while women and children were first evacuated from a sinking ship. We reserve the word hero for people who act against their own best-interest and are compelled by duty to act in the service of others (police, firefighters, and soldiers come to mind). Volition, here, overrides reflexive survival tendencies.

The determinist and the automaton theorist argue that if only we had complete knowledge of all antecedents, and the degree of their influence, there would be no element to be found that is self-originating, unconditioned, or in any way outside of the influence of normal cause–effect sequences. The determinist, nonetheless, argues that such a lack should not deter us from believing in absolute determinism and a rejection of freedom of choice. Carpenter was not convinced of this and neither was William James, whom he influenced.

12.2 DETERMINISM IN PSYCHOLOGY

William James' dilemma

During a visit to Germany (late 1860s) a debate was raging over free will versus determinism which James was drawn into (Menand, 2001). As a scientist, he accepted that humans are thoroughly natural and completely conditioned by physical law; that meant that what was willed was determined. At the same time, he was convinced that humans act rationally, with reason and for reasons, and that how one confronts the world, including scientifically, is based on belief of some sort. Reasons and beliefs, though, as a basis for acting, are inconsistent with absolute determinism. James left Germany believing in both and suffered an intellectual struggle that left him deeply depressed. By late 1869 he had read a book by Renouvier that defended freedom and spurred him to experiment on himself. According to Renouvier, necessity is an incoherent doctrine. If every belief is determined, one cannot judge the correctness of the belief in the determination of all beliefs, since it too is determined. Nor could one explain why people believe opposite things like free will or determinism. The only option Renouvier saw was to believe in the freedom to believe and to believe therefore in free will. To James this meant that free will was defined as the maintenance of a belief simply because one chose to when other beliefs were possible. He therefore decided his first choice would be to believe in free will.

James (1884) wrote that one cannot prove free will, but he asked his readers to accept it since he wanted others to benefit from Renouvier as he had (his depression had lifted). Determinism, he argued, espouses a form of pessimism and no good could come from it since it meant no one could be held to account for their actions. There would be no responsibility and no reason for guilt, praise, or blame, and regret would be a meaningless word. Determinism belittles humanity and renders humans inconsequential. Just as he had questioned the lack of utility of consciousness in Huxley's epiphenomenalism, he wondered what value the sense of personal choice, effort, and intent had. Determinism, itself, was an unproven scientific postulate that was maintained by the belief in its eventual proof once enough evidence was marshaled. Until it was, either assertion was possible. In the end, belief in determinism or free will was a choice and James (1892) decided to accept both until the matter was settled. For scientific purposes he proposed that determinism should be admitted, but in matters of personal conduct and ethics he would accept free will.

One other area, habits and their reconditioning, also bears mention here. Whereas Huxley conceived of habits as mechanical action patterns, James (1887) drew upon Carpenter's secondary automatism theory and argued that most habits were originally voluntary in their formation, involving consciousness and will. That they became mechanical did not mean they always were. At the same time, they must have originally rested upon some impulsive or reflexive activity from which they were developed. All habits rest upon the plasticity of the original organic, native conditions (James, 1890/1950). With the organic constitution as the starting point, the individual is subject to biological determinism, but experience and learning modify what was given by nature. Societal conditions impose limitations and one is conditioned to adapt to local circumstances by developing serviceable habits. Customs, dialects, manners, attitudes, prejudices, values, all set patterns to which the individual accommodates. Socialization was habit-forming. Once formed, habits no longer require attention or monitoring. They unfold naturally, with little or no consciousness. Consciousness is freed for other demands. "It is a general principle in Psychology," James wrote, "that consciousness deserts all processes where it can no longer be of use" (1890/1950, p. 496). That is the point of automaticity.

It is altogether possible that habits may prove undesirable to their holder (smoking is an obvious example). As James (1887) wrote, "Could the young but realize how soon they will become walking bundles of habits, they would give more heed to their conduct while in the plastic state" (pp. 450–451). Once set, that did not mean that habits could not be broken. To that end, James offered some maxims for developing desired habits (which are a matter of choice in their adoption).

- One must first muster as much initiative as possible and establish conditions supporting success by removing incompatible circumstances.

- Make a public pledge to render it difficult to renege.

- Allow no exceptions until the habit has been firmly set.

In time they will become secondary automatisms. (Box 12.1 introduces a modern variation on James.)

James (1884) distinguished between determinism (which he called 'hard determinism') and 'soft determinism' (or **compatibilism**), which repudiated the fatalism inherent in the hard form. Compatibilism was not a denial of necessity, or a lawful order to natural phenomena, but it was a rejection of the impossibility of human agency. Freedom involved an appreciation of necessity. Understanding the laws of gravity, for instance, supported freedom of movement without stupidly walking off cliffs. One is still bound by natural law and is not free, for example, to deny the necessity of food, unless one chooses to expire. As James put it: "… sometimes we are free and sometimes we are not" (p. 198).

BOX 12.1
BREAKING THE COMPLAINING HABIT

Will Bowen (2007), a minister in Kansas City, came to the realization that he was creating his own conditions of misery through his widespread complaining, griping, and gossiping, and was determined to change his behavior. He would include his parishioners in the process since he believed they likely could benefit as well. According to Bowen, people complain 15–30 times a day, on average, and are making themselves unnecessarily miserable as result. Not only are they making themselves wretched and stressed, they make those around them uncomfortable too. He developed a procedure to break the habit and wrote a book—*A complaint free world: How to stop complaining and start enjoying the life you always wanted.* The aim was, if one chose, to shift from destructive to constructive thinking. The premise was that if you change your thinking you can change your world. So Bowen developed the complaint free challenge which was really quite simple: go 21 days without complaining (including criticizing, gossiping, and being sarcastic). To help in the process and to stay focused, participants would wear a purple bracelet on one wrist. There were four rules:

- Wear the bracelet.
- Switch it to the other wrist each time you catch yourself complaining and restart the count (it keeps you aware).
- If you catch someone else who has taken up the challenge complaining it is all right to tell them, BUT switch the bracelet to the other wrist and start over—that was a complaint about their complaining.
- Stay with it.

It can take from four to eight months to break the complaining habit. Be aware that this is not a test of James' maxims, but it is in the same spirit.

Freud's determinism

Sigmund Freud (1856–1939) was trained as a neurologist, specializing in nervous disorders, and his training in medicine and science was the foundation for his theorizing in psychology (Hall and Lindzey, 1978). Due to this he developed a firm belief in the determinism pervading the scientific community. It became a foundation in his psychological theorizing. To Freud, the psychological was an aspect of natural phenomena and was explicable in terms of materialism and mechanism (McAdams, 1994). When he discussed mind it was not conceived of as something immaterial, a mental substance, but a process rooted in biology (Rycroft, 1968). It was a dynamic entity, a web of adaptive responses, intrinsically connected to bodily processes.

As an organism the body is an energy system that takes in food and converts that into energy to maintain the bodily processes of respiration, circulation, neural activity, perceiving, thinking, and remembering (Hall and Lindzey, 1978). The same energy innervates each and, when performing psychological functions, is called psychic energy. Freud's psychology was bound to biology and physiology, and was consistent with the physiology of the time, wherein determinism was paramount.

Determinism is a fundamental assumption. Due to that, there are no accidents. Whatever happens is caused and that precludes free will. According to Freud, "Anyone thus breaking away from the determination of natural phenomena … has thrown over the whole scientific outlook on the world" (1924/1953, p. 32). He wrote that it was his intention to show that "… there is within you a deeply rooted belief in psychic freedom and choice, that this belief is quite unscientific, and that it must give ground before the claims of a determinism which governs even mental life" (p. 112). These deterministic processes often operate outside of consciousness (what is called 'unconscious motivation') and are responsible for the production of errors and supposedly chance actions, hence no accidents. That is why Freud placed so much emphasis on tracing psychological problems to childhood, determining causes. The aetiology of neuroses, he proposed, lay in inherited predispositions and in those that were acquired in childhood.

Not all would accept Freud's complete determinism, nor his **genetic method** of searching for causal origins in childhood. Allport (1937) proposed that there are no features of developed personality that are without hereditary influences, but that was insufficient as a full explanatory proposition. There are only the most basic beginnings of the 'psychological being' in place at birth. Hereditary material is subject from the start to modifications effected by learning (of the behaviorist variety) and the socializing influence of education (instruction, including schooling but not limited to it). Thus, given the accruing changes with learning, biological theory was best applied to the motives of infancy like instincts and drives. Under conditioning habits are formed, but habits to Allport were fixed and inflexible, too rigid and invariant to account for the malleability and adaptability in conduct. Similar habitual adaptations eventually coalesce to form traits, or general disposition to act, that are **functionally autonomous** (see **functional autonomy**) and achieve independence from formative conditions. In the process of maturation, the manifold potentialities of childhood unite into distinctive motivational systems that assume a directive driving power unto themselves (including interests, values, ideals, purposes, goals). The mature life, unlike the reactivity of childhood, involves the intelligent planning for the future. The behavioristic causal stimulus is dethroned by current interests and the fetish of the 'genetic method' is removed as an account of conduct. Motives are always contemporary and must be studied in their current context.

Functional autonomy

Social learning theory and agency

While behaviorists like Watson and Skinner were advocates of determinism, 'social learning theory,' associated with Julian Rotter (1916–2014) and Albert Bandura (1925–), allowed for cognitive learning through observation. The rewards and punishments observed in the behavior of others served to guide one's own future behavior. That led to the introduction of agency into the tradition. In the initial formulation, Bandura (1977) proposed that a person's behavior was mediated by her/his sense of 'self efficacy' (perceived ability in light of prior successes and failures). The anticipated sense of success will influence what a person attempts to do and how much effort will be expended. Rather than being merely reactive to external events the person is conceived of as actively engaging the environment. In the course of experience, cognitive representations are developed that support anticipating future outcomes and become motivating factors in engaging the world. On the other hand, a person who has a very low sense of self-efficacy may give up trying and develop 'learned helplessness' (Box 12.2 expands on this).

BOX 12.2
LEARNED HELPLESSNESS AND THE HOLOCAUST

The phenomenon of learned helplessness was identified by Seligman and Maier (1967) in their work with dogs. The animals were placed in a situation in which they were subjected to unavoidable electric shocks. Their behaviors could do nothing to alter the application of shock and they eventually gave up trying, just lying there helplessly taking the shock. Subsequently they were transferred to a situation where they were again shocked but, if they tried, they could do something to evade the shock. The dogs did nothing and just suffered. They had what the experimenters termed 'learned "helplessness".' Later research with cats, fish, rats, and humans resulted in a motivational deficit in which there was an inhibition of voluntary responses to escape (Abramson, Seligman, and Teasdale, 1978). The most striking evidence of learned helplessness in humans—the loss of will to survive in the Nazi concentration camps—was overlooked in the experimental tradition.

Viktor Frankl (1905–1997), an Austrian psychotherapist, was incarcerated by the Nazis and subsequently wrote (Frankl, 1963) of the tenacity of the sense of personal freedom under the harshest of conditions. Many of the people suffered severe deprivation and mistreatment that stripped them of their humanity, even their sense of identity. They were not valued as people nor afforded that dignity; they were vermin, something to be exterminated. Over the course of their incarceration, all values were lost to the struggle to live. Inadequate food and sleep, the never-ending abuse and stress, could break a person, and they could descend to animal level. Their status as unreal, non-human, non-entities caused many to relinquish their hold on life as they slipped into meaninglessness and pointlessness. The loss of hope and courage could be deadly, and the symptoms were clear. The person would

(Continued)

(Continued)

refuse to arise in the morning, to dress or wash, to cease responding to threats and blows by lying motionless (reminiscent of the dogs), even unbothered by being prostrate in their own excrement. They had given up (or arrived in the learned helplessness). To Frankl, this, while caused by the unending abuse, was still a choice.

Every day there were choices to be made about whether to give in, about what to think. People could still decide on their attitude toward their conditions, about their abusers trying to steal their inner freedom, and whether to keep fighting on the inside. One man did so by comforting others and gave them his meagre food; they could take his life but not his humanity. Others yielded to the fear of making decisions, of taking initiative, and gave in to their fate. They allowed apathy to take hold. Yet there were numerous cases of apathy being overcome or warded off by personal choice. People could still preserve their independence of mind and freedom of spirit. People can be robbed of everything but still retain that. What gives the person's life purpose and meaning, their spiritual freedom, cannot be stolen but it could be lost. The person who lost faith in a personal future or was bereft of a reason to live was doomed. When they did Frankl tried to help them recover it, to find a reason to live, and to carry on. Whether one succeeded or succumbed, it rested on a personal choice which was free all the same. It was that phenomenon that Frankl witnessed and he contended that it challenges notions of universal or absolute determinism.

Bandura (1989, 2006, 2008) further developed his position on the question of agency by proposing that humans have the capacity to exert self-control over their thoughts, motives, and actions. He believed that people can effect changes in themselves and in the circumstances they encounter through personal effort. Taking a compatibilist stance, he maintained that peoples' actions are neither the mechanical effect of environmental influences nor are they completely autonomous. Most human behavior is under the guidance of forethought, the formation of goals, the anticipation of outcomes, and plans for action. Thought has a major role to play in exercising control over daily life.

Thoughts to Bandura are rooted in higher brain processes and that means one has to distinguish between 'biological laws' and 'psychological laws.' Biological laws account for cerebral mechanisms and psychological laws explain how biological processes are enlisted in the service of differing purposes. With learning, humans become agents in directing their own activities, but that does not liberate them completely from determination. Freedom is not an absence of external constraints but an increasing capacity to direct activity within those constraints. One achieves that through knowledge of conditions. This is not a solitary endeavor. Human activity, historically, has produced social systems that aid in the organization and regulation of human life. People act on the environment, transforming it, recreating it, even destroying it; they have created society. That accumulates and is passed on to subsequent generations. Socialization creates humans with an emerging, increasing power for consciousness, self-awareness, and intent. Humans are more than mere mechanisms or automatons.

Experimental refutation of free will

Central to recent experimental challenges to free will is the 'Libet paradigm,' which nearly leads to an epiphenomenalist account of free will like that of Wegner and Wheatley (1999) on the illusion of mental causation (see Chapter 6). What Libet found was that the conscious intention to act was preceded by an initiation of activity in the motor cortex of the brain. That meant that the decision to act had been made by the motor cortex prior to the individual being aware of the intention, since the motor activity preceded it (Libet, Gleason, Wright, and Pearl, 1983). In the experiment, participants were asked to relax and, when ready, to flex their wrist (Libet, 1999). Measures of cerebral activity indicated a readiness potential (activity in the motor cortex) about 800ms before the person was aware of intending to

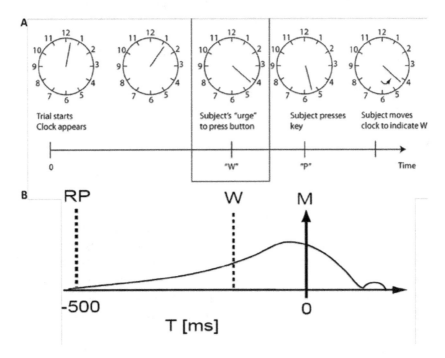

Figure 12.1 The Libet paradigm

With permission, NeuroLogica Blog

flex (around 150–200ms before actual flexion)—see Figure 12.1. It was concluded that the apparently voluntary, conscious act was actually begun unconsciously (it began with the readiness potential—RP in the figure, in the motor cortex). An element of free will remained for Libet, however, in that the person could intercede and veto the actual performance. His overall conclusion was that free will does not initiate an act but it may regulate subsequent performance. As far as Libet was concerned both determinist and non-determinist theories are speculative and one may as well assume free will until proven false since it plays such a large role in peoples' subjective experience.

While the Libet paradigm has proven popular among advocates of determinism, not all neuroscientists found the rejection of conscious intent convincing. Eccles (1985) found it tempting to accept Libet's interpretation of the readiness-potential as initiating the supposed voluntary movement and then subjective experience of intent. He preferred an alternative hypothesis. The cerebral cortex, he suggested, has a background of fluctuating activity and the readiness-potential may not indicate the cortical initiation of movement. One may, instead, interpret the spontaneous cortical fluctuations as adjustments to the conscious initiation 200ms prior to actual movement. It is possible that intent actually occurs prior to the readiness-potential and that it is merely a reflection of ongoing brain activity.

Searle (2010) also suggested a reconsideration of Libet's work. The standard interpretation, he contended, has failed to recognize that intent was already in place when the participants agreed that at some point they would flex their wrist. This set the conditions for what followed. It was a 'determining tendency' in the subsequent wrist flex. The intent existed in the readiness to perform the act and not in the isolated micro-performance alone. The readiness-potential therefore has no bearing on the truth or falsity of determinism. In the final analysis these studies are based on trivial instances of human action and do not address the larger issues. The real interest was in questions like did Hitler intend to wipe out millions of people or were his actions determined? Or did the protesting martyr who set himself aflame do so by free choice? The neuronal activity of a few milliseconds, represented by the readiness-potential, hardly addresses the larger matters.

Baumeister's (2010) critique supplements that of Searle. He wondered whether intention is reflected in brain activity immediately prior to muscular activation, in micro-level processes (of the millisecond temporal order) or in macro-level processes of a larger time frame. Imagine, he asked, that you are going for a walk. That is a decision you make but that does not mean that you subsequently, and consciously, specify the particular neurons to be activated or where their synaptic excitation will go. If consciousness is involved it is at the macro level well in advance of those immediate muscular excitations. While Baumeister did not mention it, this is reminiscent of the finding of **determining tendencies**. Ach (1905, in Boring, 1929) found that providing research participants with instructions to perform a task was sufficient for the action to be performed without any further conscious content directing the subsequent task (mathematical operations). The task is carried out unconsciously with the predisposition directing movement towards the assigned end. To, make this a little easier to grasp, I hope, when I decide I will go to the corner store I do not continually say to myself "go to the store," "go to the store," until I arrive. The decision is sufficient for me to follow through and my mind is taken up with other things without having to be constantly aware of my intention, unless interrupted or obstructed.

The cultural-historical perspective

The cultural-historical approach to psychology of Vygotsky, Luria, and Leontyev accepted determinism, but also believed a compatibilist solution to the problem of free will was possible. Their position was based on the dialectical materialist realization that freedom consisted in the ability to appreciate necessity. It is not a matter of being freed from natural law but of understanding, of operating within those constraints, and learning how to use them. Freedom of will, as judged by Engels (1877/1939), refers to a capacity to make decisions that are based on real knowledge and consists not only of knowledge but in the capacity to exercise control over oneself and nature. Freedom is the application of intelligence in the use of those laws to pursue one's purposes. Gravity, for instance, holds us fast to the surface of the planet, but with growing knowledge of natural laws, especially of the principles of aerodynamics and propulsion, humans have taken to flight and even leave the atmosphere. Humans have adapted to the demands of the environment but eventually adapted the environment to their needs. Tools, technologies, and constructions, like dams and canals, give evidence to this.

Not everyone is equally free or free in the same way. In the course of ontogenetic development, individuals adapt to their specific circumstances and appropriate the knowledge and skill needed to function in their sociocultural milieu and in their specific occupations. The socially and historically situated nature of the individual and the group limits or supports varying degrees of freedom (Cornforth, 1963). Individual freedom depends on the positive advances of the society and the opportunities afforded to utilize those possibilities. Poverty and enslavement limit one's freedom and range of opportunities in ways that wealth and power do not (recall Holzkamp's concept of 'action potence' in Chapter 9).

Within psychology, Vygotsky (1932/1987) concluded that the problem of will was a concern with how non-rational human activity is transformed in development and becomes rational. The development of free, voluntary purposes is the result of the culture-historical development of behavior (Vygotsky, 1930/1999). Rather than just a product of biological evolution, humans are products of cultural forces that have supported the mastery of nature and oneself. Unlike animals whose actions are bound to immediate biological needs and the present environment, humans acquire a capacity to anticipate and plan. Most significant to the development of individual freedom of action was the mastery of sign or word. This was an idea that Luria would develop.

What distinguishes humans from animals to Luria (1932/1967) is that humans can control the objective world and their own behavior, indirectly, by creating artificial means and techniques (language, symbols, numerics, tools, et cetera). In the course of human development the natural forms of behavior (attention, perception, memory, acting) become complicated by the cultural forms. As a result, there is an elaboration of a new relation of the individual to her/his personal behavior. It is because of the mediated, indirect nature of psychological processes that humans can change their environment and master their own behavior, making it rational and free (Leontiev and Luria, 1968). When you cross the street do you think "look right then left" in Britain or "look left then right" in North America? If so, street crossing is under rational direction. Using words to guide actions, writing lists to support memory, using strategies to perform complicated activities, would be other examples.

Whereas the central characteristic of elementary mental functions is their complete and direct determination by environmental stimulation, in the higher functions of humans the stimulation is self-generated, via the creation of artificial stimuli, and their mastery becomes the immediate cause of behavior. To Vygotsky the elementary psychophysiological processes of sensation, attention, memory, and movement are natural functions of nervous tissue but the higher functions (active/selective attention, voluntary memory, abstract thought, and voluntary movement) are not direct functions of the brain (Luria, 1971a). To understand the nature of higher psychological processes one has to go beyond the organism's natural limits and search for the roots in the historically formed environment, in the child's interactions and communication with adults, and in the objective relations among language, tools, and objects established through social history. Through communication with others, psychological processes are organized into new forms in the growing child that liberate him/her from immediate demands and support purposeful engagement with the world.

Through the mastery of significances/meanings, in the process of word usage, humans reflect the regularities in objective reality more efficiently and effectively and behavior becomes rational (Leontiev and Luria, 1968). The person ceases to be merely reactive to environmental conditions (internal and external) and becomes actively involved in the world. The move to verbal thought is the move from the sensory to the rational and guarantees a broad variety of possible connections for thought to move within (Luria, 1971a). Language as a system of meanings supports movement beyond the limits of immediately provided sense data.

While not within the cultural-historical approach, Kopp (1982) reviewed research into self-regulation and self-direction and identified its beginning in two-year-olds complying with commands. With increasing age there is a shift from external control to control from within (to self-control). This is in line with Luria's (1960, 1980) proposition that the early development of voluntary action involved the behavior of children coming under the control of verbal commands of others. Later the shared action begins to come under personal control—first as external speech to oneself and then internalized as inner speech. Kopp (1982) mentioned a child of 13 months who, while reaching for a plant, shook her head and vocalized "NO!" followed by hand withdrawal. When fully developed, ideas and plans are formulated with the support of inner speech and appropriated verbal meanings. Language incorporates the accumulated experience of humanity and is central to the child's intellectual development.

Parents name objects and thereby define their relations, expanding the child's reflections of reality in ways that are deeper and broader than those the child could form through individual experience (Luria, 1956/1971b). Knowledge is transmitted and concepts formed, experience is systematized, the immediate environment is transcended, and action is subordinated to verbal formulations through planning and guidance, becoming more voluntary and free.

Agency and levels of integration

In this final section we come full circle in that the perspective to be considered is based on the notion of 'levels of integration.' While this theory of agency is consistent with the cultural-historical approach it is basically an independent approach based on levels of integration, emergence, and compatibilism. One learns to regulate one's thoughts and experiences through the development of psychological tools (Martin and Sugarman, 2004). Such skills are developed in joint activity with others, and through the appropriation of socially developed psychological instruments (words, meanings, technologies) there is a transition from pre-reflective understanding and engagement with the world to reflective, mediated consciousness. This involves, further, a transition from reactive to active, agentic engagements. The greater one's awareness of natural laws and social restrictions of culturally sanctioned modes of conduct, the freer one is to act effectively within those constraints.

Mainstream psychology has been inclined to equate human action and experience with inanimate physics and involuntary biology but that is inconsistent with human experience (Martin, Sugarman, and Thompson, 2003). The experience of choice and the ability to act on those choices means that the onus is on psychologists to develop a consistent theory of agency instead of dismissing it. Natural science explanations simply evade the issue and engage in misguided reductionism. Experiments that remove people from their sociocultural environment and focus on independent and dependent variables, on stimuli and responses, are aligned with a deterministic perspective. In the process it bypasses and conceals actual human engagements with the world. Scientific psychology is not a natural science but a human science, and the adoption of natural science methods, applicable to rocks, chemicals, and atoms, is inappropriate. It misses the distinction between 'natural kinds' and 'human kinds.'

Scientific psychology must explain how self-determination emerges from the physical, biological, and sociocultural roots without resorting to reductionism (Martin and Sugarman, 2001). These are determining conditions, and humans, upon that basis, are not completely free but, over the course of development, they are somewhat liberated. Agency must therefore be conceived of as both determined and determining (compatibilism). Among the levels, the physical is most basic and came first, and all that follows rests upon it. Biology followed, contingent upon the physical for its elements but with its own characteristics (like the processes of natural selection). With the emergence of humans and collective practices, their inventions and constructions, institutions, and so on, the ground was laid for the emergent psychological individual. The reality of the sociocultural level at any historical moment is composed of systems of shared beliefs and practices which, once taken up, may be acted back upon. All the time they remain bound by physical and biological conditions.

Humans are historically situated; they are immersed in 'traditions of living'—linguistic, discursive, and relational practices that, as psychological beings, they are a part of. The social practices and meanings the individual appropriates and internalizes become tools through which life is interpreted. Usually these are taken for granted and unacknowledged (think of automaticity). Nonetheless, meaningful action in actual life conditions (not experimentally designed) requires sociocultural practices and rules that preclude agency being reduced to factors or conditions that are biological or physical (Martin et al., 2003). At the same time, this does not imply that there are no factors and coercions, internally and externally, that are outside of conscious control. Reduction to the sociocultural is also excluded because individuals can surpass their cultural conditioning and effect further alterations in those transforming social meanings and practices. Think of how Jesus, Buddha, Mohammed, Newton, Darwin, Einstein, and countless others have altered human life and understanding. Deliberative agency becomes possible when reflective understanding takes place, along with reason, and imagination. The person becomes intelligently self-determining, and voluntary agency is the result.

> This intelligible self-determination is what defines agency as the always-present, even if not always-exercised, capacity for understanding and deliberative reasoning that we humans use to select, frame, choose, and execute intentional behavior in the world. It is what makes human agents both determined and determining. (Martin et al., 2003, p. 134)

SUMMARY

In this chapter we have considered the free will versus determinism debate.

- According to the incompatibilist, the two stances of free will and determinism are diametrically opposed whereas the compatibilist contends that there is a degree of truth to each position and they can be harmonized.

- From its scientific standpoint psychology has favored the determinist position as the only scientifically valid option.

- The 'common sense' perspective contends that determinism is inconsistent with human experience and the encoding of human engagements with the world in linguistic forms (words like decision, choice, responsibility, and guilt).

- Whereas the scientific viewpoint conceives of humans as automata, psychologists like William James found that to be inconsistent with human life experience and, on its dismissal, dehumanizing.

- Freud preferred to align with the deterministic assumption in allegiance to scientificity.

- Neuroscientists, turning to micro-recordings of neural activity, have found evidence that suggests determining, involuntary activity, antecedent to thoughts of volition, and have interpreted that as the determination of the supposedly free choice.

- The cultural-historical approach allows that humans enter the world in subjugation to deterministic forces, but allows for a partial transcendence of those conditions through education and the appropriation of culturally developed knowledge and tools which support self-control and purposive action in the world.

SUGGESTED READINGS

Allport, G. W. (1937). The functional autonomy of motives. *The American Journal of Psychology*, *50*, 141–156.

Baumeister, R. F., Mele, A. R., and Vohs, K. D. (2010). *Free will and consciousness: How might they work?* Oxford: Oxford University Press.

Dennett, D. C. (2003). *Freedom evolves.* London: Penguin Books.

Martin, J., Sugarman, J., and Thompson, J. (2003). *Psychology and the question of agency*. Albany, NY: State University of New York Press.

Want to learn more? For links to online resources, examples of multiple choice questions, conceptual exercises and much more, visit the companion website at
https://study.sagepub.com/piekokola

GLOSSARY

Terms that appear in blue bold in the book are defined here in the glossary.

Absolute Threshold: The lowest intensity required to detect the presence of a stimulus.

Abstract Concept(s): A concept that does not have a direct connection to things and events that are available to immediate perception. (See **Concrete Concepts**.)

Abstract Thought: The mental separation (abstraction) of a quality, property, or aspect of a thing apart from the thing or bundle of qualities and properties that is connected with the **concrete**.

Act: A psychological unit (unified by its purpose) that represents the continuous reciprocal interaction (see **Mutualism**) between an organism and its environment; a concrete instance of an organism engaged with its environment incorporated within which are cognitive, emotional, and intention (purposes, goals) as inseparable qualities.

Action Impotence: Conditions of personal existence are such that one has very limited to no control over the possibilities of acting in the world and satisfying their needs and desires.

Action Potence: The possibilities/potential for action open to an individual; the degree to which an individual is free to engage in activities to satisfy personal need or constrained by the possibilities provided by society.

Activity: The function of the individual that connects the organism with its environment. In its elementary form it is reflected in instinctive (evolved) reactions of an adapted organism with its environment. In its higher form, as found with humans, it involves conscious efforts to transform its environment and is conditioned culturally (socio-historically). Activity is simply the process that connects the organism with its environment and supports orientation to that **niche**.

Agency: Possessing the power to act, to work towards an end; an autonomous, self-regulating, directive capacity.

Animism: The belief that spirits of some sort inhabit natural phenomena and objects, such as the spirit of the mountain.

Anthropocentrism: Human-centered; understood and evaluated from the perspective of human capacities and values.

Anthropomorphism: The ascription of human qualities to non-humans, such as attributing thunder to an angry human-like god.

Anti-mentalism: 1) One who opposes the tenets of mentalism, who asserts the existence of mind and rejects its reduction to physical processes; 2) the tendency to exclude or deny mind and to focus on what is objective, such as stimuli and behavior. (See **Mentalism**.)

Anti-realism: The view that objects of experience do not have an independent existence from mind.

Anti-realist: A person who maintains that there is no mind-independent reality.

Appearance versus Reality: In **ontology** the distinction between how things are in actuality, the totality of what is real, and the perception (appearance) of said reality and whether they coincide or not.

Atomism: The theory that all phenomena, including psychological phenomena, are made up of indivisible, irreducible, changeless constituents called atoms.

Atomists: Proponents of **atomism**.

Automaticity (also called 'automatic processing'): Engaging in a cognitive or motor activity with minimal attention or even conscious awareness after sufficient practice involving conscious attention.

Becoming: The universal process of change and flux, of non-constancy.

Behavior: In behavioral psychology or learning theory, the constellation of responses to (a) internal and (b) external stimulation. Behavior thus conceived is the product of (a) biological and (b) environmental determination.

Being: A state of permanence, stability, and constancy.

Biological Determinism: A form of **determinism** that proposes that behavior is caused by biological processes, e.g., physiological or biochemical causes.

Biological Reductionism: The proposition that behavior and higher mental processes can be fully explained by more basic biological processes.

Black Box: In telecommunications the processes in electronic hardware that occur between input and output; in psychology the unobservable operations of the mind.

Brain Plasticity: The ability of the brain to change its structure and function following damage or experience.

Carpentered World Theory: The theory which proposes that, as a result of growing up in human-carpentered environments composed of rectangles, squares, and straight lines, people are predisposed (having established habitual perceptual inferences) to be more susceptible to linear-based illusions like the Müller-Lyer.

Circular Argument: A fallacious form of argument in which a premise is restated as a conclusion instead of deriving the conclusion from the premise. For instance: This person behaves kindly from which I infer the trait of kindliness which explains acting kindly (Kindness → trait → Kindness or Kindness → Kindness).

Classical Conditioning: A form of elementary learning in which biologically non-significant, environmental conditions mediate between reflexive, biologically significant, stimulus conditions and an organism such that they come to assume signaling functions (indicating the potential presence of those biologically significant conditions) through repeated association. Within the context of behavioral psychology this is referred to as the forming of an association between a neutral stimulus and an unconditioned stimulus such that the neutral stimulus comes to elicit the unconditioned response.

Classical View of Concepts: The theory of conceptual structure and constitution which contends that concepts are based on necessary, defining features, or fundamental characteristics, which act as criteria for determining category membership. Many members of a category fail to possess defining features, such as birds like penguins being defined by flying, which proved problematic for classical theory.

Classical View of Perception: The laws underlying perceptual processes were independent of social and historical circumstances and could be studied within the framework of natural science, i.e., in terms of physiological processes.

Compatibilism: The view that free will and determinism are both true and not mutually exclusive (logically impossible for both to be true).

Concept of Integrative Levels: A theory of the historical evolution of matter from the original physicochemical level—the inanimate, with laws specific to it—on to the biological, or animate, and then the social level of organization. Each level is said to possess its own unique phenomena and laws and is not reducible to the earlier, base or foundational level.

Concrete: Pertaining to a particular thing in its wholeness as it presents itself in natural conditions.

Concrete Concept(s): Concepts that apply to groups of tangible objects treated as belonging together. (See **Abstract Concept.**)

Concurrent Validity: A demonstration of a close relationship between one measure of a concept/phenomenon, such as an intelligence test, and a separate, independent indicator of the same phenomenon, such as grades in school.

Connectionism: A computer modeled cognitive theory that proposes that complex cognitive phenomena can be explained as a system of links between units that represent pieces of information; such pieces are bound together into higher-order units through associative processes. These are thought to model neural processes underlying cognitive functions.

Constructionism (or social constructionism): The epistemological position that holds that knowledge is due to a social construction (created by people themselves) rather than due to an objective reality that is accessible and possesses some certain truth; reality is what people collectively make it to be rather than what it is.

Continuity Thesis: In evolutionary explanation, the principle that emergent forms and characteristics are continuous with, or develop from, prior evolved forms, and that the gap between the inorganic and organic is not unbridgeable.

Conventionalism: An epistemological strategy that asserts that certain a priori truths exist upon the basis of convention, that is, by agreement in use.

Coordinated: See **coordination**.

Coordination: As used by Dewey, the harmonious and integrated interaction of an organism within itself and with its environment.

Correspondence Rules: Rules that indicate the ways by which theoretical terms can be made to correspond with observational statements.

Cosmology: The study of the universe, its origins and constitution.

Cross-cultural Psychology: An approach to studying the impact of culture on thought and behavior that treats culture as external to, and interacting with, independent individuals, and how people are different from each other on some variable of interest.

Cultural Psychology: An approach to the study of psychological processes and behavior, conceived of as being embedded within cultural practices and traditions. Person and culture cannot be realistically separated; through engagements with culture the psychological being forms as historically conditioned.

Determining Tendencies: A predisposition to act that is due to having a goal which guides subsequent behavior. The goal may operate outside of consciousness yet directs or regulates behavior in service of the intended end.

Determinism: The proposition that any event or occurrence can be completely explained in terms of antecedent conditions.

Dialectical Materialism: A materialism that asserts the primacy of matter over mind, but which asserts the possibility of the evolution of matter and of the emergence of new phenomena and qualities, like life and mind, as the complexity of matter increases, the nature of which is tied to the further emergence of culture.

Direct Realism: The proposition that the world as it is perceived is the world as it is in its independence from the knower. It is equivalent to **naïve realism** with the exception that it is based on an awareness of the problem of knowledge of the objective. (See **Indirect Realism** and **Anti-realism**.)

Doctrine of Specific Nerve Energies: The subjective impression of the quality of sensation depends upon which nerve is stimulated rather than upon the type of physical stimulus acting on the sensory system (auditory, visual, and so on).

Dogmatic: See **Dogmatism**.

Dogmatism: The assertion of an opinion as absolute truth while lacking supporting evidence.

Double Aspect Theory (also called double aspectism): A dualistic solution to the mind–body problem that proposes that bodily phenomena and mental phenomena are two aspects of a single underlying reality and are therefore inseparable.

Dualism: A group of explanations of the **mind–body problem** that regard mind and matter as two distinct, separate entities (the relation between which requires explanation).

Dualistic: See **Dualism**.

Duhem-Quine Thesis: All statements are theoretical and, as such, are immune from being refuted by sense experience; it is always a possibility that associated assumptions can be adjusted to protect the hypothesis.

Ecological Validity: The degree to which experimental findings are applicable to ordinary life contexts; whether they generalize to the real world of daily living.

Elementalism: The separation of a whole into independent entities or parts; the splitting conceptually of what is inseparable in the concrete.

Eliminative Materialism (also called eliminativism): The theory that holds that everyday, common-sense conceptions of the mind or 'folk psychology' are wrong and that they do not actually exist; mental states like beliefs or sensory impressions are banished and eliminated, displaced by neuro-computational processes.

Emergence: As matter becomes more organized and more complex, new qualities or properties come into existence that had not been seen before.

Emergent Properties: Properties that arise from the combination of elements that are qualitatively different from, and cannot be explained by, reduction to the constituent elements.

Empiricism: An epistemological position which contends that all that is known is dependent upon experience.

Enculturation: The process whereby an individual adapts to and adopts a particular culture.

Epiphenomenalism: A dualistic solution to the mind–body problem that proposes that mind and mental phenomena are by-products of causal physical processes and that mental processes themselves have no causal efficacy.

Epistemological: See **Epistemology**.

Epistemology: A concern with knowledge and what, if anything, can be known. (See **Realism**, **Direct Realism**, **Indirect Realism**, **Naïve Realism**, **Anti-Realism**, **Skepticism**, **Relativism**, **Constructionism**, **Phenomenalism**, **Empiricism**, **Rationalism**, and **Solipsism**.)

Essence: Those characteristics of a thing that give it a unique identity; the indispensable qualities that constitute something's intrinsic nature and make it what it is.

Essentialism: A form of conceptualizing that reduces the variations in nature to a lesser number of classes that represent fixed, unchanging types that are clearly delimited from each other (see **Typology**).

Ethnocentric: See **Ethnocentrism**.

Ethnocentrism: Judging another culture or ethnic group by the standards, values, and norms of one's own.

Ethos: The beliefs, values, ideals, and understandings, the habits and practices, that characterize a particular group; the fundamental value system and dominant assumptions.

Eugenics: The science behind social agencies influencing the development of the mental and physical qualities of future generations of a race through the control of mating practices; the selective breeding of humans.

Evolutionary Psychology: A branch of psychology whose focus is the evolution of the human brain, especially the development of functionally specialized mechanisms that were designed to support adaptation to the recurring challenges that confronted hominids during the evolution of modern humans.

Excluded Middle: In logic, the proposition that with the principle of **identity** (A = A) and the principle of **non-contradiction** (A ≠ not-A) there is nothing in between.

Falsification: For something to be considered scientific it must be capable of being shown to be false.

Fatalism: The belief that what will happen is bound to happen, predetermined, and outside of personal control.

Folk Psychology: The naïve, common-sense, lay psychology forged throughout the history of unscientific humans in their misguided efforts to account for and predict human conduct.

Fossilized Behavior (fossilization): Behaviors that in their mature, developed form no longer reveal the connections to their development history nor the transformations undergone as they become automatized.

Foundation: That which serves as the basis for a theory of knowledge; a privileged set of beliefs that are taken as basic and that form the basis for reasoning toward more complicated beliefs.

Foundationalism: A perspective on epistemology that contends that beliefs are justified by being based on foundational beliefs that do not require being justified by other beliefs (such as the contention that the world is objectively accessible and knowable and the basis for knowledge of what is).

Free Will: The proposition that humans are in a position to decide for themselves how they will act without constraint by external forces or by predetermination; sometimes considered the opposite of determinism.

Functional Autonomy: The independence in purpose of many adult motives from their childhood and adolescent counterparts and which continue to influence behavior after the original motive has disappeared.

Functional Equivalence: Having a similar duty or part to play despite differences in structural composition or operation.

Functionalism: An approach to psychology that considers mental phenomena to be processes of organic beings and emphasizes the usefulness, in meeting the demands of continuing existence, of these activities or functions.

Fundamental Lexical Hypothesis: The theory that if a behavioral tendency of people in general is of sufficient significance it will likely be encoded into the lexicon (vocabulary) of the group; descriptive terms like combative or greedy reflect behavioral tendencies that can be observed in people and are represented in language.

Fuzzy Categories: In grouping natural objects into categories (a collection of things sharing some property or properties) the boundaries distinguishing members from non-members may not be well-defined. Some natural categories may be 'fuzzy sets' which contain varying degrees of membership.

General Genetic Law of Cultural Development: All higher psychological functions in child development occur twice and on two planes. First, they exist socially and interpersonally and second, after they have been **internalized**, they function internally as psychological functions.

General Intelligence: An inherited capacity that underlies various intellectual abilities.

Generalization: In the case of associative learning, the transfer of a response to other stimuli based on some similarity in stimulus properties, e.g., similar color or sound frequency.

Generalized Action Possibilities: As a result of accumulating knowledge about what can be done in the world, cultural knowledge accrues at the collective level and becomes a societal system of meanings that individuals can draw upon.

Genetic Method: The term genetic here is based on the term genesis rather than genes and refers to a search for origins, to history and development, such as Freud searching for causes of current conduct in early childhood.

Hereditarian: One who believes that the differences between individuals and groups of people, in terms of intellectual and other abilities, are predominantly due to biologically inherited potential.

Hermeneutics: Originally the interpretation of the Bible, and later texts; in psychology the interpretation of lived experience in terms of the individual's experiences and in an effort to appreciate the formative conditions in the individual's life.

Higher Mental Processes: In the cultural-historical tradition a distinction is made between the biologically-based, natural, lower, or elementary psychological capacities, such as natural memory and attention, and those that have been expanded upon by incorporating culturally developed psychological tools like language, mnemonics, and sign systems.

Holism: The notion that living beings have properties that can only be understood through reference to the whole rather than by being explained through reduction to elemental parts.

Holistic: See Holism.

Hominin (formerly hominid): Members of the human evolutionary family.

Human Kinds: An artificial category (not fixed by nature) that reflects human interests and understanding and is subject to change as interests and understanding are altered. (See **Natural Kinds.**)

Human Factors Engineering: The designing of instruments, devices, and systems so that they fit (user friendly) humans based on knowledge of physical characteristics and psychological capacities and weaknesses.

Hypostatization: The treatment of a conceptual abstraction or hypothetical construct as a real, concrete thing.

Idealism: The ontological theory that asserts the primacy of mind over matter, that what can be experienced is idea, spirit, or mind, or is derived from idea.

Identity Theory: A materialist ontology that asserts that mind and brain are identical (hence identity).

Idiographic: Pertaining to particulars, to the individual occurrence.

Immaterialism: The proposition that all that can be perceived is of idea or spirit; a rejection of things material.

Immaterialist: See **Immaterialism**.

Incommensurability: Kuhn's proposition that theories from different paradigms cannot be compared because they lack a common basis for comparison.

Incommensurable: See **Incommensurability**.

Incompatibilism: The contention that free will and determinism are mutually exclusive concepts; freedom and determinism are logically opposed by definition. The incompatibilist may opt for hard determinism and deny the possibility of free will. The libertarian, on the other hand, asserts the validity of free will and as a consequence rejects determinism (or at least complete determinism).

Incrementalism: The development of science is an aggregating process of evidence accumulating in successive increments with each subsequent stage building upon and improving its predecessors.

Indirect Realism: An epistemological position which contends that while there is an objective reality it can only be apprehended as it is mediated by sensations and mental representations.

Individualism: The theory that the psychological subject can be treated as wholly independent and free of determination by social and historical conditions.

Induction: Reasoning from the particular to the general, from specific facts or instances to general propositions.

Induction by Simple Enumeration: A form of generalization which assumes that, having noted a similarity between all examples, so far encountered, all others will, in the future, have the same similarity.

Inductive Definition: A procedure for determining the defining characteristics of a concept by examining every instance of the concept to identify the characteristics common to all particular instances.

Information Theory: In communications and signal transmission, the mathematical theory that utilizes statistical procedures to infer what may have been transmitted in garbled, distorted, or interfered-with messages, in an effort to decide the most likely missing elements, regardless of message content or meaning.

Insight: The appearance of a solution to a problem after having been without one; a sudden appreciation or awareness of a solution after having been bereft of one.

Intelligence Quotient (IQ): The ratio of mental age (MA; age level based on age norms for mental functioning) to chronological age (CA). IQ = MA/CA.

Intentionality: In act psychology, the property of pointing beyond itself, of referring to something outside of the mental act (an object or mental referent like the image or thought of something).

Interactionism: A dualistic solution to the mind–body problem that proposes mind and body are two distinct substances but which can interact and are mutually influencing.

Internalization: The incorporation of what is objective and/or social as an integral part of oneself (practices, values, beliefs) and a process of establishing subject–object connectivity. The term 'interiorization' is synonymous.

Internalize: See **Internalization**.

Interpellation: The ways in which an individual is positioned in relation to the prevailing ideology and the process by which the individual is produced as a subject by that ideology.

Intersubjective: Subjective phenomena shared between persons; common experiences.

Intersubjectively Homogeneous: Individual subjective experience is an instance of common subjective experience that supports comprehension of the experience of oneself and the other.

Introspection: The internal examination of one's conscious experiences, thoughts and feelings. In psychology this becomes a method for analyzing inner mental states and phenomena.

Irritability: In biology a capacity to be responsive to external irritants and to respond to them. To Leontyev (1940/1981a), irritability is a stage of prepsychic material evolution that involves the property of living bodies to become active in response to external influences.

Just Noticeable Difference: The smallest difference in magnitude that can be subjectively detected when comparing stimuli of different magnitude (strength).

Just So Stories: Explanations offered for some biological characteristic, behavior, or cultural practice that is unverifiable.

Justificationism: In epistemology, the warranting of a belief, the assertion of correctness or truth, because it fits within a standard of acceptability such as agreement with experience.

Labor: The form of intentional behavior through which humans act upon objects of the natural world and transform them to satisfy human requirements. It is thought that in so changing nature the human is transformed in the process.

Law of Contradiction: In logic, the principle that something cannot be equal to or identical with that which is not itself (A ≠ not-A).

Law of Identity: In logic, the principle that a thing is identical with that which is exactly the same as itself (A = A).

Levels of Organization: The theory that the universe has evolved through successively increasingly more complex levels of integration (physical, chemical, biological, socio-cultural), which have resulted in the emergence of new phenomena and laws that, while dependent on lower levels, cannot be reduced to or predicted by them.

Libertarianism: The contention that people's thoughts and actions are free and that hard determinism is false.

Logical Positivism (logical empiricism, neo-positivism): A theory of science that proposes that the only basis of knowledge is that which is based upon direct sensory experience or immediate observation, or, if not directly observable, on what can be logically related to what is observable.

Materialism: The ontological proposition that asserts the primacy of matter, that asserts that all-that-is is of matter or is derived from matter.

Materialists: See **Materialism**.

Matter: That which is traditionally contrasted with mind; a substance considered the basis of all that is.

'Mechanical' Functionalism: The solution to the mind–body problem that proposes that being designated mental depends upon the function performed in a system regardless of the physical makeup of that system (brain or machine).

Mechanism: The proposition that nature and society operate according to laws of mechanics, of the physical forces and dynamics behind matter in motion.

Mechanistic: See **Mechanism**.

Mechanistic Materialism: A materialism that proposes that natural phenomena develop according to the laws of mechanics.

Mental Chronometry (temporal measurement): A research procedure that investigates the time that it takes to perform various mental processes like discrimination and decision.

Mental Reflection: The changes in the nervous system and mental processes through which the relationship with objective phenomena resonate.

Mentalism: A perspective that emphasizes the primacy of the mind; the position that certain mental phenomena cannot be reduced to physical phenomena without there being something left over—not accounted for. (See **anti-mentalism**.)

Mesoforms: In the **Concept of Integrative Levels** the proposition that the different levels of matter (e.g., inanimate and animate), while distinct from each other, are not fully delimited. Natural boundaries are not fixed and categories are not airtight and impermeable. Intermediate forms may exist at the transition points.

Metaphysical: See **Metaphysics**.

Metaphysics: The study of first principles, the ultimate nature of things, of what is fundamental. It is concerned with what exists, for instance matter or mind, of what can be known, or if knowledge has any basis in certainty, and the origins of all that is. (See **Cosmology**, **Epistemology**, and **Ontology**.)

Method of Doubt: The procedure whereby various beliefs are examined and all those that are not indubitably certain are rejected; the aim is to determine what is incontestably certain and to use that as a foundation for knowledge.

Method of Impression: A verbal report on the presence or absence of a range of stimuli that was used by physicists to determine the range of the visible and audible spectrum. Psychophysiologists adopted the method to study **absolute thresholds** and **just noticeable differences**.

Mind: The organized system of mental processes and activities (thoughts, emotions, intentions, and **acts** or behaviors). As so conceived the mental evades the metaphysical question of mind as **substance** and the **mind–body problem**.

Mind-Body Problem: The problem of what the relation, if any, is between mind and matter and whether one or the other does or does not exist as a **substance**.

Modernity: In the social sciences, modernity refers to a period of transformation in Europe after the medieval period that was represented by cultural changes in the move to urbanization, market economies, industrialization, and scientific inquiry. Psychologically, there was a new conception of the self as independent from social position and an emphasis on individuality. Scientifically, there was an emphasis on the investigator as detached and objective and an independent reality that was knowable.

Molar: Pertaining to a segment of a stream of activity that possesses unity or is organized as a single unit over time because it serves a common purpose or end.

Molecular: Of or related to simple elements.

Monism: An ontological position which asserts that the universe is composed of, or derived from, only one substance. This contrasts with **dualism** and the proposition of two substances which are irreducible to each other and independent, such as body or matter and mind.

Monistic: See **Monism**.

Multiple Realizability: The proposition that a particular mental property, occurrence, or state could be realized (brought about) by numerous physical existences.

Multiply Realizable: see **Multiple Realizability**.

Mutualism: The symbiotic interpenetration, inseparability, and bi-directional influence of conceptual opposites like organism and environment.

Mutuality: See **Mutualism**

Naïve Realism: The common-sense assumption that the world as it is experienced is the world as it is. It is naïve in its lack of awareness of the epistemological quandary regarding access to an objective reality.

Nativism: A position that holds that the mind comes equipped with certain innate ideas.

Natural Kinds: An organization into categories (sets of things sharing characteristics) whose shared characteristics are fixed by nature. See **Human Kinds**.

Naturalism: The proposition that all that exists belongs to the realm of nature and that what the natural sciences study is all that there is; supernatural explanatory propositions are considered unacceptable.

Naturalist: See **Naturalism**.

Naturalistic: See **Naturalism**.

Nature: An individual's inborn, biological endowment acquired through hereditary transmission.

Neutral Monism: A position that rejects the proposition that the universe or reality is based upon either the physical (material) or mental but posits, instead, a single substance that is metaphysically neutral.

Niche: Beyond habitat, the physical place an organism lives, a niche refers to all those conditions that affect an organism's continued existence. Within the same habitat there may be different niches depending on the species of concern.

Nihilism: The proposition that: 1) there is nothing that exists that is knowable; 2) nothing exists but, if it did and were known, one could not communicate that.

Nominalism: The assumption that because something can be named, that something so named is an actual existent.

Nomothetic: Characterized by procedures and methods designed to discover general laws.

Nurture: All of the environmental conditions that can affect development through experience, upbringing, or education.

Objective Idealism: An idealism that maintains that objective phenomena (beyond the individual) are spiritual or mental in nature.

Observational Statements: A series of words in a scientific theory that refer to directly experienced sense data.

Occasionalism: A dualistic solution to the mind–body problem which contends that mind and body, being wholly different substances, cannot interact. An event in one substance is accompanied by a corresponding event in the other because God intervenes between the two such that a change in one substance is an occasion for God to effect a change in the other.

Ontogenesis: The developmental history of the individual organism; individual growth and development (and increases in connectedness with the environment in the sense of **activity**).

Ontogenetically: See **Ontogenesis**.

Ontological: See **Ontology**.

Ontology: The branch of **metaphysics** that has as its concern the nature of existence as well as the issue of **appearance versus reality**.

Operational Definition: The definition of something by the procedures or operations by which it is detected, demonstrated, or measured.

Operationism: The doctrine that what a scientific term means should be defined in terms of the processes by which it is detected/demonstrated or measured (see **Operational Definition**).

Optical Flow: Movement-produced changes in the optic image as one moves toward or away from objects or as objects move relative to oneself and the environment.

Organicism: A biological theory that proposes that life is constituted by a dynamic system of organization within the organism. Life cannot be explained by reduction to component parts, e.g., material particles or cells, but to how such components are organized such that the whole has determinative influence over the parts; as a theory it opposes vitalism and mechanism. Organicism is the biological version of **holism**.

Organicist: A proponent of **Organicism**.

Pantheism: The doctrine that God is identical with all phenomena and universal.

Paradigm: A theoretical framework that directs the pursuit of a science, its standards, methods, and subject matter.

Parental Investment: In evolutionary theory the time and resources that each parent invests in the rearing of offspring. In most species it is the female that commits the greatest contribution which may render her more selective in mate choices by seeking a good provider whereas males may be more liberal in the dissemination of their seed.

Perceptual Concept(s): Concepts formed on the basis of directly perceived common properties.

Phenomenalism: The view that knowledge should be limited to subjective experience.

Phenomenology: A philosophy that has as its focus the description of experience (see **Phenomenalism**).

Phylogenesis: The evolutionary origins and development of a species.

Phylogenetically: See **Phylogenesis**

Physicalism: The proposition that everything is reducible to the language of physics and that physical language is a universal language for all sciences. Sometimes considered a version of **materialism**, but materialism is a metaphysical concept rejected by logical positivists.

Physicalist: An advocate of **Physicalism**.

Pluralism: The ontological proposition that the universe is composed of many kinds of substances rather than one or two.

Pluralist: An advocate of **Pluralism**.

Positivism: A theory of science that stresses limiting science to what can be directly observed.

Postmodern: See **Postmodernism**.

Postmodernism: A 20th-century movement towards subjectivism, relativism, and skepticism regarding objective knowledge by the claim that is known is a social construction and that 'truth' is historically and culturally relative.

Postmodernity: See **Postmodernism**.

Pragmatism: An epistemological theory that proposes that 'truth' is a matter of practical engagement with reality. The truth value of any proposition requires testing in practice (action in the world) and truth or falsity is determined by success in action.

Pragmatist: See **Pragmatism**.

Pre-established Harmony: Leibniz's proposition that mind and body are completely independent but there is a harmony between them because of a higher reality that they depend upon—God, and which preordained that they correspond with each other.

Presentationalism: The epistemological proposition that mind apperceives its object directly and that knowledge is of presentations; the world is presented directly to consciousness. This contrasts with **Representationalism**.

Presentationist: See **Presentationalism**.

Presentism: In the analysis of historical subject matter (including concepts), the tendency to assume that current perspectives are consistent with past explanations; the distortion of past understandings and practices by failing to appreciate their place in historical context.

Primary Qualities: Properties that are inherent to matter, natural to it.

Problem of Induction: The problem of uncertainty that arises from **induction by simple enumeration**; regardless of how many instances of a phenomenon have been found to have certain characteristics, there is no guarantee that such observations will never be negated in the future.

Proximate Explanation: In biology the explanation of a behavior based on the immediate causal conditions.

Psychogenic: Having psychological rather than organic origins.

Psychometricians: See **Psychometrics**.

Psychometrics: The science of measuring mental characteristics.

Psychophysical Parallelism: A solution to the mind–body problem that proposes that mind and body are two separate substances, that are not in contact in any way, but that an event in one is accompanied by a corresponding (parallel) event in the other.

Psychophysics: The investigation of the general relation between the physical stimulus and mental processes (sensations and perceptions).

Psychosomatic: Involving both mind (psycho) and body (somatic); a concern with the influence of mind on body and the relation between organic conditions and psychic phenomena.

Quantity/Quality Dialectic: The proposition that, after sufficient quantitative change, a qualitative change may occur.

Rationalism: An epistemological proposal that gives precedence to reason in the pursuit of truth or knowledge.

Realism: The epistemological position which asserts the existence of an independent, objective realm which is mind-independent yet knowable. (See **Direct Realism**, **Indirect Realism**, and **Naïve Realism**.)

Realist: See **Realism**.

Reduction: See **Reductionism**.

Reductionism: An approach to the analysis of complex phenomena by explaining them in terms of simpler constituent elements, at a lower level of organization and complexity, such as explaining psychological phenomena in terms of biological phenomena or the biological in terms of chemistry.

Reductionistic: See **Reductionism**.

Reflection: The process whereby an external agent acts upon, and leaves an impression on/in, some thing (an object or organism) such that the thing acted upon is changed in some way. Reflection can range from inorganic, e.g., a depression (dent) after a collision, to mental, e.g., the change in sensory processes by stimulation or the retention of an experience as a memory and the changes in the brain that support it.

Reflex Arc: A simple pathway in the nervous system that involves a nerve impulse transmitted through a sensory neuron (evoked by some stimulus), through a connecting neuron to a motor neuron (the response).

Reflexivity: An inquiry into one's own inner biases and presuppositions and how this informs or influences one's practices and constructions of knowledge; critical self-awareness.

Reification: The tendency to consider abstract qualities as though they possessed an actual, concrete existence, as though they were real, independent things.

Reified: See **Reification**.

Relativism: The epistemological stance which holds that what is true is true relative to the individual, group, or historical epoch; the criterion of truth rests with the knower rather than objective reality (belief in which is itself relative).

Reliability: In psychological testing, the degree to which a test gives consistent results; the accuracy and dependability of a test.

Representationalism: The view that the external is not directly presented to consciousness as mental appearance but that it can be reliably inferred from such appearances. (See **Presentationalism**.)

Repression: The unconscious strategy of the ego to exclude specific psychological experiences that are anxiety arousing from conscious awareness.

Restrictive Action Potence: Action potence is restrictive when it is not available to all in society and involves benefits being confined to particular individuals and at a cost to society at large.

Scaling: The process by which one determines how much of something is present and measures it.

Scientism: The exaltation of the methods of the natural sciences over all other forms of inquiry; the belief that scientific knowledge claims alone are meaningful or valid.

Secondary Qualities: Qualities that result from primary qualities acting upon sensory registers.

Sensationalism: The view that experience is based upon sensation and that sensation is the sole source of knowledge.

Sign: An object or phenomenon that represents (symbolizes, carries the meaning of) some other object or phenomenon, that has a significance beyond itself and which it communicates.

Skeptic: One who advocates **Skepticism**.

Skepticism: The approach that doubts or maintains disbelief regarding the possibility of objective knowledge.

Social Constructionism: See **Constructionism**.

Social Darwinism: The theory that advocates an evolutionary ideology designed to improve the makeup of the individual, composing a society by allowing them to compete with each other in the struggle to survive, without social interference, so that the ablest will survive and contribute to the perfection of subsequent generations, while eliminating those least capable, just as nature intended.

Socialization: The process by which an individual acquires sensitivity to social stimuli, especially other people, and learns to act in ways that are in accordance with the group and becomes a social being, is made social.

Societal: Having reference to life in society.

Sociogenesis: Originating in and arising out of social relations and experience.

Solipsism: The proposition that the only certainty that one can have is of one's own experience or existence.

Sophist: One who practices deceptive argumentation.

Spontaneous Generation: The proposition that living forms can develop from non-living material; the living is generated spontaneously from the non-living.

Stoicism: Given complete determinism, and the predetermination of everything, including oneself, wisdom dictates acceptance of one's position and indifference to pleasure and pain.

Subjective Idealism: An idealism that maintains that whatever exists beyond one's sensory experience or perception is inaccessible to consciousness or does not exist.

Subjective Idealist: See **Subjective Idealism**.

Substance: 1) That which underlies outward phenomena; 2) that upon which all else relies for existence but which relies upon nothing for its own existence, it being primary.

Supernatural: see **Supernaturalism**.

Supernaturalism: Any belief in phenomena that exist outside of the realm of the natural.

Supervenience: A relation of dependency of one set of qualities or properties on another set of qualities or properties, such as the mental being supervenient upon the physical.

Survival of the Fittest: In the struggle for existence within a species, and given environmental demands and resource availability, those that are best suited to the environmental conditions and demands will succeed in the competition to survive.

System: A collection of components that work together as interconnected parts within an organized whole.

Teleology: An explanation given in terms of final causes or ends. The belief that all of nature has an inherent purpose or end that directs it from within. Mechanistic explanations reject inherent purpose or design. In humans, goals or purposes may be acquired rather than inherent.

Theoretical Statements: A series of words whose validity cannot be established through direct observation.

Theory Laden: The proposition that observations, no matter how objective, are initiated by theories.

Tradition of Separation and Isolation: The tendency to abstract qualitative differences and to artificially isolate the differentiated characteristics from each other (see **Reification**).

Trial and Error: A form of learning wherein an organism engages in a broad array of responses to a problem situation and gradually weakens and eliminates ineffective responses while increasing the frequency of the production of effective responses.

Turing Test: If the responses of a programmed machine cannot be distinguished from the responses of a human being, the machine may be said to think.

Twin Method: A method of estimating heritability by comparing the degree of similarity of identical and fraternal twins on some characteristic. If biologically based the identical twins should demonstrate a higher level of similarity.

Typology (in biology): The conception of a population as a species when its morphology and behavior are sufficiently demarcated from other populations. (See also **Essentialism**.)

Ultimate Explanation: In biology the explanation of a behavior or function in terms of the evolutionary forces that acted upon them.

Unconscious Inference Theory: The explanation of what is perceived as being the end result of incoming sensory information being matched against prior sensory input, and an inference made outside of consciousness as to what might be going on in the objective realm beyond the senses.

Unity of Science: The proposition of the logical positivists that physics is the basic science and, further, that all other branches of science should be reducible to the language and methods of physics (assuming **phenomenalism** as basic to all science).

Vademecum Science: A science whose principles and practices are so well established and unquestioned that they are contained within a catechism-like reference manual; preordained principles and procedures.

Validity: The demonstration that a test measures what it was intended to be a measure of.

Variable Psychology: The standard experimental-statistical method of psychology that examines the relationship between variables (independent and dependent) in the search for lawful generalizations. The subject matter is that of variables rather than persons as subjective beings in relation to their societal contexts.

Verbal Report: Traditionally, a verbal statement regarding what is being experienced consciously (central to the introspective method); in the hands of Watson, an overt response pure and simple that gave no report of conscious states, a mere production of sound.

Verifiability Principle: The meaning of a proposition is the means by which it is verified, its meaning is the method of its verification; verification determines truth or falsity of a statement; it rejects metaphysical statements as unverifiable.

Verisimilitude: The appearance of truth or truthlikeness.

Vitalism: The proposition that living entities possess properties that exceed their constituent physico-chemical properties.

Völkerpsychologie: Roughly this refers to the folks psychology, which includes cultural psychology and indigenous psychology, and is a perspective that considers individual psychology as conditioned by the prevailing cultural spirit, knowledge structures, and institutions.

REFERENCES

Abbagnano, N. (1967). Positivism. In P. Edwards (Ed.), *The encyclopedia of philosophy*(Vol. 6, pp. 414–419). New York: Macmillan.

Abramson, L. V., Seligman, M. E. P., and Teasdale, J. D. (1978). Learned helplessness in humans: Critique and reformulation. *Journal of Abnormal Psychology, 87*, 49–74.

Achtemeier, P. J. (1990). Omne verbum sonat: The New Testament and the oral environment of late Western antiquity. *Journal of Biblical Literature, 109*, 3–27.

Acton, H. B. (1951). Comte's positivism and the science of society. *Philosophy, 26*, 291–310.

Adams, H. F. (1930). An objectivity-subjectivity ratio for scales of measurement. *Journal of Social Psychology, 1*, 122–135.

Adler, A. (1927). *Understanding human nature.* Garden City, NY: Garden City Publishing.

Adler, A. (1957). The progress of mankind. *Journal of Individual Psychology, 13*, 3–13.

Alexander, F. G. and Selesnick, S. T. (1966). *The history of psychiatry: An evaluation of psychiatric thought and practice from prehistoric times to the present.* New York: Harper & Row.

Alexander, P. (1964). The philosophy of science, 1859–1910. In D. J. O'Connor (Ed.), *A critical history of Western philosophy* (pp. 402–425). New York: The Free Press.

Alexander, W. F. (1934). Research in guidance: A theoretical basis. *Occupations, 12*, 75–91.

Allen, J. M. (1869). On the real differences in the minds of men and women. *Journal of the Anthropological Society of London, 7*, cxcv–ccxix.

Allison, H. E. (1998). Spinoza, Benedict de (1632–1677). In E. Craig (Ed.), *Routledge encyclopedia of philosophy* (Vol. 9, pp. 91–107). London: Routledge.

Allport, G. W. (1924). The study of the undivided personality. *Journal of Abnormal and Social Psychology, 19*, 132–141.

Allport, G. W. (1927). Concepts of trait and personality. *Psychological Bulletin, 24*, 284–293.

Allport, G. W. (1928). A test for ascendance-submission. *Journal of Abnormal and Social Psychology, 23*, 118–136.

Allport, G. W. (1934). Book review: R. C. Perry. A group factor analysis of the adjustment questionnaire. *Character and Personality, 3*, 169–170.

Allport, G. W. (1937). *Personality: A psychological interpretation.* New York: Henry Holt.

Allport, G. W. (1942). The use of personal documents in psychological science. *Social Science Research Council Bulletin, 49*, xi–201.

Allport, G. W. (1947). Scientific models and human morals. *Psychological Review, 54*, 182–192.

Allport, G. W. (1955). *Becoming: Basic considerations for a psychology of personality.* New Haven, CT: Yale University Press.

Allport, G. W. (1961). *Pattern and growth in personality.* New York: Holt, Rinehart and Winston.

Allport, G. W. (1962). The general and the unique in psychological science. *Journal of Personality, 30*, 405–422.

Allport, G. W. and Odbert, H. S. (1936). Trait names: A psycholexical study. *Psychological Monographs, 47* (1, Whole No. 211).

Altman, I. (1987). Community psychology twenty years later: Still another crisis in psychology. *American Journal of Community Psychology, 15*, 613–627.

American Psychological Association (1953). *Ethical standards of psychologists.* Washington, DC: The American Psychological Association.

American Psychological Association (2002). Ethical principles of psychologists and code of conduct. *American Psychologist, 57*, 1060–1073.

American Psychological Association (2009). *Publication manual of the American Psychological Association* (6th ed.). Washington, DC: American Psychological Association.

Angyal, A. (1958). *Foundations for a science of personality*. Cambridge, MA: Harvard University Press. (Originally published 1941.)

Arnett, J. I. (2008). The neglected 95%: Why American psychology needs to become less American. *American Psychologist, 63*, 602–614.

Ash, M. G. (1998). *Gestalt psychology in German culture 1890–1967: Holism and the quest for objectivity.* Cambridge: Cambridge University Press.

Austin, S. and Prilleltensky, I. (2001). Diverse origins, common aims: The challenge of critical psychology. *Radical Psychology, 2*, 1–13.

Ayala, F. J. (1968). Biology as an autonomous science. *American Scientist, 56*, 207–221.

Ayers, M. (1998). Locke, John (1632–1704). In E. Craig (Ed.), *Routledge encyclopedia of philosophy* (Vol. 5, pp. 665–687). London: Routledge.

Baddeley, A. D. and Hitch, G. (1974). Working memory. In G. A. Bower (Ed.), *The psychology of learning and motivation* (Vol. 8, pp. 47–90). New York: Academic Press.

Baier, A. (1998). Hume, David (1711–1776). In E. Craig (Ed.), *Routledge encyclopedia of philosophy*. (Vol. 8, pp. 543–562). London: Routledge.

Baillargeon, R. (1986). Representing the existence and the location of hidden objects: Object permanence in 6- and 8-month-old infants. *Cognition, 23*, 21–41.

Bakan, D. (1967). *On method: Toward a reconstruction of psychological investigation.* San Francisco, CA: Jossey-Bass.

Baker, W. J. (91992). Positivism versus people: What should psychology be about? In C. W. Tolman (Ed.), *Positivism in psychology: Historical and contemporary problems* (pp. 9–16). New York: Springer-Verlag.

Bandura, A. (1977). Self-efficacy: Toward a unifying theory of behavioral change. *Psychological Review, 84*, 191–215.

Bandura, A. (1989). Human agency in social cognitive theory. *American Psychologist, 44*, 1175–1184.

Bandura, A. (2006). Toward a psychology of human agency. *Perspective on Psychological Science, 1*, 164–180.

Bandura, A. (2008). Reconstrual of 'free will' from the agentic perspective of social cognitive theory. In J. Baer, J. C. Kaufman, and R. F. Baumeister (Eds.), *Are we free? Psychology and free will* (pp. 86–127). Oxford: Oxford University Press.

Barber, T. X. (1984). Changing 'unchangeable' bodily processes by (hypnotic) suggestions: A new look at hypnosis, cognitions, imagining, and the mind–body problem. In A. A. Sheikh (Ed.), *Imagination and healing* (Imagery and human development series, pp. 69–127). Farmingdale, NY: Baywood Publishing.

Barker, R. G. (1968). *Ecological psychology: Concepts and methods for studying the environment for human behavior.* Stanford, CA: Stanford University Press.

Barnes, M. H. (1984). *In the presence of mystery: An introduction to the story of human religiousness.* Mystic, CT: Twenty-Third Publications.

Barrett, L., Dunbar, R., and Lycett, J. (2002). *Human evolutionary psychology.* Princeton, NJ: Princeton University Press.

Bartlett, F. C. (1916). An experimental study of some problems of perceiving and imaging. *British Journal of Psychology, 8*, 222–266.

Bartlett, F. C. (1920). Experiments on the reproduction of folk-stories. *Folklore, 31*, 30–47.

Bartlett, F. C. (1932). *Remembering: A study in experimental and social psychology.* Cambridge: Cambridge University Press.

Baumeister, R. F. (2010). Understanding free will and consciousness on the basis of current research findings in psychology. In R. F. Baumeister, A. R. Mele, and K. D. Vohs (Eds.), *Free will and consciousness: How might they work?* (pp. 24–42). Oxford: Oxford University Press.

Baumrind, D. (1964). Some thoughts on ethics of research: After reading Milgram's 'behavioral study of obedience.' *American Psychologist, 19*, 421–423.

Beckner, M. O. (1967). Vitalism. In P. Edwards (Ed.), *The encyclopedia of philosophy* (Vol. 8, pp. 253–256). New York: Macmillan Publishing Co., Inc. & The Free Press.

Bem, S. L. and Bem, D. J. (1971). Training the woman to know her place: The power of a nonconscious ideology. In M. H. Garskof (Ed.), *Roles women play: Readings toward women's liberation* (pp. 84–96). Belmont, CA: Brooks/Cole Publishing.

Bereczkei, T. (2000). Evolutionary psychology: A new perspective in the behavioral sciences. *European Psychologist, 5*, 175–190.

Berg, I. A. (1954). The use of human subjects in psychological research. *American Psychologist, 9*, 108–111.

Bernstein, D. A., Clarke-Stewart, A., Roy, E. J., and Wickens, C. D. (1997). *Psychology* (4th ed.). Boston, MA: Houghton Mifflin.

Bersoff, D. N. (2008). A short history of the development of the APA's ethics codes. In D. N. Bersoff (Ed.), *Ethical conflicts in psychology* (pp. 10–13). Washington, DC: American Psychological Association.

Best, J. B. (1999). *Cognitive psychology* (5th ed.). Belmont, CA: Wadsworth.

Bevan, W. (1991). Contemporary psychology: A tour inside the onion. *American Psychologist*, *46*, 475–483.

Billig, M. (1994). Repopulating the depopulated pages of social psychology. *Theory & Psychology*, *4*, 307–335.

Billig, M. (2008). *The hidden roots of critical psychology*. Los Angeles, CA: SAGE Publications.

Bills, A. G. (1938). Changing views of psychology as a science. *Psychological Review*, *45*, 377–394.

Binet, A. and Simon, T. (1916a). Upon the necessity of establishing a scientific diagnosis of inferior states of intelligence. In A. Binet and T. Simon, *The development of intelligence in children* (pp. 9–36). Baltimore, MD: Williams and Wilkins. (Originally published 1905.)

Binet, A. and Simon, T. (1916b). New methods for the diagnosis of intellectual level of subnormals. In A. Binet and T. Simon, *The development of intelligence in children* (pp. 37–90). Baltimore, MD: Williams and Wilkins. (Originally published 1905.)

Binet, A. and Simon, T. (1916c). Application of the new methods to the diagnosis of the intellectual level among normal and subnormal children in institutions and primary schools. In A. Binet and T. Simon, *The development of intelligence in children* (pp. 91–181). Baltimore, MD: Williams and Wilkins. (Originally published 1905.)

Blake, R. M., Ducasse, C. J., and Madden, E. H. (1960). *Theories of scientific method: The Renaissance through the nineteenth century.* Seattle, WA: University of Washington Press.

Bleier, R. (1984). *Science and gender: A critique of biology and its theories on women.* New York: Pergamon Press.

Block, J. and Block, J. H. (1981). Studying situational dimensions: A grand perspective and some limited empiricism. In D. Magnusson (Ed.), *Toward a psychology of situations: An interactional perspective* (pp. 85–102). Hillsdale, NJ: Lawrence Erlbaum Associates.

Blumenthal, A. L. (2001). A Wundt primer: The operating characteristics of consciousness. In R. W. Rieber and D. K. Robinson (Eds.), *Wilhelm Wundt in history* (pp. 121–144). New York: Kluwer Academic/Plenum.

Boesch, C. (2005). Joint cooperative hunting among wild chimpanzees: Taking natural observations seriously. *Behavioral and Brain Sciences*, *28*, 692–692.

Boesch, C. and Boesch, H. (1989). Hunting behavior of wild chimpanzees in the Taï National Park. *American Journal of Physical Anthropology*, *78*, 547–573.

Boring, E. G. (1929). *A history of experimental psychology.* New York: Appleton-Century-Crofts.

Boring, E. G. (1933). *The physical dimensions of consciousness.* New York: The Century Company.

Boring, E. G. (1961). The beginning and growth of measurement in psychology. *Isis*, *52*, 238–257.

Borst, C. V. (1970). Editor's introduction. In C. V. Borst (Ed.), *The mind-brain identity theory* (pp. 13–29). London: Macmillan.

Bowen, W. (2007). *A complaint free world: How to stop complaining and start enjoying the life you always wanted.* New York: Three Rivers Press.

Braginsky, D. D. (1985). Psychology: Handmaiden to society. In S. Koch and D. E. Leary (Eds.), *A century of psychology as science* (pp. 880–891). New York: McGraw-Hill.

Bräuer, J. and Call, J. (2011). The magic cup: Great apes and domestic dogs (*canis familiaris*) individuate objects according to their properties. *Journal of Comparative Psychology*, *125*, 353–361.

Brazier, M. A. B. (1959). The historical development of neurophysiology. In J. Field, H. W. Magoun, and V. E. Hall (Eds.), *Handbook of physiology, Vol. 1: Neurophysiology* (pp. 1–58). Washington, DC: American Physiological Society.

Brennan, J. F. (1982). *History and systems of psychology.* Englewood Cliffs, NJ: Prentice Hall.

Brentano, F. (1998). Excerpt from *Psychology from an empirical standpoint (1874)*. In J. F. Brennan (Ed.), *Readings in the history and systems of psychology* (2nd ed, pp. 115–135). Upper Saddle River, NJ: Prentice Hall.

Bresler, D. (1984). Mind-controlled analgesia: The inner way to pain control. In A. A. Sheikh (Ed.), *Imagination and healing* (Imagery and human development series, pp. 211–230). Farmingdale, NY: Baywood Publishing.

Broadbent, D. E. (1957). A mechanical model for human attention and immediate memory. *Psychological Review*, *64*, 205–215.

Broadbent, D. E. (1958). *Perception and communication.* Oxford: Pergamon Press.

Brown, R. (1963). *Explanation in social science.* Chicago, IL: Alpine Publishing.

Brown, R. E. (2007). Alfred McCoy, Hebb, the CIA and torture. *Journal of the History of the Behavioral Sciences*, *43*, 205–213.

Brown, S. D. and Stenner, P. (2009). *Psychology without foundations: History, philosophy, and psychosocial theory.* London: SAGE Publications.

Bryan, W. L. and Harter, N. (1897). Studies in the physiology and psychology of the telegraphic language. *Psychological Review*, *4*, 27–53.

Bryan, W. L. and Harter, N. (1899). Studies on the telegraphic language: The acquisition of a hierarchy of habits. *Psychological Review*, 6, 345–375.

Bryant, J. M. (1986). Intellectuals and religion in ancient Greece: Notes on a Weberian theme. *British Journal of Sociology*, 37, 269–296.

Budge, G. S. and Katz, B. (1995). Constructing psychological knowledge: Reflections on science, scientists and epistemology in the APA Publication Manual. *Theory & Psychology*, 5, 217–231.

Buller, D. J. (2009). Four fallacies of pop evolutionary psychology. *Scientific American*, 300, 74–81.

Burnyeat, M. F. (1976). Protagoras and self-refutation in Plato's Theaetetus. *Philosophical Review*, 85, 172–195.

Burt, C. (1914). The measurement of intelligence by the Binet tests. *Eugenics Review*, 6, 36–50.

Burt, C. (1962). Francis Galton and his contributions to psychology. *British Journal of Statistical Psychology*, 15, 1–49.

Burtt, E. A. (1980). *The metaphysical foundations of modern physical science*. Atlantic Highlands, NJ: Humanities Press. (Originally published 1952.)

Burtt, H. A. (1938). *Psychology of advertising*. Boston, MA: Houghton Mifflin.

Buss, D. M. (1989). Sex differences in human mate preferences: Evolutionary hypotheses tested in 37 cultures. *Behavioral and Brain Sciences*, 12, 1–49.

Buss, D. M. (1995). Evolutionary psychology: A new paradigm for psychological science. *Psychological Inquiry*, 6, 1–30.

Byrne, R. B. (1995). *The thinking ape: Evolutionary origins of intelligence*. Oxford: Oxford University Press.

Campbell, D. T. (1960). Recommendations for APA test standards regarding construct, trait, or discriminant validity. *American Psychologist*, 15, 546–553.

Campbell, D. T. and Fiske, D. W. (1959). Convergent and discriminant validation by the multitrait-multimethod matrix. *Psychological Bulletin*, 56, 81–105.

Campbell, K. and Smith, N. J. J. (1998). Epiphenomenalism. In E. Craig (Ed.), *Routledge encyclopedia of philosophy* (Vol. 3, pp. 351–354). London: Routledge.

Campbell, R. and Wasco, S. M. (2000). Feminist approaches to social science: Epistemological and methodological tenets. *American Journal of Community Psychology*, 28, 773–791.

Cantril, H., Ames, A., Hastorf, A. H., and Ittelson, W. H. (1949a). Psychology and scientific research, II: Scientific inquiry and scientific method. *Science*, 110, 491–497.

Cantril, H., Ames, A., Hastorf, A. H., and Ittelson, W. H. (1949b). Psychology and scientific research, III: The transactional view in psychological research. *Science*, 110, 517–522.

Carlson, R. (1971). Where is the person in personality research? *Psychological Bulletin*, 75, 203–219.

Carlson, R. (1972). Understanding women: Implications for personality theory and research. *Journal of Social Issues*, 28, 17–32.

Carmichael, L. (1926). Sir Charles Bell: Contribution to the history of physiological psychology. *Psychological Review*, 33, 188–217.

Carnap, R. (1959). Psychology in physical language. In A. J. Ayer (Ed.), *Logical positivism* (pp. 165–198). New York: The Free Press. (Originally published 1932/33.)

Carpenter, W. B. (1896). *Principles of mental physiology* (7th ed.). London: Kegan Paul. Trench, Trübner & Co. (Originally published 1874.)

Cattell, J. M. (1886). The time it takes to see and name objects. *Mind*, 11, 63–65.

Cattell, J. M. (1888). The psychological laboratory at Leipsic. *Mind*, 13, 37–51.

Cattell, J. M. (1890). Mental tests and measurements. *Mind*, 15, 373–381.

Cattell, J. M. (1893). Mental measurement. *Philosophical Review*, 2, 316–332.

Cattell, J. M. and Farrand, L. (1896). Physical and mental measurements of the students of Columbia University. *Psychological Review*, 3, 618–648.

Cattell, R. B. (1966). Personality structure: The larger dimensions. In B. Semeonoff (Ed.), *Personality assessment* (pp. 323–341). Harmondsworth: Penguin Books.

Cervone, D. and Pervin, L. A. (2010). *Personality: Theory and research* (11th ed.). Hoboken, NJ: Wiley.

Chaisson, E. (1981). *Cosmic dawn: The origins of matter and life*. Boston, MA: Little, Brown and Company.

Charness, N. (1983). Age, skill, and bridge bidding: A chronometric analysis. *Journal of Verbal Learning and Verbal Behavior*, 22, 406–416.

Cherry, E. C. (1953). Some experiments on the recognition of speech, with one and with two ears. *Journal of the Acoustical Society of America*, 25, 975–979.

Chi, M. T. H., Feltovich, P. J., and Glaser, R. (1981). Categorization and representation of physics problems by experts and novices. *Cognitive Science, 5*, 121–152.

Chiel, H. J. and Beer, R. D. (1997). The brain has a body: Adaptive behavior emerges from interactions of nervous system, body and environment. *Trends in Neurosciences, 20*, 553–557.

Chomsky, N. (1956). Three models for the description of language. *IRE Transactions on Information Theory, 2*, 113–124.

Chomsky, N. (1959). Review: Verbal behavior. *Language, 35*, 26–58.

Chrisomalis, S. (2010). *Numerical notation: A comparative history.* Cambridge: Cambridge University Press.

Christopher, J. C., Wendt, D. C., Marecek, J., and Goodman, D. M. (2014). Critical cultural awareness: Contributions to a globalizing psychology. *American Psychologist, 69*, 645–655.

Churchland, P. M. (1982). Is *thinker* a natural kind? *Dialogue, 21*, 223–238.

Churchland, P. M. (1988). *Matter and consciousness: A contemporary introduction to the philosophy of mind* (rev. ed.). Cambridge, MA: The MIT Press.

Churchland, P. S. (1986). *Neurophilosophy: Toward a unified science of the mind-brain.* Cambridge, MA: The MIT Press.

Churchland, P. S. and Churchland, P. M. (1983). Stalking the wild epistemic engine. *Nous, 17*, 5–18.

Churchland, P. S. and Sejnowski, T. J. (1990). Neurophilosophy and connectionism. In W. G. Lycan (Ed.), *Mind and cognition: A reader* (pp. 224–252). Oxford: Blackwell.

Cioffi-Revilla, C. (1996). Origins and evolution of war and politics. *International Studies Quarterly, 40*, 1–22.

Clark, G. and Piggott, S. (1990). *Prehistoric societies.* London: Penguin Books. (Originally published 1965.)

Clodd, E. (1904). *The story of the alphabet.* New York: McClure, Phillips.

Comas-Díaz, L., Lykes, M. B., and Alarcón, R. D. (1998). Ethnic conflict and the psychology of liberation in Guatemala, Peru, and Puerto Rico. *American Psychologist, 53*, 778–792.

Confer, J. C., Easton, J. A., Fleischman, D. S., Goetz, C. D., Lewis, D. M. G., Perilloux, C., and Buss, D. M. (2010). Evolutionary psychology: Controversies, questions, prospects, and limitations. *American Psychologist, 65*, 110–126.

Coren, S., Ward, L. M., and Enns, J. T. (1994). *Sensation and perception* (4th ed.). Fort Worth, TX: Harcourt Brace.

Cork, J. (1949). John Dewey, Karl Marx, and democratic socialism. *The Antioch Review, 9*, 435–452.

Cork, J. (1950). John Dewey and Karl Marx. In S. Hook (Ed.), *John Dewey: Philosopher of science and freedom* (pp. 331–350). New York: The Dial Press.

Cornforth, M. (1963). *The theory of knowledge* (3rd ed.). New York: International.

Cosmides, L. and Tooby, J. (1989). Evolutionary psychology and the generation of culture, part II. Case study: A computational theory of social exchange. *Ethology and Sociobiology, 10*, 51–97.

Cowles, M. (1989). *Statistics in psychology: An historical perspective.* Hillsdale, NJ: Lawrence Erlbaum Associates.

Cowles, M. (2001). *Statistics in psychology* (2nd ed.). New York: Psychology Press.

Craik, K. J. W. (1948). Theory of human operator in control systems, II: Man as an element in a control system. *British Journal of Psychology, 38*, 142–148.

Crawford, M. and Marecek, J. (1989). Psychology reconstructs the female: 1968–1988. *Psychology of Women Quarterly, 13*, 147–165.

Creath, R. (1998). Carnap, Rudolph (1891–1970). In E. Craig (Ed.), *Routledge encyclopedia of philosophy* (Vol. 2, pp. 208–215). London: Routledge.

Crick, F. (1966). *Of molecules and men.* Seattle, WA: University of Washington Press.

Crick, F. and Asanuma, C. (1986). Certain aspects of the anatomy and physiology of the cerebral cortex. In J. L. McLelland and D. E. Rumelhart (Eds.), *Parallel distributed processing: Explorations in the microstructure of cognition, Vol. 2: Psychological and biological models* (pp. 333–371). Cambridge, MA: The MIT Press.

Crick, F. H. C. and Orgel, L. E. (1973). Directed panspermia. *Icarus, 19*, 341–346.

Cronbach, L. J. (1957). The two disciplines of scientific psychology. *American Psychologist, 12*, 671–684.

Crosby, A. W. (1997). *The measure of reality.* Cambridge: Cambridge University Press.

Crosier, B. S., Webster, G. D., and Dillon, H. M. (2012). Wired to connect: Evolutionary psychology and social networks. *Review of General Psychology, 16*, 230–239.

Crump, T. (2001). *A brief history of science as seen through the development of scientific instruments.* London: Robinson.

Dafermos, M. and Marvakis, A. (2006). Critiques in psychology—critical psychology. *Annual Review of Critical Psychology, 5*, 1–20.

Damrosch, L. (1979). Hobbes as reformation theologian: Implications of the free-will controversy. *Journal of the History of Ideas, 40*, 339–352.

Danziger, K. (1979). The positivist repudiation of Wundt. *Journal of the History of the Behavioral Sciences*, *15*, 205–230.

Danziger, K. (1983). Origins and basic principles of Wundt's *Völkerpsychologie*. *British Journal of Social Psychology*, *22*, 303–313.

Danziger, K. (1985). The methodological imperative in psychology. *Philosophy of the Social Sciences*, *15*, 1–13.

Danziger, K. (1988). A question of identity: Who participated in psychological research. In J. G. Morawski (Ed.), *The rise of experimentation in American psychology* (pp. 35–52). New Haven, CT: Yale University Press.

Danziger, K. (1990a). Generative metaphor and the history of psychological discourse. In D. F. Leary (Ed.), *Metaphors in the history of psychology* (pp. 331–356). Cambridge: Cambridge University Press.

Danziger, K. (1990b). *Constructing the subject: Historical origins of psychological research.* Cambridge: Cambridge University Press.

Danziger, K. (1993). Psychological objects, practice, and history. *Annals of Theoretical Psychology*, *8*, 15–47.

Danziger, K. (1996). The practice of psychological discourse. In C. F. Graumann and K. J. Gergen (Eds.), *Historical dimensions of psychological discourse* (pp. 17–35). Cambridge: Cambridge University Press.

Danziger, K. (2008). *Marking the mind: A history of memory.* Cambridge: Cambridge University Press.

Danziger, K. (2009). The holy grail of universality. In T. Teo, P. Stenner, A. Rutherford, E. Park, and C. Baerveldt (Eds.), *Varieties of theoretical psychology: International philosophical and practical concerns* (pp. 2–11). Concord, CA: Captus University Publications.

Danziger, K. and Dzinas, K. (1997). How psychology got its variables. *Canadian Psychology*, *38*, 43–48.

Darwin, C. (1998). *The descent of man.* Amherst, NY: Prometheus Books. (Originally published 1874.)

David, H. P., Fleischhacker, J., and Hohn, C. (1988). Abortion and eugenics in Nazi Germany. *Population and Developmental Review*, *14*, 81–112.

Davis, H. (1992). Transitive inference in rats (*Rattus norvegicus*). *Journal of Comparative Psychology*, *106*, 342–349.

Davis, P. J. and Schwartz, G. E. (1987). Repression and the inaccessibility of affective memories. *Journal of Personality and Social Psychology*, *52*, 155–162.

De Carvalho, J. E. C. and Dunker, C. I. L. (2006). Critical psychological approaches in Brazil: When, where, why. *Annual Review of Critical Psychology*, *5*, 305–312.

Deese, J. (1959). The influence of inter-item associative strength upon immediate free recall. *Psychological Reports*, *5*, 305–312.

Dennis, R. M. (1995). Social Darwinism, scientific racism, and the metaphysics of race. *Journal of Negro Education*, *64*, 243–252.

Denzin, N. K. and Lincoln, Y. S. (1994). Introduction: Entering the field of qualitative research. In N. K. Denzin and Y. S. Lincoln (Eds.), *Handbook of qualitative research* (pp. 1–17). Thousand Oaks, CA: SAGE Publications.

Derry, T. K. and Williams, T. I. (1970). *A short history of technology.* London: Oxford University Press. (Originally published 1960.)

Descartes, R. (1993). *Meditation on first philosophy in which the existence of God and the distinction of the soul from the body are demonstrated* (3rd ed.). Indianapolis, IN: Hackett Publishing. (Originally published 1641.)

Dewey, J. (1884). The new psychology. *Andover Review*, *2*, 278–289.

Dewey, J. (1896). The reflex arc concept in psychology. *Psychological Review*, *3*, 357–370.

Dewey, J. (1898). Evolution and ethics. *Monist*, *8*, 321–341.

Dewey, J. (1902). Interpretation of savage mind. *Psychological Review*, *9*, 217–230.

Dewey, J. (1916). *Essays in experimental logic.* New York: Dover Publications.

Dewey, J. (1917). The need for a social psychology. *Psychological Review*, *24*, 266–277.

Dewey, J. (1922). *Human nature and conduct: An introduction to social psychology.* New York: Henry Holt.

Dewey, J. (1928). Body and mind. *Mental Hygiene*, *12*, 1–17.

Dewey, J. (1929). *The quest for certainty: A study of the relation of knowledge and action.* New York: Minton, Balch and Company.

Dewey, J. (1938). *Logic: The theory of inquiry.* New York: Henry Holt.

Dewey, J. (1948). *Reconstruction in philosophy.* Boston, MA: The Beacon Press. (Original work published 1920.)

Dewey, J. (1958). *Experience and nature.* New York: Dover Publications. (Originally published 1925.)

Dewey, J. (1960). *How we think.* Lexington, MA: D. C. Heath. (Originally published 1910.)

Dewey, J. (1961). *Democracy and education.* New York: The Macmillan Company. (Originally published 1916.)

Dewey, J. (1989). *Freedom and culture.* Buffalo, NY: Prometheus Books. (Originally published 1939.)

Dewey, J. (1998). The existential matrix of inquiry: Cultural. In L. A. Hickman and T. M. Alexander (Eds.), *The essential Dewey, Vol. 2: Ethics, logic, psychology* (pp. 78–87). Bloomington, IN: Indiana University Press. (Originally published 1938.)

Dewey, J. and Bentley, A. F. (1949). *Knowing and the known.* Boston, MA: Beacon Press.

Dewey, J., Hook, S., and Nagel, E. (1945). Are naturalists materialists? *The Journal of Philosophy*, *42*, 515–530.

Dilman, I. (1999). *Free will: An historical and philosophical introduction*. London: Routledge.

Dilthey, W. (1972). The rise of hermeneutics. *New Literary History*, *3*, 229–244. (Originally published 1910.)

Dilthey, W. (1977a). Ideas concerning a descriptive and analytic psychology. In W. Dilthey, *Descriptive psychology and historical understanding* (pp. 23–120). The Hague, the Netherlands: Martinus Nijhoff. (Originally published 1894.)

Dilthey, W. (1977b). The understanding of other persons and their expressions of life. In W. Dilthey, *Descriptive psychology and historical understanding* (pp. 123–144). The Hague, the Netherlands: Martinus Nijhoff. (Originally published 1927.)

Dixon, M. (1971). Why women's liberation. In M. H. Garskof (Ed.), *Roles women play: Readings toward women's liberation* (pp. 165–178). Belmont, CA: Brooks/Cole Publishing.

Domjan, M. (1993). *Domjan and Burkhard's* The principles of learning and behavior (3rd ed.). (Revised by M. Domjan.) Pacific Grove, CA: Brooks/Cole.

Drever, J. (1952). *The Penguin dictionary of psychology*. Hammondsworth: Penguin Books.

Driesch, H. (1914). *The history and theory of vitalism* (C. K. Ogden, Trans.). London: Macmillan and Co.

Driver-Linn, E. (2003). Where is psychology going? Structural fault lines revealed by psychologists' use of Kuhn. *American Psychologist*, *58*, 269–278.

Duncan, A. R. C. (1952). The stoic view of life. *Phoenix*, *6*, 123–138.

Dunlap, K. (1961). Knight Dunlap. In C. Murchison (Ed.), *A history of psychology in autobiography* (Vol. 2, pp. 35–61). New York: Russell and Russell. (Originally published 1930.)

Dunnette, M. D. (1966). Fads, fashions, and folderol in psychology. *American Psychologist*, *21*, 343–352.

Dupré, J. (1988). Materialism, physicalism, and scientism. *Philosophical Topics*, *16*, 31–56.

Eagly, A. H. and Riger, S. (2014). Feminism and psychology: Critiques of methods and epistemology. *American Psychologist*, *69*, 685–702.

Ebbinghaus, H. (1911). *Psychology: An elementary text-book*. Boston, MA: D. C. Heath.

Ebbinghaus, H. (1964). *Memory: A contribution to experimental psychology*. New York: Dover Publications. (Originally published 1885.)

Eccles, J. C. (1985). Mental summation: The timing of voluntary intentions by cortical activity. *Behavioral and Brain Sciences*, *8*, 542–543.

Eccles, J. C. (1989). *Evolution of the brain: Creation of the self*. London: Routledge.

Edelman, G. (2001). Consciousness: The remembered present. *Annals of the New York Academy of Sciences*, *929*, 111–122.

Edelman, G. (2003). Naturalizing consciousness: A theoretical framework. *Proceedings of the National Academy of Sciences of the United States of America*, *100*, 5520–5524.

Egan, D. E. and Schwartz, B. J. (1979). Chunking in recall of symbolic drawings. *Memory & Cognition*, *7*, 149–158.

Einstein, A. (1996). Physics and reality. In A. Einstein, *The theory of relativity (and other essays)* (pp. 16–52). New York: Citadel Press. (Originally published 1936.)

Elliott, R., Fischer, C. T., and Rennie, D. L. (1999). Evolving guidelines for publication of qualitative research studies in psychology and related fields. *British Journal of Psychology*, *38*, 215–229.

Emery, N. J. and Clayton, N. S. (2004). The mentality of crows: Convergent evolution of intelligence in corvids and apes. *Science*, *306*, 1903–1907.

Endler, N. S. (1983). Interactionism: Personality model, but not yet a theory. In M. M. Page (Ed.), *Nebraska symposium on motivation—1982* (pp. 155–200). Lincoln, NE: University of Nebraska Press.

Endler, N. S. (1984). Interactionism. In N. S. Endler and J. M. Hunt (Eds.), *Personality and the behavioral disorders* (Vol. 1, pp. 183–217). New York: John Wiley & Sons.

Endler, N. S. and Edwards, J. (1978). Person by treatment interactions in personality research. In L. A. Pervin (Ed.), *Perspectives in interactional psychology* (pp. 141–169). New York: Plenum Press.

Endler, N. S, Hunt, J. M., and Rosenstein, A. J. (1962). An S-R inventory of anxiousness. *Psychological Monographs*, *76*, 1–33.

Engels, F. (1939). *Anti-Dühring: Herr Dühring's revolution in science* (E. Burns, Trans.). New York: International. (Originally published 1877.)

English, H. B. and English, A. C. (1958). *A comprehensive dictionary of psychological and psychoanalytical terms*. New York: David McKay.

Everitt, N. (1981). A problem for the eliminative materialist. *Mind*, *90*, 428–434.

Eysenck, M. W. (Ed.) (1990). *The Blackwell dictionary of cognitive psychology*. Oxford: Blackwell.

Eysenck, M. W. (2000). *Psychology: A student's handbook*. Hove: Psychology Press.

Fahs, B. (2011). Breaking body hair boundaries: Classroom exercises for challenging social constructions of body and sexuality. *Feminism & Psychology*, *22*, 482–506.

Falagas, M. E., Zarkadoulia, E. A., Bliziotis, I. A., and Samonis, G. (2006). Science in Greece: From the age of Hippocrates to the age of the genome. *The FASEB Journal*, *20*, 1946–1950.

Fancher, R. E. (1985). *The intelligence men: Makers of the IQ controversy*. New York: W. W. Norton.

Fancher, R. E. (1990). *Pioneers of psychology* (2nd ed.). New York: W. W. Norton.

Fancher, R. E. (2000). Spinoza, Baruch (Benedictus de). In A. E. Kazdin (Ed.), *Encyclopedia of Psychology* (Vol. 7, pp. 437–438). Washington, DC: Oxford University Press.

Fechner, G. T. (1997). Psychophysics and the mind–body relations. In L. T. Benjamin (Ed.), *A history of psychology: Original sources and contemporary research* (pp. 127–137). Boston, MA: McGraw-Hill. (Originally published 1860.)

Fee, E. (1979). Nineteenth-century craniology: The study of the female skull. *Bulletin of the History of Medicine*, *53*, 415–433.

Feingold, A. (1988). Cognitive gender differences are disappearing. *American Psychologist*, *43*, 95–103.

Ferguson, C. J. and Heene, M. (2012). A vast graveyard of undead theories: Publication bias and psychological science's aversion to the null. *Perspectives on Psychological Science*, *7*, 555–561.

Fersen, L. V., Wynne, C. D. L., Delius, J. D., and Staddon, J. E. R. (1991). Transitive inference formation in pigeons. *Journal of Experimental Psychology: Animal Behavior Processes*, *17*, 334–341.

Feyerabend, P. (1963). Materialism and the mind–body problem. *The Review of Metaphysics*, *17*, 49–66.

Feyerabend, P. (1975). 'Science.' The myth and its role in society. *Inquiry*, *18*, 167–181.

Feyerabend, P. (1988). *Against method* (rev. ed.). London: Verso. (Originally published 1975.)

Feyerabend, P. K. (1967). The mind–body problem. *Continuum*, *5*, 35–49.

Feyerabend, P. K. (1970). Against method: Outline of an anarchist theory of knowledge. *Minnesota Studies in the Philosophy of Science*, *4*, 17–130.

Fine, M. (1985). Reflections on a feminist psychology of women: Paradoxes and prospects. *Psychology of Women Quarterly*, *9*, 167–183.

Fisher, R. A. (1926). The arrangement of field experiments. *Journal of the Ministry of Agriculture of Great Britain*, *33*, 503–513.

Flanagan, J. C. (1935). *Factor analysis in the study of personality*. Stanford, CA: Stanford University Press.

Flanagan, O. J. (1984). *The science of the mind*. Cambridge, MA: The MIT Press.

Fleck, L. (1979). *Genesis and development of a scientific fact*. Chicago, IL: University of Chicago Press. (Originally published 1935.)

Fletcher, G. (1995). *The scientific credibility of folk psychology*. Mahwah, NJ: Lawrence Erlbaum Associates.

Fletcher, G. J. O. (1984). Psychology and common sense. *American Psychologist*, *39*, 203–213.

Flew, A. (1984). *A dictionary of philosophy* (2nd ed.). London: Pan Books.

Flew, A. G. N. (1964). Hume. In D. J. O'Connor (Ed.), *A critical history of Western philosophy* (pp. 253–274). New York: The Free Press.

Flynn, J. R. (1987). Massive IQ gains in 14 nations: What IQ tests really measure. *Psychological Bulletin*, *101*, 171–191.

Fodor, J. A. (1968). *Psychological explanation: An introduction to the philosophy of psychology*. New York: Random House.

Fodor, J. A. (1980). Methodological solipsism considered as a research strategy in cognitive psychology. *Behavioral and Brain Sciences*, *3*, 63–73.

Frankl, V. (1963). *Man's search for meaning: An introduction to logotherapy*. New York: Washington Square Press.

Freire, P. (1981). *Pedagogy of the oppressed*. New York: Continuum. (Originally published 1968.)

Freud, S. (1953). *A general introduction to psychoanalysis*. New York: Pocket Books. (Originally published 1924.)

Freud, S. (1977a). The dissolution of the Oedipus complex. In S. Freud (A. Richards, Ed.), *On sexuality: Three essays on the theory of sexuality and other works* (pp. 315–322). London: Penguin Books. (Originally published 1924.)

Freud, S. (1977b). Some psychical consequences of the anatomical distinction between the sexes. In S. Freud (A. Richards, Ed.), *On sexuality: Three essays on the theory of sexuality and other works* (pp. 331–343). London: Penguin Books. (Originally published 1925.)

Fry, I. (1995). Are different hypotheses on the emergence of life as different as they seem? *Biology and Philosophy*, *10*, 389–417.

Fryer, D. and Henry, E. R. (1937). *An outline of general psychology*. New York: Barnes & Noble.

Fuller, B. A. G. (1945). *A history of philosophy* (rev. ed.). New York: Henry Holt.

Funder, D. S. (2013). *The personality puzzle* (6th ed.). New York: W. W. Norton.

Galileo, G. (1957). The assayer. In S. Drake (Trans.), *Discoveries and opinions of Galileo* (pp. 231–280). Garden City, NY: Doubleday Anchor Books.

Galotti, K. M. (2014). *Cognitive psychology: In and out of the laboratory* (5th ed.). Los Angeles, CA: SAGE Publications.

Galton, F. (1879). Psychometric experiments. *Brain, 2,* 149–162.

Galton, F. (1880). Statistics of mental imagery. *Mind, 5,* 301–318.

Galton, F. (1884). Measurement of character. *Fortnightly Review, 36,* 179–185.

Galton, F. (1885). On the anthropometric laboratory at the late International Health Exhibition. *The Journal of the Anthropological Institute of Great Britain and Ireland, 14,* 202–221.

Galton, F. (1888). Co-relations and their measurement, chiefly from anthropometric data. *Proceedings of the Royal Society of London, 45,* 133–145.

Galton, F. (1904). Eugenics: Its definition, scope, and aims. *American Journal of Sociology, 10,* 1–25.

Galton, F. (1905). Studies in eugenics. *American Journal of Sociology, 11,* 11–25.

Galton, F. (1979). *Hereditary genius.* London: Julian Friedman. (Original work published 1869.)

Galton, F. (2012). The history of twins, as a criterion of the relative powers of nature and nurture. *International Journal of Epidemiology, 41,* 905–911. (Originally published 1875.)

Gardner, H. (1985). *The mind's new science: A history of the cognitive revolution.* New York: Basic Books.

Garraty, J. A. and Gay, P. (1972). *The Columbia history of the world.* New York: Harper & Row.

Gaur, A. (1992). *A history of writing* (rev. ed.). New York: Cross River Press.

Gawel, R., Oberholster, A., and Francis, I. L. (2008). A 'mouth-feel wheel': Terminology for communicating the mouth-feel characteristics of red wine. *Australian Journal of Grape and Wine Research, 6,* 203–207.

Gelb, S. A. (1986). Henry H. Goddard and the immigrants, 1910–1917: The studies and their social context. *Journal of the History of the Behavioral Sciences, 22,* 324–332.

Gergen, K. (1990). Toward a postmodern psychology. *The Humanist Psychologist, 18,* 23–34.

Gergen, K. J. (1985). The social constructionist movement in modern psychology. *American Psychologist, 40,* 266–275.

Gergen, K. J. (1997). The place of the psyche in a constructed world. *Theory and Psychology, 7,* 723–746.

Giacomin, M. and Jordan, C. H. (2016). The wax and wane of narcissism: Grandiose narcissism as a process or state. *Journal of Personality, 84,* 154–164.

Gibson, J. J. (1955). The optical expansion-pattern in aerial locomotion. *American Journal of Psychology, 68,* 480–484.

Gibson, J. J. (1966). *The senses considered as perceptual systems.* Boston, MA: Houghton Mifflin.

Gibson, J. J. (1986). *The ecological approach to visual perception.* Hillsdale, NJ: Lawrence Erlbaum Associates. (Originally published 1979.)

Gibson, J. J., Olum, P., and Rosenblatt, F. (1955). Parallax and perspective during aircraft landing. *American Journal of Psychology, 68,* 372–385.

Gigerenzer, G. (1987a). Probabilistic thinking and the fight against subjectivity. In C. Krüger, G. Gigerenzer, and M. S. Morgan (Eds.), *The probabilistic revolution. Vol. 2: Ideas in science* (pp. 11–33). Cambridge, MA: MIT Press.

Gigerenzer, G. (1987b). The probabilistic revolution in psychology—an overview. In C. Krüger, G. Gigerenzer, and M. S. Morgan (Eds.), *The probabilistic revolution. Vol. 2: Ideas in science* (pp. 7–9). Cambridge, MA: MIT Press.

Gillan, D. J. (1981). Reasoning in the chimpanzee, II: Transitive inference. *Journal of Experimental Psychology: Animal Behavior Processes, 7,* 150–164.

Gillan, D. J., Premack, D., and Woodruff, G. (1981). Reasoning in the chimpanzee, I: Analogical reasoning. *Journal of Experimental Psychology: Animal Behavior Processes, 7,* 1–17.

Giorgi, A. (1970). *Psychology as a human science: A phenomenologically based approach.* New York: Harper & Row.

Giorgi, A. (1985). Toward the articulation of psychology as a coherent discipline. In S. Koch and D. E. Leary (Eds.), *A century of psychology as science* (pp. 46–59). New York: McGraw-Hill.

Goddard, H. H. (1910). A measuring scale for intelligence. *Training School, 6,* 146–154.

Goddard, H. H. (1911). The elimination of feeble-mindedness. *Annals of the American Academy of Political and Social Science, 37,* 261–272.

Goddard, H. H. (1912). *The Kallikak family: A study in the heredity of feeble-mindedness.* New York: Macmillan.

Goddard, H. H. (1913a). The diagnosis of feeble-mindedness. Paper presented to the Chicago Medical Society, June 23, 1913. Retrieved from https://repositories.lib.utexas.edu/bitstream/handle/2152/29189/059171660538276.pdf?sequence=2

Goddard, H. H. (1913b). *Sterilization or segregation.* New York: Department of Child Helping of the Russell Sage Foundation.

Goddard, H. H. (1916a). Introduction. In A. Binet and T. Simon, *The development of intelligence in children* (pp. 5–8). Baltimore, MD: Williams and Wilkins.

Goddard, H. H. (1916b). The menace of mental deficiency from the standpoint of heredity. *Boston Medical and Surgical Journal, 175*, 269–271.

Goddard, H. H. (1917). Mental tests and the immigrant. *Journal of Delinquency, 2*, 243–277.

Goddard, H. H. (1920). *Human efficiency and levels of intelligence.* Princeton, NJ: Princeton University Press.

Goddard, H. H. (1991). Four hundred feeble-minded children classified by the Binet method. *Journal of Genetic Psychology, 152*, 437–447. (Originally published 1910.)

Goldberg, L. R. (1990). An alternative 'description of personality': The Big-Five factor structure. *Journal of Personality and Social Psychology, 59*, 1216–1229.

Gordon, H. (1970). The intelligence of English canal boat children. In I. Al-Issa and W. Dennis (Eds.), *Cross-cultural studies of behavior* (pp. 111–119). New York: Holt, Rinehart, and Winston. (Originally published 1923.)

Gould, J. B. (1974). The stoic conception of fate. *Journal of the History of Ideas, 35*, 17–32.

Gould, S. J. (1981). *The mismeasure of man.* New York: W. W. Norton.

Grady, K. E. (1981). Sex bias in research design. *Psychology of Women Quarterly, 5*, 628–636.

Green, C. D. (2001). Scientific models, connectionist networks, and cognitive science. *Theory & Psychology, 11*, 97–117.

Greenberg, G. and Harraway, M. M. (2002). *Principles of comparative psychology.* Boston, MA: Allyn and Bacon.

Greenwood, J. D. (1990). Two dogmas of neo-empiricism: The 'theory-informity' of observation and the Duhem-Quine hypothesis. *Philosophy of Science, 57*, 553–574.

Gross, R. (2007). *Themes, issues and debates in psychology* (2nd ed.). London: Hodder & Stoughton.

Grossmann, H. (2009). Descartes and the social origins of the mechanistic concept of the world. In B. Hessen and H. Grossmann (Eds.), *The social and economic roots of the scientific revolution* (pp. 157–229). Dordrecht, the Netherlands: Springer.

Grosz, E. A. (1987). Feminist theory and the challenge to knowledges. *Women's Studies International Forum, 10*, 475–480.

Groves, P. M. and Schlesinger, K. (1982). *Introduction to biological psychology* (2nd ed.). Dubuque, IA: Wm. C. Brown.

Hacking, I. (1995). The looping effect of human kinds. In D. Sperber, D. Premack, and A. J. Premack (Eds.), *Causal cognition: A multidisciplinary approach* (pp. 351–383). Oxford: Clarendon.

Hacking, I. (1999). *The social construction of what?* Cambridge, MA: Harvard University Press.

Hall, A. R. (1992). *Isaac Newton: Adventurer in thought.* Oxford: Blackwell.

Hall, C. S. (1954). *A primer of Freudian psychology.* New York: Mentor.

Hall, C. S. and Lindzey, G. (1978). *Theories of personality* (3rd ed.). New York: John Wiley & Sons.

Hall, M. (1833). On the reflex function of the medulla oblongata and the medulla spinalis. *Philosophical Transactions of the Royal Society of London, 123*, 635–665.

Hannush, M. J. (1987). John B. Watson remembered: An interview with James B. Watson. *Journal of the History of the Behavioral Sciences, 23*, 137–152.

Harlow, J. M. (1993). Recovery from the passage of an iron bar through the head. *History of Psychiatry, 4*, 274–281. (Originally published 1868.)

Harré, R. (1967). Philosophy of science, history of. In P. Edwards (Ed.), *The encyclopedia of philosophy* (Vol. 5, pp. 289–296). New York: Macmillan.

Harré, R. (2005). The relevance of the philosophy of psychology to a science of psychology. In C. E. Erneling and D. M. Johnson (Eds.), *The mind as a scientific object: Between brain and culture* (pp. 20–34). Oxford: Oxford University Press.

Harrison, R. (1943). The Thematic Apperception and Rorschach methods of personality investigation in clinical practice. *Journal of Personality, 15*, 49–74.

Hasker, W. (1998). *Occasionalism.* In E. Craig (Ed.), *Routledge encyclopedia of philosophy* (Vol. 7, pp. 87–90). London: Routledge.

Haslam, N. O. (1998). Natural kinds, human kinds, and essentialism. *Social Research, 65*, 291–314.

Haviland, W. A. (1997). *Human evolution and prehistory* (4th ed.). Fort Worth, TX: Harcourt Brace College.

Hawking, S. (1988). *A brief history of time: From the big bang to black holes.* New York: Bantam Books.

Hebb, D. O. (1966). *A textbook of psychology* (2nd ed.). Philadelphia, PA: W. B. Saunders.

Heidbreder, E. (1933). *Seven psychologies*. Englewood Cliffs, NJ: Prentice-Hall.

Heilbroner, R. (1993). *The making of economic society* (9th ed.). Englewood Cliffs, NJ: Prentice Hall.

Heinrich, J. and McElreath, R. (2003). The evolution of cultural evolution. *Evolutionary Anthropology: Issues, News, and Reviews, 12*, 123–135.

Helmholtz, H. V. (1971). The aim and progress of physical science. In R. Kahl (Ed.), *Selected writings of Hermann von Helmholtz* (pp. 223–245). Middletown, CT: Wesleyan University Press. (Originally published 1869.)

Helmholtz, H. V. (2000). *Helmholtz's treatise on physiological optics* (J. P. C. Southall, Ed.). (Translated from the third German edition; 1925 translation of 1867 original.) Stirling, VA: Thoemmes Press.

Henwood, K. and Pidgeon, N. (1995). Remaking the link: Qualitative research and feminist standpoint theory. *Feminism & Psychology, 5*, 7–30.

Hergenhahn, B. R. and Henley, T. B. (2014). *An introduction to the history of psychology* (7th ed.). Belmont, CA: Wadsworth Cengage Learning.

Herrnstein, R. J. and Boring, E. G. (1965). *A source book in the history of psychology*. Cambridge, MA: Harvard University Press.

Herrnstein, R. J. and Murray, C. (1994). *The Bell Curve: Intelligence and class structure in American life*. New York: The Free Press.

Hertz, M. R. (1934). The Rorschach Ink-Blot Test: Historical summary. *Psychological Bulletin, 32*, 33–66.

Hibberd, F. J. (2001). Gergen's social constructionism, logical positivism and the continuity of error, Part 1: Conventionalism. *Theory & Psychology, 11*, 297–321.

Hilgard, E. R. (1987). *Psychology in America: A historical survey*. San Diego, CA: Harcourt Brace Jovanovich.

Hobbes, T. (2012). *Leviathan*. New York: Start Publishing LLC. (Originally published, 1651.)

Hobbs, N. (1948). The development of a code of ethical standards for psychology. *American Psychologist, 3*, 80–84.

Hodge, C. F. (1890). A sketch of the history of reflex action, 1: Beginnings and development to the time of Charles Bell. *American Journal of Psychology, 3*, 149–167.

Hoitsma, R. K. (1925). The reliability and relationships of the Colgate Mental Hygiene Test. *Journal of Applied Psychology, 9*, 293–303.

Holcomb, H. R. (1996). Just so stories and inference to the best explanation in evolutionary psychology. *Minds and Machines, 6*, 525–540.

Hollingworth, L. S. (1914). Variability as related to sex differences in achievement: A critique. *American Journal of Sociology, 19*, 510–530.

Holt, R. R. (1962). Individuality and generalization in the psychology of personality. *Journal of Personality, 30*, 377–404.

Holzinger, K. J. (1936). Recent research on unitary mental traits. *Character and Personality, 4*, 335–343.

Holzkamp, K. (1991a). Experience of self and scientific objectivity. In C. W. Tolman and W. Maiers (Eds.), *Critical psychology: Contributions to an historical science of the subject* (pp. 65–80). Cambridge: Cambridge University Press. (Originally published 1984.)

Holzkamp, K. (1991b). Psychoanalysis and Marxist psychology. In C. W. Tolman and W. Maiers (Eds.), *Critical psychology: Contributions to an historical science of the subject* (pp. 81–101). Cambridge: Cambridge University Press. (Originally published 1984.)

Holzkamp, K. (1992). On doing psychology critically. *Theory & Psychology, 2*, 193–204.

Hookway, C. (1998). Peirce, Charles, Sanders (1839–1914). In E. Craig (Ed.), *Routledge encyclopedia of philosophy* (Vol. 7, pp. 269–284). London: Routledge.

Horney, K. (1973a). The overvaluation of love: A study of a common present-day feminine type. In K. Horney (H. Kelman, Ed.), *Feminine psychology* (pp. 182–213). New York: W. W. Norton. (Originally published 1934.)

Horney, K. (1973b). The flight from womanhood: The masculinity-complex in women as viewed by men and by women. In K. Horney (H. Kelman, Ed.), *Feminine psychology* (pp. 54–70). New York: W. W. Norton. (Originally published 1926.)

Horney, K. (1973c). The problem of feminine masochism. In K. Horney (H. Kelman, Ed.), *Feminine psychology* (pp. 214–233). New York: W. W. Norton. (Originally published 1935.)

Hornstein, G. A. (1988). Quantifying psychological phenomena: Debates, dilemmas, and implications. In J. G. Morawski (Ed.), *The rise of experimentation in American psychology* (pp. 1–34). New Haven, CT: Yale University Press.

Horowitz, I. L. (1966). The life and death of Project Camelot. *American Psychologist, 21*, 445–454.

Hothersall, D. (1995). *History of psychology* (3rd ed.). New York: McGraw-Hill.

Hoyningen-Huene, P. (1998). Kuhn, Thomas Samuel. In E. Craig (Ed.), *Routledge encyclopedia of philosophy* (Vol. 5, pp. 315–318). London: Routledge.

Huby, P. (1967). The first discovery of the freewill problem. *Philosophy, 42*, 353–362.

Hudson, W. (1960). Pictorial depth perception in subcultural groups in Africa. *Journal of Social Psychology, 52*, 183–208.

Hughes, P. (1928). *An introduction to psychology: from the standpoint of life-career* (2nd ed.). Bethlehem, PA: Lehigh University Supply Bureau.

Hume, D. (2003). *A treatise of human nature*. Mineola, NY: Dover Publications. (Originally published 1739–1740.)

Hung, E. (1997). *The nature of science: Problems and perspectives*. Belmont, CA: Wadsworth Publishing.

Hunt, H. T. (2005). Why psychology is/is not traditional science: The self-referential bases of psychological research and theory. *Review of General Psychology, 9*, 358–374.

Hunt, M. (1993). *The story of psychology*. New York: Doubleday.

Hunter, W. (1913). The delayed reaction in animals and children. *Behavior Monographs, 2*, 1–86.

Hurd, D. L. and Kipling, J. J. (1964). *The origins and growth of physical science*, Vol. 1. Harmondsworth: Penguin Books.

Hutchins, E. (1995). *Cognition in the wild*. Cambridge, MA: MIT Press.

Huxley, T. H. (1874). On the hypothesis that animals are automata and its history. *Fortnightly Review, 22*, 555–580.

Hyde, J. S. (1981). How large are cognitive gender differences? A meta-analysis using w^2 and *d*. *American Psychologist, 36*, 892–901.

Immergluck, L. (1964). Determinism-freedom in contemporary psychology: An ancient problem revisited. *American Psychologist, 19*, 270–281.

Ingber, D. E. (2003). Tensegrity I: Cell structure and hierarchical systems biology. *Journal of Cell Science, 116*, 1157–1173.

Iscoe, I. (1974). Community psychology and the competent community. *American Psychologist, 29*, 607–613.

Jahoda, G. (1993). *Crossroads between culture and mind: Continuities and change in theories of human nature*. Cambridge, MA: Harvard University Press.

James, W. (1879). Are we automata? *Mind, 4*, 1–22.

James, W. (1884). The dilemma of determinism. *Unitarian Review and Religious Magazine, 22*, 193–224.

James, W. (1887). The laws of habit. *The Popular Science Monthly, 30*, 433–451.

James, W. (1892). A plea for psychology as a 'natural science.' *Philosophical Review, 1*, 146–153.

James, W. (1905). *Talks to teachers on psychology: And to students on some of life's ideals*. New York: Henry Holt.

James, W. (1950). *The principles of psychology*, Vols 1 and 2. New York: Dover Publications. (Original work published 1890.)

Jevons, W. S. (1874). *The principles of science: A treatise on logic and scientific method* (2nd ed.). London: Macmillan.

Jones, R. V. (1967). Instruments, scientific. In J. R. Newman (Ed.), *The Harper encyclopedia of science* (pp. 598–605). New York: Harper & Row.

Jourard, S. M. (1968). *Disclosing man to himself*. Princeton, NJ: D. Van Nostrand.

Jung, C. G. (1958). *The undiscovered self*. New York: Mentor Books

Jung, C. G. (1981). *Experimental researches: The collected works of C. G. Jung*, Vol. 2. Princeton, NJ: Princeton University Press.

Kagan, J. (2009). Historical selection. *Review of General Psychology, 13*, 77–88.

Kalmar, I. (1987). The *Völkerpsychologie* of Lazarus and Steinthal and the modern concept of culture. *Journal of the History of Ideas, 48*, 671–690.

Kanazawa, S. (2010). Evolutionary psychology and intelligence research. *American Psychologist, 65*, 279–289.

Kantor, J. (1979). Psychology: Science or nonscience? *Psychological Record, 29*, 155–163.

Kaufman, Y. and Klein, S. T. (2005). Semi-lossless text compression. *International Journal of Foundations of Computer Science, 16*, 1167–1178.

Kaye, J. (1988). The impact of money on the development of fourteenth century scientific thought. *Journal of Medieval History, 14*, 251–270.

Keeton, W. T. (1967). *Biological science*. New York: W. W. Norton & Company.

Keeton, W. T. and Gould, J. L. (1986). *Biological science* (4th ed.). New York: W. W. Norton.

Kelley, T. L. (1928). *Crossroads in the mind of man*. Stanford, CA: Stanford University Press.

Kelly, G. A. (1955). *A theory of personality: The psychology of personal constructs*. New York: W. W. Norton.

Kelly, J. (1971). Qualities for the community psychologist. *American Psychologist, 26*, 897–903.

Kelman, H. C. (1967). Human use of human subjects: The problem of deception in social psychological experiments. *Psychological Bulletin, 67*, 1–11.

Kendler, H. H. (2005). Psychology and phenomenology. *American Psychologist, 60*, 318–324.

Kendregan, C. P. (1966). Sixty years of compulsory eugenic sterilization: Three generations of imbeciles and the constitution of the United States. *Chicago-Kent Law Review, 43*, 123–143.

Kevles, D. J. (1999). Eugenics and human rights. *British Medical Journal, 319*, 435–438.

Kimble, G. A. (1961). *Hilgard and Marquis' conditioning and learning* (rev. 2nd ed.). New York: Appleton-Century-Crofts.

Kimble, G. A. (1985). Conditioning and learning. In S. Koch and D. E. Leary (Eds.), *A century of psychology as science* (pp. 284–321). New York: McGraw-Hill.

Kimble, G. A. and Perlmuter, L. C. (1970). The problem of volition. *Psychological Review, 77*, 361–384.

Kitchener, R. F. (1996). Skinner's theory of theories. In W. O'Donohue and R. F. Kitchener (Eds.), *The philosophy of psychology* (pp. 108–125). London: SAGE Publications.

Kitzinger, C. (1991). Politicizing psychology. *Feminism & Psychology, 1*, 49–54.

Klee, R. (1997). *Introduction to the philosophy of science: Cutting nature at its seams.* New York: Oxford University Press.

Knight, R. P. (1946). Determinism, freedom, and psychotherapy. *Psychiatry: Journal for the Study of Interpersonal Processes, 9*, 251–262.

Koch, S. (1964). Psychology and emerging conceptions of knowledge as unitary. In T. W. Wann (Ed.), *Behaviorism and phenomenology: Contrasting bases for modern psychology* (pp. 1–45). Chicago, IL: University of Chicago Press.

Koch, S. (1971). Reflections on the state of psychology. *Social Research, 38*, 669–709.

Koch, S. (1973). Psychology cannot be a coherent science. In F. W. Watson (Ed.), *Within/without: Behaviorism and humanism* (pp. 80–91). Monterey, CA: Brooks/Cole Publishing.

Koch, S. (1981). The nature and limits of psychological knowledge: Lessons of a century qua 'science.' *American Psychologist, 36*, 257–269.

Koch, S. (1985a). Foreword: Wundt's creature at age zero–and as centenarian. In S. Koch and D. E. Leary, *A century of psychology as science* (pp. 7–35). New York: McGraw-Hill.

Koch, S. (1985b). The nature and limits of psychological knowledge: Lessons of a century qua science. In S. Koch and D. E. Leary, *A century of psychology as science* (pp. 75–97). New York: McGraw-Hill.

Koch, S. (1985c). Afterword. In S. Koch and D. E. Leary, *A century of psychology as science* (pp. 928–950). New York: McGraw-Hill.

Köhler, W. (1947). *Gestalt psychology: An introduction to new concepts in modern psychology.* New York: Mentor.

Köhler, W. (1957). *The mentality of apes.* London: Penguin Books. (Originally published 1925.)

Kolb, B. and Whishaw, I. Q. (1990). *Fundamentals of human neuropsychology* (3rd ed.). New York: W. H. Freeman.

Kolb, B. and Whishaw, I. Q. (1998). Brain plasticity and behavior. *Annual Review of Psychology, 49*, 43–64.

Kopp, C. B. (1982). Antecedents of self-regulation: A developmental perspective. *Developmental Psychology, 18*, 199–214.

Krause, M. S. (1970). Use of social situations for research purposes. *American Psychologist, 25*, 748–753.

Kuhn, T. S. (1962). *The structure of scientific revolutions.* Chicago, IL: The University of Chicago Press.

Kvale, S. (1990). Postmodern psychology: A contradictio in adjecto? *The Humanistic Psychologist, 18*, 35–54.

La Mettrie, J. O. de. (2004). *Man a machine.* (Original work published 1748.) Retrieved 13 October 2004 from http://www.cscs.umich.edu/~crshalizi/LaMettrie/Machine/

Lahav, N., Nir, S., and Elitzur, A. C. (2001). The emergence of life on earth. *Progress in Biophysics & Molecular Biology, 75*, 75–120.

Lakatos, I. (1970). Falsification and the methodology of scientific research programmes. In I. Lakatos (Ed.), *Criticism and the growth of knowledge* (Vol. 4, pp. 91–195). Cambridge: Cambridge University Press.

Lakatos, I. (1974). Popper on demarcation and induction. In P. A. Schilpp (Ed.), *The philosophy of Karl Popper* (pp. 241–273). La Salle, IL: Open Court.

Lamprecht, S. P. (1955). *Our philosophical traditions: A brief history of philosophy in Western civilization.* New York: Appleton-Century-Crofts.

Langdridge, D. (2007). *Phenomenological psychology: Theory, research and method.* Harlow: Pearson/Prentice-Hall.

Langenhove, L. V. (1995). The theoretical foundations of experimental psychology and its alternatives. In J. A. Smith, R. Harré, and L. V. Langenhove (Eds.), *Rethinking psychology* (pp. 10–23). London: SAGE Publications.

Lanham, U. (1968). *Origins of modern biology*. New York: Columbia University Press.

Lashley, K. S. (1967). The problem of serial order in behavior. In L. A. Jeffress (Ed.), *Cerebral mechanisms in behavior: The Hixon symposium* (pp. 112–146). New York: Hafner Publishing Company. (Originally published 1951.)

Lawrence, E. (2011). *Henderson's dictionary of biology* (15th ed.). Harlow: Pearson.

Leakey, R. E. (1981). *The making of mankind*. New York: E. P. Dutton.

Leakey, R. E. and Lewin R. L. (1992). *Origins reconsidered*. New York: Anchor Books.

Lenin, V. I. (1947). *Materialism and empirio-criticism*. Moscow: Progress Publishers.

Lenoir, T. (1986). Models and instruments in the development of electrophysiology: 1945–1912. *Historical Studies in the Physical and Biological Sciences, 17*, 1–54.

Leont'ev, A. N. (1974–75). The problem of activity in psychology. *Soviet Psychology, 13*, 4–33.

Leontiev, A. N. and Luria, A. R. (1968). The psychological ideas of L. S. Vygotskii. In B. B. Wolman (Ed.), *Historical roots of contemporary psychology* (pp. 338–367). New York: Harper & Row.

Leontyev, A. N. (1981a). The problem of the origin of sensation. In A. N. Leontyev, *Problems of the development of the mind* (pp. 7–155). Moscow: Progress Publishers. (Doctoral dissertation, 1940.)

Leontyev, A. N. (1981b). An outline of the evolution of the psyche. In A. N. Leontyev, *Problems of the development of the mind* (pp. 156–327). Moscow: Progress Publishers. (Originally published 1947.)

Lerner, R. M. (1976). *Concepts and theories of human development*. Reading, MA: Addison-Wesley Publishing.

Levine, M. (1974). Scientific method and the adversary model: Some preliminary thoughts. *American Psychologist, 29*, 661–677.

Levine, M. W. and Shefner, J. M. (1981). *Fundamentals of sensation and perception*. Reading, MA: Addison-Wesley Publishing.

Lewin, R. and Foley, R. A. (2004). *Principles of human evolution* (2nd ed.). Malden, MA: Blackwell.

Lewis, R. (1995). *Beginnings of life* (2nd ed.). Dubuque, IA: Wm. C. Brown Publishers.

Lewis-Williams, D. (2002). *The mind in the cave*. London: Thames & Hudson.

Libet, B. (1999). Do we have free will? *Journal of Consciousness Studies, 6*, 47–57.

Libet, B., Gleason, C. A., Wright, E. W., and Pearl, D. K. (1983). Time of conscious intention to act in relation to onset of cerebral activity (readiness-potential). *Brain, 106*, 623–642.

Lilienfield, S. O., Wood, J. M., and Garb, H. N. (2000). The scientific status of projective techniques. *Psychological Science in the Public Interest, 1*, 27–66.

Lloyd-Jones, H. (2001). Ancient Greek religion. *Proceedings of the American Philosophical Society, 145*, 456–464.

Lorge, I. (1935). Personality traits by fiat, 1: The analysis of the total trait scores and keys of the Bernreuter personality inventory. *Journal of Educational Psychology, 26*, 273–278.

Lott, B. (1985). The potential enrichment of social/personality psychology through feminist research and vice versa. *American Psychologist, 40*, 155–164.

Lundberg. G. A. (1926). Case work and the statistical method. *Social Forces, 5*, 61–65.

Luria, A. R. (1960). Verbal regulation of behavior. In M. Brazier (Ed.), *The central nervous system and behavior* (pp. 359–423). New York: Josiah Macy, Jr. Foundation.

Luria, A. R. (1966/1967). L. S. Vygotsky and the problem of functional localization. *Soviet Psychology, 5*, 53–57.

Luria, A. R. (1967). *The nature of human conflicts: Or emotion, conflict and will*. New York: Washington Square Press. (Originally published 1932.)

Luria, A. R. (1971a). Towards the problem of the historical nature of psychological processes. *International Journal of Psychology, 6*, 259–272.

Luria, A. R. (1971b). *Speech and the development of mental processes in the child*. Harmondsworth: Penguin Education.

Luria, A. R. (1976). *Cognitive development: Its cultural and social foundations*. Cambridge, MA: Harvard University Press.

Luria, A. R. (1979). *The making of mind*. Cambridge, MA: Harvard University Press.

Luria, A. R. (1980). *Higher cortical functions in man* (2nd ed.). New York: Basic Books.

Luria, A. R. (1982). *Language and cognition*. Washington, DC: V. H. Winston and Sons.

Maccoby, E. E. and Jacklin, C. N. (1974). *The psychology of sex differences*. Stanford, CA: Stanford University Press.

Mach, E. (1897). *Contributions to the analysis of the sensations*. Chicago, IL: Open Court Publishing. (Originally published 1890.)

Mach, E. (1976). *Knowledge and error: Sketches on the psychology of enquiry*. Dordrecht, the Netherlands: D. Reidel Publishing. (Originally published 1897.)

MacLeod, R. B. (1944). The phenomenological approach to social psychology. *Psychological Review, 54,* 193–210.

Madigan, R., Johnson, S., and Linton, P. (1995). The language of psychology: APA style as epistemology. *American Psychologist, 50,* 428–436.

Magee, B. (1973). *Karl Popper.* New York: Viking Press.

Magnusson, D. and Allen, V. L. (1983). Implications and applications of an interactional perspective for human development. In D. Magnusson and V. L. Allen (Eds.), *Human development: An interactional perspective* (pp. 369–387). New York: Academic Press.

Magnusson, D. and Ekehammar, B. (1978). Similar situations—similar behavior: A study of the intraindividual congruence between situation perception and situation reaction. *Journal of Research in Personality, 12,* 41–48.

Maier, R. (1998). *Comparative animal behavior: An evolutionary and ecological approach.* Boston, MA: Allyn and Bacon.

Maiers, W. (1987). The historical approach of critical psychology: Another case of 'paradigm promotion'? In W. Baker, M. Hyland, H. Van Rapport, and A. W., Staats (Eds.), *Current issues in theoretical psychology* (pp. 175–188). Amsterdam, the Netherlands: Elsevier Science Publishers.

Marr, M. J. (1985). 'Tis the gift to be simple: A retrospective appreciation of Mach's *The Science of Mechanics. Journal of Experimental Analysis of Behavior, 44,* 129–138.

Martin, J. (1996). The 'top ten' problems of psychology. *History and Philosophy of Psychology Bulletin, 8,* 4–10.

Martin, J. and Sugarman, J. (2001). Interpreting human kinds: Beginnings of a hermeneutic psychology. *Theory & Psychology, 11,* 193–207.

Martin, J. and Sugarman, J. (2004). The political disposition of self as a kind of understanding. In W. E. Smythe and A. Baydala (Eds.), *Studies of how the mind publicly enfolds into being* (pp. 175–198). Lewiston, NY: The Edwin Mellen Press.

Martin, J. and Sugarman, J. (2009). Does interpretation in psychology differ from interpretation in natural science? *Journal for the Theory of Social Behavior, 39,* 19–37.

Martin, J., Sugarman, J., and Thompson, J. (2003). *Psychology and the question of agency.* Albany, NY: State University of New York Press.

Mason, M. K. (1942). Learning to speak after six and one-half years of silence. *Journal of Speech Disorders, 12,* 41–48.

May, R. (1958). *Existence: A new dimension in psychiatry and psychology.* New York: Basic Books.

May, R. (1966). Sex differences in fantasy patterns. *Journal of Projective Techniques and Personality Assessment, 30,* 576–586.

Mayr, E. (1987). The ontological status of species: Scientific progress and philosophical terminology. *Biology and Philosophy, 2,* 145–166.

Mayr, E. (1996). The autonomy of biology: The position of biology among the sciences. *The Quarterly Review of Biology, 71,* 97–106.

Mayr, E. (1997). *This is biology: The science of the living world.* Cambridge, MA: The Belknap Press of the Harvard University Press.

Mayr, E. (2004). *What makes biology unique?* New York: Cambridge University Press.

Mazlish, B. (1967). Comte, Auguste. In P. Edwards (Ed.), *The encyclopedia of philosophy* (Vol. 2, pp. 173–177). New York: Macmillan.

McAdams, D. P. (1994). *The person: An introduction to personality psychology* (2nd ed.). Fort Worth, TX: Harcourt Brace College.

McBurney, D. H. (1997). *Research methods* (4th ed.). Pacific Grove, CA: Brooks/Cole.

McClelland, D. C. (1951). *Personality.* New York: Holt, Rinehart, and Winston.

McCloskey, M. E. and Glucksberg, S. (1978). Natural categories: Well defined or fuzzy sets? *Memory & Cognition, 6,* 462–472.

McCrae, R. R. and Costa, P. T. (1985). Updating Norman's 'Adequate taxonomy': Intelligence and personality dimensions in natural language and in questionnaires. *Journal of Personality and Social Psychology, 49,* 710–721.

McCrae, R. R. and Costa, P. T. (2003). *Personality in adulthood: A five factor theory* (2nd ed.). New York: The Guilford Press.

McCulloch, W. B. and Pitts, W. (1943). A logical calculus of the ideas immanent in nervous activity. *Bulletin of Mathematical Biophysics, 5,* 115–133.

McDougall, W. (1950). *An introduction to social psychology* (30th ed.). London: Methuen. (Originally published 1908.)

Medin, D. L., Ross, B. H., and Markman, A. B. (2001). *Cognitive psychology* (3rd ed.). Fort Worth, TX: Harcourt College Publishers.

Menand, L. (2001). *The metaphysical club.* New York: Farrar, Straus, and Giroux.

Michell, J. (1997). Quantitative science and the definition of *measurement* in psychology. *British Journal of Psychology*, *88*, 355–383.

Michell, J. (1999). *Measurement in psychology: Critical history of a methodological concept.* Cambridge: Cambridge University Press.

Michell, J. (2003). The quantitative imperative: Positivism, naïve realism and the place of qualitative methods in psychology. *Theory & Psychology*, *13*, 5–31.

Milgram, S. (1963). Behavioral study of obedience. *Journal of Abnormal and Social Psychology*, *67*, 371–378.

Milgram, S. (1977). Subject reaction: The neglected factor in the ethics of experimentation. *Hastings Center Report*, *7*, 19–23.

Mill, J. S. (1973). *A system of logic: Ratiocinative and inductive: Being a connected view of the principles of evidence and the methods of scientific investigation.* Toronto: University of Toronto Press. (Originally published 1843.)

Mill, J. S. (1988). *The subjection of women.* Indianapolis, IN: Hackett Publishing. (Originally published 1869.)

Miller, G. A. (1956). The magical number seven, plus or minus two: Some limits on our capacity for processing information. *Psychological Review*, *63*, 81–97.

Mischel, W. (1986). *Introduction to personality* (4th ed.). New York: Holt, Rinehart and Winston.

Mishler, E. G. (1979). Meaning in context: Is there any other kind? *Harvard Educational Review*, *49*, 1–19.

Mitroff, I. I. (1974). Norms and counter-norms in a select group of the Apollo moon scientists: A case study of the ambivalence of scientists. *American Sociological Review*, *39*, 579–595.

Moane, G. (2003). Bridging the personal and the political: Practices for a liberation psychology. *American Journal of Community Psychology*, *31*, 91–101.

Mobius, J. P. (1901). The physiological mental weakness of women. *Alienist and Neurologist*, *22*, 624–642.

Montero, M. and Montenegro, M. (2006). Critical psychology in Venezuela. *Annual Review of Critical Psychology*, *5*, 257–268.

Moravia, S. (1995). *The enigma of the mind: The mind–body problem in contemporary thought* (S. Staton, Trans.). Cambridge, UK: Cambridge University Press.

Morawski, J. (2007). Scientific selves: Discerning the subject and the experimenter in experimental psychology in the United States. 1900–1935. In M. Ash and T. Stern (Eds.), *Psychology's territories: Historical and contemporary perspectives from different disciplines* (pp. 129–148). Mahwah, NJ: Lawrence Erlbaum Associates.

Morawski, J. G. (1982). Assessing psychology's moral heritage through our neglected utopias. *American Psychologist*, *37*, 1082–1095.

Mørck, L. L. and Huniche, L. (2006). Critical psychology in a Danish context. *Annual Review of Critical Psychology*, *5*, 1– 19.

Mørck, L. L., Hussain, K., Møller-Andersen, C., Özüpek, T., Palm, A., and Vorbeck, I. H. (2013). Praxis development in relation to gang conflicts in Copenhagen, Denmark. *Outlines—Critical Practice Studies*, *14*, 79–105.

Morgan, C. L. (1926). *Life, mind, and spirit.* London: Williams and Norgate.

Morgan, C. L. (1998). Introduction to comparative psychology. In D. Robinson (Ed.), *The mind* (pp. 260–264). Oxford: Oxford University Press. (Originally published 1884.)

Morgan, W. G. (2002). Origin and history of the earliest Thematic Apperception Test pictures. *Journal of Personality Assessment*, *79*, 422–445.

Morse, S. J. (2008). Determinism and the death of folk psychology: Two challenges to responsibility from neuroscience. *Minnesota Journal of Law, Science & Technology*, *9*, 1–36.

Much, N. (1995). Cultural psychology. In J. A. Smith, R. Harré, and L. V. Langenhove (Eds.), *Rethinking psychology* (pp. 97–121). London: SAGE Publications.

Mulaik, S. A. (1987). A brief history of the philosophical foundations of exploratory factor analysis. *Multivariate Behavioral Research*, *22*, 267–305.

Müller, J. (1997). The specific energies of nerves. In L. T. Benjamin (Ed.), *A history of psychology: Original sources and contemporary research* (pp. 66–73). Boston, MA: McGraw-Hill. (Originally published 1838.)

Munn, N. L. (1971). *The evolution of the human mind.* Boston, MA: Houghton Mifflin.

Munsterberg, H. (1894). Studies from the Harvard Psychological Laboratory. *Psychological Review*, *1*, 34–60.

Murch, G. M. (1973). *Visual and auditory perception.* Indianapolis, IN: The Bobbs-Merrill Company.

Murphy, G. (1967). Pythagorean number theory and its implications for psychology. *American Psychologist*, *22*, 423–431.

Murray, H. A. (1951). Uses of the Thematic Apperception Test. *American Journal of Psychiatry*, *107*, 577–581.

Murray, H. A. (1962). *Explorations in personality.* New York: Science Editions, Inc. (Originally published 1938.)

Myers, G. E. (1992). William James and contemporary psychology. In M. E. Donnelly (Ed.), *Reinterpreting the legacy of William James* (49–64). Washington, DC: American Psychological Association.

Nadler, S. (1998). *Malebranche, Nicholas (1638–1715)*. In E. Craig (Ed.), *Routledge encyclopedia of philosophy* (Vol. 6, pp. 56–66). London: Routledge.

Naletov, I. (1984). *Alternative to positivism*. Moscow: Progress Publishers.

Neisser, U. (1996). Remembering as doing. *Behavioral and Brain Sciences, 19*, 203–204.

Neisser, U. (2000). Memory: What are the important questions? In U. Neisser and I. E. Hyman (Eds.), *Memory observed: Remembering in natural contexts* (2nd ed.) (pp. 3–18). New York: Worth. (Originally published 1978.)

Newell, A., Shaw, J. C., and Simon, H. A. (1958). Elements of a theory of human problem solving. *Psychological Review, 65*, 151–166.

Newell, A. and Simon, H. A. (1956). The logic theory machine—A complex information processing system. *IRE Transactions on Information Theory, 2*, 61–79.

Nicolas, S., Gounden, Y., and Levine, Z. (2011). The memory of two great mental calculators: Charcot and Binet's neglected 1893 experiments. *American Journal of Psychology, 124*, 235–242.

Nightingale, D. J. and Cromby, J. (2001). Critical psychology and the ideal of individualism. *Journal of Critical Psychology, Counseling, and Psychotherapy, 1*, 117–128.

Nissen, M. (2000). Practice research: Critical psychology in and through practices. *Annual Review of Critical Psychology, 2*, 145–179.

Nissen, M. (2003). Objective subjectification: The antimethod of social work. *Mind, Culture, and Activity, 10*, 332–349.

Nissen, M. (2012). *The subjectivity of participation: Articulating social work practice with youth in Copenhagen*. New York: Palgrave Macmillan.

Norenzayan, A. and Heine, S. J. (2005). Psychological universals: What are they and how can we know? *Psychological Bulletin, 131*, 763–784.

Novikoff, A. (1945). The concept of integrative levels and biology. *Science, 101*, 209–215.

O'Keefe, T. (2010). *Epicureanism*. Berkeley, CA: University of California Press.

Olson, D. R. (1993). How writing represents speech. *Language & Communication, 13*, 1–17.

Palmer, D. K. (2004). On the organism-environment distinction in psychology. *Behavior and Philosophy, 32*, 317–347.

Palmer, J. A. (2000). Skeptical investigation. *Ancient Philosophy, 20*, 351–375.

Pappas, G. S. (1998). Epistemology, history of. In E. Craig (Ed.), *Routledge encyclopedia of philosophy* (Vol. 3, pp. 371–384). London: Routledge.

Park, M. A. (2000). *Introducing anthropology: An integrative approach*. Mountain View, CA: Mayfield Publishing.

Parker, I. (1999). Critical psychology: Critical links. *Annual Review of Critical Psychology, 1*, 3–18.

Parker, I. (2006). Critical psychology and critical practice in Britain. *Annual Review of Critical Psychology, 5*, 89–100.

Partington, J. R. (1960). *A short history of chemistry* (3rd ed.). New York: Harper & Brothers. (Originally published 1937.)

Patrick, G. T. W. (1895). The psychology of women. *Popular Science, 47*, 209–225.

Pearson, K. (1906). On the relationship of intelligence to size and shape of head, and to other physical and mental characteristics. *Biometrika, 5*, 105–146.

Pepperberg, I. M. (1998). Cognitive capacities of birds. In G. Greenberg and M. M. Haraway (Eds.), *Comparative psychology: A handbook* (pp. 376–385). New York: Garland Publishers.

Peters, R. S. (Ed.) (1962). *Brett's history of psychology* (rev. ed.). Cambridge, MA: The MIT Press. (Original work written 1921.)

Petrovsky, A. V. (1985). *Studies in psychology: The individual and the collective*. Moscow: Progress Publishers.

Petrovsky, A. V. (1989). *Psychology*. Moscow: Progress Publishers.

Phillips, D. C. and Orton, R. (1983). The new causal principle of cognitive learning theory: Perspectives on Bandura's 'Reciprocal Determinism'. *Psychological Review, 90*, 158–165.

Piekkola, B. (2011). Traits across cultures: A neo-Allportian perspective. *Journal of Theoretical and Philosophical Psychology, 31*, 2–24.

Plutchik, R. (1970). Operationism as methodology. In D. P. Schultz (Ed.), *The science of psychology: Critical reflections* (pp. 87–97). New York: Appleton-Century-Crofts.

Popkin, R. H. and Stroll, A. (1993). *Philosophy made simple* (2nd ed.). New York: Doubleday.

Popper, K. R. (1959). *The logic of scientific discovery*. New York: Harper & Row. (Originally published 1934.)

Power, A. (2013). *Roger Bacon and the defense of Christendom.* Cambridge: Cambridge University Press.

Price, H. H. (1960). Some objections to behaviorism. In S. Hook (Ed.), *Dimensions of mind* (pp. 79–84). New York: Collier Books.

Prilleltensky, I. and Fox, D. (1997). Introducing critical psychology: Values, assumptions, and the status quo. In D. Fox and I. Prilleltensky (Eds.), *Critical psychology: An introduction* (pp. 3–20). London: SAGE Publications.

Prilleltensky, I. and Gonick, L. (1996). Polities change, oppression remains: On the psychology and politics of oppression. *Political Psychology*, *17*, 127–148.

Putnam, H. (1967). The mental life of some machines. In H. Casteňada (Ed.), *Intentionality, minds, and perception: Discussions on contemporary philosophy* (pp. 177–200). Detroit, MI: Wayne State University Press.

Putnam, H. (1975). The nature of mental states. In H. Putnam (Ed.), *Mind, language and reality: Philosophical papers* (Vol. 2, pp. 429–440). Cambridge, MA: Cambridge University Press. (Originally published 1967.)

Quin, C. E. (1994). The soul and the pneuma in the function of the nervous system after Galen. *Journal of the Royal Society of Medicine*, *87*, 393–395.

Rahmani, L. (1973). *Soviet psychology: Philosophical, theoretical, and experimental issues.* New York: International Universities Press.

Rapaport, D. (1942). Principles underlying projective techniques. *Journal of Personality*, *10*, 213–219.

Raush, H. L., Dittmann, A. T., and Taylor, T. J. (1959). Person, setting, and change in social interaction. *Human Relations*, *12*, 361–377.

Razran, G. H. S. (1939). A quantitative study of meaning by a conditioning salivary technique (semantic conditioning). *Science*, *90*, 89–90.

Reid, T. (1788). *Essays on the active powers of man.* London: G. G. J. & J. Robinson.

Reitman, J. S. (1976). Skilled perception in Go: Deducing memory structures from inter-response times. *Cognitive Psychology*, *8*, 336–356.

Report of the Secretary (1909). Proceedings of the fourth annual meeting of the Southern Society for Philosophy and Psychology, Baltimore, MD., December 30 and 31, 1908. *Psychological Bulletin*, *6*, 56–67.

Rey, G. (1998). Eliminativism. In E. Craig (Ed.), *Routledge encyclopedia of philosophy* (pp. 263–266). London: Routledge.

Reymert, M. L. and Hartman, M. L. (1933). A qualitative and quantitative analysis of a mental test. *American Journal of Psychology*, *45*, 87–105.

Richards, G. (1996). *Putting psychology in its place.* London: Routledge.

Richardson, K. (2002). What IQ tests test. *Theory & Psychology*, *12*, 283–314.

Rieber, R. W. and Salzinger, K. D. (Eds.) (1998) *Psychology: Theoretical-historical perspectives* (2nd ed.). Washington, DC: American Psychological Association.

Riger, S. (1992). Epistemological debates, feminist voices: Science, social values, and the study of women. *American Psychologist*, *47*, 730–740.

Rivers, W. H. R. (1905). Observations on the sense of the Todas. *British Journal of Psychology*, *1*, 321–396.

Roberts, W. A. (1998). *Principles of animal cognition.* Boston, MA: McGraw-Hill.

Robinson, D. N. (1981). *An intellectual history of psychology* (rev. ed.). Madison, WI: The University of Wisconsin Press.

Robinson, D. N. (1982). *Toward a science of human nature: Essays on the psychologies of Mill, Hegel, Wundt, and James.* New York: Columbia University Press.

Robinson, D. N. (2000a). Philosophy of psychology at the turn of the century. *American Psychologist*, *55*, 1018–1021.

Robinson, D. N. (2000b). Paradigms and the 'myth of framework': How science progresses. *Theory & Psychology*, *10*, 39–47.

Rogers, A. K. (1910). *A student's history of philosophy.* New York: Macmillan.

Rogers, J. A. (1972). Darwinism and social Darwinism. *Journal of the History of Ideas*, *33*, 265–280.

Rogoff, B. (1984). Introduction: Thinking and learning in social contexts. In B. Rogoff and J. Lave (Eds.), *Everyday cognition: Its development in social context* (pp. 1–8). Cambridge, MA: Harvard University Press.

Rogoff, B. and Lave, J. (1984). *Everyday cognition: Its development in social context.* Cambridge, MA: Harvard University Press.

Romanes, G. J. (1887). Mental differences between men and women. *Nineteenth Century*, *21*, 654–672.

Romanyshyn, R. D. (1971). Method and meaning in psychology: The method has been the message. *Journal of Phenomenological Psychology*, *2*, 93–113.

Rorty, R. (1965). Mind-body identity, privacy, and categories. *The Review of Metaphysics*, *19*, 24–54.

Rose, S. (2000). Escaping evolutionary psychology. In H. Rose and S. Rose (Eds.), *Alas, poor Darwin: Arguments against evolutionary psychology* (pp. 247–265). London: Jonathan Cape.

Rose, S., Lewontin, R. C., and Kamin, L. J. (1984). *Not in our genes.* Harmondsworth: Penguin.

Rosenthal, D. M. and Frank, J. D. (1956). Psychotherapy and the placebo effect. *Psychological Bulletin, 53,* 294–302.

Roth, L. M. (1948). A study of mosquito behavior: An experimental laboratory study of the sexual behavior of Aedes aegypti (Linnaeus). *American Midland Naturalist, 40,* 265–352.

Rumelhart, D. E., Hinton, G. E., and McClelland, J. L. (1986). A general framework for parallel distributed processing. In D. E. Rumelhart and J. L. McClelland, *Parallel distributed processing: Explorations in the microstructure of cognition, Vol. 1: Foundations* (pp. 45–76). Cambridge, MA: The MIT Press.

Runes, D. D. (1977). *Dictionary of philosophy.* Totowa, NJ: Littlefield Adams.

Russell, B. (1932). *Education and the social order.* London: George Allen & Unwin.

Rycroft, C. (1968). *A critical dictionary of psychoanalysis.* Harmondsworth: Penguin Books.

Sahakian, W. S. (1975). *History and systems of psychology.* New York: John Wiley & Sons.

Sampson, E. E. (1977). Psychology and the American ideal. *Journal of Personality and Social Psychology, 35,* 767–782.

Sampson, E. E. (1981). Cognitive psychology as ideology. *American Psychologist, 36,* 730–743.

Sampson, E. E. (1983). *Justice and the critique of pure psychology.* New York: Plenum Press.

Sanford, F. H. and Capaldi, E. J. (Eds.) (1964). *Philosophies, methods, and approaches.* Belmont, CA: Wadsworth Publishing.

Sapir, E. (1932). Cultural anthropology and psychiatry. *Journal of Abnormal and Social Psychology, 27,* 229–242.

Sarton, G. (1952). *A history of science: Ancient science through the golden age of Greece.* New York: John Wiley & Sons.

Scarr, S. (1985). Constructing psychology: Making facts and fables of our times. *American Psychologist, 40,* 499–512.

Schepartz. L. A. (1993). Language and modern human origins. *Yearbook of Physical Anthropology, 36,* 91–126.

Schmandt-Besserat, S. (1986). The origins of writing: An archaeologist's perspective. *Written Communication, 3,* 31–45.

Schwartz, L. A. (1932). Social-situation pictures in the psychiatric interview. *American Journal of Orthopsychiatry, 2,* 124–133.

Scribner, S. (1984). Literacy in three metaphors. *American Journal of Education, 93,* 6–21.

Scrupin, R. and DeCorse, C. R. (2008). *Anthropology: A global perspective* (6th ed.). Upper Saddle River, NJ: Pearson Prentice-Hall.

Searle, J. R. (1980). Minds, brains, programs. *The Behavioral and Brain Sciences, 3,* 417–424.

Searle, J. R. (1990). Is the brain's mind a computer program? *Scientific American, 262,* 26–31.

Searle, J. R. (2010). Consciousness and the problem of free will. In R. F. Baumeister, A. R. Mele, and K. D. Vohs (Eds.), *Free will and consciousness: How might they work?* (pp. 121–134). Oxford: Oxford University Press.

Segall, M. H., Campbell, D. T., and Herskovits, M. J. (1966). *The influence of culture on visual perception.* Indianapolis, IN: Bobbs-Merrill.

Seitz, J. and O'Neill, P. (1996). Ethical decision-making and the code of ethics of the Canadian Psychological Association. *Canadian Psychology, 37,* 23–30.

Seligman, M. E. P. and Maier, S. F. (1967). Failure to escape from traumatic shock. *Journal of Experimental Psychology, 74,* 1–9.

Shafir, I. P. (2006). Reflections on the emergence of a critical psychology in Chile. *Annual Review of Critical Psychology, 5,* 269–280.

Shannon, C. E. and Weaver, W. W. (1964). *The mathematical theory of communication.* Urbana, IL: The University of Illinois Press. (Originally published 1949.)

Sherif, C. W. (1979). Bias in psychology. In J. A. Sherman and E. T. Beck (Eds.), *The prism of sex: Essays in the sociology of knowledge* (pp. 93–133). Madison, WI: The University of Wisconsin Press.

Shiffrin, R. M. and Atkinson, R. C. (1969). Storage and retrieval processes in long-term memory. *Psychological Review, 76,* 179–193.

Shotter, J. (1990). Getting in touch: The metamethodology of a postmodern science of mental life. *The Humanistic Psychologist, 18,* 7–22.

Simon, D. P. and Simon, H. A. (1978). Individual differences in solving physics problems. In R. S. Siegler (Ed.), *Children's thinking: What develops* (pp. 325–348). Hillsdale, NJ: Lawrence Erlbaum.

Simon, H. A. (1996). Computational theories of cognition. In W. O'Donohue and R. F. Kitchener (Eds.), *The philosophy of psychology* (pp. 160–172). London: SAGE Publications.

Simon, H. A. (2000). Artificial intelligence. In A. E. Kazdin (Ed.), *Encyclopedia of psychology* (pp. 248–255). Oxford: Oxford University Press.

Singer, C. (1950). *A history of biology* (rev. ed.). New York: Henry Schuman. (Originally published 1931.)

Skaggs, E. B. (1927). Some critical comments on certain prevailing concepts and methods used in mental testing. *Journal of Applied Psychology, 11,* 503–508.

Skeels, H. M. (1966). Adult status of children with contrasting early life experience: A follow-up. *Monographs of the Society for Research in Child Development, 31,* 1–65.

Skeels, H. M. and Dye, M. D. (1939). A study of the effects of differential stimulation on mentally retarded children. *American Journal of Mental Deficiency, 63,* 114–136.

Skinner, B. F. (1931). The concept of the reflex in the description of behavior. *The Journal of General Psychology, 5,* 427–458.

Skinner, B. F. (1957). *Verbal behavior.* New York: Appleton-Century-Crofts.

Skinner, B. F. (1960). Pigeons in a pelican. *American Psychologist, 15,* 28–37.

Skinner, B. F. (1965). *Science and human behavior.* New York: The Free Press. (Originally published 1953.)

Skinner, B. F. (1974). *About behaviorism.* New York: Vintage Books.

Skinner, B. F. (1985). Cognitive science and behaviorism. *British Journal of Psychology, 76,* 291–301.

Slamecka, N. J. (1985). Ebbinghaus: Some associations. *Journal of Experimental Psychology: Learning, Memory, and Cognition, 11,* 414–435.

Sloan, T. (2000). Editor's introduction. *Critical psychology: Voices for change* (pp. xiv–xxvi). London: Macmillan.

Smith, J. A., Harré, R., and Langenhove, L. V. (1995). Introduction. In J. A. Smith, R. Harré, and L. V. Langenhove (Eds.), *Rethinking psychology* (pp. 1–9). London: SAGE Publications.

Smith, R. (2005). The history of psychological categories. *Studies in History and Philosophy of Biological and Biomedical Sciences, 36,* 55–94.

Smith-Rosenberg, C. and Rosenberg, C. (1973). The female animal: Medical and biological views of woman and her role in nineteenth-century America. *Journal of American History, 60,* 332–356.

Snyderman, M. and Herrnstein, R. J. (1983). Intelligence tests and the Immigration Act of 1924. *American Psychologist, 38,* 986–995.

Sobel, C. P. (2001). *The cognitive sciences: An interdisciplinary approach.* Mountain View, CA: Mayfield Publishing.

Solomon, E. P., Berg, L. R., and Martin, D. W. (2008). *Biology* (8th ed.). Australia: Brooks/Cole.

Southall, J. P. C. (Ed.) (2000). *Helmholtz's treatise on physiological optics, Vol. III: The perceptions of vision.* Sterling, VA: Thoemmes Press. (Original edition translated in 1925 from Helmholtz 1867.)

Spence, J. T. (1985). Achievement American style: The rewards and costs of individualism. *American Psychologist, 40,* 1285–1295.

Sperry, R. W. (1952). Neurology and the mind-brain problem. *American Scientist, 40,* 291–312.

Sperry, R. W. (1969a). Toward a theory of mind. *Proceedings of the National Academy of Sciences, 63,* 230–231.

Sperry, R. W. (1969b). A modified concept of consciousness. *Psychological Review, 76,* 532–536.

Sperry, R. W. (1970). An objective approach to subjective phenomena: Further explanations of a hypothesis. *Psychological Review, 77,* 585–590.

Sperry, R. W. (1976). Mental phenomena as causal determinants in brain function. In G. Globus, G. Maxwell, and I. Savodnik (Eds.), *Consciousness and the brain: A scientific and philosophical inquiry* (pp. 163–177). New York: Plenum Press.

Sperry, R. W. (1980). Mind-brain interaction: Mentalism, yes; dualism, no. *Neuroscience, 5,* 195–206.

Sperry, R. W. (1984). Consciousness, personal identity, and the divided brain. *Neuropsychologia, 22,* 661–673.

Stace, W. T. (1920). *A critical history of Greek philosophy.* London: Macmillan.

Stace, W. T. (1955). *The philosophy of Hegel.* New York: Dover Publications. (Originally published 1924.)

Stam, H. J. (1992). The demise of logical positivism: Implications of the Duhem-Quine thesis for psychology. In C. W. Tolman (Ed.), *Positivism in psychology: Historical and contemporary problems* (pp. 17–24). New York: Springer-Verlag.

Stander, P. E. (1992). Foraging dynamics of lions in a semi-arid environment. *Canadian Journal of Zoology, 70,* 8–21.

Stevens, S. S. (1935). The operational basis of psychology. *American Journal of Psychology, 43,* 323–330.

Stevens, S. S. (1939). Psychology and the science of science. *Psychological Bulletin, 36,* 221–263.

Strick, J. E. (2000). *Sparks of life: Darwinism and the Victorian debates over spontaneous generation.* Cambridge, MA: Harvard University Press.

Stroud, B. (1980). Berkeley v. Locke on primary qualities. *Philosophy, 55,* 149–166.

Sturm, T. (2006). Is there a problem with mathematical psychology in the eighteenth century? A fresh look at Kant's old argument. *Journal of the History of the Behavioral Sciences, 42,* 353–377.

Sumner, F. (1922). The organism and its environment. *Scientific Monthly, 14*, 223–233.

Super, C. M. and Harkness, S. (1986). The developmental niche: A conceptualization at the interface of child and culture. *International Journal of Behavioral Development, 9*, 545–569.

Symonds, P. M. (1924). The present status of character measurement. *Journal of Educational Psychology, 15*, 484–498.

Symonds, P. M. (1931). *Diagnosing personality and* conduct. New York: D. Appleton-Century.

Tavolga, W. N. (1969). *Principles of animal behavior.* New York: Harper & Row.

Tavris, C. (1993). The mismeasure of woman. *Feminism & Psychology, 3*, 149–168.

Tavris, C. and Wade, C. (1997). *Psychology in perspective* (2nd ed.). New York: Longman.

Taylor, C. (1985). *Human agency and language: Philosophical papers 1.* Cambridge: Cambridge University Press.

Taylor, R. (1967). Determinism. In P. Edwards (Ed.), *The encyclopedia of philosophy* (pp. 359–373). New York: Macmillan Publishing Company, Inc. & The Free Press.

Teleki, G. (1975). Primate subsistence patterns: Collector-predators and gatherer-hunters. *Journal of Human Evolution, 4*, 125–184.

Teo, T. (1995). Society, subject, and development: Analysis of categories in German critical thought. In I. Lubek, R. van Hezewijk, G. Pheterson, and C. W. Tolman (Eds.), *Trends and issues in theoretical psychology* (pp. 353–358). New York: Springer.

Teo, T. (1998). Klaus Holzkamp and the rise and decline of German Critical Psychology. *History of Psychology, 1*, 235–253.

Teo, T. (2003). Wilhelm Dilthey (1833–1911) and Eduard Spranger (1882–1963) on the developing person. *The Humanist Psychologist, 31*, 74–94.

Teo, T. (2013). Backlash against American psychology: An indigenous reconstruction of the history of German Critical Psychology. *History of Psychology, 16*, 1–18.

Terman, L. M. (1922). Were we born that way? *World's Work, 44*, 655–660.

Thomas, A. and Chess, S. (1977). *Temperament and development.* Oxford: Brunner/Mazel.

Thomson, J. F. (1964). Berkeley. In D. J. O'Connor (Ed.), *A critical history of Western philosophy* (pp. 236–252). New York: The Free Press.

Thorndike, E. L. (1934). Unity or purity in traits and tests. *Occupations, 12*, 57–59.

Thorndike, E. L., Terman, L. M., Freeman, F. N., Colvin, S. S., Pinter, R., Ruml, B., and Pressey, S. L. (1921). *Journal of Educational Psychology, 12*, 123–147.

Thorndike, L. (1914). Roger Bacon and experimental method in the Middle Ages. *Philosophical Review, 23*, 271–298.

Thorpe, L. P. (1938). *Psychological foundations of personality.* New York: McGraw-Hill.

Thurnwald, R. C. (1936). Civilization and culture: A contribution toward analysis of the mechanism of culture. *American Sociological Review, 1*, 387–395.

Tibbetts, P. (1977). Feyerabend's 'against method': The case for methodological pluralism. *Philosophy of the Social Sciences, 7*, 265–275.

Tichý, P. (1974). On Popper's definitions of verisimilitude. *British Journal for the Philosophy of Science, 25*, 155–160.

Tinbergen, N. (1989). *The study of instinct.* Oxford: Oxford University Press. (Originally published 1951.)

Tinklepaugh, O. L. (1928). An experimental study of representative factors in monkeys. *Journal of Comparative Psychology, 8*, 197–236.

Titchener, E. B. (1898). The postulates of a structural psychology. *Philosophical Review, 7*, 449–465.

Titchener, E. B. (1971). *Experimental psychology. A manual of laboratory practice, Vol 1: Qualitative experiments.* New York: Johnson Reprint Corporation. (Originally published 1902.)

Tolman, C. W. (1980). Metatheoretical constructivism: A materialist evaluation. *Canadian Psychology, 21*, 7–13.

Tolman, C. W. (1987). The comparative psychology of A. N. Leontyev (USSR). In E. Tobach (Rd.), *Historical perspectives and the international status of comparative psychology* (pp. 203–209). Hillsdale, NJ: Lawrence Erlbaum Associates.

Tolman, C. W. (1989). What's critical about *Kritische Psychologie*? *Canadian Psychology, 30*, 628–635.

Tolman, C. W. (1992). Watson's positivism: Materialist or phenomenalist? In C. W. Tolman (Ed.), *Positivism in psychology: Historical and contemporary problems* (pp. 83–102). New York: Springer-Verlag.

Tolman, C. W. (1994). *Psychology, society, and subjectivity: An introduction to German critical psychology.* London: Routledge.

Tolman, C. W. (1996). The critical psychological view of subject and subjectivity. In C. W. Tolman, F. Cherry, R. van Hezewijk, and I. Lubek (Eds.), *Problems of theoretical psychology* (pp. 49–54). Toronto: Captus University Publications.

Tolman, C. W. (2009). Holzkamp's critical psychology as a science from the standpoint of the human subject. *Theory & Psychology, 19*, 149–160.

Tolman, C. W. (2011). Personal communication.

Tolman, E. C. and Honzik, C. H. (1930). Introduction and removal of reward, and maze performance in rats. *University of California Publications in Psychology, 4*, 257–275.

Toulmin, S. and Leary, D. E. (1985). The cult of empiricism in psychology and beyond. In S. Koch and D. E. Leary (Eds.), *A century of psychology as science* (pp. 594–617). New York: McGraw-Hill.

Treisman, A. M. (1964). Verbal cues, language, and meaning in selective attention. *American Journal of Psychology, 77*, 206–219.

Triandis, H. C. (2000). Dialectics between cultural and cross-cultural psychology. *Asian Journal of Social Psychology, 3*, 185–195.

Turing, A. M. (1936). On computable numbers, with an application to the Entscheidungsproblem. *Proceedings of the London Mathematical Society, 42*, 230–265.

Turing, A. M. (1950). I—Computing machinery and intelligence. *Mind, 59*, 433–460.

Turk, A., Meislich, H., Brescia, F., and Arents, J. (1968). *Introduction to chemistry.* New York: Academic Press.

Twain, M. (1966). *Pudd'nhead Wilson.* New York: Airmont Publishing. (Originally published 1894.)

Tyler, L. T. and Malessa, R. (2000). The Goltz-Ferrier debates and the triumph of cerebral localizationalist theory. *Neurology, 55*, 1015–1024.

Tyson, N. D. and Goldsmith, D. (2004). *Origins: Fourteen billion years of cosmic evolution.* New York: W. W. Norton.

Unger, R. K. (1983). Through the looking glass: No wonderland yet! (The reciprocal relationship between methodology and models of reality.) *Psychology of Women Quarterly, 8*, 9–21.

Urmson, J. O. and Rée, J. (Eds.) (1989). *The concise encyclopedia of Western philosophy and philosophers.* London: Unwin Hyman.

Valencia, N. M. and Mesa, A. M. E. (2006). Critical construction in Columbia. *Annual Review of Critical Psychology, 5*, 342–353.

Van der Veer, R. and Valsiner, J. (1991). *Understanding Vygotsky: A quest for synthesis.* Oxford: Blackwell.

Vernon, P. E. (1937). The Stanford-Binet as a psychometric method. *Journal of Personality, 6*, 99–113.

von Neumann, J. (1967). The general and logical theory of automata. In L. A. Jeffress (Ed.) *Cerebral mechanisms in behavior: The Hixon symposium* (pp. 1–41). New York: Hafner Publishing Company. (Originally published 1951.)

Vygotsky, L. S. (1977). The development of higher psychological functions. *Soviet Psychology, 16*, 60–73.

Vygotsky, L. S. (1978). *Mind in society.* Cambridge, MA: Harvard University Press.

Vygotsky, L. (1986). *Thought and language* (newly revised). Cambridge, MA: The MIT Press. (Originally published 1934.)

Vygotsky, L. S. (1987). Lectures on psychology. In R. W. Rieber and A. S. Carton (Eds.), *The collected works of L. S. Vygotsky, Vol. 1: Problems of general psychology* (pp. 289–358). New York: Plenum Press. (Based on lectures delivered in 1932.)

Vygotsky, L. S. (1994). The problem of the environment. In R. Van der Veer and J. Valsiner (Eds.), *The Vygotsky reader* (pp. 338–354). Oxford: Blackwell. (Originally published 1930.)

Vygotsky, L. S. (1997). The historical meaning of the crisis in psychology: A methodological investigation. In R. W. Rieber and J. Wollock (Eds.), *The collected works of L. S. Vygotsky, Vol. 3: Problems of the theory and history of psychology.* New York: Plenum Press. (Originally unpublished manuscript written 1927.)

Vygotsky, L. S. (1999). Tool and sign in the development of the child. In R. W. Rieber (Ed.), *The collected works of L. S. Vygotsky, Vol.6: Scientific legacy* (pp. 3–68). New York: Plenum Press. (Originally written 1930.)

Vygotsky L. S. and Luria, A. R. (1993). *Studies on the history of behavior: Ape, primitive, and child* (V. I. Golod and J. E. Knox, Eds. and Trans.). Hillsdale, NJ: Lawrence Erlbaum Associates. (Originally published 1930.)

Wallston, B. S. (1981). What are the questions in psychology of women? A feminist approach to research. *Psychology of Women Quarterly, 5*, 597–617.

Walsh, R. T. (1987). The evolution of the research relationship in community psychology. *American Journal of Community Psychology, 15*, 773–788.

Washburn, S. L. (1959). Speculations on the interrelations of the history of tools and biological evolution. *Human Biology, 31*, 21–31.

Waterfield, R. (2000). *The first philosophers: The presocractics and sophists.* Oxford: Oxford University Press.

Watkins, J. W. N. (1955). Philosophy and politics in Hobbes. *The Philosophical Quarterly, 5*, 125–146.

Watson, J. B. (1913a). Psychology as the behaviorist views it. *Psychological Review, 20*, 158–177.

Watson, J. B. (1913b). Image and affection in behavior. *The Journal of Philosophy, Psychology, and Scientific Methods, 16*, 421–428.

Watson, J. B. (1928). *Psychological care of infant and child.* New York: W. W. Norton.

Watson, J. B. (1966). *Behaviorism*. Chicago, IL: Phoenix Books. (Originally published 1924.)

Watson, J. B. and Rayner, R. (1920). Conditioned emotional reactions. *Journal of Experimental Psychology, 3*, 1–14.

Watzlawick, P., Beavin, J. H., and Jackson, D. D. (1967). *Pragmatics of human communication*. New York: W. W. Norton.

Weaver, W. (1964). Recent contributions to the mathematical theory of communication. In C. E. Shannon and W. W. Weaver, *The mathematical theory of communication*. Urbana, IL: The University of Illinois Press (pp. 1–28). (Originally published 1949.)

Wegner, D. M. and Wheatley, T. (1999). Apparent mental causation: Sources of the experience of will. *American Psychologist, 54*, 480–492.

Weir, A. A. S., Chappell, J., and Kacelnik, A. (2002). Shaping of hooks in New Caledonian crows. *Science, 297*, 981.

Weisstein, N. (1971). Psychology constructs the female, or the fantasy life of the male psychologist. In M. H. Garskof (Ed.), *Roles women play: Readings toward women's liberation* (pp. 68–83). Belmont, CA: Brooks/Cole Publishing.

Wells, D. C. (1909). Some questions concerning the higher education of women. *American Journal of Sociology, 14*, 731–739.

West, M. J. and King, A. P. (1987). Settling nature and nurture into an ontogenetic niche. *Developmental Psychobiology, 20*, 549–562.

Westkott, M. (1979). Feminist criticism of the social sciences. *Harvard Educational Review, 49*, 422–430.

Wheeler, L. R. (1932). The intelligence of East Tennessee mountain children. *Journal of Educational Psychology, 23*, 351–370.

Wheeler, L. R. (1942). A comparative study of the intelligence of East Tennessee mountain children. *Journal of Educational Psychology, 33*, 321–334.

White, L. A. (1942). On the use of tools by primates. *Journal of Comparative Psychology, 34*, 369–374.

Whitehead, A. N. (1925). *Science and the modern world: Lowell lectures, 1925*. New York: Macmillan.

Wiener, N. (1961). *Cybernetics or the control and communication in the animal and the machine* (2nd ed.). Cambridge, MA: The MIT Press. (Originally published 1948.)

Wilcox, S. and Katz, S. (1984). Can indirect realism be demonstrated in the psychological laboratory? *Philosophy of the Social Sciences, 14*, 149–157.

Wilkinson, L. and the Task Force on Statistical Inference (1999). Statistical methods in psychology journals: Guidelines and explanations. *American Psychologist, 54*, 594–604.

Wilkinson, S. (1988). The role of reflexivity in feminist psychology. *Women's Studies International Forum, 11*, 493–502.

Wilkinson, S. (1989). The impact of feminist research. *Philosophical Psychology, 2*, 261–269.

Wilkinson, S. (1999). Focus groups: A feminist method. *Psychology of Women Quarterly, 23*, 221–244.

Willingham, D. B. (2001). *Cognition: The thinking animal*. Upper Saddle River, NJ: Prentice-Hall.

Willis, T. R. (1957). Scientific method in psychology: I. *British Journal of Statistical Psychology, 11*, 97–104.

Wiltshire, D. (1978). *The social and political thought of Herbert Spencer*. Oxford: Oxford University Press.

Windelband, W. (1998). History and natural science. *Theory & Psychology, 8*, 5–22. (Originally presented 1894.)

Winston, A. S. (1988). *Cause* and *experiment* in introductory psychology: An analysis of R. S. Woodworth's textbooks. *Teaching of Psychology, 15*, 79–83.

Winston, A. S. (1990). Robert Session Woodworth and the 'Columbia Bible': How the psychology experiment was redefined. *American Journal of Psychology, 103*, 391–401.

Winston, A. S. (2001). Cause into function: Ernst Mach and the reconstruction of explanation in psychology. In C. D. Green, M. Shore, and T. Teo (Eds.), *The transformation of psychology* (pp. 107–131). Washington, DC: American Psychological Association.

Winston, A. S. (2004). Controlling the metalanguage: Authority and acquiescence in the history of method. In A. C. Brock, J. Louw, and W. V. Hoorn (Eds.), *Rediscovering the history of psychology: Essays inspired by the work of Kurt Danziger* (pp. 53–73). New York: Kluwer Academic/Plenum.

Winston, A. S. and Blais, D. J. (1996). What counts as an experiment? A transdisciplinary analysis of textbooks, 1930–1970. *American Journal of Psychology, 109*, 599–616.

Winthrop, H. (1960). The Pythagorean complex in the behavioral sciences. *Journal of Genetic psychology, 96*, 301–319.

Wissler, C. (1901). The correlation of mental and physical tests. *Psychological Review: Monograph Supplements, 3*, i–62.

Woodworth, R. S. (1910). Racial differences in mental traits. *Science, 31*, 171–186.

Woodworth, R. S. (1931). *Contemporary schools of psychology*. London: Methuen and Co.

Woodworth, R. S. (1938). *Experimental psychology*. New York: Henry Holt.

Wooley, H. T. (1910). A review of the recent literature on the psychology of sex. *Psychological Bulletin, 7*, 335–342.

Worrall, J. (1998). Lakatos, Imre (1922–1974). In E. Craig (Ed.), *Routledge encyclopedia of philosophy* (Vol. 5, pp. 342–345). London: Routledge.

Wright, M. R. (2009). *Introducing Greek philosophy.* London: Routledge, Taylor & Francis Group.

Wynn, T. and McGraw, W. C. (1989). An ape's view of the Oldowan. *Man, 24,* 383–398.

Wynne, C. D. L. (2001). *Animal cognition: The mental lives of animals.* Houndmills: Palgrave Macmillan.

Yaroshevsky, M. (1990). *A history of psychology* (R. English, Trans.). Moscow: Progress Publishers.

Yates, F. A. (1992). *The art of memory.* London: Pimlico. (Originally published 1966.)

Yeh, B. J. and Lim, W. A. (2007). Synthetic biology: Lessons from the history of synthetic organic chemistry. *Nature Chemical Biology, 3,* 521–525.

Yule, G. U. (1912). *An introduction to the theory of statistics* (2nd ed.). London: Charles Griffin.

INDEX